Approaches and Methods in Language Teaching

Approaches and Methods in Language Teaching

Third Edition

Jack C. Richards and
Theodore S. Rodgers

CAMBRIDGE
UNIVERSITY PRESS

CAMBRIDGE
UNIVERSITY PRESS

University Printing House, Cambridge, CB2 8BS, United Kingdom

Cambridge University Press is part of the University of Cambridge.

It furthers the University's mission by disseminating knowledge in the pursuit of education,
learning and research at the highest international levels of excellence.

www.cambridge.org
Information on this title: www.cambridge.org/9781107675964

© Cambridge University Press 1986, 2001, 2014

First published 1986
Second edition 2001
Third edition 2014
Reprinted 2016

Printed in Italy by Rotolito Lombarda S.p.A.

A catalogue record for this publication is available from the British Library

Library of Congress Cataloguing in Publication data
Richards, Jack C.
Approaches and methods in language teaching / Jack C. Richards and
Theodore S. Rodgers. –Third Edition.
    p.   cm.
Includes index.
ISBN 978-1-107-67596-4 (Paperback)
1. Language and languages–Study and teaching.
I. Rodgers, Theodore S. (Theodore Stephen), 1934– II. Title.

P51.R467 2014
418.0071–dc23

2013041790

Contents

Acknowledgments

The authors and publishers acknowledge the following sources of copyright material and are grateful for the permissions granted. While every effort has been made, it has not always been possible to identify the sources of all the material used, or to trace all copyright holders. If any omissions are brought to our notice, we will be happy to include the appropriate acknowledgments on reprinting.

Cambridge University Press for the text on pp. 114–115 from *Interchange Level 3 Student's Book 4th edition* by Jack C. Richards, Jonathan Hull and Susan Proctor, copyright © Cambridge University Press 2013. Reproduced with permission;

Cambridge University Press for the text on pp. 137–138 from *Ecosystems: Keeping the Balance Fieldbook Pack* by Natàlia Maldonado Martín, Rosa Bergadà Llobet, Núria Carrillo Monsó, Lídia Jové Roda, Pilar Olivares Aguilar, copyright © Cambridge University Press 2012. Reproduced with permission;

Alex Orbe for the artwork on p. 137. Reproduced with permission;

Televisio de Catalunya for the video still on p. 138. Reproduced with permission;

Theodore S. Rodgers for the text on p. 145 from *Teacher training for Whole Language in ELT* by Theodore S. Rodgers, April 1993. Paper given at City University of Hong Kong Seminar. Reproduced with permission;

Cambridge University Press for the text on p. 173 from *Ventures 1 Student's Book 2nd edition* by Gretchen Bitterlin, Dennis Johnson, Donna Price, Sylvia Ramirez and K. Lynn Savage, copyright © Cambridge University Press 2014. Reproduced with permission;

Palgrave Macmillan for the text on p. 192–193 from 'Integrating Task-based Learning Into a Business English Programme' by Patricia Pullin Stark, from *Teachers Exploring Tasks in English Language Teaching*, edited by Corony Edwards and Jane Willis, published by Palgrave Macmillan, 2005. Reproduced with permission of Palgrave Macmillan;

Georgetown University Press for the text on p. 199 from 'Implementing task-based assessment in a TEFL environment' by Cláudio Passos de Oliveira, from *Task-Based Instruction in Foreign Language Education: Practices and Programs* edited by Betty Lou Leaver and Jane R. Willis. Copyright © 2004 by Georgetown University Press, www.press.georgetown.edu. Reprinted with permission;

Text on pp. 208–209 from *Text Based Syllabus Design* by Susan Feez, National Centre for English Language Teaching and Research, published by Macquarie University, 1998;

Marshall Cavendish International for the text on pp. 213–214 adapted from *Marshall Cavendish English Pupil Book 4*, published by Marshall Cavendish Education, 2012. Copyright © 2012 Marshall Cavendish International (Singapore) Private Limited;

Rolf Palmberg for the text on p. 233 from *Multiple Intelligences Revisited* by Rolf Palmberg, ESLDepot.com, 2011. Reproduced with permission;

Pearson Education for the tables on pp. 235–236 and 239–240 adapted from 'An introduction to multiple intelligences theory and second language learning' by Mary Ann Christison, from *Understanding Learning Styles in the Second Language Classroom* edited by Joy M. Reid, published by Pearson Education, copyright © 1998. Reproduced by permission of Pearson Education, Inc., Upper Saddle River, New Jersey;

Academy Publisher Inc. for the table on pp. 253–254 from 'Cooperative Language Learning and Foreign Language Learning and Teaching' by Yan Zhang, from *Journal of Language Teaching and Research, Vol 1, No 1*, published by Academy Publisher, 2010. Reproduced with permission;

Text on p. 272 from *The Natural Approach: Language Acquisition in the Classroom* by Stephen D. Krashen and Tracy D. Terrell, published by Pergamon Press, 1983;

Text on pp. 284–5 from *Learning Another Language through Actions: The Complete Teacher's Guide Book 2nd edition* by James J. Asher, published by Sky Oaks Productions, 1977;

Text on pp. 294–299 from a Peace Corps Syllabus for teaching volunteers Thai by Joel Wiskin;

Cambridge University Press for the text on pp. 317–319 and 324–325 from 'Lozanov and the teaching text' by Grethe Hooper Hansen, from *Materials Development in Language Teaching 2nd Edition* edited by B. Tomlinson, copyright © Cambridge University Press 2011. Reproduced with permission;

SAGE Publications for the extracts on pp. 363–379 adapted from 'Curriculum Approaches in Language Teaching: Forward, Central and Backward Design' by Jack C. Richards, from *RELC Journal*, published by SAGE Publications, 2013. Reproduced with permission.

Introduction to the third edition

The first two editions of this book were published in the Cambridge Language Teaching Library series, with the first edition produced in 1986 followed by a second edition in 2001. *Approaches and Methods in Language Teaching* has been widely referred to by teachers and teachers in training for an account of the major teaching approaches and methods that have been used in language teaching from the late nineteenth century to the present day. Despite the advances that have been made in our understanding of language teaching and learning in the last few decades, the language teaching profession continues to explore new instructional designs and pedagogies. Language teaching today reflects the changed status of English as an international language, which has accelerated the demand for more effective approaches to language teaching. Innovations in technology, the growing trend to begin teaching English at primary level as well as the use of English as a medium of instruction in many university programs prompt an ongoing review of past and present practices as teachers and teacher educators search for effective activities and resources for their classrooms. And despite the belief that contemporary approaches to language teaching rely less on standard approaches and methods and more on post-method conceptions of teaching – new teaching proposals continue to appear (such as Content and Language Integrated Learning, or CLIL, text- and task-based teaching as well as the Common European Framework of Reference). Familiarity with these as well as with earlier traditions in language teaching are important components of the professional knowledge expected of today's language teachers. For these reasons a third edition of *Approaches and Methods* seemed appropriate.[1] As we prepared the third edition, we were reminded that not everything that is new is necessarily better and that today's teachers could continue to benefit from a text that provides a guide to this rich repository of instructional practices in our field.

A number of changes have been incorporated into the third edition.

- The book is now divided into four parts, with the final part presenting three new chapters focusing on approaches and methods in relation to the teaching and learning process. These chapters seek to show how current views of the roles of learners and teachers in the language teaching process prompt alternative conceptualizations of the status of approaches and methods, and also how approaches and methods can be viewed in relation to the processes of curriculum development.
- Part I of the book, *Major trends in twentieth-century language teaching*, has been updated, with the theoretical framework for the book presented in Chapter 2. Many chapters in the book now offer fuller descriptions of approach, design, and procedure.

---

[1] New material for the third edition has been mainly prepared by JCR.

- The chapters presenting current approaches and methods have been moved from Part III to Part II of the book, reflecting their continuity with the major twentieth-century trends. Chapter 5, Communicative Language Teaching, has been expanded significantly, as has Chapter 6, which now includes the approach known as CLIL, along with Content-Based Instruction. Chapter 8 now covers not only Competency-Based Instruction but also the broader standards and outcomes movements and the Common European Framework of Reference. A new chapter on Text-Based Instruction has been added.
- Several chapters in Part III, *Alternative twentieth-century approaches and methods*, have been expanded, with fuller descriptions of the underlying framework. (One chapter from the second edition, Neurolinguistic Programming [NLP], has not been included since NLP is not a language teaching method, but rather a humanistic philosophy based on popular psychology and, as such, does not meet the criteria for inclusion as an approach or method.)
- Discussion questions have been added to all chapters, allowing the reader to synthesize the material, and a comprehensive table comparing approaches and methods has been added as an appendix. Textbook samples of a number of approaches and methods have been provided, as well. While these samples may not reflect the approach or method in its pure form, and may combine features of more than one method, they provide realistic examples of how the approaches and methods have been interpreted by materials writers.

While we considered not including some of the "innovative" methods of the 1970s and 1980s that attract little interest today, reviewers felt that retaining them provided a useful historical perspective on method trends; hence, they have been included in this edition.

We are grateful for the anonymous reviewers for their feedback on this edition and who provided many useful suggestions, to Hayo Reinders for help with discussion questions, and to Debbie Goldblatt and Jacqueline French for their skillful editorial guidance. We also wish to thank Karen Momber and Joanna Garbutt of Cambridge University Press for their support in bringing this edition to fruition.

Part I *Major trends in twentieth-century language teaching*

Language teaching came into its own as a profession in the twentieth century. The whole foundation of contemporary language teaching was developed during the early part of the twentieth century, as applied linguists and others sought to develop principles and procedures for the design of teaching methods and materials, drawing on the developing fields of linguistics and psychology to support a succession of proposals for what were thought to be more effective and theoretically sound teaching methods. Language teaching in the twentieth century was characterized by frequent change and innovation and by the development of sometimes competing language teaching ideologies. Much of the impetus for change in approaches to language teaching came about from changes in teaching methods. The method concept in teaching – the notion of a systematic set of teaching practices based on a particular theory of language and language learning – is a powerful one, and the quest for better methods was a preoccupation of many teachers and applied linguists throughout the twentieth century. Methods typically make the same claim, namely that they reflect a correct understanding of language learning and that adopting the newest method will lead to better results than the method that preceded it. The chapters in Part I examine the developments that led to the first major paradigm in modern language teaching – the adoption of grammar-based teaching methods that came to be known as the structural approach or Situational Language Teaching in the United Kingdom, and Audiolingualism in the United States. In Chapter 1, we outline the historical precedents to language teaching in the first part of the twentieth century and provide a rationale for the study of approaches and methods and their impact on trends and practices in language teaching. In Chapter 2, we introduce a model, or framework, for the description of approaches and methods, one that identifies three levels of organization underlying approaches and methods that we refer to as *approach, design,* and *procedure.* These levels of organization are used throughout the book. In Chapter 3, we describe one of the most important British language teaching proposals of the twentieth century, the Oral Approach or Situational Language Teaching, a method that continues to be widely used today in textbooks and teaching materials, though in the somewhat modified form of Presentation-Practice-Production, or PPP. In Chapter 4, we describe the method known as Audiolingualism, an American teaching method that has similarly left a lasting and continuing legacy in terms of commonly used teaching procedures that focus on structure and pattern practice.

1 A brief history of early developments in language teaching

Introduction

By the beginning of the twentieth century, language teaching was emerging as an active area of educational debate and innovation. Although language teaching has a very long history, the foundations of contemporary approaches to language teaching were developed during the early part of the twentieth century, as applied linguists and others sought to develop principles and procedures for the design of teaching methods and materials, drawing on the developing fields of linguistics and psychology. This led to a succession of proposals for what were thought to be more effective and theoretically sound language teaching methods. Language teaching in the twentieth century was characterized at different times by change and innovation and by the development of competing language teaching ideologies. The impetus for change in approaches to language teaching is generally a response to increased demand for speakers of second and foreign languages. World War II, for example, prompted the need for new ways of teaching oral skills in foreign languages, as we discuss in Chapter 4. Large-scale movement of people through immigration as well as the internationalization of education since the 1950s also created a demand for new types of language programs. And in more recent times, globalization, the rise of the Internet, and the global spread of English has also prompted a reassessment of language teaching policies and practices. This chapter, in briefly reviewing the history of language teaching methods, provides a background for the discussion of past and present methods and suggests the issues we will refer to in analyzing these methods.

The emergence of methods

Efforts to improve the effectiveness of language teaching have often focused on changes in teaching methods. Throughout history such changes have reflected changes in the goals of language teaching, such as a move toward oral proficiency rather than reading comprehension as the goal of language study; they have also reflected changes in theories of the nature of language and of language learning. The method concept in teaching – the notion of a systematic set of teaching practices based on a particular theory of language and language learning – is a powerful though controversial one, and the quest for better methods was a preoccupation of many teachers and applied linguists throughout the twentieth century. From a historical perspective, we are able to see that the concerns that have prompted recent innovations in language teaching, such as Task-Based Language Teaching (Chapter 9) and Content and Language Integrated Learning, or CLIL (Chapter 6), are similar to those that have always been at the center of discussions on how to teach foreign languages. Common to each method is the belief that the teaching practices it supports provide a more effective and theoretically sound basis for teaching than the methods that preceded it. Today's controversies reflect contemporary responses to questions that have often been asked throughout the history of language teaching – questions about how to improve the quality of teaching and learning in language teaching classrooms.

The influence of Latin

We live in a bilingual and multilingual world. From both a contemporary and a historical perspective, bilingualism or multilingualism is the norm rather than the exception. It is fair, then, to say that throughout history foreign language learning has always been an important practical concern. Whereas today English is the world's most widely studied foreign or second language, 500 years ago it was Latin, for it was the dominant language of education, commerce, religion, and government in the Western world. In the sixteenth century, however, French, Italian, and English gained in importance as a result of political changes in Europe, and Latin gradually became displaced as a language of spoken and written communication.

As the status of Latin diminished from that of a living language to that of an "occasional" subject in the school curriculum, the study of Latin took on a different function. The study of classical Latin (the Latin in which the works of Virgil, Ovid, and Cicero were written) and an analysis of its grammar and rhetoric became the model for foreign language study from the seventeenth to the nineteenth centuries. Children entering "grammar school" in the sixteenth, seventeenth, and eighteenth centuries in England were initially given a rigorous introduction to Latin grammar, which was taught through rote learning of grammar rules, study of declensions and conjugations, translation, and practice in writing sample sentences, sometimes with the use of parallel bilingual texts and dialogue (Kelly 1969; Howatt 1984). Once basic proficiency was established, students were introduced to the advanced study of grammar and rhetoric. School learning must have been a deadening experience for children, for lapses in knowledge were often met with brutal punishment. There were occasional attempts to promote alternative approaches to education; Roger Ascham and Montaigne in the sixteenth century and Comenius and John Locke in the seventeenth century, for example, had made specific proposals for curriculum reform and for changes in the way Latin was taught (Kelly 1969; Howatt 1984), but since Latin (and, to a lesser extent, Greek) had for so long been regarded as the classical and therefore most ideal form of language, it was not surprising that ideas about the role of language study in the curriculum reflected the long-established status of Latin.

The decline of Latin also brought with it a new justification for teaching Latin. Latin was said to develop intellectual abilities, and the study of Latin grammar became an end in itself.

> When once the Latin tongue had ceased to be a normal vehicle for communication, and was replaced as such by the vernacular languages, then it most speedily became a "mental gymnastic," the supremely "dead" language, a disciplined and systematic study of which was held to be indispensable as a basis for all forms of higher education.
>
> (V. Mallison, cited in Titone 1968: 26)

As "modern" languages began to enter the curriculum of European schools in the eighteenth century, they were taught using the same basic procedures that were used for teaching Latin. Textbooks consisted of statements of abstract grammar rules, lists of vocabulary, and sentences for translation. Speaking the foreign language was not the goal, and oral practice was limited to students reading aloud the sentences they had translated. These sentences were constructed to illustrate the grammatical system of the language and consequently bore no relation to the language of real communication. Students labored over translating sentences such as the following:

> The philosopher pulled the lower jaw of the hen.
> My sons have bought the mirrors of the Duke.
> The cat of my aunt is more treacherous than the dog of your uncle.
>
> (Titone 1968: 28)

By the nineteenth century, this approach based on the study of Latin had become the standard way of studying foreign languages in schools. A typical textbook in the mid-nineteenth century thus consisted of chapters or lessons organized around grammar points. Each grammar point was listed, rules on its use were explained, and it was illustrated by sample sentences.

> Nineteenth-century textbook compilers were mainly determined to codify the foreign language into frozen rules of morphology and syntax to be explained and eventually memorized. Oral work was reduced to an absolute minimum, while a handful of written exercises, constructed at random, came as a sort of appendix to the rules. Of the many books published during this period, those by Seidenstücker and Plötz were perhaps the most typical … [Seidenstücker] reduced the material to disconnected sentences to illustrate specific rules. He divided his text carefully into two parts, one giving the rules and necessary paradigms, the other giving French sentences for translation into German and German sentences for translation into French. The immediate aim was for the student to apply the given rules by means of appropriate exercises … In [Plötz's] textbooks, divided into the two parts described above, the sole form of instruction was mechanical translation. Typical sentences were: "Thou hast a book. The house is

beautiful. He has a kind dog. We have a bread [*sic*]. The door is black. He has a book and a dog. The horse of the father was kind."

(Titone 1968: 27)

This approach to foreign language teaching became known as the Grammar-Translation Method.

The Grammar-Translation Method

As the names of some of its leading exponents suggest (Johann Seidenstücker, Karl Plötz, H. S. Ollendorf, and Johann Meidinger), Grammar Translation was the offspring of German scholarship, the object of which, according to one of its less charitable critics, was "to know everything about something rather than the thing itself" (W. H. D. Rouse, quoted in Kelly 1969: 53). Grammar Translation was in fact first known in the United States as the Prussian Method. (A book by B. Sears, an American classics teacher, published in 1845 was titled *The Ciceronian or the Prussian Method of Teaching the Elements of the Latin Language* [Kelly 1969].) The principal characteristics of the Grammar-Translation Method were these:

1. The goal of foreign language study is to learn a language in order to read its literature or in order to benefit from the mental discipline and intellectual development that result from foreign language study. Grammar Translation is a way of studying a language that approaches the language first through detailed analysis of its grammar rules, followed by application of this knowledge to the task of translating sentences and texts into and out of the target language. It hence views language learning as consisting of little more than memorizing rules and facts in order to understand and manipulate the morphology and syntax of the foreign language. "The first language is maintained as the reference system in the acquisition of the second language" (Stern 1983: 455).
2. Reading and writing are the major focus; little or no systematic attention is paid to speaking or listening.
3. Vocabulary selection is based solely on the reading texts used, and words are taught through bilingual word lists, dictionary study, and memorization. In a typical Grammar-Translation text, the grammar rules are presented and illustrated, a list of vocabulary items is presented with their translation equivalents, and translation exercises are prescribed.
4. The sentence is the basic unit of teaching and language practice. Much of the lesson is devoted to translating sentences into and out of the target language, and it is this focus on the sentence that is a distinctive feature of the method. Earlier approaches to foreign language study used grammar as an aid to the study of texts in a foreign language. But this was thought to be too difficult for students in secondary schools, and the focus on the sentence was an attempt to make language learning easier (see Howatt 1984: 131).
5. Accuracy is emphasized. Students are expected to attain high standards in translation, because of "the high priority attached to meticulous standards of accuracy which, as well

as having an intrinsic moral value, was a prerequisite for passing the increasing number of formal written examinations that grew up during the century" (Howatt 1984: 132).

6. Grammar is taught deductively – that is, by presentation and study of grammar rules, which are then practiced through translation exercises. In most Grammar-Translation texts, a syllabus was followed for the sequencing of grammar points throughout a text, and there was an attempt to teach grammar in an organized and systematic way.

7. The student's native language is the medium of instruction. It is used to explain new items and to enable comparisons to be made between the foreign language and the student's native language.

Grammar Translation dominated European and foreign language teaching from the 1840s to the 1940s, and in modified form it continues to be widely used in some parts of the world today. At its best, as Howatt (1984) points out, it was not necessarily the horror that its critics depicted it as. Its worst excesses were introduced by those who wanted to demonstrate that the study of French or German was no less rigorous than the study of classical languages. This resulted in the type of Grammar-Translation courses remembered with distaste by thousands of school learners, for whom foreign language learning meant a tedious experience of memorizing endless lists of unusable grammar rules and vocabulary and attempting to produce perfect translations of stilted or literary prose. Although the Grammar-Translation Method often creates frustration for students, it makes few demands on teachers. It is still used in situations where understanding literary texts is the primary focus of foreign language study and there is little need for a speaking knowledge of the language. Contemporary texts for the teaching of foreign languages at the college level still sometimes reflect Grammar-Translation principles. These texts are frequently the products of people trained in literature rather than in language teaching or applied linguistics. Consequently, though it may be true to say that the Grammar-Translation Method is still widely practiced, it has no advocates. It is a method for which there is no theory. There is no literature that offers a rationale or justification for it or that attempts to relate it to issues in linguistics, psychology, or educational theory. However, its continued use in some part of the world may be due to (a) the limited command of spoken English of language teachers, (b) the fact that this was the method their teachers used, (c) it gives teachers a sense of control and authority in the classroom, and (d) it works well in large classes. Jin and Cortazzi (2011: 558–9) offer the following explanation for the continued use of Grammar Translation and other traditional teaching approaches in some parts of the world:

> TAs (traditional approaches) have persisted for longer in most developing parts of the world than in more economically developed ones, due to the slower development of educational systems and language teacher training, cultural perceptions and different ways of change, limited learning resources and finance.

But in Europe in the mid and late nineteenth century, opposition to the Grammar-Translation Method gradually developed in several countries. This Reform Movement, as it was referred to, laid the foundations for the development of new ways of teaching languages and raised controversies that have continued to the present day.

Language teaching innovations in the nineteenth century

Toward the middle of the nineteenth century, several factors contributed to a questioning and rejection of the Grammar-Translation Method. Increased opportunities for communication among Europeans created a demand for oral proficiency in foreign languages. Initially, this created a market for conversation books and phrase books intended for private study, but language teaching specialists also turned their attention to the way English and modern European languages were being taught in secondary schools. Increasingly, the public education system was seen to be failing in its responsibilities. In Germany, England, France, and other parts of Europe, new approaches to language teaching were developed by individual language teaching specialists, each with a specific method for reforming the teaching of modern languages. Some of these specialists, such as C. Marcel, T. Prendergast, and F. Gouin, did not manage to achieve any lasting impact, though their ideas are of historical interest.

The Frenchman C. Marcel (1793–1896) referred to child language learning as a model for language teaching, emphasized the importance of meaning in learning, proposed that reading be taught before other skills, and tried to locate language teaching within a broader educational framework. The Englishman T. Prendergast (1806–1886) was one of the first to record the observation that children use contextual and situational cues to interpret utterances and that they use memorized phrases and "routines" in speaking. He proposed the first "structural syllabus," advocating that learners be taught the most basic structural patterns occurring in the language. In this way he was anticipating a more scientific approach to language study, an issue that was to be taken up in the 1920s and 1930s, as we shall see in Chapter 3. The Frenchman F. Gouin (1831–1896) is perhaps the best known of these mid-nineteenth-century reformers. Gouin developed an approach to teaching a foreign language based on his observations of children's use of language. He believed that language learning was facilitated through using language to accomplish events consisting of a sequence of related actions. His method used situations and themes as ways of organizing and presenting oral language – the famous Gouin "series," which includes sequences of sentences related to such activities as chopping wood and opening the door. Gouin established schools to teach according to his method, and it was quite popular for a time. In the first lesson of a foreign language, the following series would be learned:

I walk toward the door.	I walk.
I draw near to the door.	I draw near.
I draw nearer to the door.	I draw nearer.
I get to the door.	I get to.
I stop at the door.	I stop.
I stretch out my arm.	I stretch out.

I take hold of the handle.	I take hold.
I turn the handle.	I turn.
I open the door.	I open.
I pull the door.	I pull.
The door moves.	moves
The door turns on its hinges	turns
The door turns and turns.	turns
I open the door wide.	I open.
I let go of the handle.	I let go.

(Titone 1968: 35)

Gouin's emphasis on the need to present new teaching items in a context that makes their meaning clear, and the use of gestures and actions to convey the meanings of utterances, are practices that later became part of such approaches and methods as Situational Language Teaching (Chapter 3) and Total Physical Response (Chapter 15).

The work of individual language specialists like these reflects the changing climate of the times in which they worked. Educators recognized the need for speaking proficiency rather than reading comprehension, grammar, or literary appreciation as the goal for foreign language programs; there was an interest in how children learn languages, which prompted attempts to develop teaching principles from observation of (or, more typically, reflections about) child language learning. But the ideas and methods of Marcel, Prendergast, Gouin, and other innovators were developed outside the context of established circles of education and hence lacked the means for wider dissemination, acceptance, and implementation. They were writing at a time when there was not sufficient organizational structure in the language teaching profession (i.e., in the form of professional associations, journals, and conferences) to enable new ideas to develop into an educational movement. This began to change toward the end of the nineteenth century, however, when a more concerted effort arose in which the interests of reform-minded language teachers and linguists coincided. Teachers and linguists began to write about the need for new approaches to language teaching, and through their pamphlets, books, speeches, and articles, the foundation for more widespread pedagogical reforms was laid. This effort became known as the Reform Movement in language teaching.

The Reform Movement

Language teaching specialists such as Marcel, Prendergast, and Gouin had done much to promote alternative approaches to language teaching, but their ideas failed to receive widespread support or attention. From the 1880s, however, practical-minded linguists such as Henry Sweet in England, Wilhelm Viëtor in Germany, and Paul Passy in France began to provide the intellectual leadership needed to give reformist ideas greater credibility and acceptance. The discipline of linguistics was revitalized. Phonetics – the scientific analysis and description of the sound systems of languages – was established, giving new insights into speech processes. Linguists emphasized that speech, rather than the written word, was the primary form of language. The International Phonetic Association was founded in 1886, and its International Phonetic Alphabet (IPA) was designed to enable the sounds of any language to be accurately transcribed. One of the earliest goals of the association was to improve the teaching of modern languages. It advocated

1. the study of the spoken language;
2. phonetic training in order to establish good pronunciation habits;
3. the use of conversation texts and dialogues to introduce conversational phrases and idioms;
4. an inductive approach to the teaching of grammar;
5. teaching new meanings through establishing associations within the target language rather than by establishing associations with the native language.

Linguists too became interested in the controversies that emerged about the best way to teach foreign languages, and ideas were fiercely discussed and defended in books, articles, and pamphlets. Henry Sweet (1845–1912) argued that sound methodological principles should be based on a scientific analysis of language and a study of psychology. In his book *The Practical Study of Languages* (1899), he set forth principles for the development of teaching method. These included

1. careful selection of what is to be taught;
2. imposing limits on what is to be taught;
3. arranging what is to be taught in terms of the four skills of listening, speaking, reading, and writing;
4. grading materials from simple to complex.

In Germany, the prominent scholar Wilhelm Viëtor (1850–1918) used linguistic theory to justify his views on language teaching. He argued that training in phonetics would enable teachers to pronounce the language accurately. Speech patterns, rather than grammar, were the fundamental elements of language. In 1882 he published his views in an influential pamphlet, *Language Teaching Must Start Afresh,* in which he strongly criticized the inadequacies of Grammar Translation and stressed the value of training teachers in the new science of phonetics.

Viëtor, Sweet, and other reformers in the late nineteenth century shared many beliefs about the principles on which a new approach to teaching foreign languages should be based, although they often differed considerably in the specific procedures they advocated for teaching a language. In general the reformers believed that

1. the spoken language is primary and that this should be reflected in an oral-based methodology;
2. the findings of phonetics should be applied to teaching and to teacher training;
3. learners should hear the language first, before seeing it in written form;
4. words should be presented in sentences, and sentences should be practiced in meaningful contexts and not be taught as isolated, disconnected elements;

5. the rules of grammar should be taught only after the students have practiced the grammar points in context – that is, grammar should be taught inductively;
6. translation should be avoided, although the native language could be used in order to explain new words or to check comprehension.

These principles provided the theoretical foundations for a principled approach to language teaching, one based on a scientific approach to the study of language and of language learning. They reflect the beginnings of the discipline of applied linguistics – that branch of language study and research concerned with the scientific study of second and foreign language teaching and learning. The writings of such scholars as Sweet, Viëtor, and Passy provided suggestions on how these applied linguistic principles could best be put into practice. None of these proposals assumed the status of a method, however, in the sense of a widely recognized and uniformly implemented design for teaching a language. But parallel to the ideas put forward by members of the Reform Movement was an interest in developing principles for language teaching out of naturalistic principles of language learning, such as are seen in first language acquisition. This led to what have been termed *natural methods* and then ultimately to the development of what came to be known as the Direct Method.

The Direct Method

Gouin had been one of the first of the nineteenth-century reformers to attempt to build a methodology around observation of child language learning. Other reformers toward the end of the century likewise turned their attention to naturalistic principles of language learning, and for this reason they are sometimes referred to as advocates of a "natural" method. In fact, at various times throughout the history of language teaching, attempts have been made to make second language learning more like first language learning. In the sixteenth century, for example, Montaigne described how he was entrusted to a guardian who addressed him exclusively in Latin for the first years of his life, since Montaigne's father wanted his son to speak Latin well. Among those who tried to apply natural principles to language classes in the nineteenth century was L. Sauveur (1826–1907), who used intensive oral interaction in the target language, employing questions as a way of presenting and eliciting language. He opened a language school in Boston in the late 1860s, and his method soon came to be referred to as the Natural Method.

Sauveur and other believers in the Natural Method argued that a foreign language could be taught without translation or the use of the learner's native language if meaning was conveyed directly through demonstration and action. The German scholar F. Franke wrote on the psychological principles of direct association between forms and meanings in the target language (1884) and provided a theoretical justification for a monolingual approach to teaching. According to Franke, a language could best be taught by using it actively in the classroom. Rather than using analytical procedures that focus on explanation of grammar rules in classroom teaching, teachers must encourage direct and spontaneous use of the foreign language in the classroom. Learners would then be able to induce rules of grammar. The teacher replaced the textbook in the early stages of learning. Speaking began with systematic attention to pronunciation. Known words could be used to teach new vocabulary, using mime, demonstration, and pictures.

These natural language learning principles provided the foundation for what came to be known as the Direct Method, which refers to the most widely known of the natural methods. Enthusiastic supporters of the Direct Method introduced it in France and Germany (it was officially approved in both countries at the turn of the century), and it became widely known in the United States through its use by Sauveur and Maximilian Berlitz in successful commercial language schools. (Berlitz, in fact, never used the term; he referred to the method used in his schools as the Berlitz Method.) In practice it stood for the following principles and procedures:

1. Classroom instruction was conducted exclusively in the target language.
2. Only everyday vocabulary and sentences were taught.
3. Oral communication skills were built up in a carefully graded progression organized around question-and-answer exchanges between teachers and students in small, intensive classes.
4. Grammar was taught inductively.
5. New teaching points were introduced orally.
6. Concrete vocabulary was taught through demonstration, objects, and pictures; abstract vocabulary was taught by association of ideas.
7. Both speech and listening comprehension were taught.
8. Correct pronunciation and grammar were emphasized.

These principles are seen in the following guidelines for teaching oral language, which are still followed in contemporary Berlitz schools:

> Never translate: demonstrate
> Never explain: act
> Never make a speech: ask questions
> Never imitate mistakes: correct
> Never speak with single words: use sentences
> Never speak too much: make students speak much
> Never use the book: use your lesson plan
> Never jump around: follow your plan
> Never go too fast: keep the pace of the student
> Never speak too slowly: speak normally
> Never speak too quickly: speak naturally
> Never speak too loudly: speak naturally
> Never be impatient: take it easy

(cited in Titone 1968: 100–1)

The Direct Method was quite successful in private language schools, such as those of the Berlitz chain, where paying clients had high motivation and the use of native-speaking teachers was the norm. But despite pressure from proponents of the method, it was difficult to implement in public secondary school education. It overemphasized and distorted the similarities between naturalistic first language learning and classroom foreign language learning and failed to consider the practical realities of the classroom. In addition, it lacked a rigorous basis in applied linguistic theory, and for this reason it was often criticized by the more academically based proponents of the Reform Movement. The Direct Method represented the product of enlightened amateurism. It was perceived to have several drawbacks. It required teachers who were native speakers or who had native-like fluency in the foreign language. It was largely dependent on the teacher's skill, rather than on a textbook, and not all teachers were proficient enough in the foreign language to adhere to the principles of the method. Critics pointed out that strict adherence to Direct Method principles was often counterproductive, since teachers were required to go to great lengths to avoid using the native language, when sometimes a simple, brief explanation in the student's native language would have been a more efficient route to comprehension.

The Harvard psychologist Roger Brown has documented similar problems with strict Direct Method techniques. He described his frustration in observing a teacher performing verbal gymnastics in an attempt to convey the meaning of Japanese words, when translation would have been a much more efficient technique (Brown 1973: 5).

By the 1920s, use of the Direct Method in noncommercial schools in Europe had consequently declined. In France and Germany it was gradually modified into versions that combined some Direct Method techniques with more controlled grammar-based activities. The European popularity of the Direct Method in the early part of the twentieth century caused foreign language specialists in the United States to attempt to have it implemented in US schools and colleges, although they decided to move with caution. A study begun in 1923 on the state of foreign language teaching concluded that no single method could guarantee successful results. The goal of trying to teach conversation skills was considered impractical in view of the restricted time available for foreign language teaching in schools, the limited skills of teachers, and the perceived irrelevance of conversation skills in a foreign language for the average American college student. The study – published as the Coleman Report – argued that a more reasonable goal for a foreign language course would be a reading knowledge of a foreign language, achieved through the gradual introduction of words and grammatical structures in simple reading texts. The main result of this recommendation was that reading became the goal of most foreign language programs in the United States (Coleman 1929). The emphasis on reading continued to characterize foreign language teaching in the United States until World War II.

Although the Direct Method enjoyed popularity in Europe, not everyone embraced it enthusiastically. The British applied linguist Henry Sweet recognized its limitations. It offered innovations at the level of teaching procedures but lacked a thorough methodological basis. Its main focus was on the exclusive use of the target language in the classroom, but it failed to address many issues that Sweet thought more basic. Sweet and other applied linguists argued for the development of sound methodological principles that could serve as the basis for teaching techniques. In the 1920s and 1930s, applied linguists systematized the principles proposed earlier by the Reform Movement and so laid the foundations for what developed into the British, or Oral Approach to teaching English as a foreign language, which emphasized the need to grade language items according to difficulty and to teach language through a focus on its core structures and grammar (see Chapter 3). Subsequent developments led to Audiolingualism (Chapter 4) in the United States and Situational Language Teaching (Chapter 3) in Britain.

However, what assumptions underlie the concept of *method* in language teaching as it emerged as a significant educational issue in the nineteenth and twentieth centuries? We have seen from this historical survey some of the questions that prompted innovations and new directions in language teaching in the past:

1. What should the goals of language teaching be? Should a language course try to teach conversational proficiency, reading, translation, or some other skill?
2. What is the basic nature of language, and how will this affect the way we teach it?
3. What are the principles for the selection of language content in language teaching?
4. What principles of organization, sequencing, and presentation best facilitate learning?
5. What should the role of the first language or languages be?
6. What language acquisition processes do learners use in mastering a language, and can these be incorporated into a method?
7. What teaching techniques and activities work best and under what circumstances?

Particular teaching approaches and methods differ in the way they have addressed these issues from the late nineteenth century to the present, as we shall see throughout this book. The Direct Method can be regarded as the first language teaching method to have caught the attention of teachers and language teaching specialists, and it offered a methodology that appeared to move language teaching into a new era. It marked the beginning of what we can refer to as the "methods era."

The methods era

One of the lasting legacies of the Direct Method was the notion of "method" itself. The controversy over the Direct Method was the first of many debates over how second and foreign languages should be taught. The history of language teaching throughout much of the twentieth century and into the twenty-first century saw the rise and fall of a variety of language teaching approaches and methods, the major examples of which are described in this book. The distinction between an approach and a method will be covered in depth in Chapter 2; for the purposes of this chapter, however, the terms are used indistinguishably. Common to most approaches and methods are the following assumptions:

- An approach or method refers to a theoretically consistent set of teaching procedures that define good practice in language teaching.
- Particular approaches and methods, if followed precisely, will lead to more effective levels of language learning than alternative ways of teaching.
- Teacher training should include preparing teachers to understand and use the best available language teaching methods.

The different teaching approaches and methods that have emerged since the 1950s and 1960s, while often having very different characteristics in terms of goals, assumptions about how a second language is learned, and preferred teaching techniques, have in common the belief that if language learning is to be improved, it will come about through changes and improvements in teaching methodology. This notion has been reinforced by professional organizations that endorse particular teaching approaches and methods, by academics who support some and reject others, by publishers who produce and sell textbooks based on the latest teaching approaches and methods, and by teachers who are constantly looking for the "best" method of teaching a language. Lange (1990: 253) comments:

> Foreign language teacher development ... has a basic orientation to methods of teaching. Unfortunately, the latest bandwagon "methodologies" come into prominence without much study or understanding, particularly those that appear easiest to immediately apply in the classroom or those that are supported by a particular "guru." Although concern for method is certainly not a new issue, the current attraction to "method" stems from the late 1950s, when foreign language teachers were falsely led to believe that there was a method to remedy the "language teaching and learning problems."

Hunter and Smith (2012: 430) suggest that the notion of methods has also been established by the fact that accounts (such as this one) represent "a general tendency in the profession to 'package up' the past by assigning methods labeled to bounded periods of history. Past methods are presented as fixed sets of procedures and principles, with little attention paid to the contexts in which these were developed, the way alternatives were debated at the time, or indeed the extent to which there was continuity with previous period." This should be kept in mind in reading the accounts presented here.

Notwithstanding the note of caution above, debate over the teaching methods and approaches that will be covered in this book has been a dominant theme in language teaching since the 1950s. The 1950s and 1960s saw the emergence of the Audiolingual Method and the Situational Method, which were both superseded by the Communicative Approach (Chapter 5). During the same period, other methods attracted smaller but equally enthusiastic followers, including the Silent Way (Chapter 16), the Natural Approach (Chapter 14), and Total Physical Response (Chapter 15). Since the 1980s and 1990s, Content-Based Instruction (Chapter 6), and task-based and text-based approaches (Chapters 9 and 10) were developed as well as movements such as Competency-Based Language Teaching (Chapter 8) that focus on the outcomes of learning rather than methods of teaching. Other approaches such as Cooperative Language Learning (Chapter 13), Whole Language (Chapter 7), and Multiple Intelligences (Chapter 12), originally developed in general education, have been extended to second language settings. And more recently CLIL (Chapter 6) has attracted considerable interest in Europe, as has the Common European Framework of Reference which shifts focus to the outcomes of learning.

At the same time, applied linguists have also questioned the assumptions implicit in the views of teaching underlying the concept of approaches and methods. For example, Holliday (1994) argued that a communicative approach, as taught to teachers who are native speakers of English, reflects a view of teaching and learning that is culturally bound and reflects assumptions from dominant Western cultures – Britain, Australasia, and North America (see Chapter 20). Kumaravadivelu presents a more radical critique of the influence of Western methods, also known as "inner-circle" based or "center-based" methods, which take as their starting point "the native speaker's language competence, learning styles, communication patterns, conversational maxims, cultural beliefs, and even accent":

> Briefly, Center-produced methods are based on idealized concepts geared toward idealized contexts. Since language learning and teaching needs, wants, and situations are unpredictably numerous, no idealized teaching method can visualize all the variables in advance to provide situation-specific suggestions that practicing teachers need to tackle the challenges that confront the practice of their everyday teaching. As a predominantly top-down exercise, the conception and construction of methods have been largely guided by a one-size-fits-all cookie-cutter approach that assumes a common clientele with common goals.
>
> (Kumaravadivelu 2012: 18)

Others have suggested that the history of methods is often presented as evidence of self-proclaimed progress, with little consideration of the successes achieved by teachers using superseded methods that are depicted as "failures." Since the 1990s, many applied linguists and language teachers have consequently moved away from a belief that newer and therefore "better" approaches and methods are the solution to problems in language teaching. Alternative ways of understanding the nature of language teaching have emerged that are sometimes viewed as characterizing the "post-methods era" (Chapter 20). These newer approaches to understanding language teaching are discussed in Part IV of this book.

Approaches and methods in teacher preparation programs

Despite the changing status of approaches and methods in language teaching, the study of past and present teaching methods continues to form a component of many teacher preparation programs. This is discussed more fully in Chapter 20. There are several reasons why methods are a component of many teacher-education programs. The study of approaches and methods

- provides teachers with a view of how the field of language teaching has evolved and forms part of the disciplinary knowledge expected of language teachers today;
- introduces teachers to the issues and options that are involved in planning and developing a language course;
- introduces a variety of principles and procedures that teachers can review and evaluate in relation to their own knowledge, beliefs, and practice.

This is the orientation we adopt toward the teaching approaches and methods described in this book. In order to understand the fundamental nature of methods in language teaching, however, it is necessary to conceptualize the notion of approach and method more systematically. This is the aim of the next chapter, in which we present a model for the description, analysis, and comparison of methods. This model will be used as a framework for our subsequent discussions and analyses of particular language teaching methods and philosophies.

Conclusion

In this chapter, we have looked at the emergence of methods, which in the early years included an emphasis on Latin and the Grammar-Translation Method. The Reform Movement then led to an emphasis on the spoken language and development of the Direct Method, a "natural method" emphasizing native-speaker input as a way for the learner to induce language patterns in the target language. Criticisms that the Direct Method lacked a thorough methodological underpinning led to the birth of the "methods era" and the many approaches and methods that will be covered in this book. More recently, some educators have criticized the better-known approaches and methods as "Western-centric," and applied linguists have begun to conceptualize new ways of understanding language.

Discussion questions

1. What changes in approaches to language teaching have you experienced? What prompted the changes you have witnessed?

2. Have you ever been trained in, or have you ever studied, the use of a "new" language teaching method? What are your recollections of the experience? Has it had a lasting impact on your approach to teaching?

3. "The goal of foreign language study is to learn a language in order to ... benefit from the mental discipline and intellectual development that result from foreign language study" (p. 6). What do you think are examples of this "mental discipline" and "intellectual development"? Are these relevant to language learning today?

4. Have you experienced grammar-translation instruction yourself? How was your experience? Were there any aspects of it that you enjoyed or thought were useful for your own teaching?

5. Review the beliefs of Viëtor, Sweet, and other reformers in the late nineteenth century presented on page 10. To what extent do these differ from your own?

6. Can you think of situations where the use of translation and a heavy reliance on the learner's first language can be fruitful?

7. What are some ways in which first and second language learning are similar? In what ways are they different?

8. The Coleman Report, published in 1929, recommended a focus on reading as the basis of language instruction. In some countries today, language classes meet for only two or

three hours per week and most of the learners will not move or travel overseas. Could a similar argument be made for a focus on reading skills?

9. What do you think is the value of studying approaches and methods, including older and more current ones? What factors contributed to the development of the methods era? Do you perceive a Western bias in current approaches and methods that you are familiar with?

References and further reading

Brown, H. D. 1993. *Principles of Language Learning and Teaching*. 3rd edn. Englewood Cliffs, NJ: Prentice Hall.

Brown, R. 1973. *A First Language*. Cambridge, MA: Harvard University Press.

Coleman, A. 1929. *The Teaching of Modern Foreign Languages in the United States*. New York: Macmillan.

Cook, V. 2011. Teaching English as a foreign language in Europe. In Eli Hinkel (ed.), *Handbook of Research in Second Language Teaching and Learning*, Vol. II. New York: Routledge. 140–54.

Darian, K. C. 1971. *Generative Grammar, Structural Linguistics, and Language Teaching*. Rowley, MA: Newbury House.

Franke, F. 1884. *Die Praktische Spracherlernung auf Grund der Psychologie und der Physiologie der Sprache Dargestellt*. Leipzig: O. R. Reisland.

Holliday, A. 1994. The house of TESEP and the communicative approach: the special needs of state English language education. *ELT Journal* 48(1): 3–11.

Howatt, A. P. R. 1984. *A History of English Language Teaching*. Oxford: Oxford University Press.

Howatt, T. 1997. Talking shop: transformation and change in ELT. *ELT Journal* 5(3): 263–8.

Hunter, D., and R. Smith. 2012. Unpackaging the past: "CLT" through ELTJ keywords. *ELT Journal* 66(4): 430–9.

Jin, L., and M. Cortazzi. 2011. Re-evaluating traditional approaches to second language teaching and learning. In E. Hinkel (ed.), *Handbook of Research in Second Language Teaching and Learning*, Vol. II. New York: Routledge. 558–75.

Kelly, L. 1969. *25 Centuries of Language Teaching*. Rowley, MA: Newbury House.

Kumaravadivelu. B. 2012. Individual identity, cultural globalization, and teaching English as an international language: the case for an epistemic break. In L. Alsagoff, S. L. McKay, G. Hu, and W. A. Renandya (eds.), *Principles and Practices for Teaching English as an International Language*. New York: Routledge. 9–27.

Lange, D. 1990. A blueprint for a teacher development program. In J. C. Richards and D. Nunan (eds.), *Second Language Teacher Education*. New York: Cambridge University Press. 245–68.

Larsen-Freeman, D. 1998. Expanding roles of learners and teachers in learner-centered instruction. In W. Renandya and G. Jacobs (eds.), *Learners and Language Learning*. Singapore: SEAMEO Regional Language Center. 207–26.

Mackey, W. F. 1965. *Language Teaching Analysis*. London: Longman.

Marcella, F. 1998. *The Historical Development of ESL Materials in the United States*. ERIC document (ED425653).

Richards, J. C. 1985. The secret life of methods. In J. C. Richards, *The Context of Language Teaching*. New York: Cambridge University Press. 32–45.

Stern, H. H. 1983. *Fundamental Concepts of Language Teaching*. Oxford: Oxford University Press.

Sweet, H. 1899. *The Practical Study of Languages*. Repr. London: Oxford University Press.

Titone, R. 1968. *Teaching Foreign Languages: An Historical Sketch*. Washington, DC: Georgetown University Press.

Waters, A. 2012. Trends and issues in ELT methods and methodology. *ELT Journal* 66(4): 440–9.

2 The nature of approaches and methods in language teaching

Introduction

We saw in the preceding chapter that the changing rationale for foreign language study and the classroom techniques and procedures used to teach languages have reflected responses to a variety of historical issues and circumstances. Tradition was for many years the guiding principle. The Grammar-Translation Method reflected a time-honored and scholarly view of language and language study. At times, the practical realities of the classroom determined both goals and procedures, as with the determination of reading as the goal in US schools and colleges in the late 1920s. At other times, theories derived from linguistics, psychology, or a mixture of both were used to develop a philosophical and practical basis for language teaching, as with the various reformist proposals of the nineteenth century. As the study of teaching methods and procedures in language teaching assumed a more central role within applied linguistics in the latter part of the twentieth century, various attempts have been made to conceptualize the nature of methods and to explore more systematically the relationship between theory and practice within a method. In this chapter we will clarify the relationship between approach and method and present a model for the description, analysis, and comparison of methods.

Approach and method

When linguists and language specialists sought to improve the quality of language teaching in the late nineteenth century, they often did so by referring to general principles and theories concerning how languages are learned, how knowledge of language is represented and organized in memory, or how language itself is structured. The early applied linguists, such as Henry Sweet (1845–1912), Otto Jespersen (1860–1943), and Harold Palmer (1877–1949) (see Chapters 1 and 3), elaborated principles and theoretically accountable approaches to the design of language teaching programs, courses, and materials, though many of the specific practical details were left to be worked out by others. They sought a rational answer to questions such as those regarding principles for the selection and sequencing of vocabulary and grammar, though none of these applied linguists saw in any existing method the ideal embodiment of their ideas.

In describing methods, the difference between a philosophy of language teaching at the level of theory and principles and a set of derived procedures for teaching a language is central. In an attempt to clarify this difference, a scheme was proposed by the American applied linguist Edward Anthony in 1963. He identified three levels of conceptualization and organization, which he termed *approach*, *method*, and *technique*:

> The arrangement is hierarchical. The organizational key is that techniques carry out a method which is consistent with an approach ...
>
> ... An approach is a set of correlative assumptions dealing with the nature of language teaching and learning. An approach is axiomatic. It describes the nature of the subject matter to be taught ...
>
> ... Method is an overall plan for the orderly presentation of language material, no part of which contradicts, and all of which is based upon, the selected approach. An approach is axiomatic, a method is procedural.
>
> Within one approach, there can be many methods ...
>
> ... A technique is implementational – that which actually takes place in a classroom. It is a particular trick, stratagem, or contrivance used to accomplish an immediate objective. Techniques must be consistent with a method, and therefore in harmony with an approach as well.
>
> (Anthony 1963: 63–7)

According to Anthony's model, approach is the level at which assumptions and beliefs about language and language learning are specified; method is the level at which theory is put into practice and at which choices are made about the particular skills to be taught, the content to be taught, and the order in which the content will be presented; technique is the level at which classroom procedures are described.

Anthony's model serves as a useful way of distinguishing between different degrees of abstraction and specificity found in different language teaching proposals. Thus, we can see that the proposals of the Reform Movement were at the level of approach and that the Direct Method is one method derived from this approach. The so-called Reading Method, which evolved as a result of the Coleman Report (see Chapter 1), should really be described in the plural – reading methods – since a number of different ways of implementing a reading approach have been developed.

Other ways of conceptualizing approaches and methods in language teaching have also been proposed. Mackey, in his book *Language Teaching Analysis* (1965), elaborated perhaps the most well known model of the 1960s, one that focuses primarily on the levels of method and technique. Mackey's model of language teaching analysis concentrates on the dimensions of selection, gradation, presentation, and repetition underlying a method. In fact, despite the title of Mackey's book, his concern is primarily with the analysis of textbooks and their underlying principles of organization. His model does not address the level of approach, nor does it deal with the actual classroom behaviors of teachers and learners, except as these are represented in textbooks. Hence, it cannot really serve as a basis for comprehensive analysis of either approaches or methods.

Although Anthony's original proposal has the advantage of simplicity and comprehensiveness and serves as a useful way of distinguishing the relationship between underlying theoretical principles and the practices derived from them, it does not give sufficient attention to the nature of a method itself. Nothing is said about the roles of teachers and learners assumed in a method, for example, nor about the role of instructional materials or the form these materials are expected to take. Nor does it account for how an approach may be realized in a method, or for how method and technique are related. In order to provide a more comprehensive model for the discussion and analysis of approaches and methods, we have revised and extended the original Anthony model. The primary areas needing further clarification are, using Anthony's terms, method and technique. We see approach and method treated at the level of *design,* that level in which objectives, syllabus, and content are determined, and in which the roles of teachers, learners, and instructional materials are specified. The implementation phase (the level of technique in Anthony's model) we refer to by the slightly more comprehensive term *procedure.* Thus, a method is theoretically related to an approach, is organizationally determined by a design, and is practically realized in procedure. In the remainder of this chapter, we will elaborate on the relationship between approach, design, and procedure, using this framework to compare particular methods and approaches in language teaching. In the remaining chapters of the book, we will use the model presented here as a basis for describing a number of widely used approaches and methods.

1 Approach

Following Anthony, *approach* refers to theories about the nature of language and language learning that serve as the source of practices and principles in language teaching. In other words, it refers to the "philosophy," or belief system, that a method reflects. We will examine the linguistic and psycholinguistic aspects of approach in turn.

Theory of language

Language is a very complex phenomenon and is studied from the perspective of many different disciplines, including linguistics, literature, psychology, anthropology, and sociology. Not surprisingly, a number of different theoretical views of language and the nature of language proficiency explicitly or implicitly inform current as well as less recent approaches and methods in language teaching. Here we will briefly review models of language that have influenced language teaching methods and approaches. These include the Cognitive model, the Structural model, the Functional model, the Interactional model, the Sociocultural model, the Genre model, and the Lexical model.

Cognitive model

A *cognitive view* of language is based on the idea that language reflects properties of the mind. Atkinson (2011: 4–5) identifies a number of core features and assumptions of a cognitive view of language, or "cognitivism":

1. Mind as a computer – a set of operations that take in input, process it, and produce output, as with a computer
2. Representationalism – processes that the mind engages in to store internal representations of external events
3. Learning as abstract knowledge acquisition – i.e. abstracting the rules of the competence that underlies linguistic performance, as Noam Chomsky put it.

Chomsky's theory of universal grammar, or UG, first proposed in the 1980s is a well-developed example of a cognitive model of language. According to UG theory, our minds contain a mental grammar that consists of universal *principles* that are common to all languages, and *parameters* that vary according to different languages. The Grammar-Translation Method can perhaps be understood as an early example of a cognitive view of language since it reflects the idea that the learner has built up knowledge of the principles of language by abstracting its rules though a study of grammar and through translation-based activities. More recently, the short-lived language teaching theory in the 1960s known as the cognitive-code approach (Chapter 4) reflected a similar understanding of language – one in which grammar played a central role. It referred to the organization of language teaching around grammar while allowing for meaningful use and practice of the language. Methods such as the Silent Way (Chapter 16) can also be seen as reflecting a cognitive orientation to language. We will say more about cognitive approaches when we turn to language learning theories below.

Structural model

Another way of conceptualizing language and one that has had a wide application in language teaching is the *structural view*, the view that language is a system of structurally related elements for the coding of meaning. The target of language learning is seen to be the mastery of elements of this system, which are generally defined in terms of phonological units (e.g., phonemes), grammatical units (e.g., clauses, phrases, sentences), grammatical operations (e.g., adding, shifting, joining, or transforming elements), and lexical items (e.g., function words and structure words). As we see in Chapter 4, the Audiolingual Method embodies this particular view of language as do such methods as Situational Language Teaching (Chapter 3) and Total Physical Response (Chapter 15).

Functional model

A different model of language and one which takes a number of different forms is the *functional view*, the view that language is a vehicle for the expression of functional meanings and for performing real-world activities. Functional models of language are linked to the concept of communicative competence – knowing how language is used to achieve different kinds of communicative purposes (see Chapter 5) or, as defined by Brown (1994: 227):

> That aspect of our competence which enables us to convey and interpret messages and to negotiate meanings interpersonally within specific contexts ... [The] knowledge that enables a person to communicate functionally and interactionally.

The communicative movement in language teaching subscribes to this view of language (see Chapter 5) as does Competency-Based Language Teaching (Chapter 8). Functional approaches emphasize the semantic and communicative dimension rather than merely the grammatical characteristics of language, and lead to a specification and organization of language teaching content by categories of meaning and function rather than by elements of structure and grammar. The Threshold Level syllabus developed by the Council of Europe (Chapter 5) spelled out the implications of this view of language for syllabus design as does the Common European Framework of Reference, which describes language in terms of sets of the competencies a learner is able to express through language (Chapter 8). The English for Specific Purposes (ESP) movement likewise begins not from a structural theory of language but from a functional account of learner needs.

Interactional model

Yet another perspective on language can be called the *interactional view*. It sees language as a vehicle for the realization of interpersonal relations and for the performance of social transactions between individuals. Language is seen as a tool for the creation and maintenance of social relations. Areas of inquiry being drawn on in the development of interactional approaches to language teaching include second language acquisition, interaction analysis, conversation analysis, and ethnomethodology. Interactional theories focus on the patterns of moves, acts, negotiation, and interaction found in conversational and other kinds of exchanges and which are central to an understanding of discourse (Chapter 5). "Interaction" has been central to theories of second language learning and pedagogy since the 1980s. Rivers (1987: 4) defined the interactive perspective in language education: "Students achieve facility in *using* a language when their attention is focused on conveying and receiving authentic messages (that is, messages that contain information of interest to both speaker and listener in a situation of importance to both)." Negotiation of meaning is believed to play a central role in interactive views of language and is central to current teaching proposals, including Task-Based Language Teaching (Chapter 9) and CLIL (see below).

Sociocultural model

A related view of language is referred to as a *sociocultural* model. Sociocultural theory views language as a communicative activity in which the social context is central. Knowledge is constructed through social interaction with others and reflects the learner's culture, customs, and beliefs as well as the collaborative activities people are engaged in. A sociocultural view of language is sometimes said to undergird accounts of Task-Based

Language Teaching, Content-Based Instruction (Chapter 6), and Cooperative Language Learning (Chapter 13).

Genre model

Another functional model of language is the genre-based approach. *Genre* refers to an area of human activity where there are norms of language usage, such as in science, business, medicine, literature. Texts are the units of discourse that occur in different genres such as narratives, descriptions, and explanations (see Chapter 10). This model owes much to the work of the Australian school of applied linguistics, drawing on the work of Halliday and others. The main concepts of this model of language can be summarized as follows (Feez 1998: 5):

- Language is a resource for making meaning.
- The resource of language consists of a set of interrelated systems.
- Language users draw on this resource each time they use language.
- Language users create texts to create meaning.
- Texts are shaped by the social context in which they are used.
- The social context is shaped by the people using language.

The genre and text approach is seen in Text-Based Instruction (Chapter 10) as well as in Content-Based Instruction and CLIL (Chapter 6). It has also had an impact on the teaching of both English for Specific Purposes and English for Academic Purposes (Paltridge 2006).

Lexical model

The *lexical view* of language prioritizes the role of lexis and lexical chunks or phrases in language and highlights the interrelatedness of grammar and vocabulary. Rather than seeing lexis and grammar as discrete, they are viewed as being intrinsically related (Schmitt 2004; O'Keefe, McCarthy, and Carter 2007). Drawing on the findings of corpus studies, advocates of lexical models of language suggest that grammatical competence arises out of phrase- and lexically-based learning and argue for a greater role for vocabulary as well as lexical phrases and chunks in language teaching. This view is reflected most directly in the Lexical Approach (Chapter 11), but is also compatible with aspects of Content-Based Instruction and CLIL.

The accounts above provide a very brief description of some of the different models of language that are reflected in language teaching methods. However, in themselves they are incomplete and need to be complemented by theories of language learning. It is to this dimension that we will turn next.

Theory of learning

Although specific theories of the nature of language may provide the basis for a particular teaching method, all methods reflect, either explicitly or implicitly, a theory of language learning. Language learning theories account for the cognitive, personal, interpersonal, and social processes learners make use of in second language learning. We will describe the theories of learning assumed in different methods throughout this book. Research on second language acquisition has led to the development of a rich and diverse set of theories to explain how languages are learned, and different methods draw on different learning theories, and often more than one. These have included *behaviorism, cognitive-code learning*, the *creative-construction hypothesis, skill learning, interactional theory, constructivism, sociocultural learning theory* (or social constructivism), as well as the role of *individual factors* in language learning.

Behaviorism

This theory was based on the view that learning is a process in which specific behaviors are acquired in response to specific stimuli. Correct responses are reinforced and increase the chance of the behavior becoming learned (Skinner 1957). Learning was said to involve habit formation through repetition and reinforcement. This theory provided the basis for the Audiolingual Method (see Chapter 4). Language was taught through extensive drilling and repetition exercises and through making use of activities that minimized the chances of producing mistakes.

Cognitive-code learning

This view was developed in the 1960s as an alternative to behaviorism and emphasized that language learning was a cognitive process depending on both deductive and inductive learning as well as meaningful practice. Students are taught grammatical rules which they then apply in practice. Learning is seen to depend on cognitive processing and mental effort. The PPP approach (Presentation-Practice-Production) used in Situational Language Teaching can be linked to cognitive-code learning, as well as to methods such as the Silent Way.

Creative-construction hypothesis

This theory, first proposed in the 1970s but still implicit in current theories of second language acquisition, suggests that learning is not simply a question of reproducing input but a creative process that has common features regardless of the learner's language background, and that this accounts for the similarities seen in the language produced by linguistically diverse second language learners. Errors are seen as evidence of learning rather than signs of faulty learning. Communicative Language Teaching reflects this view of learning and introduced the concept of fluency work in teaching, where the communication of meaning rather than a grammatically precise use of language is the focus. It is also implicit in Task-Based Language Teaching.

Skill learning

Skills are integrated sets of behaviors that are learned through practice. They are made up of individual components that may be learned separately and that come together as a whole to constitute skilled performance. Skill learning theory suggests that complex uses of language are made up of a hierarchy of skills. Initially, skills are often consciously managed and directed by the learner, such as learning how to make a class presentation in English. This is called *controlled processing* (Ortega 2009). Over time skills can become automatic and do not require conscious attention. This is called *automatic processing*. Learning involves development from *controlled* to *automatic processing*, that is, the cumulative learning of skills. Many language teaching methods treat language learning, at least in part, as skill-based learning.

Interactional theory

This theory argues that learning is an interactive process and depends on learners working together to achieve mutual understanding. Central to this view of learning is the concept of negotiation of meaning – the modification of input learners receive when they communicate with more advanced learners or native speakers and the kind of feedback they receive from their interlocutors. More competent speakers will typically modify their input by using known vocabulary, speaking more slowly, saying things in different ways, adjusting the topic, avoiding idioms, using a slower rate of speech, using stress on key words, repeating key elements, using simpler grammatical structures, paraphrasing and elaborating, and so on. In this way modified input facilitates both understanding and learning. These processes in a sense "teach" the language, and the role of instruction is to support these interactive processes in the classroom. Both Communicative Language Teaching and Task-Based Language Teaching reflect aspects of interactional theory.

Constructivism

Constructivism is another learning theory that has had a powerful influence on education and on theories of second language learning. It draws on the work of Jean Piaget and John Dewey on child development as well as on the work of Lev Vygotsky. Rather than viewing learning as a passive process and the result of the internalization of outside knowledge (i.e., as a process of transmission), learning is seen as something that results from the learner's internal construction of meaning (Williams and Burden 1997). Knowledge does not exist independently of the meaning constructed from experience by the learner or community of learners. Constructivism emphasizes that learners are actively involved in their own process of learning. It is a dynamic process that has both cognitive dimensions, as the organizer reorganizes new knowledge on the basis of existing knowledge, and social dimensions, as the learner interacts with others and solves problems through dialogue. (This latter social view of constructivism is now referred to as sociocultural learning theory and is discussed below.) Constructivist approaches to learning emphasize student-centered and project-based learning where students pose questions, explore multiple interpretations of meaning, and where the teacher acts as facilitator and guide. Constructivist theories of learning are seen in concepts such as restructuring, schema theory, and scaffolding (see below) and can also be seen in Communicative Language Teaching, Community Language Learning (Chapter 17), Cooperative Language Learning and Whole Language (Chapter 7).

Sociocultural learning theory (also known as social constructivism)

This theory can be seen as an extension of both constructivism and interactional theory and views language learning as resulting from dialogue between a learner and a more knowledgeable other person. The term *sociocultural* means that learning takes place in a particular social setting (e.g. a classroom), in which there is interaction between people (teachers and students), objects (texts, books, images), and culturally organized activities and events (instructional acts and sequences). Learning is a process of guided participation, mediated through the direction of a more knowledgeable other. Through repeated participation in a variety of joint activities, the novice gradually develops new knowledge and skills (Rogoff 1990). A process referred to as scaffolding plays an important part in sociocultural learning theory (Lave and Wenger 1991). In the classroom, scaffolding is the process of interaction between two or more people as they carry out a classroom activity and where one person (e.g., the teacher or another learner) has more advanced knowledge than the other (the learner) (Swain, Kinnear, and Steinman 2010). During the process, interaction proceeds as a kind of joint problem-solving activity between teacher and student. Collaborative dialogue "scaffolds" the learning process by initially providing support (the "scaffold") and gradually removing support as learning develops. Many current teaching proposals, such as CLIL and text-based and task-based instruction, attribute an important role to the process of scaffolded learning.

Individual factors

The attributes individual learners bring to language learning can also have an important influence on learning, and teaching methods often seek to take account of these attributes. These include *learning style preferences* (such as whether a learner likes to learn in groups or prefers learning alone); *affective factors* such as shyness, anxiety, enthusiasm, and other emotions that language learning may elicit and that may influence the learner's willingness to communicate; *motivation*, which refers to the learner's attitude, desire, interest in, and willingness to invest effort in learning a second language; *learning strategies* – the ways in which learners plan, manage, and evaluate their own learning – for example, monitoring their language development over time and identifying areas that need additional effort and improvement. Strategies are discussed in Chapter 19.

Methods may seek to address individual learning factors by attempting to match teaching strategies to learning styles, by enhancing motivation through the choice of content that is of high interest value or relevance (as with Content-Based Instruction); by delaying speaking and focusing on comprehension skills in an introductory language course in order to address the issue of anxiety (as in the Natural Approach – Chapter 14); or by using group-based learning (as with Cooperative Language Learning). Methods may also seek to develop and guide learners' use of particular learning strategies (as seen in Task-Based Language Teaching).

Relationship between language theory and learning theory

There often appear to be natural affinities between certain theories of language and theories of language learning; however, one can imagine different pairings of language theory and learning theory that might work as well as those we observe. The linking of structuralism (a linguistic theory) to behaviorism (a learning theory) produced Audiolingualism. That particular link was not inevitable, however. Cognitive-code proponents (see Chapter 4), for example, attempted to link a more sophisticated model of structuralism to a more mentalistic and less behavioristic brand of learning theory.

At the level of approach, we are hence concerned with theoretical principles. With respect to language theory, we are concerned with a model of language competence and an account of the basic features of linguistic organization and language use. With respect to learning theory, we are concerned with an account of the central processes of learning and an account of the conditions believed to promote successful language learning. These principles may or may not lead to "a" method. Teachers may, for example, develop their own teaching procedures, informed by a particular view of language and a particular theory of learning. They may constantly revise, vary, and modify teaching/learning procedures on the basis of the performance of the learners and their reactions to instructional practice. A group of teachers holding similar beliefs about language and language learning (i.e., sharing a similar approach) may each implement these principles in different ways. Approach does not specify procedure. Theory does not dictate a particular set of teaching techniques and activities. What links theory with practice (or approach with procedure) is what we have called design.[1]

2 Design

In order for an approach to lead to a method, it is necessary to develop a design for an instructional system. *Design* is the level of method analysis in which we consider (a) what the objectives of a method are; (b) how language content is selected and organized within the method, that is, the syllabus model the method incorporates; (c) the types of learning tasks and teaching activities the method advocates; (d) the roles of learners; (e) the roles of teachers; and (f) the role of instructional materials.

Objectives

Different theories of language and language learning influence the focus of a method; that is, they determine what learning outcomes a method sets out to achieve. The specification of particular learning outcomes, however, is a product of design, not of approach. Some methods focus primarily on oral skills and say that reading and writing skills are secondary and derive from transfer of oral skills. Some methods set out to teach general communication skills and give greater priority to the ability to express oneself meaningfully and to make oneself understood than to grammatical accuracy or perfect pronunciation. Others

---

[1] We should also note that focus on variations in instructional methodology is not unique to language teaching. Mathematics and science instruction, particularly in the 1960s, adopted revised notions of effective subject matter instruction. These notions were typically labeled "inquiry," "discovery," and "constructivist" approaches to education. From a pedagogical perspective, inquiry-oriented teaching is often contrasted with more traditional expository methods and reflects the constructivist model of learning, often referred to as active learning, so strongly held among science educators today. As noted above, according to constructivist models, learning is the result of ongoing changes in our mental frameworks as we attempt to make meaning out of our experiences (Osborne and Freyberg 1985). In classrooms where students are encouraged to make meaning, they are generally involved in "developing and restructuring [their] knowledge schemes through experiences with phenomena, through exploratory talk and teacher intervention" (Driver 1989).

may place a greater emphasis on accurate grammar and pronunciation from the very beginning. Some methods set out to teach the basic grammar and vocabulary of a language. Still others may define their objectives less in linguistic terms than in terms of learning behaviors, that is, in terms of the processes or abilities the learner is expected to acquire as a result of instruction. Gattegno writes, for example, "Learning is not seen as the means of accumulating knowledge but as the means of becoming a more proficient learner in whatever one is engaged in" (1972: 89). This process-oriented objective may be offered in contrast to the linguistically oriented or product-oriented objectives of more traditional methods. The degree to which a method has process-oriented or product-oriented objectives may be revealed in how much emphasis is placed on vocabulary acquisition and grammatical proficiency and in how grammatical or pronunciation errors are treated in the method. Many methods that claim to be primarily process-oriented in fact show overriding concerns with grammatical and lexical attainment and with accurate grammar and pronunciation. Different ways of conceptualizing the relationship between learning outcomes and methods are discussed in Chapter 21.

The syllabus

All methods of language teaching involve the use of the target language. All methods thus involve overt or covert decisions concerning the selection of language items or features (words, sentence patterns, tenses, constructions, functions, topics, texts, etc.) that are to be used within a course or method. Decisions about the choice of language content relate to both subject matter and linguistic matter. In straightforward terms, one makes decisions about what to talk about (subject matter) and how to talk about it (linguistic matter). ESP and content-based courses, for example, are necessarily subject matter focused. Structurally and language-based methods, such as Situational Language Teaching, the Audiolingual Method, the Lexical Approach, and Text-Based Instruction, are necessarily linguistically focused. Methods typically differ in what they see as the relevant language and subject matter around which language teaching should be organized and the principles used in sequencing content within a course. Content issues involve the principles of selection that ultimately shape the syllabus adopted in a course as well as the instructional materials that are used, together with the principles of gradation the method adopts. For example, in courses for young learners, concrete topics are likely to be introduced before abstract ones. With adults, course topics related to immediate needs are likely to precede those related to other issues. In grammar-based courses, matters of sequencing and gradation are generally determined according to the difficulty of items, their frequency, and/or their usefulness in the classroom. In communicative or functionally oriented courses (e.g., in ESP programs or task-based courses), sequencing may be according to the learners' perceived communicative needs in terms of functional focus.

Traditionally, the term *syllabus* has been used to refer to the form in which linguistic material is specified in a course or method. Inevitably, the term has been more closely associated with methods that are product-centered rather than with those that are process-centered. Syllabuses and syllabus principles for Audiolingual, Structural-Situational, and communicative methods, as well as in ESP and text-based approaches to language program design, can be readily identified. The syllabus underlying the Situational and Audiolingual methods consists of a list of grammatical items and constructions, often together with an associated list of vocabulary items (Fries and Fries 1961; Alexander et al. 1975). Notional-functional syllabuses (Chapter 5) specify the communicative content of a course in terms of functions, notions, topics, grammar, and vocabulary. Text-based approaches organize courses in terms of text-types such as reports, recounts, and narratives. Such syllabuses are usually determined in advance of teaching and for this reason have been referred to as "a priori syllabuses." (For examples of "a posteri syllabus" types see below.)

A number of taxonomies of syllabus types in language teaching have been proposed: for example, Richards (2001) lists ten basic syllabus types – grammatical, lexical, functional, situational, topical or content-based, competency-based, skills-based, task-based, text-based, and integrated. These can usually be linked to specific approaches or methods: Oral/Situational (situational); Audiolingual (grammatical), Communicative Language Teaching (functional), Task-Based Language Teaching (task-based), and so on. However, for some of the approaches and methods discussed in this book we have had to infer syllabus assumptions since no explicit syllabus specification is given (See Chapter 21). This is particularly true where content organization rather than language organization or pedagogical issues determines syllabus design, as with Content-Based Instruction.

The term *syllabus*, however, is less frequently used in process-based methods, in which considerations of language content are often secondary. Community Language Learning, also known as Counseling-Learning, for example, has no language syllabus as such. Neither linguistic matter nor subject matter is specified in advance. Learners select content for themselves by choosing topics they want to talk about. These are then translated into the target language and used as the basis for interaction and language practice. To find out what linguistic content had in fact been generated and practiced during a course organized according to Counseling-Learning principles, it would be necessary to record the lessons and later determine what items of language had been covered. This would be an *a posteriori* approach to syllabus specification; that is, the syllabus would be determined from examining lesson protocols. The same is true with more recent teaching proposals such as "Dogme" (see Chapter 21), where the syllabus also results from interaction between teachers and students.

Types of learning and teaching activities

The objectives of a method, whether defined primarily in terms of product or process, are attained through the instructional process, through the organized and directed interaction of teachers, learners, and materials in the classroom. Differences among methods at the level of approach manifest themselves in the choice of different kinds of learning and teaching activities in the classroom. Teaching activities that focus on grammatical accuracy may be quite different from those that focus on communicative skills. Activities designed to activate specific second language acquisition processes (such as "noticing") will differ from those directed toward mastery of particular features of grammar. The activity types that a method advocates – the third component in the level of design in method analysis – often serve to distinguish methods and approaches most clearly. Audiolingualism, for example, makes extensive use of dialogues and pattern practice. Communicative Language Teaching makes use of activities that involve an "information gap" and "information transfer"; that is, learners work on the same activity, but each learner has different information needed to complete the activity. In Task-Based Language Teaching, learners work on specially designed tasks or tasks that reflect real-world uses of language, and in text-based approaches students work with authentic texts. Older methods such as the Silent Way also make use of specially designed problem-solving activities that involve the use of special charts and colored rods.

Different philosophies at the level of approach may be reflected both in the use of different kinds of activities and in different uses for particular activity types. For example, interactive games were often used in audiolingual courses for motivation and to provide a change of pace from pattern-practice drills. In Communicative Language Teaching and Task-Based Language Teaching, the same games may be used to introduce or provide practice for particular types of interactive exchanges. Differences in activity types in methods may also involve different arrangements and groupings of learners. A method that stresses oral chorus drilling will require different groupings of learners in the classroom from a method that uses problem-solving/information-exchange activities involving pair work. Activity types in methods thus specify what classroom techniques and procedures the method advocates, such as dialogue, drills, question and answer, responding to commands, group problem-solving, information-exchange activities, task-work, text analysis, role plays, and simulations.

Because of the different assumptions they make about learning processes, syllabuses, and learning activities, methods also assume different roles and functions for learners, teachers, and instructional materials within the instructional process. These constitute the next three components of design in method analysis.

Learner roles

The design of an instructional system will be considerably influenced by how learners are regarded. A method reflects explicit or implicit responses to questions concerning the learners' contribution to the learning process. This is seen in the types of activities learners carry out, the degree of control learners have over the content of learning, the patterns of learner groupings adopted, the degree to which learners influence the learning of others, and the view of the learner as processor, performer, initiator, problem-solver, or other.

The emergence of learner-centered approaches to teaching in the 1980s redefined the role of the learner. Rather than being a passive recipient of teaching – a view that was reflected in older traditions such as Audiolingualism – learners were assigned much more power and autonomy in learning and the great diversity of learners was acknowledged (see Chapter 19). The emergence of what were termed humanistic methods during this period reflected another dimension to a focus on the learner. Humanistic methods were those which emphasized the development of human values, growth in self-awareness and the understanding of others, sensitivity to human feelings and emotions, and active student involvement in learning and the way learning takes place. Community Language Learning and the Silent Way are often mentioned examples of this learner-centeredness as is the more recent Multiple Intelligences (Chapter 12).

A different interpretation of learner-centeredness emerged at the same time under the rubric of individualized approaches to language teaching. This was based on the assumption that people learn in different ways, that they can learn from a variety of different sources, and that they may have different goals and objectives in language learning – assumptions that are now part of the perspective known as learner autonomy (see Chapter 19). Other learner roles have also emerged in more recent methods. The role of the learner as a participant in dialogue and interpersonal communication is central to functional and task-based methods, while the learner as an active processor of language and information and one who draws on prior knowledge, schema, and innate cognitive processes is also reflected in Task-Based Language Teaching as well as in Content-Based Instruction and CLIL. In examining the different approaches and methods in this book, we will describe the different roles they assume for learners.

Teacher roles

Learner roles in an instructional system are closely linked to the teacher's roles and function. Teacher roles are similarly related ultimately to assumptions about both language and language learning at the level of approach. Some methods are totally dependent on the teacher as a source of knowledge and direction; others see the teacher's role as catalyst, consultant, guide, and model for learning; still others try to "teacher-proof" the instructional system by limiting teacher initiative and by building instructional content and direction into texts or lesson plans. Teacher and learner roles define the type of interaction characteristic of classrooms in which a particular method is being used and consequently the kinds of learning processes and opportunities for learning that are provided for.

Teacher roles in methods are related to the following issues: (a) the types of functions teachers are expected to fulfill, whether that of practice director, counselor, or model, for example; (b) the degree of control the teacher has over how learning takes place; (c) the degree to which the teacher is responsible for determining the content of what is taught; and (d) the interactional patterns that develop between teachers and learners. Methods typically depend critically on teacher roles and their realizations. In the classical Audiolingual Method, the teacher is regarded as the primary source of language and of language learning, and in more recent methods such as Task-Based Language Teaching and Text-Based Instruction a very direct role for the teacher is assumed. But less teacher-directed learning may still demand very specific and sometimes even more demanding roles for the teacher. The role of the teacher in Cooperative Language Learning, for example, requires teachers who are confident enough to step back from teacher-fronted teaching and adopt the role of a facilitator. Only teachers who are thoroughly sure of their role and the concomitant learner's role will risk departure from the security of traditional textbook-oriented and teacher-fronted teaching.

For some methods, the role of the teacher has been specified in detail. Individualized approaches to learning define roles for the teacher that create specific patterns of interaction between teachers and learners in classrooms. These are designed to shift gradually the responsibility for learning from the teacher to the learner. Community Language Learning sees the teacher's role as that of psychological counselor, the effectiveness of the teacher's role being a measure of counseling skills and attributes – warmth, sensitivity, and acceptance.

As these examples suggest, the potential role relationships of learner and teacher are many and varied. They may be asymmetrical relationships, such as those of conductor to orchestra member, therapist to patient, coach to player. Some contemporary methodologies have sought to establish more symmetrical kinds of learner–teacher relationships, such as friend to friend, colleague to colleague, teammate to teammate. The role of the teacher will ultimately reflect both the objectives of the method and the learning theory on which the method is predicated, since the success of a method may depend on the degree to which the teacher can provide access to the learning processes and content or create the conditions for successful language learning.

The role of instructional materials

The last component within the level of design concerns the role of instructional materials within the instructional system. What is specified with respect to objectives, content (i.e., the syllabus), learning activities, and learner and teacher roles suggests the function for materials within the system. The syllabus defines linguistic content in terms of language elements – structures, topics, notions, functions, or tasks. It also defines the goals for language learning in terms of listening, speaking, reading, or writing skills. The instructional materials in their turn further specify subject matter content, even where no syllabus exists, and define or suggest the intensity of coverage for syllabus items, allocating the amount of time, attention, and detail particular syllabus items or tasks require. Instructional materials also define or imply the day-to-day learning objectives that collectively constitute the goals of the syllabus. Materials designed on the assumption that learning is initiated and monitored by the teacher must meet quite different requirements from those designed for student self-instruction or for peer tutoring. Some methods require the instructional use of existing materials, found materials, and realia. Some assume teacher-proof materials that even poorly trained teachers with imperfect control of the target language can teach with. Some materials require specially trained teachers with near-native competence in the target language. Some are designed to replace the teacher, so that learning can take place independently. Some materials dictate various interactional patterns in the classroom; others inhibit classroom interaction; still others are noncommittal about interaction between teacher and learner and learner and learner.

The role of instructional materials within a method or instructional system will reflect decisions concerning the primary goal of materials (e.g., to present content, to practice content, to facilitate communication between learners, or to enable learners to practice content without the teacher's help), the form of materials (e.g., textbook, DVDs, computer software), the relation of materials to other sources of input (i.e., whether they serve as the major source of input or only as a minor component of it), and the abilities of teachers (e.g., their competence in the language or degree of training and experience).

A particular design for an instructional system may imply a particular set of roles for materials in support of the syllabus and the teachers and learners. For example, the role of instructional materials within a functional/communicative methodology includes allowing for interpretation, expression, and negotiation of meaning; focusing on understandable, relevant, and interesting exchanges of information, rather than on the presentation of grammatical form, and for involving different kinds of texts and different media, which the learners can use to develop their competence through a variety of different activities and tasks. Within the framework of autonomous learning (see Chapter 19), materials allow learners to progress at their own rates of learning and use different styles of learning; they also provide opportunities for independent study and use, and to provide opportunities for self-evaluation and progress in learning.

In Task-Based Language Teaching, classroom materials provide examples of tasks learners will need to use language beyond the classroom, or they create the need for nego-tiation of meaning and interaction. In Text-Based Instruction, materials model the features of texts and initiate the process by which learners engage in the creation of their own texts. And in CLIL and Content-Based Instruction, materials are the vehicles for the communica-tion of the content that serves as the basis of the lesson.

3 Procedure

The last level of conceptualization and organization within a method is what we will refer to as *procedure*. This encompasses the actual moment-to-moment techniques, practices, and behav-iors that operate in teaching a language according to a particular approach or method. It is the level at which we describe how a method realizes its approach and design in classroom behavior. At the level of design, we saw that a method will advocate the use of certain types of teaching activities as a consequence of its theoretical assumptions about language and learning. At the level of procedure, we are concerned with how these tasks and activities are integrated into les-sons and used as the basis for teaching and learning. There are three dimensions to a method at the level of procedure: (a) the use of teaching activities (drills, dialogues, information gap activities, etc.) to present new language and to clarify and demonstrate formal, communicative, or other aspects of the target language; (b) the ways in which particular teaching activities are used for practicing language; and (c) the procedures and techniques used in giving feedback to learners concerning the form or content of their utterances or sentences.

Essentially, then, procedure focuses on the way a method handles the presentation, practice, and feedback phases of teaching. Figure 2.1 below demonstrates the relationship between approach, design, and procedure, the final step in implementing a method.

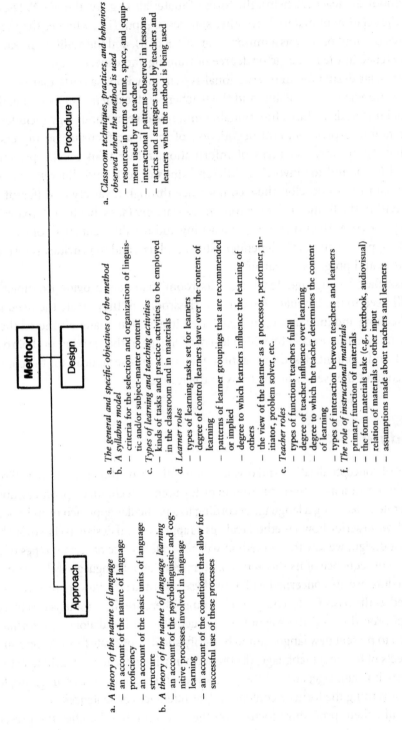

Method

Approach

a. *A theory of the nature of language*
   – an account of the nature of language proficiency
   – an account of the basic units of language structure
b. *A theory of the nature of language learning*
   – an account of the psycholinguistic and cognitive processes involved in language learning
   – an account of the conditions that allow for successful use of these processes

Design

a. *The general and specific objectives of the method*
b. *A syllabus model*
   – criteria for the selection and organization of linguistic and/or subject-matter content
c. *Types of learning and teaching activities*
   – kinds of tasks and practice activities to be employed in the classroom and in materials
d. *Learner roles*
   – types of learning tasks set for learners
   – degree of control learners have over the content of learning
   – patterns of learner groupings that are recommended or implied
   – degree to which learners influence the learning of others
   – the view of the learner as a processor, performer, initiator, problem solver, etc.
e. *Teacher roles*
   – types of functions teachers fulfill
   – degree of teacher influence over learning
   – degree to which the teacher determines the content of learning
   – types of interaction between teachers and learners
f. *The role of instructional materials*
   – primary function of materials
   – the form materials take (e.g., textbook, audiovisual)
   – relation of materials to other input
   – assumptions made about teachers and learners

Procedure

a. *Classroom techniques, practices, and behaviors observed when the method is used*
   – resources in terms of time, space, and equipment used by the teacher
   – interactional patterns observed in lessons
   – tactics and strategies used by teachers and learners when the method is being used

Figure 2.1 Summary of elements and sub-elements that constitute a method

In Situational Language Teaching, a sequence of five activities is often used:

1. *Presentation.* The new structure is introduced and presented.
2. *Controlled practice.* Learners are given intensive practice in the structure, under the teacher's guidance and control.
3. *Free practice.* The students practice using the structure without any control by the teacher.
4. *Checking.* The teacher elicits use of the new structure to check that it has been learned.
5. *Further practice.* The structure is now practiced in new situations or in combination with other structures.

In Communicative Language Teaching (Chapter 5), the following sequence of activities is often used:

1. *Pre-communicative activities.* Accuracy-based activities which focus on presentation of structures, functions, and vocabulary.
2. *Communication activities.* Fluency-based activities which focus on information-sharing and information-exchange.

Text-based lessons or units (Chapter 10) often contain the following five-stage sequence of activities:

1. *Building the context* (the situations in which a particular text-type is used and its purpose are discussed)
2. *Modeling and deconstructing the text* (the teacher shows how the text is constructed and what its linguistic and discourse features are)
3. *Joint construction of the text* (teacher and students jointly create a new text following the format of the model text)
4. *Independent construction of the text* (students create their own texts)
5. *Links to related texts* (similarities and differences between other types of texts are discussed).

We expect methods to be most obviously idiosyncratic at the level of procedure, though classroom observations often reveal that teachers do not necessarily follow the procedures a method prescribes. Over time they adapt the procedures to their own preferred teaching style.

Why is an approach or method adopted?

Throughout this book we will examine a number of language teaching approaches and methods that have been used in recent and less recent times, as well as some that are still very current. The fact that so many different instructional designs for second language teaching have been proposed over a relatively short period of time poses the question of why the language teaching field is subject to the many contrasting views of teaching that we find reflected in different methods.

Factors responsible for the rise and fall of methods

What factors appear to be responsible for the rise and fall of methods? We would suggest that a number of factors are involved, including the following.

Paradigm shifts

As with other fields of education, language teaching is subject to the influences of changes in the theories found in the supporting disciplines of linguistics, psychology, and second language learning. Chomsky's attack on behaviorism (Chapter 3) and his theory of linguistic competence was an example of such a shift – one that had a significant impact on approaches to language teaching. The emergence of the field of second language acquisition similarly prompted a shift in thinking about the nature of second language learning and new approaches to language teaching that led to the Natural Approach and Task-Based Language Teaching. Communicative Language Teaching similarly was adopted as evidence of a new paradigm of understanding about language teaching and learning.

Support networks

The support networks available in promoting or explaining a new teaching approach or method are also crucial. Here a ministry or department of education, key educational administrators, leading academics, and professional bodies and organizations can play an important role in promoting a new approach or method. The fact that the Common European Framework of Reference (Chapter 8) is the product of an important European organization (the Council of Europe) has done much to give it a sense of legitimacy, as was similarly the case with earlier proposals from the Council of Europe – the Threshold Level – that provided a framework for Communicative Language Teaching (Chapter 5).

Practicality

A method that is simple to understand, that requires little time to master, that appears to conform to common sense, and that can be used in many different kinds of situations is more likely to find advocates than one that is difficult to understand and that requires special training and resources. Total Physical Response and Text-Based Instruction would be examples in the former category while the Silent Way and Task-Based Language Teaching would be examples of the second.

Teacher's language proficiency

Many of the world's language teachers are not native speakers of the languages they teach but nonetheless often achieve very good results. However, a method that assumes a native-speaker level of proficiency on the part of the teacher is unlikely to find advocates in some countries. The Direct Method proved difficult for many teachers for this reason, and more recent methods such as Task-Based Language Teaching and CLIL may also be difficult for some teachers to use for the same reason.

Used as the basis for published materials and tests

Some instructional designs can readily be used as the basis for syllabuses, courses, text-books, and tests. Millions of textbooks have been sold based on the principles of methods such as Audiolingualism and Communicative Language Teaching, and approaches and methods such as Text-Based Instruction and Content-Based Instruction have similarly been used as the basis for textbooks. These together with the principles they are based on will generally be widely promoted by publishers and their representatives to secure their adoption in schools. However, approaches and methods that do not provide the basis for published coursebooks and syllabuses, such as the Natural Approach and Task-Based Language Teaching, are unlikely to achieve similar prominence, since they are more dependent on the efforts of individual teachers for their application than published resources. Many language tests today are linked to the Common European Framework of Reference – a fact that further consolidates its influence. The use of a method as the basis for technology-supported learning will also help consolidate its impact and uptake.

Compatibility with local traditions

Styles of teaching and learning differ significantly in different parts of the world and conceptions of good teaching differ from culture to culture (Tsui 2009). In some cultures a good teacher is one who controls and directs learners and who maintains a respectful distance between the teacher and the learners. Learners are the more or less passive recipients of the teacher's expertise. Teaching is viewed as a teacher-controlled and teacher-directed process. In other cultures the teacher may be viewed more as a facilitator. The ability to form close interpersonal relations with students is highly valued and there is a strong emphasis on individual learner creativity and independent learning. Students may even be encouraged to question and challenge what the teacher says. Methods that are learner-centered and that encourage autonomous learning (Chapter 19) may not be suited to contexts where teachers are unfamiliar with this style of teaching and learning.

A checklist for the adoption of an approach or method

The extent to which new approaches and methods become widely accepted and have a lasting impact on teachers' practices hence depends on the relative ease or difficulty of introducing the changes the approach or method requires. Curriculum changes are of many different kinds. They may affect teachers' pedagogical values and beliefs, their understanding of the nature of language or second language learning, or their classroom practices and uses of teaching materials. Some changes may be readily accepted, others resisted. The following questions will therefore affect the extent to which a new approach or method is adopted:

- What advantages does the new approach or method offer? Is it perceived to be more effective than current practices?
- How compatible is it with teachers' existing beliefs and attitudes and with the organization and practices within classrooms and schools?

- Who recommends it? Is it supported by the recommendations of authorities and experts?
- Is the new approach or method very complicated and difficult to understand and use?
- Has it been tested out in some schools and classrooms before teachers are expected to use it?
- Have the benefits of the new approach or method been clearly communicated to teachers and institutions?
- How clear and practical is the new approach or method? Are its expectations stated in ways that clearly show how it can be used in the classroom?

Conclusion

The model presented in this chapter demonstrates that any language teaching method can be described in terms of the issues identified here at the levels of approach, design, and procedure. Very few methods are explicit with respect to all of these dimensions, however. In the remaining chapters of this book, we will attempt to make each of these features of approach, design, and procedure explicit with reference to the major language teaching approaches and methods in use today. In so doing, we will often have to infer from what method developers have written in order to determine precisely what criteria are being used for teaching activities, what claims are being made about learning theory, what type of syllabus is being employed, and so on.

The model presented here is not intended to imply that methodological development proceeds neatly from approach, through design, to procedure. It is not clear whether such a developmental formula is possible, and our model certainly does not describe the typical case. Methods can develop from the level of approach or from that of procedure. A novel theory of language or language learning might prompt attempts to develop a teaching method from it. Or one could, perhaps, stumble on or invent a set of teaching procedures that appear to be successful and then later develop a design and a theoretical approach that explain or justify the procedures. Some methodologists would resist calling their proposals a method, although, if descriptions are possible at each of the levels described here, we would argue that what is advocated has, in fact, the status of a method. Let us now turn to the major approaches and teaching methods that are in use today and examine them according to how they reflect specific decisions at the levels of approach, design, and procedure.

Discussion questions

1. How would you explain, in your own words, the difference between an approach, a method, and a technique?

2. Match the models of language below with their descriptions.

Sociocultural	Language is a system of structurally related elements for the coding of meaning, such as phonemes and grammar.
Interactional	Language is a vehicle for the expression of functional meanings and for performing real-world activities.

Cognitive	Language is the acquisition of abstract knowledge and involves properties of the mind.
Genre	Language is a communicative activity in which the social context, customs, and beliefs are central.
Lexical	Language is considered primarily through the role of lexis and lexical chunks or phrases.
Functional	Language is a vehicle for the realization of interpersonal relations.
Structural	Language is governed by discourse-specific norms and texts for different purposes.

3. What theories of learning are reflected in the materials or textbooks you use in your teaching?

4. Which approaches and methods have been popular in your country in the past? Can you identify the reasons for their success?

5. What do you understand by the concept of *scaffolded learning*? Why might dialogue with a more knowledgeable other be important to sociocultural learning theory?

6. How important to do you think practice is in language learning? How can practice affect learning and language use?

7. Do your learners have particular learning style preferences? How can these be identified and, if necessary, supported or modified?

8. What are the different components of design? Why is each one important? What are some examples of how design translates into procedure?

9. What are some factors that determine whether an approach or method is adopted? Which of these do you feel are the most important?

References and further reading

Alexander, L. G., W. S. Allen, R. A. Close, and R. J. O'Neill. 1975. *English Grammatical Structure.* London: Longman.

Anthony, E. M. 1963. Approach, method and technique. *English Language Teaching* 17: 63–7.

Asher, J. 1977. *Learning Another Language through Actions: The Complete Teacher's Guidebook.* Los Gatos, CA: Sky Oakes Productions.

Atkinson, D. 2002. Towards a sociocognitive approach to second language acquisition. *Modern Language Journal* 86(4): 525–45.

Atkinson, D. 2011. *Alternative Approaches to Second Language Acquisition.* New York: Routledge.

Bosco, F. J., and R. J. Di Pietro. 1970. Instructional strategies: their psychological and linguistic bases. *International Review of Applied Linguistics* 8: 1–19.

Breen, M. P., and C. Candlin. 1980. The essentials of a communicative curriculum in language teaching. *Applied Linguistics* 1(2): 89–112.

Brown, H. D. 1994. *Teaching by Principles: An interactive Approach to Language Pedagogy*. Englewood Cliffs, NJ: Prentice Hall.

Brown, J. 1995. *The Elements of the Language Curriculum*. Boston: Heinle and Heinle.

Carrell, P., A. Devine, and D. Esky. 1988. *Interactive Approaches to Second Language Reading*. Cambridge: Cambridge University Press.

Curran, C. A. 1972. *Counseling-Learning: A Whole-Person Model for Education*. New York: Grune and Stratton.

Curran, C. A. 1976. *Counseling-Learning in Second Languages*. Apple River, IL: Apple River Press.

Driver, R. 1989. Students' conceptions and the learning of science. *International Journal of Science Education* 11(5): 481–90.

Feez, S. 1998. *Text-Based Syllabus Design*. Sydney: Macquarie University.

Finocchiaro, M., and C. Brumfit. 1983. *The Functional-Notional Approach: From Theory to Practice*. New York: Oxford University Press.

Fries, C. C., and A. C. Fries. 1961. *Foundations for English Teaching*. Tokyo: Kenkyusha.

Gattegno, C. 1972. *Teaching Foreign Languages in Schools: The Silent Way*. 2nd edn. New York: Educational Solutions.

Gattegno, C. 1976. *The Common Sense of Teaching Foreign Languages*. New York: Educational Solutions.

Haury, D. 1993. *Teaching Science through Inquiry*. ERIC/SCMEE Digest. Available at: http://www.uhu.es/gaia-inm/invest_escolar/httpdocs/biblioteca_pdf/14_HAURY[1].1993%20TEACHING%20SCIENCE%20THROUGH%20INQUIRY.pdf

Holliday, A. 1994. *Appropriate Methodology*. Cambridge: Cambridge University Press.

Johnson, F., and C. B. Paulston. 1976. *Individualizing in the Language Classroom*. Cambridge, MA: Jacaranda.

Johnson, K. 1982. *Communicative Syllabus Design and Methodology*. Oxford: Pergamon.

Krashen, S. D. 1981. *Second Language Acquisition and Second Language Learning*. Oxford: Pergamon.

Lave, J., and Wenger E. 1991. *Situated Learning: Legitimate Peripheral Participation*. Cambridge: Cambridge University Press.

Long, M., and G. Crookes. 1992. Three approaches to task-based syllabus design. *TESOL Quarterly* 226(1) (Spring): 27–56.

Mackey, W. F. 1965. *Language Teaching Analysis*. London: Longman.

Ortega, L. 2009. *Understanding Second Language Acquisition*. London: Hodder Education.

Osborne, R., and P. Freyberg. 1985. *Learning in Science: The Implications of Children's Science*. Portsmouth, NH: Heinemann Educational Books.

O'Keefe, A., M. McCarthy, and R. Carter 2007. *From Corpus to Classroom*. Cambridge: Cambridge University Press.

Oxford, R. 1997. Cooperative learning, collaborative learning and interaction: three communicative strands in the language classroom. *Modern Language Journal* 81(4): 443–56.

Paltridge, B. 2006. *Discourse Analysis*. London: Continuum.

Prabhu, N. 1983. Procedural syllabuses. Paper presented at the RELC Seminar. Singapore: Regional Language Centre.

Prabhu, N. 1990. There is no best method – why? *TESOL Quarterly* 24: 161–76.

Richards J. C. 1990. Beyond methods. In J. C. Richards, *The Language Teaching Matrix*. New York: Cambridge University Press. 35–49.

Richards J. C. 2001. *Curriculum Development in Language Teaching*. New York: Cambridge University Press.

Rivers, W. M. (ed.). 1987. *Interactive Language Teaching*. Cambridge: Cambridge University Press.

Robinson, P. 1980. *ESP (English for Specific Purposes)*. Oxford: Pergamon.

Rodgers, T. 1990. After methods, what? In S. Aninan (ed.), *Language Teaching Methodology for the Nineties*. Singapore: SEAMEO Regional Language Centre. 1–21.

Rogoff, B. 1990. *Apprenticeship in Thinking*. New York: Oxford University Press.

Schmitt, N. (ed.). 2004. *Formulaic Sequences: Acquisition, Processing and Use*. Amsterdam: John Benjamins.

Skinner, B. F. 1957. *Verbal Behavior*. New York: Appleton-Century-Crofts.

Spolsky, B. 1998. *Conditions for Second Language Learning: Introduction to a General Theory*. Oxford: Oxford University Press.

Stevick, E. W. 1980. *Teaching Languages: A Way and Ways*. Rowley, MA: Newbury House.

Swain, M., P. Kinnear, and L. Steinman. 2010. *Sociocultural Theory in Second Language Education*. Bristol: Multilingual Matters.

Terrell, T. D. 1977. A natural approach to the acquisition and learning of a language. *Modern Language Journal* 61(7): 325–36.

Tsui, A. B. M. 2009. Teaching expertise: approaches, perspectives and characteristics. In A. Burns and J. C. Richards (eds.), *The Cambridge Guide to Second Language Teacher Education*. Cambridge: Cambridge University Press. 190–7.

Warschauer, M., and R. Kern (eds.). 1999. *Network-Based Language Teaching: Concepts and Practices*. New York: Cambridge University Press.

Wilkins, D. A. 1976. *Notional Syllabuses*. Oxford: Oxford University Press.

Yalden, J. 1987. *Principles of Course Design for Language Teaching*. Cambridge: Cambridge University Press.

Williams, M., and R. Burden. 1997. *Psychology for Language Teachers: A Social Constructivist Approach*. Cambridge: Cambridge University Press.

3 The Oral Approach and Situational Language Teaching

Few language teachers today are familiar with the terms *Oral Approach* or *Situational Language Teaching*, which both refer to an approach to language teaching developed by British applied linguists, the first dating from the 1920s and 1930s and the second from the 1950s and 1960s. Even though neither term is commonly used today, the impact of the Oral Approach has been long-lasting, and it shaped the design of many widely used English as a Second/Foreign Language (ESL/EFL) textbooks and courses, particularly those published in the United Kingdom. Situational Language Teaching, a type of oral approach, continued to be popular well into the 1980s, and some of these textbooks are still used today. One of the most successful ESL courses published, *Streamline English* (Hartley and Viney 1978), reflected the classic principles of Situational Language Teaching, as did many other series that have been widely used, such as *Access to English* (Coles and Lord 1975), *Kernel Lessons Plus* (O'Neill 1973) and many of L. G. Alexander's widely used textbooks, for example, *New Concept English* (1967). Perhaps the biggest legacy of the Oral Approach was the PPP lesson format: Presentation-Practice-Production, which will be discussed further below. Hundreds of thousands of teachers worldwide have been trained to use this lesson format, and it continues to be seen in language textbooks today. This chapter will explore the development of the Oral Approach in Britain. In the next chapter, we will look at related developments in the United States.

Introduction

The origins of this approach began with the work of British applied linguists in the 1920s and 1930s. Beginning at this time, a number of outstanding applied linguists developed the basis for a principled approach to methodology in language teaching. Two of the leaders in this movement were Harold Palmer (1877–1949) and A. S. Hornby (1898–1978), two of the most prominent figures in British twentieth-century language teaching. Both were familiar with the work of such prominent linguists of the time as the Danish grammarian Otto Jespersen and the phonetician Daniel Jones, as well as with the Direct Method. They attempted to develop a more scientific foundation for an oral approach to teaching English than was evidenced in the Direct Method. The result was a systematic study of the principles and procedures that could be applied to the selection and organization of the content of a language course (Palmer 1917, 1921).

Vocabulary selection

One of the first aspects of method design to receive attention was the role of vocabulary. In the 1920s and 1930s, several large-scale investigations of foreign language vocabulary were undertaken. The impetus for this research came from two quarters. First, there was a general consensus among language teaching specialists, such as Palmer, that vocabulary was one of the most important aspects of foreign language learning. A second influence was the increased emphasis on reading skills as the goal of foreign language study in some countries. This had been the recommendation of the Coleman Report (Chapter 1) and also the independent conclusion of another British language teaching specialist, Michael West, who had examined the role of English in India in the 1920s. Vocabulary was seen as an essential component of reading proficiency.

This led to the development of principles for vocabulary selection, which were to have a major practical impact on the teaching of English in subsequent decades. Frequency counts showed that a core of 2,000 or so words occurred frequently in written texts and that a knowledge of these words would greatly assist in reading a foreign language. Palmer, West, and other specialists produced a guide to the English vocabulary needed for teaching English as a foreign language, *The Interim Report on Vocabulary Selection* (Faucett et al. 1936), based on frequency as well as other criteria. This was later revised by West and published as *A General Service List of English Words* (1953b), which became a standard reference in developing teaching materials. These efforts to introduce a scientific and rational basis for choosing the vocabulary content of a language course represented the first attempts to establish principles of syllabus design in language teaching.

Grammar control

Parallel to the interest in developing rational principles for vocabulary selection was a focus on the grammatical content of a language course. Palmer had emphasized the problems of grammar for the foreign learner. Much of his work in Japan, where he directed the Institute for Research in English Teaching from 1922 until World War II, was directed toward developing classroom procedures suited to teaching basic grammatical patterns through an oral approach. His view of grammar was very different from the abstract model of grammar seen in the Grammar-Translation Method, however, which was based on the assumption that one universal logic formed the basis of all languages and that the teacher's responsibility was to show how each category of the universal grammar was to be expressed in the foreign language. Palmer viewed grammar as the underlying sentence patterns of the spoken language. Palmer, Hornby, and other British applied linguists analyzed English and classified its major grammatical structures into sentence patterns (later called "substitution tables"), which could be used to help internalize the rules of English sentence structure. The following is an example of a sentence pattern:

Pattern: S–Vtr–DO (Subject + Transitive Verb + Direct Object)
The dog **catches** the ball.
The baby **likes** bananas.

Dogs **chase** cats.

That man **teaches** English.

The scientist **performed** an experiment.

A classification of English sentence patterns was incorporated into the first dictionary for students of English as a second or foreign language, developed by Hornby, Gatenby, and Wakefield and published in 1953 as *The Advanced Learner's Dictionary of Current English*. A number of pedagogically motivated descriptions of English grammar were undertaken, including *A Grammar of Spoken English on a Strictly Phonetic Basis* (Palmer and Blandford 1939), *A Handbook of English Grammar* (Zandvoort 1945), and Hornby's *Guide to Patterns and Usage in English* (1954a), which became a standard reference source of basic English sentence patterns for textbook writers. With the development of systematic approaches to the lexical and grammatical content of a language course and with the efforts of such specialists as Palmer, West, and Hornby in using these resources as part of a comprehensive methodological framework for the teaching of English as a second or foreign language, the foundations for the British approach in TEFL/TESL – the Oral Approach – were firmly established.

The Oral Approach and Situational Language Teaching

Palmer, Hornby, and other British applied linguists from the 1920s onward developed an approach to methodology that involved systematic principles of *selection* (the procedures by which lexical and grammatical content was chosen), *gradation* (principles by which the organization and sequencing of content were determined), and *presentation* (techniques used for presentation and practice of items in a course). Although Palmer, Hornby, and other English teaching specialists had differing views on the specific procedures to be used in teaching English, their general principles were referred to as the Oral Approach to language teaching. This was not to be confused with the Direct Method (Chapter 1), which, although it used oral procedures, lacked a systematic basis in applied linguistic theory and practice.

> An oral approach should not be confused with the obsolete Direct Method, which meant only that the learner was bewildered by a flow of ungraded speech, suffering all the difficulties he would have encountered in picking up the language in its normal environment and losing most of the compensating benefits of better contextualization in those circumstances.
>
> (Pattison 1964: 4)

Situational Language Teaching is a type of oral approach, as will be explained. The Oral Approach, described in detail below, was the accepted British approach to English language teaching by the 1950s. It is described in the standard methodology textbooks of the period, such as French (1948–1950), Gurrey (1955), Frisby (1957), and Billows (1961). Its principles are seen in Hornby's famous *Oxford Progressive English Course for Adult Learners* (1954–1956) and in many other more recent textbooks. One of the most active proponents of the Oral Approach in the 1960s was the Australian George Pittman. Pittman and his colleagues were responsible for developing an influential set of teaching materials based on the Situational Approach, a more modern version of the early Oral Approach, which were widely used in Australia, New Guinea, and the Pacific territories. Pittman was also responsible for the situationally based materials developed by the Commonwealth Office of Education in Sydney, used in the English programs for immigrants in Australia. These were published for worldwide use in 1965 as the series *Situational English*. Materials by Alexander and other leading British textbook writers also reflected the principles of Situational Language Teaching as they had evolved over a 20-year period. The main characteristics of the Oral Approach were as follows:

1. Language teaching begins with the spoken language. Material is taught orally before it is presented in written form.
2. The target language is the language of the classroom.
3. New language points are introduced and practiced situationally.
4. Vocabulary selection procedures are followed to ensure that an essential general service vocabulary is covered.
5. Items of grammar are graded following the principle that simple forms should be taught before complex ones.
6. Reading and writing are introduced once a sufficient lexical and grammatical basis is established.

It was the third principle that became a key feature of the approach in the 1960s, and it was then that the term *situational* was used increasingly in referring to the Oral Approach. Hornby himself used the term the *Situational Approach* in the title of an influential series of articles published in *English Language Teaching* in 1950. Later, the terms *Structural- Situational Approach* and *Situational Language Teaching* came into common usage. To avoid further confusion, we will use the term *Situational Language Teaching* (SLT) to include the Structural-Situational and Oral approaches that predominated in the 1950s and beyond. How can SLT be characterized at the levels of approach, design, and procedure?

Approach

Theory of language

The theory of language underlying SLT can be characterized as a type of British structural model or "structuralism." Underlying every language was a system of grammatical patterns and structures that had to be mastered in learning a language. Speech was regarded as the basis of language, and structure was viewed as being at the heart of speaking ability. Palmer, Hornby, and other British applied linguists had prepared pedagogical descriptions of the basic grammatical structures of English, and these were to be followed in developing methodology. "Word order, structural words, the few inflexions of English, and content words, will form the material of our teaching" (Frisby 1957: 134). In terms of language theory, there was little to distinguish such a view from that proposed by American linguists, such as Charles Fries, who viewed grammar, or "structure," and basic sentence patterns as the starting point for language teaching (Chapter 4). Indeed, Pittman drew heavily on Fries's theories of language in the 1960s, but American theory was largely unknown to British applied linguists in the 1950s. The British theoreticians, however, had a different focus to their version of structuralism – the notion of "situation." "Our principal classroom activity in the teaching of English structure will be the oral practice of structures. This oral practice of controlled sentence patterns should be given in situations designed to give the greatest amount of practice in English speech to the pupil" (Pittman 1963: 179).

The theory that knowledge of structures must be linked to situations in which they could be used gave SLT one of its distinctive features. This may have reflected the functional trend in British linguistics since the 1930s. Many British linguists had emphasized the close relationship between the structure of language and the context and situations in which language is used. Beginning in the 1930s, British linguists, such as J. R. Firth, followed by M. A. K. Halliday, developed powerful views of language in which meaning, context, and situation were given a prominent place: "The emphasis now is on the description of language activity as part of the whole complex of events which, together with the participants and relevant objects, make up actual situations" (Halliday, McIntosh, and Strevens 1964: 38). Thus, in contrast to American structuralist views on language (see Chapter 4), language was viewed as purposeful activity related to goals and situations in the real world. "The language which a person originates ... is always expressed for a purpose" (Frisby 1957: 16).

Theory of learning

The theory of learning underlying SLT is a type of behaviorist habit-learning theory. Frisby, for example, cites Palmer's views as authoritative: "As Palmer has pointed out, there are three processes in learning a language – receiving the knowledge or materials, fixing it in the memory by repetition, and using it in actual practice until it becomes a personal skill" (1957: 136). French likewise saw language learning as habit formation: "The fundamental is correct speech habits ... The pupils should be able to put the words, without hesitation and almost without thought, into sentence patterns which are correct. Such speech habits can be cultivated by blind imitative drill" (1950, III: 9).

Like the Direct Method, SLT adopts an inductive approach to the teaching of grammar. The meaning of words or structures is not to be given through explanation in either the native language or the target language but is to be induced from the way the form is used in a situation. "If we give the meaning of a new word, either by translation into the home language or by an equivalent in the same language, as soon as we introduce it, we weaken the impression which the word makes on the mind" (Billows 1961: 28). Explanation is therefore discouraged, and the learner is expected to deduce the meaning of a particular structure or vocabulary item from the situation in which it is presented. Extending structures and vocabulary to new situations takes place by generalization. The learner is expected to apply the language learned in a classroom to situations outside the classroom. This is how child language learning is believed to take place, and the same processes are thought to occur in second and foreign language learning, according to practitioners of SLT.

Design
Objectives

The objectives of the SLT method are to teach a practical command of the four basic skills of language, goals it shares with most methods of language teaching. But the skills are approached through structure. Accuracy in both pronunciation and grammar is regarded as crucial, and errors are to be avoided at all costs. Automatic control of basic structures and sentence patterns is fundamental to reading and writing skills, and this is achieved through speech work. "Before our pupils read new structures and new vocabulary, we shall teach orally both the new structures and the new vocabulary" (Pittman 1963: 186). Writing likewise derives from speech.

> Oral composition can be a very valuable exercise ... Nevertheless, the skill with which this activity is handled depends largely on the control of the language suggested by the teacher and used by the children ... Only when the teacher is reasonably certain that learners can speak fairly correctly within the limits of their knowledge of sentence structure and vocabulary may he [sic] allow them free choice in sentence patterns and vocabulary.
>
> (Pittman 1963: 188)

The syllabus

Basic to the teaching of English in SLT is a structural syllabus and a word list. A structural syllabus is a list of the basic structures and sentence patterns of English, arranged according to their order of presentation. In SLT, structures are always taught within sentences, and vocabulary is chosen according to how well it enables sentence patterns to be taught. "Our early course will consist of a list of sentence patterns [statement patterns, question patterns, and request or command patterns] ... will include as many structural words as possible, and sufficient content words to provide us with material upon which to base our language practice" (Frisby 1957: 134). Frisby (1957: 134) gives an example of the typical structural syllabus around which situational teaching was based:

	Sentence pattern	Vocabulary
1st lesson	This is ... That is ...	book, pencil, ruler, desk
2nd lesson	These are ... Those are ...	chair, picture, door, window
3rd lesson	Is this ... ? Yes it is. Is that ... ? Yes it is.	watch, box, pen, blackboard

The syllabus was not therefore a situational syllabus in the sense that this term is sometimes used (i.e., a list of situations and the language associated with them). Rather, situation refers to the manner of presenting and practicing sentence patterns, as we shall see later. The word *situation* is understood as encompassing such areas as pictures or realia, actions, and drills, as we will explain.

Types of learning and teaching activities

SLT employs a situational approach to presenting new sentence patterns and a drill-based manner of practicing them:

> our method will ... be situational. The situation will be controlled carefully to teach the new language material ... in such a way that there can be no doubt in the learner's mind of the meaning of what he hears ... almost all the vocabulary and structures taught in the first four or five years and even later can be placed in situations in which the meaning is quite clear.
>
> (Pittman 1963: 155–6)

By *situation* Pittman means the use of concrete objects, pictures, and realia, which together with actions and gestures can be used to demonstrate the meanings of new language items:

> The form of new words and sentence patterns is demonstrated with examples and not through grammatical explanation or description. The meaning of new words and sentence patterns is not conveyed through translation. It is made clear visually (with objects, pictures, action and mime). Wherever possible model sentences are related and taken from a single situation.
>
> (Davies, Roberts, and Rossner 1975: 3)

The practice techniques employed generally consist of guided repetition and substitution activities, including chorus repetition, dictation, drills, and controlled oral-based reading and writing tasks. Other oral-practice techniques are sometimes used, including pair practice and group work.

Learner roles

In the initial stages of learning, the learner is required simply to listen and repeat what the teacher says and to respond to questions and commands. The learner has no control over the content of learning and is often regarded as likely to succumb to undesirable behaviors unless skillfully manipulated by the teacher. For example, the learner might lapse into faulty grammar or pronunciation, forget what has been taught, or fail to respond quickly enough; incorrect habits are to be avoided at all costs (see Pittman 1963). Later, more active participation is encouraged. This includes learners initiating responses and asking each other questions, although teacher-controlled introduction and practice of new language is stressed throughout (Davies et al. 1975).

Teacher roles

The teacher's function is threefold. In the presentation stage of the lesson, the teacher serves as a model, setting up situations in which the need for the target structure is created and then modeling the new structure for students to repeat. Then the teacher "becomes more like the skillful conductor of an orchestra, drawing the music out of the performers" (Byrne 1976: 2). The teacher is required to be a skillful manipulator, using questions, commands, and other cues to elicit correct sentences from the learners. Lessons are hence teacher-directed, and the teacher sets the pace.

During the practice phase of the lesson, students are given more of an opportunity to use the language in less controlled situations, but the teacher is ever on the lookout for grammatical and structural errors that can form the basis of subsequent lessons. Organizing review is a primary task for the teacher, according to Pittman, who summarizes the teacher's responsibilities as dealing with

1. timing
2. oral practice, to support the textbook structures
3. revision [i.e., review]
4. adjustment to special needs of individuals
5. testing
6. developing language activities other than those arising from the textbook

(Pittman 1963: 177–8)

The teacher is essential to the success of the method, since the textbook serves to present activities for the teacher to carry out in class.

The role of instructional materials

SLT is dependent on both a textbook and visual aids. The textbook contains tightly organized lessons planned around different grammatical structures. Visual aids may be produced by the teacher or may be commercially produced; they consist of wall charts, flashcards, pictures, stick figures, and so on. The visual element together with a carefully graded grammatical syllabus is a crucial aspect of SLT, hence the importance of the textbook. In principle, however, the textbook should be used "only as a guide to the learning process. The teacher is expected to be the master of his textbook" (Pittman 1963: 176).

Procedure

Classroom procedures in SLT vary according to the level of the class, but procedures at any level aim to move from controlled to freer practice of structures and from oral use of sentence patterns to their automatic use in speech, reading, and writing. Pittman (1963: 173) gives an example of a typical lesson plan:

> The first part of the lesson will be stress and intonation practice ... The main body of the lesson should then follow. This might consist of the teaching of a structure. If so, the lesson would then consist of four parts:
>
> 1. pronunciation
> 2. revision (to prepare for new work if necessary)
> 3. presentation of new structure or vocabulary
> 4. oral practice (drilling)
> 5. reading of material on the new structure, or written exercises

Davies et al. (1975: 56) give sample lesson plans for use with SLT. The structures being taught in the following lesson are "This is a ..." and "That's a ..."

Teacher:	(holding up a watch) Look. This is a watch. (2 ×) (pointing to a clock on wall or table) That's a clock. (2 ×) That's a clock. (2 ×) This is a watch. (putting down watch and moving across to touch the clock or pick it up) This is a clock. (2 ×) (pointing to watch) That's a watch. (2 ×) (picking up a pen) This is a pen. (2 ×) (drawing large pencil on blackboard and moving away) That's a pencil. (2 ×) Take your pens. All take your pens. (students all pick up their pens)
Teacher:	Listen. This is a pen. (3 ×) This. (3 ×)
Students:	This. (3 ×)
A student:	This. (6 ×) Teacher: This is a pen.
Students:	This is a pen. (3 ×)
A student:	(moving pen) This is a pen. (6 ×)
Teacher:	(pointing to blackboard) That's a pencil. (3 ×) That. (3 ×)
Students:	That. (3 ×)
A student:	That. (6 ×)
Teacher:	That's a pencil.
Students:	(all pointing at blackboard) That's a pencil. (3 ×)
A student:	(pointing at blackboard) That's a pencil. (6 ×)
Teacher:	Take your books. (taking a book himself) This is a book. (3 ×)
Students:	This is a book. (3 ×)
Teacher:	(placing notebook in a visible place) Tell me ...
Student 1:	That's a notebook.

You can now begin taking objects out of your box, making sure they are as far as possible not new vocabulary items. Large objects may be placed in visible places at the front of the classroom. Smaller ones distributed to students.

These procedures illustrate the techniques used in presenting new language items in situations. Drills, as mentioned, are likewise related to "situations." Pittman illustrates oral drilling on a pattern, using a box full of objects to create the situation. The pattern being practiced is "There's a NOUN + of + (noun) in the box." The teacher takes objects out of the box and the class repeats:

> There's a tin of cigarettes in the box.
> There's a packet of matches in the box.
> There's a reel of cotton in the box.
> There's a bottle of ink in the box.
> There's a packet of pins in the box.
> There's a pair of shoes in the box.
> There's a jar of rice in the box.
>
> (Pittman 1963: 168)

The teacher's kit, a collection of items and realia that can be used in situational language practice, is hence an essential part of the teacher's equipment.

Davies et al. likewise give detailed information about teaching procedures to be used with SLT. The sequence of activities they propose consists of the following:

1. Listening practice in which the teacher obtains his students' attention and repeats an example of the patterns or a word in isolation clearly, several times, probably saying it slowly at least once (where ... is ... the ... pen?), separating the words.
2. Choral imitation in which students all together or in large groups repeat what the teacher has said. This works best if the teacher gives a clear instruction like "Repeat," or "Everybody" and hand signals to mark time and stress.
3. Individual imitation in which the teacher asks several individual students to repeat the model he has given in order to check their pronunciation.
4. Isolation, in which the teacher isolates sounds, words, or groups of words which cause trouble and goes through techniques 1–3 with them before replacing them in context.
5. Building up to a new model, in which the teacher gets students to ask and answer questions using patterns they already know in order to bring about the information necessary to introduce the new model.
6. Elicitation, in which the teacher, using mime, prompt words, gestures, etc., gets students to ask questions, make statements, or give new examples of the pattern.
7. Substitution drilling, in which the teacher uses cue words (words, pictures, numbers, names, etc.) to get individual students to mix the examples of the new patterns.
8. Question-answer drilling, in which the teacher gets one student to ask a question and another to answer until most students in the class have practiced asking and answering the new question form.

9. Correction, in which the teacher indicates by shaking his head, repeating the error, etc., that there is a mistake and invites the student or a different student to correct it. Where possible the teacher does not simply correct the mistake himself. He gets students to correct themselves so they will be encouraged to listen to each other carefully.

(Davies et al. 1975: 6–7)

Davies et al. then go on to discuss how follow-up reading and writing activities are to be carried out.

The PPP lesson format

One of the most enduring legacies of SLT at the procedure level is what came to be known as the PPP lesson format – Presentation-Practice-Production – widely popular well into the 1990s and still used today. Its main features can be characterized as follows:

- *Presentation.* A text, audio, or visual is used by the teacher to present the grammar in a controlled situation.
- *Practice.* A controlled practice phase follows where the learner says the structure correctly, using such activities as drills and transformations, gap-fill or cloze activities, and multiple-choice questions.
- *Production.* In the production phase, the learner transfers the structure to freer communication through dialogues and other activities, where there is more than one correct answer.

Critics have argued, however, that not all learners effectively manage this transfer and that controlled practice does not prepare them adequately for freer production. The implications of these criticisms will be explored in Chapter 5.

Conclusion

In this chapter, we have reviewed the Oral Approach and its later manifestation, Situational Language Teaching, as it developed in Britain, and have seen how the design and procedure emphasized accuracy and repetition in controlled situations. Procedures associated with SLT in the 1950s and 1960s were an extension and further development of well-established techniques advocated by proponents of the earlier Oral Approach in the British school of language teaching. The essential features of SLT are seen in the PPP lesson model that thousands of teachers who studied for the RSA/Cambridge Certificate in TEFLA were required to master in the 1980s and early 1990s, with a lesson having three phases: Presentation (introduction of a new teaching item in context), Practice (controlled practice of the item), and Production (a freer practice phase) (Willis and Willis 1996). SLT provided the methodology of major teacher-training texts throughout the 1980s and beyond (e.g., Hubbard et al. 1983), and, as we noted, textbooks written according to the principles of SLT were widely used in many parts of the world. In the mid-1960s, however, applied linguists began to call into question the view of language, language learning, and language teaching underlying SLT. We discuss this reaction and how it led to Communicative Language Teaching in Chapter 5. But because the principles of SLT, with its strong emphasis on oral practice, grammar, and sentence patterns, conform to the intuitions of many language teachers and offer a practical methodology suited to countries where national EFL/ESL syllabuses continue to be grammatically based, it continues to be used in some parts of the world today, even though it may not be widely acknowledged.

Discussion questions

1. Does the PPP lesson cycle play any role in your current teaching?

2. Have you experienced or observed any limitations of the PPP cycle?

3. Like the Direct Method, the Oral Approach was inductive and, in its pure form, did not explain grammar. What do you think might be some pros and cons to this approach to grammar?

4. "In the mid-1960s, however, applied linguists began to call into question the view of language, language learning, and language teaching underlying SLT" (p. 55). Can you think of reasons why (aspects of) SLT may still be useful and relevant in certain teaching contexts today?

5. On page 47 is a list with the main characteristics of the Oral Approach. Point (2) is "The target language is the language of the classroom." Can you think of reasons why in some situations this might be difficult to implement?

6. Point (5) is "Items of grammar are graded following the principle that simple forms should be taught before complex ones." Can you think of situations where it would be sensible to break this general rule?

7. Point (6) is "Reading and writing are introduced once a sufficient lexical and grammatical basis is established." Can you think of situations where it would be sensible to focus on reading and/or writing sooner?

8. Look at the list below that summarizes the teacher's responsibilities in the Oral Approach. How does this compare with your own list of teaching responsibilities?

    1. timing
    2. oral practice, to support the textbook structures
    3. revision [i.e., review]
    4. adjustment to special needs of individuals
    5. testing
    6. developing language activities other than those arising from the textbook

    (Pittman 1963: 177–8)

9. Looking at the structure 'there's a + noun" and the way that it is presented in a situational course, how would you teach it?

> There's a tin of cigarettes in the box.
> There's a packet of matches in the box.
> There's a reel of cotton in the box.
> There's a bottle of ink in the box.
> There's a packet of pins in the box.
> There's a pair of shoes in the box.
> There's a jar of rice in the box.

(Pittman 1963: 168)

10. "The Oral Approach ... was the accepted British approach to English language teaching by the 1950s. Its principles are seen ... in many other more recent textbooks" (pp. 46–7). Select a textbook published after 2000 and look at the table in the appendix at the end of the book, summarizing the key characteristics of the Oral Approach. Do you find any aspects of the Oral Approach in the textbook?

References and further reading

Alexander, L. G. 1967. *New Concept English*, 4 vols. London: Longman.

Billows, F. L. 1961. *The Techniques of Language Teaching*. London: Longman.

Byrne, D. 1976. *Teaching Oral English*. London: Longman.

Coles, M., and B. Lord. 1975. *Access to English*. Oxford: Oxford University Press.

Commonwealth Office of Education. 1965. *Situational English*. London: Longman.

Cook, V. 2011. Teaching English as a foreign language in Europe. In E. Hinkel (ed.), *Handbook of Research in Second Language Teaching and Learning*, Vol. II. New York: Routledge. 140–54.

Davies, P., J. Roberts, and R. Rossner. 1975. *Situational Lesson Plans*. Mexico City: Macmillan.

Faucett, L., M. West, H. E. Palmer, and E. L. Thorndike. 1936. *The Interim Report on Vocabulary Selection for the Teaching of English as a Foreign Language*. London: P. S. King.

French, F. G. 1948–1950. *The Teaching of English Abroad*, 3 vols. Oxford: Oxford University Press.

Frisby, A. W. 1957. *Teaching English: Notes and Comments on Teaching English Overseas*. London: Longman.

Gatenby, E. V. 1944. *English as a Foreign Language*. London: Longman.

Gauntlett, J. O. 1957. *Teaching English as a Foreign Language*. London: Macmillan.

Gurrey, P. 1955. *Teaching English as a Foreign Language*. London: Longman.

Halliday, M. A. K., A. McIntosh, and P. Strevens. 1964. *The Linguistic Sciences and Language Teaching*. London: Longman.

Hartley, B., and P. Viney. [1978] 1999. *Streamline English*. Oxford: Oxford University Press.

Hodgson, F. M. 1955. *Learning Modern Languages*. London: Routledge and Kegan Paul.

Hornby, A. S. 1950. The situational approach in language teaching: a series of three articles in English. *Language Teaching* 4: 98–104, 121–8, 150–6.

Hornby, A. S. 1954. *A Guide to Patterns and Usage in English*. London: Oxford University Press.

Hornby, A. S. 1954–1956. *Oxford Progressive English Course for Adult Learners*, 3 vols. London: Oxford University Press.

Hornby, A. S., E. V. Gatenby, and H. Wakefield. 1953. *The Advanced Learner's Dictionary of Current English*. London: Oxford University Press.

Howatt, A. P. R. 1984. *A History of English Language Teaching*. Oxford: Oxford University Press.

Hubbard, P., H. Jones, B. Thornton, and R. Wheeler. 1983. *A Training Course for TEFL*. Oxford: Oxford University Press.

Jespersen, O. E. 1933. *Essentials of English Grammar*. London: Allen and Unwin.

Mennon, T. K. N., and M. S. Patel. 1957. *The Teaching of English as a Foreign Language*. Baroda, India: Acharya.

Morris, I. 1954. *The Art of Teaching English as a Living Language*. London: Macmillan.

O'Neill, R. 1973. *Kernel Lessons Plus*. London: Longman.

Palmer, H. E. [1917] 1968. *The Scientific Study and Teaching of Languages*. Repr. London: Oxford University Press.

Palmer, H. E. 1921. *Principles of Language Study*. New York: World Book Co.

Palmer, H. E. 1923. *The Oral Method of Teaching Languages*. Cambridge: Heffer.

Palmer, H. E. 1934. *Specimens of English Construction Patterns*. Tokyo: Department of Education.

Palmer, H. E. 1938. *Grammar of English Words*. London: Longman.

Palmer, H. E. 1940. *The Teaching of Oral English*. London: Longman.

Palmer, H. E., and F. G. Blandford. 1939. *A Grammar of Spoken English on a Strictly Phonetic Basis*. Cambridge: Heffer.

Pattison, B. 1952. *English Teaching in the World Today*. London: Evans.

Pattison, B. 1964. Modern methods of language teaching. *English Language Teaching* 19(1): 2–6.

Pittman, G. 1963. *Teaching Structural English*. Brisbane: Jacaranda.

Richards, J. C., B. Ho, and K. Giblin. 1996. Learning how to teach in the RSA Cert. In D. Freeman and J. Richards (eds.), *Teacher Learning in Language Teaching*. New York: Cambridge University Press. 242–59.

Situational English for Newcomers to Australia. Sydney: Longman.

West, M. (ed.). 1953a. *A General Service List of English Words*. London: Longman.

West, M. 1953b. *The Teaching of English: A Guide to the New Method Series*. London: Longman.

White, R. 1988. *The ELT Curriculum*. Oxford: Blackwell.

Willis, J., and D. Willis (eds.). 1996. *Challenge and Change in Language Teaching*. Oxford: Heinemann.

Zandvoort, R. W. 1945. *A Handbook of English Grammar*. Groningen: Wolters.

4 The Audiolingual Method

Introduction

The Coleman Report in 1929 recommended a reading-based approach to foreign language teaching for use in US schools and colleges (Chapter 1). This emphasized teaching the comprehension of texts. Teachers taught from books containing short reading passages in the foreign language, preceded by lists of vocabulary. Rapid silent reading was the goal, but in practice teachers often resorted to discussing the content of the passage in English. Those involved in the teaching of English as a second or foreign language in the United States between the two world wars used either a modified Direct Method approach, a reading-based approach, or a reading-oral approach (Darian 1972). Unlike the approach that was being developed by British applied linguists during the same period (Chapter 3), there was little attempt to treat language content systematically. Sentence patterns and grammar were introduced at the whim of the textbook writer. There was no standardization of the vocabulary or grammar that was included. Neither was there a consensus on what grammar, sentence patterns, and vocabulary were most important for beginning, intermediate, or advanced learners.

However, the entry of the United States into World War II had a significant effect on language teaching there. To supply the US government with personnel who were fluent in German, French, Italian, Chinese, Japanese, Malay, and other languages, and who could work as interpreters, code-room assistants, and translators, it was necessary to set up a special language training program. The government commissioned US universities to develop foreign language programs for military personnel. Thus, the Army Specialized Training Program (ASTP) was established in 1942. Fifty-five American universities were involved in the program by the beginning of 1943.

The objective of the army programs was for students to attain conversational proficiency in a variety of foreign languages. Since this was not the goal of conventional foreign language courses in the United States, new approaches were necessary. Linguists, such as Leonard Bloomfield at Yale, had already developed training programs as part of their linguistic research that were designed to give linguists and anthropologists mastery of American Indian languages and other languages they were studying. Textbooks did not exist for such languages. The technique Bloomfield and his colleagues used was sometimes known as the "informant method," since it used a native speaker of the language – the informant – who served as a source of phrases and vocabulary and who provided sentences for imitation, and a linguist, who supervised the learning experience. The linguist did not necessarily know the language but was trained in eliciting the basic structure of the language from the informant. Thus, the students and the linguist were able to take part in guided conversation with the informant, and together they gradually learned how to speak the language, as well as to understand much of its basic grammar. Students in such courses studied 10 hours a day, six days a week. There were generally 15 hours of drill with native speakers and 20 to 30 hours of private study spread over two to three 6-week sessions. This was the system adopted by the army, and in small classes of mature and highly motivated students, excellent results were often achieved.

The ASTP lasted only about two years but attracted considerable attention in the popular press and in the academic community. For the next ten years the "Army Method" and its suitability for use in regular language programs were discussed. But the linguists who developed the ASTP were not interested primarily in language teaching. The "methodology" of the Army Method, like the Direct Method, derived from the intensity of contact with the target language rather than from any well-developed methodological basis. It was a program that was innovative mainly in terms of the procedures used and the intensity of teaching rather than in terms of its underlying theory. However, it did convince a number of prominent linguists of the value of an intensive, oral-based approach to the learning of a foreign language.

Linguists and applied linguists during this period were becoming increasingly involved in the teaching of English as a second or foreign language. The United States had now emerged as a major international power. There was a growing demand for foreign expertise in the teaching of English. Thousands of foreign students entered the USA to study in universities, and many of these students required training in English before they could begin their studies. These factors led to the emergence of the American approach to ESL, which by the mid-1950s had become Audiolingualism.

In 1939, the University of Michigan developed the first English Language Institute in the United States; it specialized in the training of teachers of English as a foreign language and in teaching English as a second or foreign language to international students. Charles Fries, director of the institute, was trained in structural linguistics, and he applied the principles of structural linguistics to language teaching. Fries and his colleagues rejected approaches such as those of the Direct Method, in which learners are exposed to the language, use it, and gradually absorb its grammatical patterns. For Fries, grammar, or "structure," was the starting point. The structure of the language was identified with its basic sentence patterns and grammatical structures. The language was taught by systematic attention to pronunciation and by intensive oral drilling of its core sentence patterns. Pattern practice was an essential classroom technique. "It is these basic patterns that constitute the learner's task. They require drill, drill, and more drill, and only enough vocabulary to make such drills possible" (Hockett 1959).

Michigan was not the only university involved in developing courses and materials for teaching English. A number of other similar programs were established, some of the earliest being at Georgetown University and American University, Washington, DC, and at the University of Texas, Austin. US linguists were becoming increasingly active, both within the United States and abroad, in supervising programs for the teaching of English

(Moulton 1961). In 1950, the American Council of Learned Societies, under contract to the US State Department, was commissioned to develop textbooks for teaching English to speakers of a wide range of foreign languages. The format the linguists involved in this project followed was known as the "general form": a lesson began with work on pronunciation, morphology, and grammar, followed by drills and exercises. The guidelines were published as *Structural Notes and Corpus: A Basis for the Preparation of Materials to Teach English as a Foreign Language* (American Council of Learned Societies 1952). This became an influential document and together with the "general form" was used as a guide to developing English courses for speakers of ten different languages (the famous *Spoken Language* series), published between 1953 and 1956 (Moulton 1961).

In many ways the methodology used by US linguists and language teaching experts during this period sounded similar to the British Oral Approach, although the two traditions developed independently. The American approach differed, however, in its strong alliance with American structural linguistics (described in more detail below) and its applied linguistic applications, particularly contrastive analysis, explained below. Fries set forth his principles of structural linguistics in *Teaching and Learning English as a Foreign Language* (1945), in which the problems of learning a foreign language were attributed to the conflict of different structural systems (i.e., differences between the grammatical and phonological patterns of the native language and the target language). Contrastive analysis of the two languages would allow potential problems of interference to be predicted and addressed through carefully prepared teaching materials. Thus was born a major industry in American applied linguistics – systematic comparisons of English with other languages, with a view toward solving the fundamental problems of foreign language learning.

The approach developed by linguists at Michigan and other universities became known variously as the Oral Approach, not to be confused with the Oral Method of the 1920s as developed in Britain (Chapter 3), the Aural-Oral Approach, and the Structural Approach. It advocated aural training first, then pronunciation training, followed by speaking, reading, and writing. Language was identified with speech, and speech was approached through structure. This approach influenced the way languages were taught in the United States throughout the 1950s. As an approach to the teaching of English as a second or foreign language, the new orthodoxy was promoted through the University of Michigan's journal *Language Learning*. This was a period when expertise in linguistics was regarded as a necessary and sufficient foundation for expertise in language teaching. Not surprisingly, the classroom materials produced by Fries and linguists at Yale, Cornell, and elsewhere evidenced considerable linguistic analysis but very little pedagogy. They were widely used, however, and the applied linguistic principles on which they were based were thought to incorporate the most advanced scientific approach to language teaching. If there was any learning theory underlying the Aural-Oral materials, it was a commonsense application of the idea that practice makes perfect. There is no explicit reference to then-current learning theory in Fries's work. It was the incorporation of the linguistic principles of the Aural-Oral Approach with state-of-the-art psychological learning theory in the mid-1950s that led to the method that came to be known as Audiolingualism.

The emergence of the Audiolingual Method resulted from the increased attention given to foreign language teaching in the United States toward the end of the 1950s. The need for a radical change and rethinking of foreign language teaching methodology (most of which was still linked to the Reading Method) was prompted by the launching of the first Russian satellite in 1957. The US government acknowledged the need for a more intensive effort to teach foreign languages in order to prevent Americans from becoming isolated from scientific advances made in other countries. The National Defense Education Act (1958), among other measures, provided funds for the study and analysis of modern languages, for the development of teaching materials, and for the training of teachers. Teachers were encouraged to attend summer institutes to improve their knowledge of foreign languages and to learn the principles of linguistics and the new linguistically based teaching methods. Language teaching specialists set about developing a method that was applicable to conditions in US colleges and university classrooms. They drew on the earlier experience of the army programs and the Aural-Oral or Structural Approach developed by Fries and his colleagues, adding insights taken from behaviorist psychology. This combination of structural linguistic theory, contrastive analysis, aural-oral procedures, and behaviorist psychology led to the Audiolingual Method. Audiolingualism (the term was coined by Professor Nelson Brooks in 1964) claimed to have transformed language teaching from an art into a science, which would enable learners to achieve mastery of a foreign language effectively and efficiently. The method was widely adopted for teaching foreign languages in North American colleges and universities. It provided the methodological foundation for materials for the teaching of foreign languages at the college and university level in the United States and Canada, and its principles formed the basis of such widely used series as the *Lado English Series* (Lado 1977) and *English 900* (English Language Services 1964). Although the method began to fall from favor in the late 1960s for reasons we shall discuss later, practices and materials based on audiolingual principles – particularly the use of drills and repetition-based exercises – continue to be used by some teachers today. A description of the methods used to teach Thai in a leading language center in Thailand (the AUA) states:

> The teaching methodology employed for the AUA Thai courses is an outgrowth of the philosophy that for the students to speak Thai well they must be able to understand and produce the tones of the language correctly and accurately. In order to accomplish this goal, a method of "focused practice" is used. Practical vocabulary and grammar patterns are introduced and drilled before students are asked to engage in short or long dialogs and conversations. A large percentage of the class is spent in having the teacher model sounds, patterns and sentences and the students practicing those drills. Language items are not initially introduced for communicative purposes, but to introduce to the learner the problem sounds and patterns to increase fluency. Within each lesson, dialogs are practiced to help the students to be conversational in order to function outside of the classroom. Communicative activities are added when necessary to integrate the language items learned.

The role of the teacher, other than presenting the material in a logical and non-threatening way, is to not only provide the sounds but also monitor the performance of the students so that mistakes are corrected in a timely and non-intrusive manner. The student must take an active role in producing the sounds through repetition and substitution drills. In all activities the student must work cooperatively with the other students in the class to practice the patterns and for longer dialog and conversations to be creative by adding items needed in real situations.

(AUA Language Center, Chiang Mai Thailand 2012)

Let us examine the features of the Audiolingual Method at the levels of approach, design, and procedure.

Approach

Theory of language

The theory of language underlying Audiolingualism was derived from a view proposed by American linguists in the 1950s – a view that came to be known as *structural linguistics*. Linguistics had emerged as a flourishing academic discipline in the 1950s, and the structural theory of language constituted its backbone. Structural linguistics had developed in part as a reaction to traditional grammar. Traditional approaches to the study of language had linked the study of language to philosophy and to a mentalist approach to grammar. Grammar was considered a branch of logic, and the grammatical categories of Indo-European languages were thought to represent ideal categories in languages. Many nineteenth-century language scholars had viewed modern European languages as corruptions of classical grammar, and languages from other parts of the world were viewed as primitive and underdeveloped.

The reaction against traditional grammar was prompted by the movement toward positivism and empiricism, which Darwin's *On the Origin of Species* had helped promote, and by an increased interest in non-European languages on the part of scholars. A more practical interest in language study emerged. As linguists discovered new sound types and new patterns of linguistic invention and organization, a new interest in phonetics, phonology, morphology, and syntax developed. By the 1930s, the scientific approach to the study of language was thought to consist of collecting examples of what speakers said and analyzing them according to different levels of structural organization rather than according to categories of Latin grammar. A sophisticated methodology for collecting and analyzing data developed, which involved transcribing spoken utterances in a language phonetically and later working out the phonemic, morphological (stems, prefixes, suffixes, etc.), and syntactic (phrases, clauses, sentence types) systems underlying the grammar of the language. Language was viewed as a system of structurally related elements for the encoding of meaning, the elements being phonemes, morphemes, words, structures, and sentence types. The term *structural* referred to these characteristics: (a) Elements in a language were thought of as being linearly produced in a rule-governed (structured) way; (b) Language samples could be exhaustively described at any structural level of description (phonetic, phonemic, morphological, etc.); (c) Linguistic levels were thought of as systems within systems – that is, as being pyramidally structured: phonemic systems led to morphemic systems, and these in turn led to the higher-level systems of phrases, clauses, and sentences. Learning a language, it was assumed, entails mastering the elements or building blocks of the language and learning the rules by which these elements are combined, from phoneme to morpheme to word to phrase to sentence. The phonological system defines those sound elements that contrast meaningfully with one another in the language (phonemes), their phonetic realizations in specific environments (allophones), and their permissible sequences (phonotactics). The phonological and grammatical systems of the language constitute the organization of language and by implication the units of production and comprehension. The grammatical system consists of a listing of grammatical elements and rules for their linear combination into words, phrases, and sentences. Rule-ordered processes involve addition, deletion, and transposition of elements.

An important tenet of structural linguistics was that the primary medium of language is oral: Speech is language. Since many languages do not have a written form and we learn to speak before we learn to read or write, it was argued that language is "primarily what is spoken and only secondarily what is written" (Brooks 1964). Therefore, it was assumed that speech had a priority in language teaching. This was contrary to popular views of the relationship of the spoken and written forms of language, since it had been widely assumed that language existed principally as symbols written on paper, and that spoken language was an imperfect realization of the pure written version.

This scientific approach to language analysis appeared to offer the foundations for a scientific approach to language teaching. In 1961, the American linguist William Moulton, in a report prepared for the Ninth International Congress of Linguists, proclaimed the linguistic principles on which language teaching methodology should be based: "Language is speech, not writing … A language is a set of habits … Teach the language, not about the language … A language is what its native speakers say, not what someone thinks they ought to say … Languages are different" (quoted in Rivers 1964: 5). But a method cannot be based simply on a theory of language. It also needs to refer to the psychology of learning and to learning theory. It is to this aspect of Audiolingualism that we now turn.

Theory of learning

The language teaching theoreticians and methodologists who developed Audiolingualism not only had a convincing and powerful theory of language to draw upon but were also working in a period when a prominent school of American psychology – known as behavioral psychology – claimed to have tapped the secrets of all human learning, including language learning. Behaviorism, like structural linguistics, is another antimentalist, empirically based approach to the study of human behavior. To the behaviorist, the human being is an organism capable of a wide repertoire of behaviors. The occurrence of these behaviors is dependent on three crucial elements in learning: a *stimulus*, which serves to elicit behavior; a *response* triggered by a stimulus; and *reinforcement*, which serves to mark the

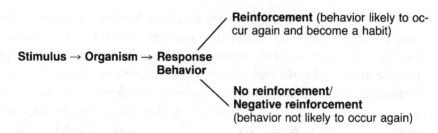

Figure 4.1 The behaviorist learning process

response as being appropriate (or inappropriate) and encourages the repetition (or suppression) of the response in the future (see Skinner 1957; Brown 1980). A representation of this can be seen in Figure 4.1.

Reinforcement is a vital element in the learning process, because it increases the likelihood that the behavior will occur again and eventually become a habit. To apply this theory to language learning is to identify the organism as the foreign language learner, the behavior as verbal behavior, the stimulus as what is taught or presented of the foreign language, the response as the learner's reaction to the stimulus, and the reinforcement as the extrinsic approval and praise of the teacher or fellow students or the intrinsic self-satisfaction of target language use. Language mastery is represented as acquiring a set of appropriate language stimulus-response chains.

The descriptive practices of structural linguists suggested a number of hypotheses about language learning, and hence about language teaching as well. For example, since linguists normally described languages beginning with the phonological level and finishing with the sentence level, it was assumed that this was also the appropriate sequence for learning and teaching. Since speech was now held to be primary and writing secondary, it was assumed that language teaching should focus on mastery of speech and that writing or even written prompts should be withheld until reasonably late in the language learning process. Since the structure is what is important and unique about a language, early practice should focus on mastery of phonological and grammatical structures rather than on mastery of vocabulary.

Out of these various influences emerged a number of learning principles, which became the psychological foundations of Audiolingualism and came to shape its methodological practices. Among the more central are the following:

1. Foreign language learning is basically a process of mechanical habit formation. Good habits are formed by giving correct responses rather than by making mistakes. By memorizing dialogues and performing pattern drills, the chances of producing mistakes are minimized. Language is verbal behavior – that is, the automatic production and comprehension of utterances – and can be learned by inducing the students to do likewise.

2. Language skills are learned more effectively if the items to be learned in the target language are presented in spoken form before they are seen in written form. Aural-oral training is needed to provide the foundation for the development of other language skills.

3. Analogy provides a better foundation for language learning than analysis. Analogy involves the processes of generalization and discrimination. Explanations of rules are therefore not given until students have practiced a pattern in a variety of contexts and are thought to have acquired a perception of the analogies involved. Drills can enable learners to form correct analogies. Hence the approach to the teaching of grammar is essentially inductive rather than deductive.

4. The meanings that the words of a language have for the native speaker can be learned only in a linguistic and cultural context and not in isolation. Teaching a language thus involves teaching aspects of the cultural system of the people who speak the language.

(Rivers 1964: 19–22)

In advocating these principles, proponents of Audiolingualism were drawing on the theory of a well-developed school of American psychology – behaviorism. The prominent Harvard behaviorist B. F. Skinner had elaborated a theory of learning applicable to language learning in his influential book *Verbal Behavior* (1957), in which he stated, "We have no reason to assume … that verbal behavior differs in any fundamental respect from non-verbal behavior, or that any new principles must be invoked to account for it" (1957: 10). Armed with a powerful theory of the nature of language and of language learning, audiolingualists could now turn to the design of language teaching courses and materials.

Design

Audiolingualists demanded a complete reorientation of the foreign language curriculum. Like the nineteenth-century reformers, they advocated a return to speech-based instruction with the primary objective of oral proficiency, and dismissed the study of grammar or literature as the goal of foreign language teaching. "A radical transformation is called for, a new orientation of procedures is demanded, and a thorough house cleaning of methods, materials, texts and tests is unavoidable" (Brooks 1964: 50).

Objectives

Brooks distinguishes between short-range and long-range objectives of an audiolingual program. Short-range objectives include training in listening comprehension, accurate pronunciation, recognition of speech symbols as graphic signs on the printed page, and ability to reproduce these symbols in writing (Brooks 1964: 111). "These immediate objectives imply three others: first, control of the structures of sound, form, and order in the new language; second, acquaintance with vocabulary items that bring content into these structures; and third, meaning, in terms of the significance these verbal symbols have for those who speak the language natively" (p. 113). Long-range objectives "must be language as the native speaker uses it … There must be some knowledge of a second language as it is possessed by a true bilingualist" (p. 107).

In practice this means that the focus in the early stages is on oral skills, with gradual links to other skills as learning develops. Oral proficiency is equated with accurate pronunciation and grammar and the ability to respond quickly and accurately in speech situations. The teaching of listening comprehension, pronunciation, grammar, and vocabulary are all related to development of oral fluency. Reading and writing skills may be taught, but they are dependent on prior oral skills. Language is primarily speech in audiolingual theory, but speaking skills are themselves dependent on the ability to accurately perceive and produce the major phonological features of the target language, fluency in the use of the key grammatical patterns in the language, and knowledge of sufficient vocabulary to use with these patterns.

The syllabus

Audiolingualism is a linguistic, or structure-based, approach to language teaching. The starting point is a linguistic syllabus, which contains the key items of phonology, morphology, and syntax of the language arranged according to their order of presentation. These may have been derived in part from a *contrastive analysis* of the differences between the native language and the target language, since these differences are thought to be the cause of the major difficulties the learner will encounter. In addition, a lexical syllabus of basic vocabulary items is usually specified in advance. In *Foundations for English Teaching* (Fries and Fries 1961), for example, a corpus of structural and lexical items graded into three levels is proposed, together with suggestions as to the situations that could be used to contextualize them.

The language skills are taught in the order of listening, speaking, reading, and writing. Listening is viewed largely as training in aural discrimination of basic sound patterns. The language may be presented entirely orally at first; written representations are usually withheld from learners in early stages.

> The learner's activities must at first be confined to the audiolingual and gestural-visual bands of language behavior …
>
>   Recognition and discrimination are followed by imitation, repetition and memorization. Only when he is thoroughly familiar with sounds, arrangements, and forms does he center his attention on enlarging his vocabulary … Throughout he concentrates upon gaining accuracy before striving for fluency.
>
> (Brooks 1964: 50)

When reading and writing are introduced, students are taught to read and write what they have already learned to say orally. An attempt is made to minimize the possibilities for making mistakes in both speaking and writing by using a tightly structured approach to the presentation of new language items. At more advanced levels, more complex reading and writing tasks may be introduced.

Types of learning and teaching activities

Dialogues and drills form the basis of audiolingual classroom practices. Dialogues provide the means of contextualizing key structures and illustrate situations in which structures might be used as well as some cultural aspects of the target language. Dialogues are used for repetition and memorization. Correct pronunciation, stress, rhythm, and intonation are emphasized. After a dialogue has been presented and memorized, specific grammatical patterns in the dialogue are selected and become the focus of various kinds of drill and pattern-practice exercises.

The use of drills and pattern practice is a distinctive feature of the Audiolingual Method. Various kinds of drills are used. Brooks (1964: 156–61) includes the following:

Repetition. The student repeats an utterance aloud as soon as he has heard it. He does this without looking at a printed text. The utterance must be brief enough to be retained by the ear. Sound is as important as form and order.

EXAMPLE
This is the seventh month. –This is the seventh month.

After a student has repeated an utterance, he may repeat it again and add a few words, then repeat that whole utterance and add more words.

EXAMPLES
I used to know him. –I used to know him.
I used to know him *years ago.* –used to know him *years ago when we were in school …*

Inflection. One word in an utterance appears in another form when repeated.

EXAMPLES
I bought the *ticket.* –I bought the *tickets.*
He bought the candy. –*She* bought the candy.
I called the young *man.* –I called the young *men …*

Replacement. One word in an utterance is replaced by another.

EXAMPLES
He bought *this house* cheap. –He bought *it* cheap.
Helen left early. –*She* left early.
They gave their *boss* a watch. –They gave *him* a watch …

Restatement. The student rephrases an utterance and addresses it to someone else, according to instructions.

EXAMPLES
Tell him to wait for you. –Wait for me.
Ask her how old she is. –How old are you?
Ask John when he began. –John, when did you begin? …

Completion. The student hears an utterance that is complete except for one word, then repeats the utterance in completed form.

EXAMPLES
I'll go my way and you go … –I'll go my way and you go *yours.*
We all have … own troubles. –We all have *our* own troubles …

Transposition. A change in word order is necessary when a word is added.

EXAMPLES

I'm hungry. (so). –So *am* I.
I'll never do it again. (neither). –Neither *will* I ...

Expansion. When a word is added, it takes a certain place in the sequence.

EXAMPLES

I know him. (hardly). –I *hardly* know him.
I know him. (well). –I know him *well* ...

Contraction. A single word stands for a phrase or clause.

EXAMPLES

Put your hand *on the table.* –Put your hand *there.*
They believe *that the earth is flat.* –They believe *it* ...

Transformation. A sentence is transformed by being made negative or interrogative or through changes in tense, mood, voice, aspect, or modality.

EXAMPLES

He knows my address.
He doesn't know my address.
Does he know my address?
He used to know my address.
If he had known my address.

Integration. Two separate utterances are integrated into one.

EXAMPLES

They must be honest. This is important. –It is important that they be honest.
I know that man. He is looking for you. –I know the man who is looking for you ...

Rejoinder. The student makes an appropriate rejoinder to a given utterance. He is told in advance to respond in one of the following ways:

Be polite.
Answer the question.
Agree.
Agree emphatically.
Express surprise.
Express regret.
Disagree.
Disagree emphatically.
Question what is said.
Fail to understand.

BE POLITE. EXAMPLES

Thank you. –You're welcome.
May I take one? –Certainly.

ANSWER THE QUESTION. EXAMPLES

What is your name? –My name is Smith.
Where did it happen? –In the middle of the street.

AGREE. EXAMPLES
He's following us. –I think you're right.
This is good coffee. –It's very good ...

Restoration. The student is given a sequence of words that have been culled from a sentence but still bear its basic meaning. He uses these words with a minimum of changes and additions to restore the sentence to its original form. He may be told whether the time is present, past, or future.

EXAMPLES
students/waiting/bus –The students are waiting for the bus.
boys/build/house/tree –The boys built a house in a tree ...

Learner roles

Learners are viewed as organisms that can be directed by skilled training techniques to produce correct responses. In accordance with behaviorist learning theory, teaching focuses on the external manifestations of learning rather than on the internal processes. Learners play a reactive role by responding to stimuli and thus have little control over the content, pace, or style of learning. They are not encouraged to initiate interaction, because this may lead to mistakes. The fact that in the early stages learners do not always understand the meaning of what they are repeating is not perceived as a drawback, for by listening to the teacher, imitating accurately, and responding to and performing controlled tasks, they are learning a new form of verbal behavior.

Teacher roles

In Audiolingualism, as in Situational Language Teaching, the teacher's role is central and active; it is a teacher-dominated method. The teacher models the target language, controls the direction and pace of learning, and monitors and corrects the learners' performance. The teacher must keep the learners attentive by varying drills and tasks and choosing relevant situations to practice structures. Language learning is seen to result from active verbal interaction between the teacher and the learners. Failure to learn results only from the improper application of the method, for example from the teacher not providing sufficient practice or from the learner not memorizing the essential patterns and structures; but the method itself is never to blame. Brooks (1964: 143) argues that the teacher must be trained to do the following:

- Introduce, sustain, and harmonize the learning of the four skills in this order: hearing, speaking, reading and writing.
- Use – and not use – English in the language classroom.
- Model the various types of language behavior that the student is to learn.
- Teach spoken language in dialogue form.
- Direct choral response by all or parts of the class.
- Teach the use of structure through pattern practice.
- Guide the student in choosing and learning vocabulary.

- Show how words relate to meaning in the target language.
- Get the individual student to talk.
- Reward trials by the student in such a way that learning is reinforced.
- Teach a short story and other literary forms.
- Establish and maintain a cultural island.
- Formalize on the first day the rules according to which the language class is to be conducted, and enforce them.

The role of instructional materials

Instructional materials in the Audiolingual Method assist the teacher to develop language mastery in the learner. They are primarily teacher oriented. A student textbook is often not used in the elementary phases of a course where students are primarily listening, repeating, and responding. At this stage in learning, exposure to the printed word may not be considered desirable, because it diverts attention from the aural input. The teacher, however, will have access to a teacher's book that contains the structured sequence of lessons to be followed and the dialogues, drills, and other practice activities. When textbooks and printed materials are introduced to the student, they provide the texts of dialogues and cues needed for drills and exercises.

Technology had an important role to play in Audiolingualism, and when it first became popular tape recorders and audiovisual equipment often had central roles in an audiolingual course. If the teacher was not a native speaker of the target language, the tape recorder provided accurate models for dialogues and drills. The language laboratory was also an innovation that was essential in an audiolingual course. It provides the opportunity for further drill work and to receive controlled error-free practice of basic structures. It also adds variety by providing an alternative to classroom practice. A recorded lesson in the audio program may first present a dialogue for listening practice, allow for the student to repeat the sentences in the dialogue line by line, and provide follow-up fluency drills on grammar or pronunciation.

Procedure

Since Audiolingualism is primarily an oral approach to language teaching, it is not surprising that the process of teaching involves extensive oral instruction. The focus of instruction is on immediate and accurate speech; there is little provision for grammatical explanation or talking about the language. As far as possible, the target language is used as the medium of instruction, and translation or use of the native language is discouraged. Classes of ten or fewer are considered optimal, although larger classes are often the norm. Brooks (1964: 142) lists the following procedures that the teacher should adopt in using the Audiolingual Method:

- The modeling of all learnings by the teacher.
- The subordination of the mother tongue to the second language by rendering English inactive while the new language is being learned.
- The early and continued training of the ear and tongue without recourse to graphic symbols.

- The learning of structure through the practice of patterns of sound, order, and form, rather than by explanation.
- The gradual substitution of graphic symbols for sounds after sounds are thoroughly known.
- The summarizing of the main principles of structure for the student's use when the structures are already familiar, especially when they differ from those of the mother tongue …
- The shortening of the time span between a performance and the pronouncement of its rightness or wrongness, without interrupting the response. This enhances the factor of reinforcement in learning.
- The minimizing of vocabulary until all common structures have been learned.
- The study of vocabulary only in context.
- Sustained practice in the use of the language only in the molecular form of speaker-hearer-situation.
- Practice in translation only as a literary exercise at an advanced level.

In a typical audiolingual lesson, the following procedures would be observed:

1. Students first hear a model dialogue (either read by the teacher or on tape) containing the key structures that are the focus of the lesson. They repeat each line of the dialogue, individually and in chorus. The teacher pays attention to pronunciation, intonation, and fluency. Correction of mistakes of pronunciation or grammar is direct and immediate. The dialogue is memorized gradually, line by line. A line may be broken down into several phrases if necessary. The dialogue is read aloud in chorus, one half saying one speaker's part and the other half responding. The students do not consult their book throughout this phase.
2. The dialogue is adapted to the students' interest or situation, through changing certain key words or phrases. This is acted out by the students.
3. Certain key structures from the dialogue are selected and used as the basis for pattern drills of different kinds. These are first practiced in chorus and then individually. Some grammatical explanation may be offered at this point, but this is kept to an absolute minimum.
4. The students may refer to their textbook, and follow-up reading, writing, or vocabulary activities based on the dialogue may be introduced. At the beginning level, writing is purely imitative and consists of little more than copying out sentences that have been practiced. As proficiency increases, students may write out variations of structural items they have practiced or write short compositions on given topics with the help of framing questions, which will guide their use of the language.
5. Follow-up activities may take place in the language laboratory, where further dialogue and drill work is carried out.

An example of an audiolingual lesson may be found in the appendix to this chapter.

The decline of Audiolingualism

Audiolingualism reached its period of most widespread use in the 1960s and was applied both to the teaching of foreign languages in the United States and to the teaching of English as a second or foreign language. It led to such widely used courses as *English 900* and the *Lado English Series*, as mentioned earlier, as well as to texts for teaching the major European languages. But then came criticism on two fronts. On the one hand, the theoretical foundations of Audiolingualism were attacked as being unsound in terms of both language theory and learning theory. On the other hand, practitioners found that the practical results fell short of expectations. Students were often found to be unable to transfer skills acquired through Audiolingualism to real communication outside the classroom, and many found the experience of studying through audiolingual procedures to be boring and unsatisfying.

The theoretical attack on audiolingual beliefs resulted from changes in American linguistic theory in the 1960s. The MIT linguist Noam Chomsky rejected the structuralist approach to language description as well as the behaviorist theory of language learning. "Language is not a habit structure. Ordinary linguistic behavior characteristically involves innovation, formation of new sentences and patterns in accordance with rules of great abstractness and intricacy" (Chomsky 1966: 153). Chomsky's theory of transformational grammar proposed that the fundamental properties of language derive from innate aspects of the mind and from how humans process experience through language. His theories were to revolutionize American linguistics and focus the attention of linguists and psychologists on the mental properties people bring to bear on language use and language learning. Chomsky also proposed an alternative theory of language learning to that of the behaviorists. Behaviorism regarded language learning as similar in principle to any other kind of learning. It was subject to the same laws of stimulus and response, reinforcement and association. Chomsky argued that such a learning theory could not possibly serve as a model of how humans learn language, since much of human language use is not imitated behavior but is created anew from underlying knowledge of abstract rules. Sentences are not learned by imitation and repetition but "generated" from the learner's underlying "competence."

Suddenly the whole audiolingual paradigm was called into question: pattern practice, drilling, memorization. These might lead to language-like behaviors, but they were not resulting in competence. This created a crisis in American language teaching circles. Temporary relief was offered in the form of a theory derived in part from Chomsky – cognitive-code learning. In 1966, John B. Carroll, a psychologist who had taken a close interest in foreign language teaching, wrote:

> The audio-lingual habit theory which is so prevalent in American foreign language teaching was, perhaps fifteen years ago, in step with the state of psychological thinking of that time, but it is no longer abreast of recent developments. It is ripe for major revision, particularly in the direction of joining it with some of the better elements of the cognitive-code learning theory.
>
> (1966a: 105)

This referred to a view of learning that allowed for a conscious focus on grammar and that acknowledged the role of abstract mental processes in learning rather than defining learning simply in terms of habit formation. Practice activities should involve meaningful learning and language use. Learners should be encouraged to use their innate and creative abilities to derive and make explicit the underlying grammatical rules of the language. For a time in the early 1970s, there was a considerable interest in the implication of the cognitive-code theory for language teaching (e.g., see Jakobovits 1970; Lugton 1971). But no clear-cut methodological guidelines emerged, nor did any particular method incorporating this view of learning. The term *cognitive code* is still sometimes invoked to refer to any conscious attempt to organize materials around a grammatical syllabus while allowing for meaningful practice and use of language.

The lack of an alternative to Audiolingualism led in the 1970s and 1980s to a period of adaptation, innovation, experimentation, and some confusion. Several alternative method proposals appeared in the 1970s that made no claims to any links with mainstream language teaching and second language acquisition research. These included Total Physical Response (Chapter 15) and the Silent Way (Chapter 16). These methods attracted some interest at first but have not continued to attract significant levels of acceptance. Other proposals since then have reflected developments in general education and other fields outside the second language teaching community, such as Whole Language (Chapter 7), Multiple Intelligences (Chapter 12), Competency-Based Language Teaching (Chapter 8), and Cooperative Language Learning (Chapter 13). Mainstream language teaching since the 1980s, however, has generally drawn on contemporary theories of language and second language acquisition as a basis for teaching proposals. The current approaches and methods covered in Part II of this book, including Communicative Language Teaching, Content-Based Instruction, Task-Based Language Teaching, and the Lexical Approach are representative of this last group, as is the Natural Approach in Part III. The concern for grammatical accuracy that was a focus of Audiolingualism has not disappeared, however, and continues to provide a challenge for contemporary applied linguistics (see Doughty and Williams 1998).

Conclusion

Audiolingualism holds that language learning is like other forms of learning. Since language is a formal, rule-governed system, it can be formally organized to maximize teaching and learning efficiency. Audiolingualism thus stresses the mechanistic aspects of language learning and language use. There are many similarities between Situational Language Teaching and Audiolingualism. The order in which the language skills are introduced, and the focus on accuracy through drill and practice in the basic structures and sentence patterns of the target language, might suggest that these methods drew from each other. In fact, however, SLT was a development of the earlier Direct Method (see Chapter 1) and does not have the strong ties to linguistics and behavioral psychology that characterize Audiolingualism. To summarize, Audiolingualism reflects the view that speech can be approached through structure and that practice makes perfect. Errors are understood through contrastive analysis with the student's first language. SLT also approached language teaching through structure or patterns, but situations (exemplified through realia) were primary, and contrastive analysis was not an underlying focus. At the level of design, the syllabus, learner and teacher roles, and instructional materials tend to be quite similar. The procedure bears many similarities, as well, although Audiolingualism tended to be more rigorous. Thus, the similarities of the two methods reflect similar views about the nature of language and of language learning, though these views were in fact developed from quite different traditions.

However, despite the criticisms made of Audiolingualism and the emergence of Communicative Language Teaching in the 1970s, audiolingual practices are still used in some parts of the world. Williams and Burden (1997: 12) offer the following explanation for the dominance Audiolingualism achieved and for its continued presence in places today:

> There are a number of possible practical reasons for this. In many countries teachers are not provided with a professional training; in some contexts the prerequisite for teaching is a primary education. It can be quicker and easier to teach teachers to use the steps involved in an audiolingual approach: presentation, practice, repetition and drills. Teachers can also follow the steps provided in their coursebook in a fairly mechanical way. Teachers who lack confidence tend to be less frightened of these techniques, whereas allowing language to develop through meaningful interaction in the classroom can be considerably daunting, and requires teachers with some professional knowledge. An audiolingual methodology can also be used by teachers whose own knowledge of the target language is limited.

Discussion questions

1. Read the description of the teaching methodology of the Thai school on pages 61–2. Which, if any, of the principles and practices mentioned can also be found in courses you are teaching or language courses you are familiar with?

2. "Language items are not initially introduced for communicative purposes, but to introduce to the learner the problem sounds and patterns to increase fluency" (p. 61). To what extent do you feel it is possible to move from a focus on individual linguistic aspects to developing fluency? How would you assess this progression?

3. A tenet of the Audiolingual Method is its emphasis on speaking over writing: language is "primarily what is spoken and only secondarily what is written" (Brooks 1964). Do you agree with this statement? Is there perhaps a similar bias in some current textbooks you are familiar with? If so, how does this impact how you teach learners for whom reading and writing is their main purpose for learning the language?

4. In the model in Figure 4.1 (p. 64) "no reinforcement/negative reinforcement" is said to lead to behavior not likely to occur again. Consider the students in one of the classes you have taught or observed. Can you think of examples of errors that learners continued to make despite negative reinforcement or a lack of reinforcement? Why do you think that is?

5. Long-range objectives of Audiolingualism "must be language as the native speaker uses it" (p. 65). Do you think this is reasonable? Can you think of situations where this may not be desirable?

6. The Oral Approach, as developed in the United States, and the Audiolingual Method place a lot of emphasis on contrastive analysis to determine similarities and dissimilarities between languages. Do you find that words that are similar between two languages are always easier to learn than words that are different?

7. "An audiolingual methodology can also be used by teachers whose own knowledge of the target language is limited" (p. 74). What is your opinion on this rationale? Is this an acceptable reason to use audiolingual methodology? Why/Why not? And more broadly, to what extent should the choice of a method or textbook be based on the knowledge of the target language of the teachers who will use it?

8. With a colleague, select a textbook you are both familiar with and decide how you would use it in a course. What, if any, ongoing influences of Audiolingualism can you find?

9. Pages 67–9 include 12 types of drill activities. In Audiolingualism the main purpose of these activities was to provide as much repetition as possible. However, such activities can also be used for other purposes. Can you think of any? One has been given as an example:

Drill technique	Uses
Repetition	
Inflection	
Restoration	
Replacement	
Restatement	
Completion	
Transposition	
Expansion	
Contraction	
Transformation	
Integration	practicing the use of relative pronouns
Rejoinder	

10. Audiolingualism is based on a theory of behaviorism and habit formation. Do you agree that "practice makes perfect"? Do you see a role for drills in language learning, or do you feel the decline of Audiolingualism was inevitable?

11. Review the description of PPP in Chapter 3 and compare it to the typical audiolingual lesson on page 71 of this chapter. What similarities and differences do you perceive in the procedure for Situational Language Teaching and Audiolingualism?

References and further reading

Allen, V. F. 1965. *On Teaching English to Speakers of Other Languages*. Champaign, IL: National Council of Teachers of English.

American Council of Learned Societies. 1952. *Structural Notes and Corpus: A Basis for the Preparation of Materials to Teach English as a Foreign Language*. Washington, DC: American Council of Learned Societies.

Bloch, B., and G. Trager. 1942. *Outline of Linguistic Analysis*. Baltimore: Linguistic Society of America.

Bloomfield, L. 1933. *Language*. New York: Holt.

Brooks, N. 1964. *Language and Language Learning: Theory and Practice*. 2nd edn. New York: Harcourt Brace.

Brown, H. D. 1980. *Principles of Language Learning and Teaching*. Englewood Cliffs, NJ: Prentice Hall.

Carroll, J. B. 1953. *The Study of Language: A Surveyor of Linguistics and Related Disciplines in America*. Cambridge, MA: Harvard University Press.

Carroll, J. B. 1966a. The contributions of psychological theory and educational research to the teaching of foreign languages. In A. Valdman (ed.), *Trends in Language Teaching*. New York: McGraw-Hill. 93–106.

Carroll, J. B. 1966b. Research in foreign language teaching: the last five years. In R. G. Mead Jr. (ed.), *Language Teaching: Broader Contexts*. Northeast Conference Reports on the Teaching of Foreign Languages: Reports of the Working Committees. New York: MLA Materials Center. 12–42.

Chastain, K. 1969. The audio-lingual habit theory versus the cognitive code learning theory: some theoretical considerations. *International Review of Applied Linguistics* 7: 79–106.

Chastain, K. 1971. *The Development of Modern Language Skills: Theory to Practice*. Chicago: Rand McNally.

Chomsky, N. 1957. *Syntactic Structures*. The Hague: Mouton.

Chomsky, N. 1959. A review of B. F. Skinner's *Verbal Behavior*. *Language* 35(1): 26–58.

Chomsky, N. 1965. *Aspects of the Theory of Syntax*. Cambridge, MA: MIT Press.

Chomsky, N. 1966. Linguistic theory. Repr. in J. P. B. Allen and P. Van Buren (eds.), *Chomsky: Selected Readings*. London: Oxford University Press. 152–9.

Darian, S. G. 1972. *English as a Foreign Language: History, Development, and Methods of Teaching*. Norman: University of Oklahoma Press.

Doughty, C., and J. Williams (eds.). 1998. *Focus on Form in Classroom Second Language Acquisitions*. Cambridge: Cambridge University Press.

English Language Services. 1964. *English 900*. New York: Collier Macmillan.

Fries, C. C. 1945. *Teaching and Learning English as a Foreign Language*. Ann Arbor: University of Michigan Press.

Fries, C. C., and A. C. Fries. 1961. *Foundations for English Teaching*. Tokyo: Kenkyusha.

Gagne, R. M. 1962. Military training and principles of learning. *American Psychologist* 17(2): 83–91.

Hilgard, E. R. 1975. *Theories of Learning*. 2nd edn. New York: Appleton-Century-Crofts.

Hockett, C. F. 1958. *A Course in Modern Linguistics*. New York: Macmillan.

Hockett, C. F. 1959. The objectives and process of language teaching. Repr. in D. Byrne (ed.), *English Teaching Extracts*. London: Longman, 1969.

Hughes, J. P. 1968. *Linguistics and Language Teaching*. New York: Random House.

Howatt, A. P. R., and H. Widdowson. 2004. *A History of English Language Teaching*. 2nd edn. Oxford: Oxford University Press.

Jakobovits, L. A. 1970. *Foreign Language Learning: A Psycholinguistic Analysis of the Issues*. Rowley, MA: Newbury House.

Kirsch, C. 2008. *Teaching Foreign Languages in the Primary School: Principles and Practice*. London: Continuum.

Knight. P. 2001. The development of EFL methodologies. In C. Candlin and N. Mercer (eds.), *English Language Teaching in Its Social Context*. London: Routledge. 147–66.

Lado, R. 1957. *Linguistics across Cultures: Applied Linguistics for Language Teachers*. Ann Arbor: University of Michigan Press.

Lado, R. 1961. *Language Testing*. London: Longman.

Lado, R. 1977. *Lado English Series*, 7 vols. New York: Regents.

Lugton, R. (ed.). 1971. *Toward a Cognitive Approach to Second Language Acquisition*. Philadelphia: Center for Curriculum Development.

Matthew, R. J. 1947. *Language and Area Studies in the Armed Services: Their Future and Significance*. Washington, DC: American Council on Education.

Modern Language Association. 1962. *Reports of Surveys and Studies in the Teaching of Modern Foreign Languages*. New York: Modern Language Teaching Association.

Moulton, W. G. 1961. Linguistics and language teaching in the United States: 1940–1960. In C. Mohrmann, A. Sommerfelt, and J. Whatmough (eds.), *Trends in European and American Linguistics, 1930–1960*. Utrecht: Spectrum. 82–109.

Moulton, W. G. 1963. What is structural drill? *International Journal of American Linguistics* 29(2, pt. 3): 3–15.

Moulton, W. 1966. *A Linguistic Guide to Language Learning*. New York: Modern Language Association.

Parker, W. 1962. *The National Interest and Foreign Languages*. Washington, DC: Department of State.

Rivers, W. M. 1964. *The Psychologist and the Foreign Language Teacher*. Chicago: University of Chicago Press.

Rivers, W. M. 1981. *Teaching Foreign Language Skills*. Chicago: University of Chicago Press.

Skinner, B. F. 1957. *Verbal Behavior*. New York: Appleton-Century-Crofts.

Smith, H. L. 1956. *Linguistics Science and the Teaching of English*. Cambridge, MA: Harvard University Press.

Stack, E. 1969. *The Language Laboratory and Modern Language Teaching*. New York: Oxford University Press.

Stern, H. H. 1983. *Fundamental Concepts of Language Teaching*. Oxford: Oxford University Press.

Tarvin, W., and A. Al Arishi. 1990. Literature in EFL: communicative alternatives to audiolingual assumptions. *Journal of Reading* 34(1): 30–6.

United States Office of Education. 1963. *The Language Development Program*. Washington, DC: US Government Printing Office.

Williams, M., and R. Burden 1997. *Psychology for Language Teachers: A Social Constructivist Approach*. Cambridge: Cambridge University Press.

Zimmerman, C. B. 1997. Historical trends in second language vocabulary instruction. In J. Coady and T. Huckin (eds.), *Second Language Vocabulary Acquisition*. Cambridge: Cambridge University Press. 5–19.

Appendix: An audiolingual lesson

Objectives

Students will learn the past tense forms of common verbs.

Students will describe past events using the past tense.

Students will ask and answer *Wh*-question and *Yes-No* questions using the past tense.

1. Dialog. Listen and practice.
   A. What did you do last night?
   B. I ¹ <u>watched TV for a while</u> and I ² <u>went online to talk to friends</u>.
   A. Did you ³ <u>watch the movie</u> on channel 9?
   B. No, I didn't.
   A. What time did you go to bed?
   B. At about 10.30.

2. Practice the dialog again. Use these phrases to replace the ones in the dialog.
   (a) ¹ read for a while
        ² watched a DVD
        ³ watch the football
   (b) ¹ went for a walk
        ² called my sister in Toronto
        ³ watch the documentary

3. Complete the sentences with the past tense of the verbs.
   I _____ (get up) early today.
   I _____ (watch) a good movie on TV last night.
   I _____ (meet) my friends on Sunday.
   I _____ (go) shopping on the weekend.
   I _____ (buy) a camera last week.
   I _____ (check) my messages this morning.
   I _____ (have) breakfast at home.

4. Drills.
   a) Ask and answer.

What did you do ...	on Friday night?
	on Saturday morning?
	on Saturday night?
	on Sunday?

I ...	went down town.
	slept in.
	stayed in.
	played basketball.

b) Answer with "Yes, I did", or "No, I didn't".
 Did you watch TV last night?
 Did you study yesterday?
 Did you go shopping on Saturday?
 Did you play any sport this week?
 Did you get up early this morning?
 Did you check your e-mail this morning?
 Did you have breakfast this morning?

c) Ask and answer.
 What time did you ...   go to bed last night?
                          get up this morning?
                          have breakfast today?
                          come to class today?

Part II   *Current approaches and methods*

The chapters in Part II bring the description of approaches and methods up to the present time and describe some of the directions mainstream language teaching has followed since the emergence of communicative methodologies in the 1980s.

Communicative Language Teaching (CLT), which we examine in Chapter 5, marks the beginning of a major paradigm shift within language teaching in the twentieth century, one whose ramifications continue to be felt today. The general principles of CLT are still widely accepted in language teaching today, although as we demonstrate in this chapter, these principles have been open to various interpretations, and those favoring the approach may weigh the value of fluency and accuracy in different ways. Aspects of CLT may also be used to support other approaches and methods. In Chapter 6, we consider Content-Based Instruction (CBI) and Content and Language Integrated Learning (CLIL). The first (CBI) can be regarded as a logical development of some of the core principles of CLT, particularly those that relate to the role of meaning in language learning. Because CBI provides an approach that is particularly suited to prepare ESL students to enter elementary, secondary, or tertiary education, it is widely used in English-speaking countries around the world, particularly in the United States. CLIL, a related approach, has become popular in Europe; both approaches involve a merging of content and language. In Chapter 7, we look at the Whole Language movement that developed in the 1980s as a response to teaching the language arts. As an approach aimed at younger learners, it may be contrasted with the more modern-day CBI and CLIL.

Chapters 8 through 11 examine, like CBI, CLIL, and Whole Language, a number of other special-purpose approaches, in the sense that they have specific goals in mind or reflect principles of language learning that have a more limited application. In Chapter 8, we describe Competency-Based Language Teaching (CBLT), standards, and the Common European Framework of Reference (CEFR), all reflecting the outcomes movement that has become increasingly important in recent years as programs strive for accountability and a focus on standards in teaching and learning. In Chapter 9, we look at Task-Based Language Teaching (TBLT), an approach that aims to replace a conventional language-focused syllabus with one organized around communicative tasks as units of teaching and learning. In Chapter 10, we present Text-Based Instruction (TBI), an approach that derives from genre theory and emphasizes the importance of spoken and written texts in teaching. In Chapter 11, we review the Lexical Approach, which developed in the 1990s and sees multi-word lexical units, or "chunks," as the basic building blocks of language proficiency.

The final two chapters describe teaching approaches that are derived from particular theories of learners and learning, theories that have been applied across the curriculum and which were not developed specifically as the basis for teaching languages. In Chapter 12, we describe Multiple Intelligences, a learner-centered view of learning that focuses on the uniqueness of the individual. In Chapter 13, we consider Cooperative Language Learning (CLL), which derived from the collaborative or cooperative learning movement in mainstream education and emphasizes group activities and peer support. All of the chapters in Part II combine to give the reader an overview of approaches and methods still in use, which may be used either individually or in combination.

5 Communicative Language Teaching

Introduction

The development of Communicative Language Teaching

There are two interacting sources of influence that shape the field of language teaching, which have accounted for its recent history and which will no doubt determine the direction it takes in years to come. One comes from outside the profession and reflects the changing status of English in the world. Increasingly, essential features of contemporary societies are an English-proficient workforce in many key sectors of the economy as well as the ability of people from all walks of life to access the educational, technical, and knowledge resources that proficiency in English makes available. Consequently, in recent years there has been a dramatic change in the scope of English language teaching worldwide and, as a result, growing demands on those charged with providing an adequate response to the impact of the global spread of English. There is increasing demand worldwide for language programs that deliver the foreign language skills and competencies needed by today's global citizens and a demand from governments for more effective approaches to the preparation of language teachers. At the same time, there has often been a perception that language teaching policies and practices are not providing an adequate response to the problem. Hence, the regular review of language teaching policies, curriculum, and approaches to both teaching and assessment that has been a feature of the field of language teaching for many years.

The second source of change is internally initiated, that is, it reflects the language teaching profession gradually evolving a changed understanding of its own essential knowledge base and associated instructional practices through the efforts of applied linguists, specialists, and teachers in the field of second language teaching and teacher education. The language teaching profession undergoes periodic waves of renewal and paradigm shifts as it continually reinvents itself through the impact of new ideas, new educational philosophies, advances in technology, and new research paradigms, and as a response to external pressures of the kind noted above. The movement and approach known as Communicative Language Teaching (CLT) is a good example of how a paradigm shift in language teaching reflects these two sources of change.

CLT was the result of a questioning of the assumptions and practices associated with Situational Language Teaching (SLT) (see Chapter 3) – up until the 1960s the major British approach to teaching English as a second or foreign language. In SLT, language was taught by practicing basic structures in meaningful situation-based activities. But just as the linguistic theory underlying Audiolingualism was rejected in the United States in the mid-1960s, British applied linguists began to call into question the theoretical assumptions underlying SLT:

> By the end of the sixties it was clear that the situational approach ... had run its course. There was no future in continuing to pursue the chimera of predicting language on the basis of situational events. What was required was a closer study of the language itself and a return to the traditional concept that utterances carried meaning in themselves and expressed the meanings and intentions of the speakers and writers who created them.
>
> (Howatt 1984: 280)

This was partly a response to the sorts of criticisms the prominent American linguist Noam Chomsky had leveled at structural linguistic theory in his influential book *Syntactic Structures* (1957). Chomsky had demonstrated that the then standard structural theories of language were incapable of accounting for the fundamental characteristic of language – the creativity and uniqueness of individual sentences. British applied linguists emphasized another fundamental dimension of language that was inadequately addressed in approaches to language teaching at that time – the functional and communicative potential of language. They saw the need to focus in language teaching on communicative proficiency rather than on mere mastery of structures. Scholars who advocated this view of language, such as Christopher Candlin and Henry Widdowson, drew on the work of British functional linguists (e.g., John Firth, M. A. K. Halliday), American work in sociolinguistics (e.g., by Dell Hymes, John Gumperz), as well as work in philosophy (e.g., by John Austin and John Searle).

The "communicative movement" in language teaching was also partly the result of changing educational realities in Europe in the 1960s and 1970s. With the increasing interdependence of European countries came the need for greater efforts to teach adults the major languages of the European Common Market. The Council of Europe, a regional organization for cultural and educational cooperation, examined the problem. Education was one of the Council of Europe's major areas of activity. It sponsored international conferences on language teaching, published books about language teaching, and was active in promoting the formation of the International Association of Applied Linguistics. The need to develop alternative methods of language teaching was considered a high priority. Thus, as mentioned earlier, the second impetus for change resulted from this need and a questioning of the underlying basis of SLT.

Versions of Communicative Language Teaching

In 1971, a group of experts began to investigate the possibility of developing language courses on a unit-credit system, a system in which learning tasks are broken down into "portions or units, each of which corresponds to a component of a learner's needs and is systematically related to all the other portions" (Van Ek and Alexander 1980: 6). The group used studies of the needs of European language learners, and in particular a preliminary document prepared by a British linguist, D. A. Wilkins (1972), which proposed a functional or communicative definition of language that could serve as a basis for developing communicative syllabuses for language teaching. Wilkins's contribution was an analysis of the communicative meanings that a language learner needs to understand and express. Rather than describe the core of language through traditional concepts of grammar and vocabulary, Wilkins attempted to demonstrate the systems of meanings that lay behind the communicative uses of language. He described two types of meanings: notional categories (concepts such as time, sequence, quantity, location, frequency) and categories of communicative function (requests, denials, offers, complaints). Wilkins later revised and expanded his 1972 document into a book titled *Notional Syllabuses* (Wilkins 1976), which had a significant impact on the development of CLT. The Council of Europe incorporated his semantic/communicative analysis into a set of specifications for a first-level communicative language syllabus. These Threshold Level specifications (Van Ek and Alexander 1980) have had a strong influence on the design of communicative language programs and textbooks in Europe.

The work of the Council of Europe; the writings of Wilkins, Widdowson, Candlin, Christopher Brumfit, Keith Johnson, and other British applied linguists on the theoretical basis for a communicative or functional approach to language teaching; the rapid application of these ideas by textbook writers; and the equally rapid acceptance of these new principles by British language teaching specialists, curriculum development centers, and even governments gave prominence nationally and internationally to what came to be referred to as the Communicative Approach, or Communicative Language Teaching (CLT). (The terms *notional-functional approach* and *functional approach* are also sometimes used.) Although the movement began as a largely British innovation, focusing on alternative conceptions of a syllabus, from the mid-1970s the scope of CLT soon expanded as it became in many parts of the world the new paradigm in language teaching. For example in Malaysia in the 1980s, the Malaysian Communicational Syllabus was the official national syllabus for over ten years and was the instructional guide for several hundreds of thousands of students in upper secondary schools. It stipulated considerable training for 50 regional key personnel who in turn trained all upper secondary language teachers for a period of two weeks. A detailed Teaching Kit, a Handbook, and textbook specifications were developed by special teams of teachers seconded to those tasks. Four series of approved commercial textbooks were produced and distributed within a year of the introduction of the Communicational Syllabus. The plan and its realization received a number of detailed evaluation studies (Rodgers 1984).

Both American and British proponents typically described CLT as an approach (and not a method) that aimed to (a) make communicative competence the goal of language teaching and (b) develop procedures for the teaching of the four language skills that acknowledge the interdependence of language and communication. The concept of communicative competence entails a much broader understanding of language as a means of getting things accomplished in an appropriate manner. The various ways this term has been interpreted will be explained later in this chapter, but essentially, language and communication are interdependent in the sense that language must serve the purpose of communicating the speaker's objectives. The comprehensiveness of CLT thus makes it somewhat different in scope and status from any of the other approaches or methods discussed in this book. No single text or authority on it emerged, nor any single model that was universally accepted as authoritative. For some, CLT meant little more than an integration of grammatical and functional teaching. Littlewood (1981: 1) states, "One of the most characteristic features of communicative language teaching is that it pays systematic attention to functional as well as structural aspects of language." For others, it meant using procedures where learners work in pairs or groups employing available language resources in problem-solving tasks. In her discussion of communicative syllabus design, Yalden (1983) discusses six CLT design alternatives, ranging from a model in which communicative exercises are grafted onto an existing structural syllabus, to a learner-generated view of syllabus design (e.g., Holec 1980).

Howatt (1984: 279) distinguished between a "strong" and a "weak" version of CLT:

> There is, in a sense, a "strong" version of the communicative approach and a "weak" version. The weak version which has become more or less standard practice in the last ten years, stresses the importance of providing learners with opportunities to use their English for communicative purposes and, characteristically, attempts to integrate such activities into a wider program of language teaching ... The "strong" version of communicative teaching, on the other hand, advances the claim that language is acquired through communication, so that it is not merely a question of activating an existing but inert knowledge of the language, but of stimulating the development of the language system itself. If the former could be described as "learning to use" English, the latter entails "using English to learn it."

Advocates of some forms of Task-Based Language Teaching (Chapter 9) see it as an extension and fine-tuning of the principles of CLT in its strong form because task-based teaching builds teaching and learning around real-life tasks from which the aspects of communicative language use and a knowledge of grammar can emerge. The wide acceptance of the Communicative Approach from the 1980s and the relatively varied way in which it was interpreted and applied can be attributed to the fact that practitioners from different educational traditions could identify with it, and consequently interpret it, in different ways. One of its North American proponents, Savignon (1983), for example, offered as a precedent to CLT a commentary by Montaigne on his learning of Latin through conversation rather than through the customary method of formal analysis and translation. Writes Montaigne, "Without methods, without a book, without grammar or rules, without a whip and without tears, I had learned a Latin as proper as that of my schoolmaster" (Savignon 1983: 47). This anti-structural view can be held to represent the language learning version of a more general learning perspective usually referred to as "learning by doing" or "the experience approach" (Hilgard and Bower 1966). This notion of direct rather than delayed practice of communicative acts is central to most CLT interpretations. That is, unlike in SLT, communicative production is not postponed until after the mastery of forms and controlled sentence practice has occurred.

The focus on communicative and contextual factors in language use also has an antecedent in the work of the anthropologist Bronislaw Malinowski and his colleague, the linguist John Firth. British applied linguists usually credit Firth with focusing attention on discourse. Firth also stressed that language needed to be studied in the broader sociocultural context of its use, which included participants, their behavior and beliefs, the objects of linguistic discussion, and word choice. Both Michael Halliday and Dell Hymes, linguists frequently cited by advocates of CLT, acknowledge primary debts to Malinowski and Firth.

Another frequently cited dimension of CLT, its learner-centered and experience-based view of second language teaching, also has antecedents outside the language teaching tradition per se. An important American national curriculum commission in the 1930s, for example, proposed the adoption of an Experience Curriculum in English. The report of the commission began with the premise that "experience is the best of all schools … The ideal curriculum consists of well-selected experiences" (cited in Applebee 1974: 119). Like those who have urged the organization of CLT around tasks and procedures, the commission tried to suggest "the means for selection and weaving appropriate experiences into a coherent curriculum stretching across the years of school English study" (Applebee 1974: 119). Individual learners were also seen as possessing unique interests, styles, needs, and goals, which should be reflected in the design of methods of instruction. Teachers were encouraged to develop learning materials "on the basis of the particular needs manifested by the class" (Applebee 1974: 150).

Common to all versions of CLT is a theory of language teaching that starts from a communicative model of language and language use – that is, a focus on achieving a communicative purpose as opposed to a control of structure – and that seeks to translate this into a design for an instructional system, for materials, for teacher and learner roles and behaviors, and for classroom activities and techniques. Let us now consider how this is manifested at the levels of approach, design, and procedure.

Approach

Theory of language

The Communicative Approach in language teaching starts from a functional theory of language – one that focuses on language as a means of communication. The goal of language teaching is to develop what Hymes (1972) referred to as "communicative competence." Hymes coined this term in order to contrast a communicative view of language and Chomsky's theory of competence. Chomsky (1965: 3) held that linguistic theory is concerned primarily with an ideal speaker-listener in a completely homogeneous speech community, who knows its language perfectly and is unaffected by such grammatically irrelevant conditions as memory limitation, distractions, shifts of attention and interest, and errors (random or characteristic) in applying his knowledge of the language in actual performance.

For Chomsky, the focus of linguistic theory was to characterize the abstract abilities speakers possess that enable them to produce grammatically correct sentences in a language. It was based on a cognitive view of language. Hymes held that such a view of linguistic theory was sterile, that linguistic theory needed to be seen as part of a more general theory incorporating communication and culture. Hymes's theory of communicative competence was a definition of what a speaker needs to know in order to be communicatively competent in a speech community. In Hymes's view, a person who acquires communicative competence acquires both knowledge and ability for language use with respect to the following:

1. whether (and to what degree) something is formally possible
2. whether (and to what degree) something is feasible in virtue of the means of implementation available
3. whether (and to what degree) something is appropriate (adequate, happy, successful) in relation to a context in which it is used and evaluated
4. whether (and to what degree) something is in fact done, actually performed, and what its doing entails

(1972: 281)

This theory of what knowing a language entails offers a much more comprehensive view than Chomsky's cognitive view of competence – a theory of language that deals primarily with abstract grammatical knowledge.

Another linguistic theory of communication favored in CLT theory was Halliday's functional account of language use. Here the term *functional* is expanded to encompass the categories given below, as well as *speech acts*, another term for functions in the sense used by Wilkins to describe what we do with language (complain, apologize, etc.). "Linguistics … is concerned … with the description of speech acts or texts, since only through the study of language in use are all the functions of language, and therefore all components of meaning, brought into focus" (Halliday 1975: 145). In a number of influential books and papers, Halliday elaborated a powerful theory of the functions of language, which complements Hymes's view of communicative competence for many writers on CLT (e.g., Brumfit and Johnson 1979; Savignon 1983). He described (1975: 11–17) seven basic functions that language performs for children learning their first language:

1. The instrumental function: using language to get things
2. The regulatory function: using language to control the behavior of others

3. The interactional function: using language to create interaction with others
4. The personal function: using language to express personal feelings and meanings
5. The heuristic function: using language to learn and to discover
6. The imaginative function: using language to create a world of the imagination
7. The representational function: using language to communicate information.

Learning a second language now was similarly viewed by proponents of CLT as acquiring the linguistic means to perform these seven basic kinds of functions.

Another theorist frequently cited for his views on the communicative nature of language is Henry Widdowson. In his book *Teaching Language as Communication* (1978), Widdowson presented a view of the relationship between linguistic systems and their communicative values in text and discourse. He focused on the communicative acts underlying the ability to use language for different purposes. In other words, Widdowson's focus was a practical one, as opposed to a purely philosophical one, and emphasized the learner's use of speech acts or functions for a communicative purpose.

A more pedagogically influential analysis of communicative competence was presented in an important paper by Canale and Swain (1980), in which four dimensions of communicative competence are identified: grammatical competence, sociolinguistic competence, discourse competence, and strategic competence. *Grammatical competence* refers to what Chomsky calls linguistic competence and what Hymes intends by what is "formally possible." It is the domain of grammatical and lexical capacity. *Sociolinguistic competence* refers to an understanding of the social context in which communication takes place, including role relationships, the shared information of the participants, and the communicative purpose for their interaction. *Discourse competence* refers to the interpretation of individual message elements in terms of their interconnectedness and of how meaning is represented in relationship to the entire discourse or text. *Strategic competence* refers to the coping strategies that communicators employ to initiate, terminate, maintain, repair, and redirect communication. The usefulness of the notion of communicative competence is seen in the many attempts that have been made to refine the original notion of communicative competence since it was first introduced (e.g. Savignon 1983). Sociocultural learning theory has replaced earlier views of communicative competence in many current accounts of second language learning (see Chapter 2) because of its more comprehensive understanding of the role of social context in discourse.

At the level of language theory, CLT has a rich, if somewhat eclectic, theoretical base. Some of the characteristics of this communicative view of language follow:

1. Language is a system for the expression of meaning.
2. The primary function of language is to allow interaction and communication.
3. The structure of language reflects its functional and communicative uses.
4. The primary units of language are not merely its grammatical and structural features, but categories of functional and communicative meaning as exemplified in discourse.

5. Communicative competence entails knowing how to use language for a range of different purposes and functions as well as the following dimensions of language knowledge:

- Knowing how to vary use of language according to the setting and the participants (e.g., knowing when to use formal and informal speech or when to use language appropriately for written as opposed to spoken communication)
- Knowing how to produce and understand different types of texts (e.g., narratives, reports, interviews, conversations)
- Knowing how to maintain communication despite having limitations in one's language knowledge (e.g., through using different kinds of communication strategies).

Theory of learning

Several of the learning theories presented in Chapter 2 can be said to underpin CLT, as will be explained below. However, in early accounts of CLT, little was written about learning theory when compared to the amount written about communicative dimensions of language. Neither Brumfit and Johnson (1979) nor Littlewood (1981), for example, offered any discussion of learning theory. Elements of an underlying learning theory can be discerned in some CLT practices, however. One such element might be described as the communication principle: activities that involve real communication promote learning. A second element is the task principle: activities in which language is used for carrying out meaningful tasks promote learning (Johnson 1982). A third element is the meaningfulness principle: language that is meaningful to the learner supports the learning process. Learning activities are consequently selected according to how well they engage the learner in meaningful and authentic language use (rather than merely mechanical practice of language patterns). These principles, we suggest, can be inferred from CLT practices (e.g., Littlewood 1981; Johnson 1982) and inform the design of textbooks and courses since the 1980s that are based on CLT. These and a variety of other more recent learning principles relevant to the claims of CLT are summarized in Skehan (1998) and further discussed in relation to Task-Based Language Teaching in Chapter 19.

Later accounts of CLT, however, identified theories of language learning processes that are compatible with the Communicative Approach. Savignon (1983) surveyed second language acquisition research as a source for learning theories and considers the role of linguistic, social, cognitive, and individual variables in language acquisition. Johnson (1984) and Littlewood (1984) proposed an alternative learning theory that they also saw as compatible with CLT – a skill-learning model of learning. According to this theory, the acquisition of communicative competence in a language is an example of skill development. This involves both a cognitive and a behavioral aspect:

> The cognitive aspect involves the internalisation of plans for creating appropriate behaviour. For language use, these plans derive mainly from the language system – they include grammatical rules, procedures for selecting vocabulary, and social

conventions governing speech. The behavioural aspect involves the automation of these plans so that they can be converted into fluent performance in real time. This occurs mainly through practice in converting plans into performance.

(Littlewood 1984: 74)

Other learning theories that can be cited to support CLT are the creative-construction hypothesis, and particularly interactional theory and sociocultural learning theory, which were referred to above and in Chapter 2. From these perspectives language learning is seen to result from processes of the following kind:

- Interaction between the learner and users of the language
- Collaborative creation of meaning
- Creating meaningful and purposeful interaction through language
- Negotiation of meaning as the learner and his or her interlocutor arrive at understanding
- Learning through attending to the feedback learners get when they use the language
- Paying attention to the language one hears (the input) and trying to incorporate new forms into one's developing communicative competence
- Trying out and experimenting with different ways of saying things
- Learning as social mediation between the learner and another during which socially acquired knowledge becomes internal to the learner
- Learning facilitated through scaffolding by an expert or fellow learner (Vygotsky 1978)
- Learning through collaborative dialogue centering on structured cooperative tasks (Cook 2008).

More recent teaching approaches, such as Task-Based Language Teaching (Chapter 9) and CLIL (Chapter 6), also emphasize many of these processes, particularly the use of strategies to arrive at a shared understanding of meaning.

Design

Objectives

Objectives in CLT courses and materials may relate either to very general language learning goals, or to those linked to learners with very specific needs. In the case of the former, objectives will reflect the type of syllabus framework used, such as whether the course is organized around a topic-based, function-based, or skill-based syllabus. In either case objectives will normally seek to operationalize the notion of communicative competence into more specific descriptions of learning outcomes. In recent years objectives for communicative courses are often linked to the learning outcomes described in the Common European Framework of Reference (see Chapter 8). For example, in *Four Corners 2* (Richards and Bohlke 2012) the learning outcomes or objectives listed for the first two units are as follows:

Unit 1: My interests
Students can:

- ask and talk about interests
- ask for repetition
- ask someone to speak more slowly
- ask and talk about sports and exercise habits
- talk about free-time activities.

Unit 2: Descriptions
Students can:

- ask and talk about someone's personality
- say they think something is true and not true
- ask and talk about people's appearance
- describe their personality and appearance.

The syllabus also specifies the grammar, vocabulary, functions, and other skills used to achieve these learning outcomes. In the case of courses developed for learners with more specific needs, objectives will be specific to the contexts of teaching and learning. These needs may be in the domains of listening, speaking, reading, or writing, each of which can be approached from a communicative perspective. Curriculum or instructional objectives for a particular course would reflect specific aspects of communicative competence according to the learner's proficiency level and communicative needs.

The syllabus

Discussions of the nature of the syllabus have been central in CLT, and various versions have been proposed.

The notional-functional syllabus

We have seen that one of the first, and ultimately influential, syllabus models was described as a notional syllabus (Wilkins 1976), which specified the semantic-grammatical categories (e.g., frequency, motion, location) and the categories of communicative function that learners need to express. The Council of Europe expanded and developed it into a syllabus that included descriptions of the objectives of foreign language courses for European adults, the situations in which they might typically need to use a foreign language (e.g., travel, business), the topics they might need to talk about (e.g., personal identification, education, shopping), the functions they needed language for (e.g., describing something, requesting information, expressing agreement and disagreement), the notions made use of in communication (e.g., time, frequency, duration), as well as the vocabulary and grammar needed. The result was published as *Threshold Level English* (Van Ek and Alexander 1980) and was an attempt to specify what was needed in order to be able to achieve a reasonable degree of communicative proficiency in a foreign language, including the language items needed to realize this "threshold level." Rather than simply specifying the grammar and vocabulary that learners needed to master, it was argued that a syllabus should identify the following aspects of language use in order to be able to develop the learner's communicative competence:

1. as detailed a consideration as possible of the *purposes* for which the learner wishes to acquire the target language. For example, using English for business purposes, in the hotel industry, or for travel.
2. some idea of the *setting* in which they will want to use the target language. For example in an office, on an airplane, or in a store.
3. the socially defined *role* the learners will assume in the target language, as well as the role of their interlocutors. For example as a traveler, as a salesperson talking to clients, or as a student in a school setting.
4. the *communicative events* in which the learners will participate: everyday situations, vocational or professional situations, academic situations, and so on. For example, making telephone calls, engaging in casual conversation, or taking part in a meeting.
5. the *language functions* involved in those events, or what the learner will be able to do with or through the language. For example, making introductions, giving explanations, or describing plans.
6. the *notions* or concepts involved, or what the learner will need to be able to talk about. For example, leisure, finance, history, religion.
7. the skills involved in the "knitting together" of discourse: *discourse and rhetorical skills.* For example, storytelling, giving an effective business presentation.
8. the *variety* or varieties of the target language that will be needed, such as American, Australian, or British English, and the levels in the spoken and written language which the learners will need to reach.
9. the *grammatical* content that will be needed.
10. the *lexical content* or vocabulary that will be needed.

(Van Ek and Alexander 1980)

Since the description and dissemination of Threshold Level specifications for various languages, three additional communicative levels have been added – two pre-Threshold levels: Breakthrough and Waystage, and one post-Threshold level: Vantage (Council of Europe 2011).

Discussion of syllabus theory and syllabus models in CLT has been extensive. Wilkins's original notional syllabus model was soon criticized by British applied linguists as merely replacing one kind of list (e.g., a list of grammar items) with another (a list of notions and functions). It specified products, rather than communicative processes. Widdowson (1979: 254) argued that notional-functional categories provide

only a very partial and imprecise description of certain semantic and pragmatic rules which are used for reference when people interact. They tell us nothing about the procedures people employ in the application of these rules when they are actually engaged in communicative activity. If we are to adopt a communicative approach to teaching which takes as its primary purpose the development of the ability to do things with language, then it is discourse which must be at the center of our attention.

Other syllabus proposals

There have been numerous proposals and models for what a syllabus might look like in CLT throughout the 1980s. Yalden (1983) described the major current communicative syllabus types, summarized below:

Type	Reference
1. structures plus functions	Wilkins (1976)
2. functional spiral around a structural core	Brumfit (1980)
3. structural, functional, instrumental	Allen (1980)
4. functional	Jupp and Hodlin (1975)
5. notional	Wilkins (1976)
6. interactional	Widdowson (1979)
7. task-based	Prabhu (1983)
8. learner-generated	Candlin (1976)

Prabhu believed that a task-based approach was the most appropriate model for syllabus design in CLT because meaningful tasks can encourage the development of communicative competence through information-sharing (see Chapter 9).

> The only form of syllabus which is compatible with and can support communicational teaching seems to be a purely procedural one – which lists, in more or less detail, the types of tasks to be attempted in the classroom and suggests an order of complexity for tasks of the same kind.
>
> (Prabhu 1987: 4)

This approach to a syllabus has been developed in Task-Based Language Teaching – which many see as an extension of the principles of CLT. Other more radical proposals suggested that the syllabus concept be abolished altogether in its accepted forms, arguing that only learners can be fully aware of their own needs, communicational resources, and desired learning pace and path, and that each learner must create a personal, albeit implicit, syllabus as part of learning. In other words, the syllabus is not predetermined but is an outcome of the kinds of communication and learning that occur in the classroom. This approach is described more fully in the final chapter of this book. Brumfit (1980) represents a more conservative approach, one which favors a grammatically based syllabus around which notions, functions, and communicational activities are grouped.

English for Specific Purposes

Advocates of CLT also recognized that many learners needed English in order to use it in specific occupational or educational settings – they needed English for Specific Purposes (ESP). For such learners it would be more efficient to teach them the specific kinds of language and communicative skills needed for particular roles (e.g., that of nurse, engineer, flight attendant, pilot, biologist, etc.) rather than just to concentrate on more and more general English. This led to the process of *needs analysis* (described more fully in Chapter 21) – the use of observation, surveys, interviews, situation analysis, analysis of language samples collected in different settings – in order to determine the kinds of communication learners would need to master if they were in specific occupational or educational roles and the language features of particular settings. The focus of needs analysis was to determine the particular characteristics of a language when it is used for specific rather than general purposes. Such differences might include

- differences in vocabulary choice;
- differences in grammar;
- differences in the kinds of texts commonly occurring;
- differences in functions;
- differences in the need for particular skills.

Munby's Communicative Syllabus Design (1978) presented a detailed model for conducting needs analysis in ESP course design. ESP courses soon began to appear addressing the language needs of university students, nurses, engineers, restaurant staff, doctors, hotel staff, airline pilots, and so on.

Types of learning and teaching activities

As well as rethinking the nature of a syllabus, the Communicative Approach to teaching prompted a rethinking of classroom teaching methodology. It was argued that learners learn a language through the process of communicating in it, and that communication that is meaningful to the learner provides a better opportunity for learning than a grammar-based approach. Activities were needed that reflected the following principles:

- Make real communication the focus of language learning.
- Provide opportunities for learners to experiment and try out what they know.
- Be tolerant of learners' errors as they indicate that the learner is building up his or her communicative competence.
- Provide opportunities for learners to develop both accuracy and fluency.
- Link the different skills such as speaking, reading, and listening together, since they usually occur together in the real world.
- Let students induce or discover grammar rules.

In applying these principles in the classroom, new classroom techniques and activities were needed as well as new roles for teachers and learners in the classroom. Instead of making use of activities that demanded accurate repetition and memorization of sentences and grammatical patterns, activities that required learners to negotiate meaning – a term used to refer to the processes speakers use to arrive at a shared understanding of meaning – and to interact meaningfully, and that developed fluency in language use were required. The range of exercise types and activities compatible with a communicative approach is unlimited, provided that such exercises enable learners to attain the communicative objectives of the curriculum and engage learners in communication. Classroom activities are often designed to focus on completing tasks that are mediated through language or involve negotiation of information and information-sharing – a feature that has become the primary characteristic of Task-Based Language Teaching. Littlewood (1981) distinguished between "functional communication activities" and "social interaction activities" as major activity types in CLT. Functional communication activities include such tasks as learners comparing sets of pictures and noting similarities and differences; working out a likely sequence of events in a set of pictures; discovering missing features in a map or picture; one learner communicating behind a screen to another learner and giving instructions on how to draw a picture or shape, or how to complete a map; following directions; and solving problems from shared clues. Social interaction activities include conversation and discussion sessions, dialogues and role plays, simulations, skits, improvisations, and debates.

One of the goals of second-language learning is to develop fluency, accuracy, and appropriacy in language use. Fluency is natural language use occurring when a speaker engages in meaningful interaction and maintains comprehensible and ongoing communication despite limitations in his or her communicative competence. In CLT fluency was addressed through classroom activities in which students must correct misunderstandings and work to avoid communication breakdowns. Fluency practice can be contrasted with accuracy practice, which focuses on creating correct examples of language use. The differences between these two kinds of activities may be summarized as follows:

Activities focusing on *fluency*
- reflect natural use of language;
- concentrate on achieving communication through negotiation of meaning;
- require meaningful use of language;
- require the use of communication strategies;
- produce language that may not be predictable;
- seek to link language use to context.

Activities focusing on *accuracy*
- reflect classroom use of language;
- concentrate on the formation of correct examples of language;
- practice language out of context;
- practice small samples of language;

- do not require meaningful communication;
- control choice of language.

Teachers were recommended to use a balance of fluency activities and accuracy and to use accuracy activities to support fluency activities. Accuracy work could come either before or after fluency work. For example, based on students' performance on a fluency task, the teacher could assign accuracy work to deal with grammatical or pronunciation problems the teacher observed while students were carrying out the task, or develop a follow-up focus on appropriacy of language use (e.g., the difference between formal and casual speech). While dialogues, grammar, and pronunciation drills did not usually disappear from textbooks and classroom materials at this time, they now appeared as part of a sequence of activities that moved back and forth between accuracy activities and fluency activities.

The dynamics of classrooms also changed. Instead of a predominance of teacher-fronted teaching, teachers were encouraged to make greater use of small-group work, often involving an "information gap" (students negotiating to obtain information that they do not have). Pair and group activities gave learners greater opportunities to use the language and to develop fluency. Common activity types in CLT include:

- *Jig-saw activities.* The class is divided into groups and each group has part of the information needed to complete an activity. The class must fit the pieces together to complete the whole.
- *Task-completion activities.* Puzzles, games, map-reading, and other kinds of classroom tasks in which the focus is on using one's language resources to complete a task.
- *Information-gathering activities.* Student-conducted surveys, interviews, and searches in which students are required to use their linguistic resources to collect information.
- *Opinion-sharing activities.* Activities where students compare values, opinions, beliefs, such as a ranking task in which students list six qualities in order of importance when choosing a date or spouse.
- *Information-transfer activities.* Taking information that is presented in one form, and representing it in a different form. For example, students may read instructions on how to get from A to B, and then draw a map showing the sequence, or they may read information about a subject and then represent it as a graph.
- *Reasoning gap activities.* Deriving some new information from given information through the process of inference, practical reasoning, etc. For example, working out a teacher's timetable on the basis of given class timetables.
- *Role plays.* Students are assigned roles and improvise a scene or exchange based on given information or clues.

Learner roles

The emphasis in CLT on the processes of communication, rather than mastery of language forms, leads to different roles for learners from those found in more traditional second language classrooms. Breen and Candlin (1980: 110) describe the learner's role within CLT in the following terms:

> The role of learner as negotiator – between the self, the learning process, and the object of learning – emerges from and interacts with the role of joint negotiator within the group and within the classroom procedures and activities which the group undertakes. The implication for the learner is that he should contribute as much as he gains, and thereby learn in an interdependent way.

Learners now had to participate in classroom activities that were based on a cooperative rather than individualistic approach to learning. Students had to become comfortable with listening to their peers in group work or pair work tasks, rather than relying on the teacher for a model. They were expected to take on a greater degree of responsibility for their own learning. In the pure form of CLT, often there is no text, grammar rules are not presented, classroom arrangement is nonstandard, students are expected to interact primarily with each other rather than with the teacher, and correction of errors may be absent or infrequent. (Modified forms do aim to balance fluency and accuracy, as defined above.) The cooperative (rather than individualistic) approach to learning stressed in CLT may likewise be unfamiliar to learners. CLT methodologists consequently recommend that learners learn to see that failed communication is a joint responsibility and not the fault of speaker or listener. Similarly, successful communication is an accomplishment jointly achieved and acknowledged.

Teacher roles

The types of classroom activities proposed in CLT also implied new roles in the classroom for teachers, who now had to assume the role of facilitator and monitor. Rather than being a model for correct speech and writing and one with the primary responsibility of making sure students produced plenty of error-free sentences, the teacher had to develop a different view of learners' errors and of his or her own role in facilitating language learning. Breen and Candlin (1980: 99) described teacher roles in the following terms:

> The teacher has two main roles: the first role is to facilitate the communication process between all participants in the classroom, and between these participants and the various activities and texts. The second role is to act as an independent participant within the learning-teaching group. The latter role is closely related to the objectives of the first role and arises from it. These roles imply a set of secondary roles for the teacher; first, as an organizer of resources and as a resource himself, second as a guide within the classroom procedures and activities … A third role for the teacher is that of researcher and learner, with much to contribute in terms of appropriate knowledge and abilities, actual and observed experience of the nature of learning and organizational capacities.

Other roles assumed for teachers are needs analyst, counselor, and group process manager. Observers have pointed out that these roles may not be compatible with the traditional roles teachers are expected to play in some cultures (see below).

Needs analyst

The CLT teacher assumes a responsibility for determining and responding to learner language needs. This may be done informally and personally through one-to-one sessions with students, in which the teacher talks through such issues as the student's perception of his or her learning style, learning assets, and learning goals. It may be done formally through administering a needs assessment instrument, such as those exemplified in Savignon (1983). Typically, such formal assessments contain items that attempt to determine an individual's motivation for studying the language. For example, students might respond on a five-point scale (*strongly agree* to *strongly disagree*) to statements such as the following:

> I want to study English because …
> I think it will someday be useful in getting a good job.
> It will help me better understand English-speaking people and their way of life.
> One needs a good knowledge of English to gain other people's respect.
> It will allow me to meet and converse with interesting people.
> I need it for my job.
> It will enable me to think and behave like English-speaking people.

On the basis of such needs assessments, teachers are expected to plan group and individual instruction that responds to the learners' needs. A good example of how this process was applied in a national language program for immigrants in Australia was given in Nunan (1988).

Counselor

Another role assumed by several CLT approaches is that of counselor, similar to the way this role is defined in Community Language Learning (Chapter 17). In this role, the teacher-counselor is expected to exemplify an effective communicator seeking to maximize the meshing of speaker intention and hearer interpretation, through the use of paraphrase, confirmation, and feedback.

Group process manager

CLT procedures often require teachers to acquire less teacher-centered classroom management skills. It is the teacher's responsibility to organize the classroom as a setting for communication and communicative activities. Guidelines for classroom practice (e.g., Littlewood 1981; Finocchiaro and Brumfit 1983) suggest that during an activity the teacher monitors, encourages, and suppresses the inclination to supply gaps in lexis, grammar, and strategy but notes such gaps for later commentary and communicative practice. At the conclusion of group activities, the teacher leads in the debriefing of the activity, pointing out alternatives and extensions and assisting groups in self-correction discussion. Critics have pointed out, however, that this may be an unfamiliar role for teachers in some cultures. The focus on fluency and comprehensibility in CLT may cause anxiety among teachers accustomed to seeing error suppression and correction as the major instructional responsibility, and who see their primary function as preparing learners to take standardized or other kinds of tests. A continuing teacher concern has been the possible negative effect in pair or group work of imperfect modeling and student error. In CLT with low-level learners, students may develop fluency at the expense of accuracy and complexity (see below).

The role of instructional materials

A wide variety of materials have been used to support communicative approaches to language teaching. Practitioners of CLT view materials as a way of influencing the quality of classroom interaction and language use. Materials thus have the primary role of promoting communicative language use. We will consider four kinds of materials currently used in CLT and label these text-based, task-based, realia-based, and technology-supported.

Text-based materials

There are numerous textbooks designed to direct and support CLT. Their tables of contents sometimes suggest a kind of grading and sequencing of language practice not unlike those found in structurally organized texts. Some of these are in fact written around a largely structural syllabus, with slight reformatting to justify their claims to be based on a communicative approach. Others, however, look very different from previous language teaching texts. Morrow and Johnson's *Communicate* (1979), for example, had none of the usual dialogues, drills, or sentence patterns and uses visual cues, taped cues, pictures, and sentence fragments to initiate conversation. Watcyn-Jones's *Pair Work* (1981) consisted of two different texts for pair work, each containing different information needed to enact role plays and carry out other pair activities. More recent courses published by international publishers still often cite CLT as providing the methodological framework for the course, for example, *Interchange*, 4th edition (Richards, Hull, and Proctor 2012) and *Four Corners* (Richards and Bohlke 2012). Typically this means the use of an integrated syllabus that draws on the Common European Framework of Reference, which specifies outcomes for various language levels (see Chapter 8), and which includes functions, topics, grammar, vocabulary and the four skills, as noted above.

Task-based materials

A variety of games, role plays, simulations, and task-based communication activities have been prepared to support CLT classes. These typically are in the form of one-of-a-kind items: exercise handbooks, cue cards, activity cards, pair-communication practice materials, and student-interaction practice booklets. In pair-communication materials, there are typically two sets of material for a pair of students, each set containing different kinds of information. Sometimes the information is complementary, and partners must fit their respective parts of the "jigsaw" into a composite whole. Others assume different role relationships for the partners (e.g., an interviewer and an interviewee). Still others provide drills and practice material in interactional formats.

Realia-based materials

Many proponents of CLT have advocated the use of "authentic," "from-life" materials in the classroom. These might include language-based realia, such as signs, magazines, advertisements, and newspapers, or graphic and visual sources around which communicative activities can be built, such as maps, pictures, symbols, graphs, and charts. Different kinds of objects can be used to support communicative exercises, such as a plastic model to assemble from directions.

Technology-supported materials

CLT emphasizes the need for teaching to be organized around authentic and meaningful uses of language that are linked to the learner's communicative needs. The goals are to develop fluent, accurate, and appropriate language use through the use of a communicative curriculum built around functional and interactional uses of language. These uses more often require interaction in the modes of reading and writing than in listening and speaking. In a traditional classroom these aims are realized through a variety of activities that, as mentioned, involve negotiation of meaning, natural language use, and the development of communication strategies. However, the classroom context is often an artificial setting for authentic communication to be realized. Technology, on the other hand, provides opportunities for accessing authentic language input, combining texts, images, audio, and video. Chat rooms, discussion boards, and teleconferencing are tools that can be used to encourage authentic interaction. It creates situations in which learners have to employ and expand their communicative resources, supported by the ability to link sound, word, texts, and images in the process. Chat rooms, discussion boards, teleconferencing can all be used in this way. Access to authentic materials and collaboration on tasks with learners in different locations and utilizing different forms of communication can enhance the learning experience. Topics, functions, and activities in a coursebook can be extended through follow-up work in the multimedia lab or at home from a computer, where students work with real examples of the interactions and transactions they practiced in the classroom. Research on computer-mediated communication suggests it has a number of characteristics that reflect the assumptions of CLT (Erben, Ban, and Casteneda 2009: 84–5). These include

- increased participation on the part of the students;
- increased access to comprehensible input;
- increased opportunities for negotiation of meaning;
- group-based learning since CLT creates a context for interaction;
- the creation of a social learning environment that promotes language learning.

Procedure

Because communicative principles can be applied to the teaching of any skill, at any level, and because of the wide variety of classroom activities and exercise types discussed in the literature on CLT, description of typical classroom procedures used in a lesson based on

CLT principles is not feasible. Nevertheless, CLT procedure did evolve from the existing procedures in place for Situational Language Teaching and other earlier methods, and the Presentation-Practice-Production (or PPP) format (see Chapter 3) continued to be used by some proponents of CLT. Savignon (1983) discusses techniques and classroom management procedures associated with a number of CLT classroom procedures (e.g., group activities, language games, role plays), but neither these activities nor the ways in which they are used are exclusive to CLT classrooms. Finocchiaro and Brumfit offer a lesson outline for teaching the function "making a suggestion" for learners in the beginning level of a secondary school program that suggests that CLT procedures are evolutionary rather than revolutionary:

1. Presentation of a brief dialog or several mini-dialogs, preceded by a motivation (relating the dialog situation[s] to the learners' probable community experiences) and a discussion of the function and situation – people, roles, setting, topic, and the informality or formality of the language which the function and situation demand. (At beginning levels, where all the learners understand the same native language, the motivation can well be given in their native tongue.)

2. Oral practice of each utterance of the dialog segment to be presented that day (entire class repetition, half-class, groups, individuals) generally preceded by your model. If mini-dialogs are used, engage in similar practice.

3. Questions and answers based on the dialog topic(s) and situation itself. (Inverted *wh* or *or* questions.)

4. Questions and answers related to the students' personal experiences but centered around the dialog theme.

5. Study one of the basic communicative expressions in the dialog or one of the structures which exemplify the function. You will wish to give several additional examples of the communicative use of the expression or structure with familiar vocabulary in unambiguous utterances or mini-dialogs (using pictures, simple real objects, or dramatization) to clarify the meaning of the expression or structure ...

6. Learner discovery of generalizations or rules underlying the functional expression or structure. This should include at least four points: its oral and written forms (the elements of which it is composed, e.g., "How about + verb + ing?"); its position in the utterance; its formality or informality in the utterance; and in the case of a structure, its grammatical function and meaning ...

7. Oral recognition, interpretative activities (two to five depending on the learning level, the language knowledge of the students, and related factors).

8. Oral production activities – proceeding from guided to freer communication activities.

9. Copying of the dialogs or mini-dialogs or modules if they are not in the class text.

10. Sampling of the written homework assignment, if given.

11. Evaluation of learning (oral only), e.g., "How would you ask your friend to _____? And how would you ask me to _____?"

(Finocchiaro and Brumfit 1983: 107–8)

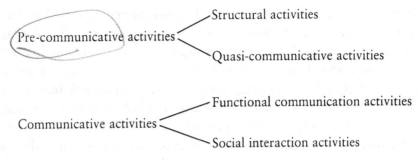

Figure 5.1 Activity types in CLT

Such procedures clearly have much in common with those observed in classes taught according to Structural-Situational and Audiolingual principles. Traditional procedures are not rejected but are reinterpreted and extended. A similar conservatism is found in many "orthodox" CLT texts, such as Alexander's *Mainline Beginners* (1978). Although each unit has an ostensibly functional focus, new teaching points are introduced with dialogues, followed by controlled practice of the main grammatical patterns. The teaching points are then contextualized through situational practice. This serves as an introduction to a freer practice activity, such as a role play or improvisation. Similar techniques are used in *Starting Strategies* (Abbs and Freebairn 1977) and in more recent series such as *Interchange* and *Four Corners*. Teaching points are often introduced in dialogue form, grammatical items are isolated for controlled practice, and then freer activities are provided. Pair and group work is suggested to encourage students to use and practice functions and forms. The methodological procedures underlying these texts reflect a sequence of activities represented in Figure 5.1 above (Littlewood 1981: 86).

Savignon (1972, 1983), however, rejected the notion that learners must first gain control over individual skills (pronunciation, grammar, vocabulary) before applying them in communicative tasks; she advocated providing communicative practice from the start of instruction – a feature that has since become central in task-based teaching.

An example of a communicative textbook lesson may be found in the appendix to this chapter.

Criticisms of CLT

Although CLT has become a widely used set of principles and procedures for the design of language courses and teaching materials, it is not without its critics. Criticisms of CLT take several different forms, including the following:

- *It promotes fossilization.* The persistence of errors in learners' language has been attributed to an over-emphasis on communication in language teaching at the expense of accuracy. The promise that the communicative classroom activities would help learners develop both communicative and linguistic competence did not always happen. Programs where there was an extensive use of "authentic communication," particularly in the early stages of learning, reported that students often developed fluency at the expense of accuracy, resulting in learners with good communication skills but a poor command of grammar and a high level of fossilization (Higgs and Clifford 1982).

- *It reflects "native-speakerism."* Holliday (1994) argued that the communicative orthodoxy taught to teachers who are native speakers of English reflects a view of teaching and learning that closely reflects culturally bound assumptions derived from the cultures of origin – Britain, Australasia, and North America (which Holliday refers to as BANA contexts). The teaching methods developed in these countries' centers reflect the kinds of learners who study in institutes and universities serving students who generally have instrumental reasons for learning English, namely for academic or professional purposes or as new settlers. Their needs, however, may be very different from learners learning English in state-based educational programs (e.g. public schools) in other parts of the world – studying in tertiary, secondary, or primary settings (referred to as TESEP contexts). Methods developed in one context will not necessarily transfer to others. As Holliday points out, most of the literature on CLT reflects a primarily BANA understanding of teaching, learning, teachers, learners, and classrooms. In these contexts, "English language teaching tends to be instrumentally oriented, in that it has grown up within a private language school ethos where there has been a considerable freedom to develop classroom methodology as a sophisticated instrument to suit the precise needs of language learners." In TESEP settings, by comparison, "English ... is taught as part of a wider curriculum and is therefore influenced and constrained by wider educational, institutional, and community forces, quite different from those in the *BANA* sector" (Holliday 1994: 4).
- *It is not applicable in different cultures of learning.* Attempts to implement CLT in non-European settings were often less than successful due to different assumptions about the nature of teaching and learning that learners in countries such as China, East Asia, and other contexts bring to learning (Ahmad and Rao 2012). Jin and Cortazzi (2011: 571) comment:

> In China in the 1980s and 1990s the national take-up of communicative approaches was slow; teachers often spoke of "the Chinese context" and of "the need for an eclectic approach," which took account of some communicative techniques but also maintained traditional approaches.

Hird (1995 cited by Liao 2000) comments:

> The teachers believed that it was not feasible to adopt CLT because China had its special characteristics. These characteristics included the teachers' inability to teach communicatively and grammar-focused examination pressure ... And maybe that is just as well because China is a vastly different English language teaching environment from the one that spawned and nurtured the communicative approach.

Observers in other regional contexts give similar accounts. Vasilopoulos (2008), describing CLT in Korea, notes:

> Many years have passed since the introduction of the CLT approach in Korea; however, despite curriculum reform and the passage of time, many remain skeptical of the effectiveness of communicative methodology in the Korean English language class room.

Chowdhry (2010) wrote that,

> In Bangladesh, students expect teachers to be authority figures and the teaching methods to conform to the traditional "lock-step" teacher-centered approach where the teacher gives orders to students, who then comply ... In the pre-university year, students are not exposed to skills development course. Hence, the more communicative approach ... seems to them foreign. Students feel tempted to discard the new style and complain that the teacher is not teaching ... They knew their status and role had suddenly been violated by something new. They are no longer familiar with the rules of this new game.

- *It reflects a Western-based top-down approach to innovation.* A more radical critique of the influence of CLT and similar Western or "center-based" methods is given by Kumaravadivelu (2012), as we saw in Chapter 1, who argues that the communicative syllabus and common procedures for its implementation do not capture the diversity of students' needs and goals.

Conclusion

In this chapter, we have considered the development of Communicative Language Teaching, the many different ways CLT has been interpreted, as well as some of the more recent criticisms. CLT is best considered an approach rather than a method. It refers to a diverse set of principles that reflect a communicative view of language and language learning and that can be used to support a wide variety of classroom procedures. Among these principles are the following:

- Learners learn a language through using it to communicate.
- Authentic and meaningful communication should be the goal of classroom activities.
- Fluency is an important dimension of communication.
- Communication involves the integration of different language skills.
- Learning is a process of creative construction and involves trial and error.

CLT appeared at a time when language teaching in many parts of the world was ready for a paradigm shift. The demand for more effective approaches to language teaching came from many quarters, including the Council of Europe and many national ministries of education. Situational Language Teaching and Audiolingualism were no longer felt to be appropriate methodologies. CLT appealed to those who sought a more humanistic approach to teaching, one in which the interactive processes of communication received priority. The rapid adoption and worldwide dissemination of the Communicative Approach also resulted from the fact that it quickly assumed the status of orthodoxy in British language teaching circles, receiving the sanction and support of leading applied linguists, language specialists, and publishers, as well as institutions such as the British Council (Richards 1985).

Since its inception CLT has passed through a number of different phases as its advocates have sought to apply its principles to different dimensions of the teaching/learning process. In its first phase, a primary concern was the need to develop a syllabus that was compatible with the notion of communicative competence. This led to proposals for the organization of syllabuses in terms of notions and functions rather than grammatical structures (Wilkins 1976). In the second phase, CLT focused on procedures for identifying learners' needs, and this resulted in proposals to make needs analysis an essential component of communicative methodology (Munby 1978). In its third phase, CLT focused on the kinds of classroom activities that could be used as the basis of a communicative methodology, such as group work, task work, and information gap activities (Prabhu 1987).

Jacobs and Farrell (2003) suggested that the CLT paradigm shift that began in the 1980s has led to eight major changes in approaches to language teaching – changes which go beyond CLT itself and can be seen reflected in other more recent language teaching approaches and proposals such as CLIL (Chapter 6), Text-Based Instruction (Chapter 10) and Task-Based Language Teaching (Chapter 9). These changes are:

1. *Learner autonomy.* Giving learners greater choice over their own learning, both in terms of the content of learning as well as processes they might employ (see Chapter 19). The use of small groups is one example of this, as well as the use of self-assessment.
2. *The social nature of learning.* Learning is not an individual private activity but a social one that depends upon interaction with others. The movement known as Cooperative Language Learning (Chapter 13) reflects this viewpoint as does sociocultural learning theory that is sometimes cited in support of both CLIL and Task-Based Language Teaching.
3. *Curricular integration.* The connection between different strands of the curriculum is emphasized, so that English is not seen as a stand-alone subject but is linked to other subjects in the curriculum. Text-Based Instruction (see below) reflects this approach and seeks to develop fluency in text-types that can be used across the curriculum. Project work in language teaching also requires students to explore issues outside of the language classroom – a feature of CLIL.
4. *Focus on meaning.* Meaning is viewed as the driving force of learning. Content-Based Instruction and CLIL reflect this view and seek to make the exploration of meaning through content the core of language learning activities (see Chapter 6).
5. *Diversity.* Learners learn in different ways and have different strengths. Teaching needs to take these differences into account rather than try to force students into a single mold. In language teaching this has led to an emphasis on developing students' use and awareness of learning strategies (see Chapter 19).

6. *Thinking skills.* Language should serve as a means of developing higher-order thinking skills, also known as critical and creative thinking. In language teaching this means that students do not learn language for its own sake but in order to develop and apply their thinking skills in situations that go beyond the language classroom.

7. *Alternative assessment.* New forms of assessment are needed to replace traditional multiple-choice and other items that test lower-order skills. Multiple forms of assessment (e.g. observation, interviews, journals, portfolios) can be used to build up a comprehensive picture of what students can do in a second language.

8. *Teachers as co-learners.* The teacher is viewed as a facilitator who is constantly trying out different alternatives (i.e., learning through doing). In language teaching this has led to an interest in action research and other forms of classroom investigation.

By the twenty-first century, the assumptions and practices of CLT seem on the one hand to be commonplace and part of a generally accepted and relatively uncontroversial canon of teaching theory and practice. They are sufficiently general to support a wide range of practices. On the other hand, language teaching today is a much more localized activity, subject to the constraints and needs of particular contexts and cultures of learning, and the use of global and generic solutions to local problems is increasingly seen as problematic. Research and documentation on local practices is needed to determine the nature of such practices and whether the philosophy of CLT is compatible with or has served as an input to local language teaching practices.

Discussion questions

1. CLT has been interpreted in different ways at the level of approach, design, and procedure. What are some of these variations? Having read this chapter, how would you define CLT to a colleague? What are some of the ways that CLT has evolved over time?

2. "There was no future in continuing to pursue the chimera of predicting language on the basis of situational events" (p. 83). Can you think of situations where it would be possible to predict to a high degree the actual language that will be used? Even where prediction is possible, can you think of disadvantages to using language that native speakers predict as the basis for a language syllabus?

3. Explain to a colleague the difference between notions and functions and how their specifications were used to underpin the communicative syllabus in Europe.

4. You read in the chapter that "Both American and British proponents typically described it as an approach (and not a method) that aimed to (a) make communicative competence the goal of language teaching and (b) develop procedures for the teaching of the four language skills that acknowledge the interdependence of language and communication." Why would they have called it an approach rather than a method (refer back to Anthony's description of approach, method, and technique on p. 21 of Chapter 2 if necessary)?

5. A colleague comes to you and is worried he or she spends too much time on grammar. Using Canale and Swain's (1980) four dimensions of communicative competence, how could you advise your colleague on balancing these four areas?

> Grammatical competence
> Sociolinguistic competence
> Discourse competence
> Strategic competence

6. What are some of the theories of learning that underpin the Communicative Approach? Can you give an example of how each theory might translate to classroom procedure?

7. You have read about the distinction between activities focusing on accuracy and those focusing on fluency. Which type of activity are the following?

> Filling in an immigration form
> Talking to a colleague over lunch
> Giving a presentation at a business meeting
> Reporting a theft to the police
> Calling out for help in an emergency

How do you feel accuracy and fluency can be balanced within CLT? Do you feel it is important to focus equally on both?

8. One purpose of a learner-generated syllabus (p. 97-8) is to give learners more control over the learning process and to encourage them to take responsibility for their own learning. How would you respond to these colleagues' concerns:

> "This would never work with my students; they have no idea what they need."
> "Maybe this works with adult learners but with my 10-year-olds it will be mayhem."
> "Sounds like a nice idea in theory, but how will I be able to make sure the students are prepared for the national exam?"

9. In the chapter you read about the difference between "functional communication activities" and "social interaction activities." Explain this difference to a colleague and give examples of such activities.

10. "CLT methodologists consequently recommend that learners learn to see that failed communication is a joint responsibility and not the fault of speaker or listener. Similarly, successful communication is an accomplishment jointly achieved and acknowledged. (p. 98)." Compare this with the way errors are treated in the Audiolingual Method (Chapter 4) or the Oral Approach (Chapter 3). How is it different?

11. At the end of the chapter a number of criticisms of CLT are discussed. Are there any that you agree with? Do you think they could be resolved in some way (e.g., by adapting CLT), or do they lead to the need for an entirely different way of language teaching?

12. Van Ek and Alexander suggested that the development of learners' communicative competence requires the syllabus to include information on the aspects of communication in the table below. Review the description of these aspects of communication on page 93. Then take a current textbook you are familiar with, and find examples of activities where each of these are implemented or communicated to the student. One example is given.

Language aspect	Implementation in the textbook
Purpose	For example: in this unit students are asked to write a letter to their lecturer, asking for an extension.
Setting	
Role	
Communicative events	
Language functions	
Notions	
Discourse and rhetorical skills	
Variety	
Grammatical content	
Lexical content	

References and further reading

Abbs, B. A., and I. Freebairn. 1977. *Starting Strategies.* London: Longman.

Alexander, L. G. 1978. *Mainline Beginners.* London: Longman.

Ahmad, S. and C. Rao. 2012. Does it work: implementing communicative language teaching approach in an EFL context. *Journal of Education and Practice* 3(12).

Allen, J. P. B. 1980. A three-level curriculum model for second language education. Mimeo, Modern Language Center, Ontario Institute for Studies in Education.

Applebee, A. N. 1974. *Tradition and Reform in the Teaching of English: A History.* Urbana, IL: National Council of Teachers of English.

Austin, J. L. 1962. *How to Do Things with Words.* Oxford: Clarendon Press.

Barnaby, B., and Y. Sun. 1989. Chinese teachers' views of Western language teaching: context informs paradigms. *TESOL Quarterly* 23(2): 219–38.

Breen, M., and C. N. Candlin. 1980. The essentials of a communicative curriculum in language teaching. *Applied Linguistics* 1(2): 89–112.

Brumfit, C. 1980. From defining to designing: communicative specifications approaches to teaching: proceedings of a European-American Seminar. Special issue of *Studies in Second Language Acquisition* 3(1): 1–9.

Brumfit, C. J., and K. Johnson (eds.). 1979. *The Communicative Approach to Language Teaching.* Oxford: Oxford University Press.

Byrne, D. 1978. *Materials for Language Teaching: Interaction Packages.* London: Modern English Publications.

Canale, M., and M. Swain. 1980. Theoretical bases of communicative approaches to second language teaching and testing. *Applied Linguistics* 1(1): 1– 47.

Candlin, C. N. 1976. Communicative language teaching and the debt to pragmatics. In C. Rameh (ed.), *Georgetown University Roundtable 1976.* Washington, DC: Georgetown University Press. 237–56.

Candlin, C. N., C. J. Bruton, and J. H. Leather. 1974. Doctor–patient communication skills. Mimeo, University of Lancaster.

Celce-Murcia, M. A., Z. Dörnyei, and S. Thurrell. 1997. Direct approaches in L2 instruction: a turning point in Communicative Language Teaching? *TESOL Quarterly* 31(1): 141–52.

Chomsky, N. 1957. *Syntactic Structures.* The Hague: Mouton.

Chomsky, N. 1965. *Aspects of the Theory of Syntax.* Cambridge, MA: MIT Press.

Chowdhry, M. R. 2010. International TESOL training and EFL contexts: the cultural disillusionment factor. *The TEFL Times.* Available at: http://www.eltworld.net/times/2010/09/international-tesol-training-and-efl-contexts-the-cultural-disillusionment-factor/

Cook, V. 2008. *Second Language Learning and Language Teaching.* 4th edn. London: Hodder Education.

Council of Europe. 2011. *Common European Framework of Reference for Languages: Learning, Teaching, Assessment.* Cambridge: Cambridge University Press.

English Language Syllabus in Malaysian Schools, Tingkatan 4 –5. 1975. Kuala Lumpur: Dewan Bahasa Dan Pustaka.

Erben, T., R. Ban, and M. Casteneda. 2009. *Teaching English Language Learners through Technology.* New York: Routledge.

Efstathiadis, S. 1987. A critique of the communicative approach to language learning and teaching. *Journal of Applied Linguistics* 3: 5–13.

Etherton, A. R. B. 1979. The communicational syllabus in Practice Case Study 1: Malaysia. *The English Bulletin* 7(2): 17–26 [Hong Kong Ministry of Education].

Finocchiaro, M., and C. Brumfit. 1983. *The Functional-Notional Approach: From Theory to Practice.* New York: Oxford University Press.

Firth, R. 1957. *Papers in Linguistics: 1934–1951.* London: Oxford University Press.

Geddes, M., and G. Sturtridge. 1979. *Listening Links.* London: Heinemann.

Green, P. 1987. *Communicative Language Testing: A Resource Book for Teacher Trainers.* Strasbourg: Council of Europe.

Gumperz, J. J., and D. Hymes (eds.). 1972. *Directions in Sociolinguistics: The Ethnography of Communication.* New York: Holt, Rinehart and Winston.

Halliday, M. A. K. 1970. Language structure and language function. In J. Lyons (ed.), *New Horizons in Linguistics.* Harmondsworth: Penguin. 140–465.

Halliday, M. A. K. 1973. *Explorations in the Functions of Language.* London: Edward Arnold.

Halliday, M. A. K. 1975. *Learning How to Mean: Explorations in the Development of Language.* London: Edward Arnold.

Henner-Stanchina, C., and P. Riley. 1978. Aspects of autonomous learning. In *ELT Documents 103: Individualization in Language Learning.* London: British Council. 75–97.

Higgs, T., and R. Clifford 1982. The push towards communication. In T. Higgs (ed.), *Curriculum, Competence, and the Foreign Language Teacher.* Skokie, IL: National Textbook Company. 57–79.

Hilgard, E. R., and G. H. Bower. 1966. *Theories of Learning.* New York: Appleton-Century-Crofts.

Hinkley, E. (ed.). 2011. *Handbook of Research in Second Language Teaching and Learning,* Vol. II. New York: Routledge.

Hird, B. 1995. How communicative can language teaching be in China? *Prospect* 10(3): 21-7.

Holec, H. 1980. *Autonomy and Foreign Language Learning.* Strasbourg: Council of Europe.

Holliday, A. 1994. The house of TESEP and the communicative approach: the special needs of English language education. *ELT Journal* 48(1): 3–11.

Howatt, A. P. R. 1984. *A History of English Language Teaching.* Oxford: Oxford University Press.

Hu, G. 2005. *Potential Cultural Resistance to Pedagogical Imports: The Case of Communicative Language Teaching in China.* Available at: http://www.freewebs.com/agapemanian/Language%20Teaching/Potential%20Cultural%20Resistance%20to%20pedagogical%20imports.pdf

Hymes, D. 1972. On communicative competence. In J. B. Pride and J. Holmes (eds.), *Sociolinguistics.* Harmondsworth: Penguin. 269–93.

Jacobs, G. M., and T. S. Farrell 2003. Understanding and implementing the CLT paradigm. *RELC Journal* 34(1): 5–30.

Jilani, W. 2004. Conditions under which English is taught in Pakistan: an applied linguistic perspective, *SARID Journal* 1(1).

Jin, L., and M. Cortazzi. 2011. Re-evaluating traditional approaches to second language teaching and learning. In Hinkley (ed.), 558–75.

Johnson, K. 1982. *Communicative Syllabus Design and Methodology.* Oxford: Pergamon.

Johnson, K. 1984. Skill psychology and communicative methodology. Paper presented at the RELC seminar, Singapore.

Johnson, K., and H. Johnson. 1998. Communicative methodology. In K. Johnson and H. Johnson (eds.), *Encylopedic Dictionary of Applied Linguistics.* Oxford: Blackwell. 68–73.

Jones, N. 1995. Business writing, Chinese students and communicative language teaching. *TESOL Journal* 4(3): 12–15.

Jupp, T. C., and S. Hodlin. 1975. *Industrial English: An Example of Theory and Practice in Functional Language Teaching.* London: Heinemann.

Kumaravadivelu. B. 2012. Individual identity, cultural globalization, and teaching English as an international language: The case for an epistemic break. In L. Alsagoff, W. Renandya, G. Hu, and S. McKay (eds.), *Principles and Practices for Teaching English as an International Language.* New York: Routledge. 9–27.

Lee, J., and B. Van Patten. 1995. *Making Communicative Language Teaching Happen.* San Francisco: McGraw-Hill.

Li, D. 1998. "It's always more difficult than you plan and imagine": teachers' perceived difficulties in introducing the Communicative Approach in South Korea. *TESOL Quarterly* 32(4): 677–703.

Liao, X. Q. 2000. How CLT became acceptable in secondary schools in China: the Internet. *TESOL Journal* 6(10).

Littlewood, W. 1981. *Communicative Language Teaching*. Cambridge: Cambridge University Press.

Littlewood, W. 1984. *Foreign and Second Language Learning: Language Acquisition Research and Its Implications for the Classroom*. Cambridge: Cambridge University Press.

Met, M. 1993. *Foreign Language Immersion Programs*. ERIC document (ED363141).

Morrow, K., and K. Johnson. 1979. *Communicate*. Cambridge: Cambridge University Press.

Munby, J. 1978. *Communicative Syllabus Design*. Cambridge: Cambridge University Press.

Nunan, D. 1988. *The Learner-Centred Curriculum: A Study in Second Language Teaching*. New York: Cambridge University Press.

Oxford, R. 1989. Language learning strategies, the communicative approach and their classroom implications. *Foreign Language Annals* 22(1): 29–39.

Pica, T. 1988. Communicative language teaching: an aid to second language acquisition? Some insights from classroom research. *English Quarterly* 21(2): 70–80.

Porter, P. A. 1983. Variations in the conversations of adult learners of English as a function of the proficiency level of the participants. Ph.D. dissertation, Stanford University.

Prabhu, N. S. [1983] 1987. *Second Language Pedagogy*. Oxford: Oxford University Press.

Richards, J. C. 1985. The secret life of methods. In J. C. Richards, *The Context of Language Teaching*. Cambridge: Cambridge University Press. 32–45.

Richards, J. C., and D. Bohlke. 2012. *Four Corners*, levels 1-4. New York: Cambridge University Press.

Richards J. C., J. Hull, and S. Proctor. 2012. *Interchange*. 4th edn. New York: Cambridge University Press.

Rodgers, T. 1979. The Malaysian communicational syllabus: a developer's reflection. *The English Bulletin* 7(3): 19–25 [Hong Kong Ministry of Education].

Rodgers, T. 1984. Communicative syllabus design and implementation: reflection on a decade of experience. *RELC Journal* (Fall): 28–52.

Savignon, S. 1972. Teaching for communicative competence: a research report. *Audiovisual Language Journal* 10(3): 153–62.

Savignon, S. 1983. *Communicative Competence: Theory and Classroom Practice*. Reading, MA: Addison-Wesley.

Savignon, S. 1991. Communicative language teaching: state of the art. *TESOL Quarterly* 25(2): 261–77.

Searle, J. R. 1969. *Speech Acts: An Essay in the Philosophy of Language*. Cambridge: Cambridge University Press.

Sinclair, J. McH., and R. M. Coulthard. 1975. *Towards an Analysis of Discourse*. Oxford: Oxford University Press.

Skehan, P. 1998. *A Cognitive Approach to Language Learning*. Oxford: Oxford University Press.

Swan, M. 1985. A critical look at the communicative approach. *English Language Teaching Journal*, pt. 1, 39(1): 2–12.

Van Ek, J. A. 1975. *The Threshold Level in a European Unit/Credit System for Modern Language Teaching by Adults*. Systems Development in Adult Language Learning. Strasbourg: Council of Europe.

Van Ek, J., and L. G. Alexander. 1980. *Threshold Level English*. Oxford: Pergamon.

Vasilopoulos, G. 2008. Adapting communicative language instruction in Korean universities. *The Internet TESOL Journal* 15(8).

Vygotsky, L. S. 1978. *Mind in Society: The Development of Higher Psychological Processes.* Cambridge, MA: Harvard University Press.

Watcyn-Jones, P. 1981. *Pair Work.* Harmondsworth: Penguin.

Wei, L. 2011. CLT in EFL context: not a universal medicine. *IDIOM* 41(2), Summer 2011: *Internet Resources.*

Wenjie, C. 2009. *Using CLT to Improve Speaking Ability of Chinese Non-English Major Students.* Available at: http//minds.wisconsin.edu/bitstream/handle/1793/34646/Cai,%20Wenjie.pdf

Widdowson, H. G. 1972. The teaching of English as communication. *English Language Teaching* 27(1): 15–18.

Widdowson, H. G. 1978. *Teaching Language as Communication.* Oxford: Oxford University Press.

Widdowson, H. G. 1979. The communicative approach and its applications. In H. G. Widdowson, *Explorations in Applied Linguistics.* Oxford: Oxford University Press. 251–64.

Wilkins, D. A. 1972. The linguistics and situational content of the common core in a unit/credit system. Ms. Strasbourg: Council of Europe.

Wilkins, D. A. 1976. *Notional Syllabuses.* Oxford: Oxford University Press.

Wilkins, D. A. 1979. Notional syllabuses and the concept of a minimum adequate grammar. In C. J. Brumfit and K. Johnson (eds.), *The Communicative Approach to Language Teaching.* Oxford: Oxford University Press. 91–8.

Wright, A. 1976. *Visual Material for the Language Teacher.* London: Longman.

Yalden, J. 1983. *The Communicative Syllabus: Evolution, Design and Implementation.* Oxford: Pergamon.

Appendix: A communicative lesson

Behind the scenes

 **SNAPSHOT**

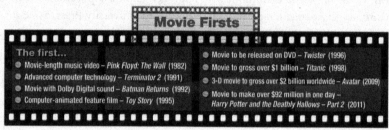

Sources: www.imdb.com; www.listology.com

Have you seen any of these movies? Did you enjoy them?
What's the most popular movie playing right now? Have you seen it? Do you plan to?
Are there many movies made in your country? Name a few of your favorites.

2 CONVERSATION *Movies are hard work!*

A ⊙ Listen and practice.

Ryan: Working on movies must be really exciting.
Nina: Oh, yeah, but it's also very hard work.
    A one-minute scene in a film can take
    days to shoot.
Ryan: Really? Why is that?
Nina: Well, a scene isn't filmed just once. Lots
    of different shots have to be taken. Only
    the best ones are used in the final film.
Ryan: So, how many times does a typical scene
    need to be shot?
Nina: It depends, but sometimes as many as
    20 times. One scene may be shot from
    five or six different angles.
Ryan: Wow! I didn't realize that.
Nina: Why don't you come visit the studio? I can
    show you how things are done.
Ryan: Great, I'd love to!

B ⊙ Listen to the rest of the conversation.
What else makes working on movies difficult?

92

3 GRAMMAR FOCUS

> **The passive to describe process** ⊙
>
> **is/are + past participle**
> A scene **isn't filmed** just once.
> Only the best shots **are used**.
>
> **Modal + be + past participle**
> One scene **may be shot** from five or six different angles.
> Lots of different shots **have to be taken**.

A The sentences below describe how a movie is made. First, complete the sentences using the passive. Then compare with a partner.

Before filming

☐ To complete the script, it has to .... (divide) into scenes, and the filming details need to .... (write out).

1 First, an outline of the script has to .... (prepare).

☐ Next, actors .... (choose), locations .... (pick), and costumes .... (design). Filming can then begin.

☐ Then the outline .... (expand) into a script.

☐ After the script .... (complete), a director must .... (hire).

During and after filming

☐ The final film you see on the screen .... (create) by the director and editor out of thousands of different shots.

☐ Soon after the film has been edited, music .... (compose) and sound effects may .... (add).

☐ After the filming .... (finish), the different shots can then .... (put together) by the editor and director.

6 Once shooting begins, different shots .... (film) separately. Scenes may .... (not shoot) in sequence.

B PAIR WORK Number the sentences in part A (before filming: from 1 to 5; during and after filming: from 6 to 9).

4 LISTENING *I love my job!*

A ⊙ Listen to an interview with a TV producer. Write down three things a producer does.

Things a producer does	Personality traits
1.	....
2.	....
3.	....

B ⊙ Listen again. What are three personality traits a producer should have? Complete the chart.

6 Content-Based Instruction and Content and Language Integrated Learning (CLIL)

Introduction

Content-Based Instruction (CBI) refers to an approach to second language teaching in which teaching is organized around the content or subject matter that students will acquire, such as history or social studies, rather than around a linguistic or other type of syllabus. Students thus learn language and content at the same time, each supporting the development of the other (Lyster 2007). While the term *Content-Based Instruction* has been commonly used to describe programs of this kind, particularly in North America, in Europe a related approach is known as *Content and Language Integrated Learning* (CLIL). The two approaches differ slightly in focus, much in the way that Situational Language Teaching and the Audiolingual Method (one developed in Europe; one in the United States) differed in focus (see Chapters 3 and 4). Both CBI and CLIL are part of a growing trend in many parts of the world to use English as a medium of instruction (Graddol 2006). They have features in common, but they are not identical. CBI often involves a language teacher teaching through English, working with a content teacher to co-teach a course, or a content teacher designing and teaching a course for ESL learners. CLIL often involves a content teacher teaching content through a second or foreign language, as does CBI, but also may involve content from subjects being used in language classes. That is, the CLIL curriculum may originate in the language class, whereas CBI tends to have as its starting point the goals of a content class. CBI emerged somewhat organically, advocated by a number of academics and educators supported by an extensive literature extending over a considerable period of time but without official sanction. CLIL, on the other hand, was officially proposed in a European Commission policy paper in which member states were encouraged to develop "teaching in schools through the medium of more than one language" (EC 1976). The acronym "CLIL" has been widely circulated within member states of the European community since 1994 and has become, by decree "the core instrument for achieving policy aims directed at creating a multilingual population in Europe" (Dalton-Puffer 2007: 1). And unlike CBI, CLIL not only aims at stimulating multilingualism of all citizens in the European community but also strives to "preserve the independence and health of local languages" (EURYDICE 2013). This is because CLIL does not represent an immersion program in an ESL setting, but rather the development of English language skills in those who will use English as a lingua franca.

Both CBI and CLIL are approaches rather than methods according to the framework used in this book, since they refer to a set of principles for the design of language courses but do not prescribe the methods that can be used with them.

Several reasons account for the expansion of programs of this kind in recent years.

1. *An application of principles of Communicative Language Teaching (CLT).* A defining principle of CLT (Chapter 5) is that classrooms should focus on real communication and the exchange of information: an ideal situation for second language learning, therefore, would be one where the subject matter of language teaching was not grammar or functions or some other language-based unit of organization, but content, that is, subject matter from outside the domain of language. The language that is being taught could be used to present subject matter, and the students would learn the language as a by-product of learning about real-world content.

2. *The basis for on-arrival and mainstreaming programs.* Since the latter part of the twentieth century, many English-speaking countries have received large numbers of immigrants as well as people displaced by upheavals in their own countries. *On-arrival programs* typically focus on the language newly arrived immigrants and others in a country need for survival. Such learners typically need to learn how to deal with differing kinds of real-world content as a basis for social survival. Content-based programs have commonly been used in these situations. Mainstreaming programs or *Programs for Students with Limited English Proficiency* (SLEP) serve especially those children whose parents might be served by the on-arrival programs, but are more generally designed to provide in-class or pullout instruction for any school-age children whose language competence is insufficient to participate fully in normal school instruction. These programs focus on giving students the language and other skills needed to enter the regular school curriculum. Such skills often involve learning how to carry out academic tasks and understand academic content through a second language. CBI was seen as an approach that would promote both academic skills development and language proficiency.

3. *Support for immersion education.* In attempts to promote language learning by majority language speakers, such as English-speaking Canadians studying French, an approach known as immersion education has been used in some countries since the 1980s. Immersion education is a type of foreign language instruction in which the regular school curriculum is taught through the medium of the foreign language. The foreign language is the vehicle for content instruction; it is not the subject of instruction. Thus, for example, an English-speaking child might enter a primary school in which the medium of instruction for all the content subjects is French. Student goals of an immersion program include: (a) developing a high level of proficiency in the foreign language; (b) developing positive attitudes toward those who speak the foreign language and toward their culture(s); (c) developing foreign language skills commensurate with expectations for a student's age and abilities; (d) gaining designated skills and knowledge in the content areas of the curriculum. Immersion programs have been adopted in many parts of North America, and alternative forms of immersion have been devised. In the United

States, immersion programs can be found in a number of languages, including French, German, Spanish, Japanese, Chinese, and Hawaiian.

4. *Promotion of bilingualism through CLIL.* In Europe the substantial increase in CLIL-based programs of different kinds is part of a policy to promote bilingualism in Europe, as reflected in the European Commission's white paper *Teaching and Learning: Towards the Learning Society* (1995) "in which a stated objective was the '1+2 policy', that is, for EU citizens to have competence in their mother tongue plus two Community foreign languages" (Llinares, Morton, and Whittaker 2012: 1). CLIL in Europe has been described as a response to globalization, the need for knowledge-driven economies and societies. According to Coyle, Hood, and Marsh (2010: 5–6): "Much CLIL classroom practice involves the learners being active participants in developing their potential for acquiring knowledge and skills (education) through a process of inquiry (research) and by using complex processes and means for problem-solving (innovation). Coyle et al. (2010: 8) cite four reasons for the spread of CLIL in Europe:

> Families wanting their children to have some competence in at least one foreign language; governments wanting to improve languages education for socio-economic advantage; at the supranational level, the European Commission wanting to lay the foundation for greater inclusion and economic strength; and finally, at the educational level, language experts seeing the potential for further integrating languages education with other subjects.

As a consequence of the factors above, different kinds of content-based and CLIL courses are now common in many parts of the world and differ significantly from traditional approaches to second and foreign language instruction. In order to understand the practices that are used in CBI and CLIL programs, it will be necessary to first examine the principles that underlie them and then look at how these are applied in language teaching programs and teaching materials. Both approaches will be considered together, except in areas where they differ.

Approach

CBI and CLIL are built around a number of core principles that can be stated as follows:

- *People learn a second language more successfully when they use the language as a means of understanding content, rather than as an end in itself.* This principle distinguishes CBI and CLIL from conventional language courses where a language syllabus is used as the basis for organization and content is chosen according to how well it supports a linguistic syllabus.
- *Content-Based Instruction better reflects learners' needs for learning a second language.* This principle reflects the fact that CBI programs serve to prepare learners for academic studies or for survival in an English language environment. CLIL programs similarly are said both to support individual development and to develop a bilingual citizenry.

- *Content provides the basis for activating both the cognitive and the interactional processes that are the starting point for second language learning.* A focus on the comprehension and expression of meaningful and engaging content is believed to activate a range of cognitive skills that are basic to learning and to intellectual as well as interactional processes that support naturalistic second language development.

Brinton (2007) provides a more detailed rationale for CBI:

1. The content-based curriculum removes the arbitrary distinction between language and content.
2. It reflects the interests and needs of the learner by taking into account the eventual uses the learner will make of the second or foreign language.
3. It offers optimal conditions for second language acquisition by exposing learners to meaningful and cognitively demanding language in the form of authentic materials and tasks.
4. It provides pedagogical accommodation to learner proficiency levels and skills.
5. It views language as learned within a larger framework of communication.
6. It holds sustained content as necessary for providing authentic, meaningful substance for students to acquire language.
7. It views rich, comprehensible input as necessary but not sufficient for the development of high-level academic language proficiency.
8. It places a high value on feedback on accuracy to help students develop target-like output.
9. It supplements exposure to input through language-enhanced instruction (e.g., skills-based instruction and consciousness raising about uses of grammar, lexis, style, and register).
10. Finally, it aims for a balanced focus on fluency and accuracy.

In the case of CLIL, principles underlying the approach refer to the fact that CLIL is believed to help achieve individual as well as educational, social, and intercultural goals for language learning. These principles, as described by Coyle et al. (2010: 42), can be summarized as follows:

- Content matter is not only about acquiring knowledge and skills, it is about the learner *creating* their own knowledge and understanding and *developing* skills (personalized learning).
- Content is related to learning and thinking processes (cognition). To enable the learner to create their own interpretation of content, it must be analyzed for its linguistic demands.
- The language learned needs to be related to the learning context, to learning *through* that language, to reconstructing the content, and, as mentioned, to related cognitive processes. This language needs to be transparent and accessible.
- Interaction in the learning context is fundamental to learning. This has implications when the learning context operates through the medium of a foreign language.

- The relationship between languages and cultures is complex. Intercultural awareness is fundamental to CLIL.
- CLIL is embedded in the wider educational context in which it is developed and therefore must take account of contextual variables (such as the overall goals of the curriculum) in order to be effectively realized.

Theory of language

A number of assumptions about the nature of language underlie CBI and CLIL. These can be summarized as follows:

1. *Lexis is central in integrating language and content.* Since specialized vocabulary registers are used to convey the meaning of different subjects or content areas, acquisition of subject-specific vocabulary is an important strand of CBI and CLIL courses. Core vocabulary for different subjects can be identified through corpus research, where language extracted from real speech, or corpora, is analyzed and used as the basis for specialized word lists such as Coxhead's Academic Word List (2000, 2010), a list of 570 word families that have high frequency in a wide range of academic texts and that are important words for students to know if they are pursuing academic studies. Llinares et al. (2012: 191) observe:

   > One special feature of learning a second language in CLIL contexts is that the vocabulary needed to represent content in the instructional register is often technical and abstract, in contrast with the type of vocabulary necessary to communicate in foreign language classes.

2. *Grammar is a resource for communicating content.* Grammar is acquired according to its role in expressing content. Grammatical progression is based on the demands of content rather than in terms of grammatical difficulty. "It uses a pragmatic as well as a linguistic approach to developing language through use" (Coyle et al. 2010: 59). This may involve the need to "integrate the grammar point through different uses across CLIL lessons, adopting a more immersive approach; explore literacy practices across the school for a more integrated approach" (ibid.).

3. *Language is text and discourse-based.* CBI and CLIL address the role of language as a vehicle for learning content as well as the role of content in the learning of language. This implies the centrality of linguistic entities longer than single sentences, because the focus of teaching is how meaning and information are communicated and constructed through texts and discourse. The linguistic units that are central are not limited to the level of sentences and sub-sentential units (clauses and phrases) but include features that account for how longer stretches of language are used and that create coherence and cohesion within genres and text-types. Language as it is used in the creation of texts is an important focus of CLIL lessons, since academic learning involves familiarity with a core set of text-types that are found in different academic disciplines. Learning how

language is used in disciplinary-based genres is central to CBI and CLIL. Llinares et al. (2012: 109) comment:

> Students need to understand and participate in the activities that build up the disciplines they study, activities that to a large extent are carried out through language. While the most obvious difference between disciplines is that of vocabulary ... Research in educational linguistics has also shown a major difference to reside in the functional structuring of discourse.

4. *Language use draws on integrated skills.* CBI and CLIL view language use as involving several skills together. In a content-based class, students are often involved in activities that link the skills, because this is how the skills are generally involved in the out-of-classroom world. Hence students might read and take notes, listen and write a summary, or respond orally to things they have read or written. And rather than viewing grammar as a separate dimension of language, grammar is seen as a component of other skills. Topic- or theme-based courses provide a good basis for an integrated skills approach because the topics selected provide coherence and continuity across skill areas and focus on the use of language in connected discourse rather than in isolated fragments. They seek to integrate knowledge, language, and thinking skills.

Theory of learning

CBI and CLIL draw on a number of assumptions about the nature of second language learning. Some of these are true of learning in other approaches to second language teaching, while others are said to be specific to CBI and CLIL (e.g., dialogic talk – see below).

1. *Comprehension is a necessary condition for second language learning to occur.* "The goal of teachers through any type of content-based program is to enable students to comprehend the curriculum presented through the second language" (Lyster 2011: 617). Making subject matter comprehensible through the way language is used is hence crucial in CBI and CLIL. In order to make content comprehensible to learners, teachers need to make the same kinds of adjustments and simplifications that native speakers make in communicating with second language learners. These modifications include using a slower rate of speech, adjusting the topic, emphasizing key words or phrases, building redundancy into their speech by using repetition, modeling, and paraphrase and giving multiple examples, definitions, and synonyms to facilitate comprehension (ibid.).

2. *Negotiation of meaning plays an important role in understanding content.* This refers to the collaboration of both teachers and learners in understanding content. Negotiation of meaning may take several forms: the meaning may be realized through several exchanges or turns rather than in a single exchange; one speaker may expand on what the other said; one speaker may provide words or expressions the other needs; one person may ask questions to clarify what another says.

3. *Learning is facilitated by corrective feedback.* Learners do not simply "pick up" language when engaged in CBI and CLIL. They also develop language awareness and language

accuracy through the kinds of corrective feedback the teacher provides. Lyster and Ranta (1997: 203) identify six types of such feedback and their functions:

Clarification request	Indication that an utterance has not been heard or understood, sometimes with the purpose of drawing attention to non-target forms
Explicit correction	Provision of the correct form, indicating that something was incorrect
Recast	Implicit correction of an utterance by means of reformulation
Elicitation	Direct elicitation of the correct form using techniques such as asking for completion
Repetition	Repetition of the error with rising intonation
Metalinguistic feedback	Reference to the well-formedness or correctness of the student's utterance without providing the correct form

4. *Learning of both content and language is facilitated by dialogic talk.* Effective discourse in CBI and CLIL classrooms is said to have the features of dialogic talk. This is described by Alexander (2008: 30) as talk which achieves "common understanding, through structures, cumulative questioning and discussion which guide and prompt, reduce choices, minimize risk and error, and expedite 'handover' of concepts and principles." Dialogic teaching is said to be an essential component of CBI and CLIL-based pedagogy "both because of its cognitive potency and the opportunities it provides for exposure to and use of rich language in the classroom" (Llinares et al. 2012: 71).

5. *Prior knowledge plays an important role in CBI.* Learners bring many different kinds of prior knowledge to learning, including knowledge about the world and knowledge about events, situations, and circumstances and the roles people play in them. They may need to use text-types (e.g., expository texts, information texts, narrative texts, recounts) that occur in their own language. They also need to access schema of different kinds in relation to the content they are studying as well as sociocultural knowledge related to situations, people, and events. Learning content in a second language can be facilitated if students are better prepared through the activation of relevant background knowledge.

6. *Scaffolded learning plays an import part in CBI and CLIL.* Scaffolding is defined as "the temporary assistance by which a teacher helps a learner know how to do something, so that the learner will be able to complete a similar task alone" (Gibbons 2002: 10). Initially, learners depend on others with more experience than themselves and gradually take on more responsibility over time for their own learning. In the classroom, scaffolding is the process of interaction between two or more people as they carry out a classroom activity and where one person (e.g., the teacher or another learner) has more advanced knowledge than the other (the learner) (Swain, Kinnear, and Steinman 2010). During the process, discourse is jointly created through the process of assisted or mediated performance, and interaction proceeds as a kind of joint problem-solving between teacher and student. While scaffolding is important in all classroom-based

Similarly, with regard to CLIL-based approaches, Mehisto, Marsh, and Frigolos (2008: 105) comment:

> The multi-faceted nature of the CLIL approach involves an extra focus on student interests; peer-cooperative work and the fostering of critical thinking among other methodological strategies. These foster the learning of content and provide increased forums for discussing and otherwise communicating about content. Those increased opportunities support language learning.

CBI and CLIL learning activities are not intrinsically different, but may differ in practice because of the age of the learners and their other needs.

Learner roles

A goal in CBI is for learners to become autonomous so that they come to "understand their own learning process and ... take charge of their own learning from the very start" (Stryker and Leaver 1993: 286). In addition, most CBI courses anticipate that students will support each other in collaborative modes of learning. This may be a challenge to those students who are accustomed to more whole-class or independent learning and teaching modes. CBI is in the "learning by doing" school of pedagogy. This assumes an active role by learners in several dimensions. Learners are expected to be active interpreters of input and to be willing to tolerate uncertainty along the path of learning, as well as to explore alternative learning strategies and seek multiple interpretations of oral and written texts.

Learners themselves may be sources of content and joint participants in the selection of topics and activities. Learners need commitment to this new kind of approach to language learning, and CBI advocates warn that some students may not find this new set of learner roles to their liking and may therefore be less than ready and willing participants in CBI courses. Some students may be overwhelmed by the quantity of new information in their CBI courses and may need additional support. Some students are reported to have experienced frustration and asked to be returned to more structured, traditional classrooms.

In CBI learners are expected to acquire language together with content through the noticing and awareness-raising activities the teacher makes use of – hence, the learner is expected to process language consciously as well as intuitively. Lyster (2011: 618) explains:

> Noticing and awareness activities ... aim to strengthen students' metalinguistic awareness, which then serves as a tool for extracting information from content-based input and thus for learning language through subject-matter instruction.

In the case of learners in CLIL programs, learner roles are seen as central to success:

> The respective roles of the teachers and students are central to CLIL, because its very nature tends to demand more student-centred approaches. Students regularly acknowledge that CLIL courses are difficult, especially at the beginning. Moreover it is certain that engaging with and learning appropriately cognitively challenging content

through another language requires a depth of processing which cannot be attained when the teacher is simply in transmission mode.

(Coyle et al. 2010: 88)

Thus, both CBI and CLIL require active participation on the part of the learner, with a goal toward learner autonomy.

Teacher roles

Both CBI and CLIL position teachers in a different, and often more demanding, role from that required in traditional forms of language and content teaching. They will often be involved in cooperating with other teachers and working collaboratively on the design of courses and materials. In the case of CBI, teachers have to familiarize themselves with, at times, difficult and unfamiliar content and often have to develop their own courses or choose and adapt materials that provide a basis for CBI. They have to keep context and comprehensibility foremost in their planning and presentations, they are responsible for selecting and adapting authentic materials for use in class, they become student needs analysts, and they have to create truly learner-centered classrooms. As Brinton et al. (1989: 3) note:

> They are asked to view their teaching in a new way, from the perspective of truly contextualizing their lessons by using content as the point of departure. They are almost certainly committing themselves to materials adaptation and development. Finally, with the investment of time and energy to create a content-based language course comes even greater responsibility for the learner, since learner needs become the hub around which the second language curriculum and materials, and therefore teaching practices, revolve.

Stryker and Leaver (1993: 293) suggest the following essential skills for any CBI instructor:

1. Varying the format of classroom instruction
2. Using group work and team-building techniques
3. Organizing jigsaw reading arrangements
4. Defining the background knowledge and language skills required for student success
5. Helping students develop coping strategies
6. Using process approaches to writing
7. Using appropriate error correction techniques
8. Developing and maintaining high levels of student esteem

CBI therefore places different demands on teachers from regular ESL teaching. Likewise, program administrators are required to make decisions about the choice and preparation of teachers and the kinds of support and resources they will need as well as developing new approaches to assessment. Hence, teachers with a high level of motivation and commitment to CBI may be essential.

In the case of CLIL, additional teacher roles have been identified (and referred to elsewhere in this chapter). Teachers are expected to modify the language they use in teaching content through a second language, to give additional support for comprehension as well as production, to facilitate dialogic and scaffolded instruction, and to provide appropriate intervention and feedback to guide both the learning of content and the learning of the second language (Llinares et al. 2012).

To summarize, ensuring that students have understood the material presented is a key focus of CLIL teachers. CBI teachers obviously have this as an important goal, as well, but may tend to focus on their own mastery and presentation of complex content.

The role of instructional materials

In both CBI and CLIL, the materials play a central role and may be specially designed materials, materials used to teach content subjects, and a variety of different forms of authentic materials. Because context- and situation-specific materials are required with both approaches, commercial textbooks are not usually available. "Since off-the-shelf-CLIL materials are in short supply, teachers often spend a considerable time developing and/or adapting existing learning resources" (Mehisto et al. 2008: 22). With CBI Crandall (2012: 152) suggests the following kinds of materials, a description that also applies to the role of materials in CLIL:

> Materials for developing the curriculum and planning CBI lessons include the use of both authentic and adapted oral and written subject matter materials (textbooks, audio and visual materials, and other learning materials) that are motivating and appropriate to the cognitive and language proficiency level of the learners or that can be made accessible through bridging activities ... These activities include the use of demonstrations, visuals, charts, graphic organizers and outlines, breaking down information into smaller chunks, pre-teaching vocabulary, and establishing background information.

Contemporary models of CBI and CLIL

The principles of CBI and CLIL can be applied to the design of courses for learners at any level of language learning. The following are examples of different applications of CBI and CLIL.

CBI courses

The four models listed below are all appropriate for university courses. Courses at the elementary and secondary levels tend to use a theme-based or adjunct approach.

Theme-based model
This is a language course in which the syllabus is organized around themes or topics such as "the modern cinema" or "cities." The language syllabus is subordinated to the more general theme. The course might be taught by a language teacher or team-taught with a content specialist. At university level a general theme such as "business and marketing" or "immigrants in a new city" might provide organizing topics for two weeks of integrated classroom

work. Language analysis and practice evolve out of the topics that form the framework for the course. A topic might be introduced through a reading, vocabulary developed through guided discussion, audio or video material on the same topic used for listening comprehension, followed by written assignments integrating information from several different sources. Most of the materials used will typically be teacher-generated and the topic treated will involve all skills. A common model at secondary or grade-school level is one in which students complete theme-based modules that are designed to facilitate their entry into the regular subject-areas classroom. These models do not provide a substitute for mainstream content classes but focus on learning strategies, concepts, tasks, and skills that are needed in subject areas in the mainstream curriculum, grouped around topics and themes such as consumer education, map skills, foods, and nutrition.

Theme-based courses also provide a framework for courses and materials in many programs outside the public school and university sector, such as the private language-school market. With theme-based courses, a set of themes might be selected as the basis for a semester's work, and each theme used as the basis for six or more hours of work in which the four skills and grammar are taught drawing on the central theme.

Sheltered model

This refers to content courses taught in the second language by a content-area specialist to a group of ESL learners who have been grouped together for this purpose. This approach is sometimes used at university level (e.g., in Canada and the United States). Since the ESL students are not in a class together with native speakers, the instructor will be required to present the content in a way which is comprehensible to second language learners and in the process use language and tasks at an appropriate level of difficulty. Typically, the instructor will choose texts of a suitable difficulty level for the learners and adjust course requirements to accommodate the learners' language capacities (e.g., by making fewer demands for written assignments).

Adjunct model

In this model, students are enrolled in two linked courses, one a content course and one a language course, with both courses sharing the same content base and complementing each other in terms of mutually coordinated assignments. These courses are often designed to prepare students for "mainstreaming" (e.g., preparing children to enter high schools in English-speaking countries or to enter an English-medium university), and will often contain a focus on the language and vocabulary of academic subjects as well as academic study skills. Such a program requires a large amount of coordination to ensure that the two curricula are interlocking, and this may require modifying both courses.

Skills-based model

This is characterized by a focus on a specific academic skill area (e.g., academic writing) that is linked to concurrent study of specific subject matter in one or more academic disciplines, and hence it has much in common with an ESP (English for Specific Purposes) or EAP (English for Academic Purposes) approach. This may mean that students write about material they are currently studying in an academic course or that the language or composition course itself simulates the academic process (e.g., mini-lectures, readings, and discussion on a topic lead into writing assignments). Students write in a variety of forms (e.g., short-essay tests, summaries, critiques, research reports) to demonstrate understanding of the subject matter and to extend their knowledge to new areas. Writing is integrated with reading, listening, and discussion about the core content and about collaborative and independent research growing from the core material.

CLIL courses

Advocates of CLIL often describe it with what one reviewer (Paran 2013: 140) refers to as "rather grandiose pronouncements." The following is typical:

> CLIL is a lifelong concept that embraces all sectors of education from primary to adults, from a few hours per week to intensive modules lasting several months. It may involve project work, examination courses, drama, puppets, chemistry practicals and mathematical investigations. In short, CLIL is flexible and dynamic, where topics and subjects – foreign languages and non-language subjects – are integrated in some kind of mutually beneficial way so as to provide value-added educational outcomes for the widest possible range of learners.
>
> (Coyle 2006: 6)

The all-encompassing nature of CLIL courses is seen in Coyle et al. (2010: 18–22), who give the following examples of CLIL courses at primary and secondary level. The first three examples pertain to primary school (ages 5–12) and the remainder to secondary school (ages 12–19).

- *Confidence-building: an introduction to key concepts.* An example is a theme-based module on climate change, which requires 15 hours of learning time involving class-based communication with learners in another country. The class teacher approaches the module using CLIL-designed materials and a networking system.
- *Development of key concepts and learner autonomy.* The example given is subject-based learning on home economics and requires 40 hours of learning time involving trans-languaging, where activities are developed through the CLIL models using bilingual materials. Subject and language teachers work together.
- *Preparation for a long-term CLIL program.* An example is an interdisciplinary approach involving a set of subjects from the natural sciences where the learners are prepared for in-depth education through the CLIL model. Subject and language teachers work together following an integrated curriculum.

At the secondary level, some logistical considerations become important, as reflected in the first two examples.

- *Dual-school education.* Schools in different countries share the teaching of a specific course or module using VoIP (Voice overInternet Protocol, e.g., Skype) technologies where the CLIL language is an additional language in both countries.

- *Bilingual education.* Learners study a significant part of the curriculum through the CLIL language for a number of years with the intention of developing required content-learning goals and advanced language skills.
- *Interdisciplinary module approach.* A specific module, for example environmental science or citizenship, is taught through CLIL involving teachers of different disciplines (e.g., mathematics, biology, physics, chemistry, and language).
- *Language-based projects.* This type differs from the models above in that it is the language teacher who takes primary responsibility for the CLIL module. This may be done through international partnerships and is an extension of both content-based and Communicative Language Teaching. The module involves authentic content learning and communication through the CLIL language, and is scaffolded through language-teacher input.
- *Specific-domain vocational CLIL.* Learners develop competence in the CLIL language so that they are able to carry out specific task-based functions which might range from customer service through to accessing and processing information in different languages. Where applicable, this is carried out by content and language teachers working in tandem. It marks a shift away from existing practice, such as teaching language for specific purposes, toward practice which seeks to achieve the same objectives through a closer tie to content teaching and learning. This model has much in common conceptually with the adjunct model used in CBI programs.

Procedure

Since CBI and CLIL refer to an approach rather than a method, no specific techniques or lesson procedures are associated with either model. In a content-driven approach, procedures typically used to teach subject matter in a content class are used, with appropriate adjustments according to the learners' level of language proficiency, as noted earlier in this chapter. In a language-driven approach, procedures more typically used in language courses (e.g., using a communicative or text-based approach) might be used.

An example of a CLIL textbook lesson may be found in the appendix to this chapter.

Conclusion

Content-based approaches in language teaching have been widely used in a variety of different settings since the 1980s and CLIL-based approached have become increasingly popular in Europe since the late 1990s. Indeed the rapid global spread of CLIL "has surprised even its most ardent advocates" (Maljers, Marsh, and Wolff 2007: 7). CBI and CLIL raise important issues for both teachers and learners. Critics have noted that most language teachers have been trained to teach language as a skill rather than to teach a content subject. Thus, language teachers may be insufficiently grounded to teach subject matter in which they have not been trained. Team-teaching proposals involving language teachers and subject-matter teachers are often considered unwieldy and likely to reduce the efficiency of both. Similarly, CLIL teachers who are unfamiliar with teaching their subject in a CLIL language may need considerable preparation and ongoing support. Both approaches involve assembling appropriate teaching materials and resources, and supporters of both approaches believe they offer considerable advantages over conventional approaches. However, in the case of CLIL, research to date does not justify the somewhat extravagant claims that are often made for it as a panacea for achieving successful learning of both language and content (Paran 2013). In recent years a growing number of researchers have begun to investigate the nature of the instructional strategies and learning in the domains of language and content in both CBI and CLIL classrooms (e.g., Duff 2001; Lyster, Collins, and Ballinger 2009; Dalton-Puffer 2007, 2011; Lyster 2011). Because of the complexity of the issues involved, the results are often inconclusive and their investigation beyond the scope of this chapter. Many factors relating to the school environment and student population may determine whether CLIL is successful. Advantages are claimed for a CLIL approach in some contexts (e.g., Austria), but not in others (e.g., Belgium [Dalton-Puffer and Smith 2007]). However, given the widespread adoption of CBI and CLIL approaches in many parts of the world, expansion in their use is expected to continue in the years to come.

Discussion questions

1. What are the basic goals of CBI and CLIL? What are some of the similarities? Can you describe some ways in which CBI and CLIL are different?

2. Are on-arrival and mainstreaming programs common in your country? Can you think of an advantage for each of these two groups of combining subject and language instruction?

3. The rationale for CLIL and CBI is not purely pedagogical; economic and political factors (such as the European Union's desire for a lingua franca) also play a role. Give both a positive (beneficial to learners) and a negative (detrimental to learners) example of these economic and political factors for each approach (CLIL and CBI).

4. Lexis lies at the core of CLIL and CBI. Much of it is technical, or specific to the subject being taught. In a sense, much of the lexis could be considered subject-specific terminology that is new to most of the learners, including L1 speakers. For example, it is unlikely that many of the learners in a science class would know the meaning of the word *refractometer*. To what extent can we still speak of language instruction in such cases? Would L2 speakers still have special needs in cases where L1 learners would find the language equally unfamiliar? And if so, how could the needs of L2 learners be taken into account? Discuss with a colleague.

5. What are the *academic* (as opposed to language-related) goals of the program described on pages 125-6?

6. Look at the examples of language (not content) goals of CLIL given on page 124. Which of these appear to be different from most non-CLIL language courses? Which appear to be the same? Discuss with a colleague.

7. You have started teaching a CBI course for the first time this semester and three weeks in some students come to you and say they are not happy with this type of instruction. Having read this chapter, what could be some of the reasons for this? How could you anticipate and deal with them?

8. CBI and CLIL courses can sometimes be rather all-encompassing (see the examples on pp. 131–2). Can you think of any downsides to this? Can you think of other downsides to the implementation of CBI and CLIL?

9. In one university in an English-speaking country, approximately 40% of the 35,000 students have English as an Additional Language (EAL). For many of these students, additional support in English is beneficial. Clearly, it would not be possible, and would probably be inefficient, to teach these students in special language classes. Take one group of students from a particular program (e.g., a student in physics in the faculty of science) and consider the following:

   a) How would you identify those students' English needs?
   b) How would you identify what possible language needs exist among L1 speakers and the overlap with the EAL students' needs?
   c) What type of CLIL provision(s) do you think would be most suitable? (You can use the table on p. 124 and the models for CBI courses presented on pp. 129–31.)
   d) How should these be implemented (Who should teach them? Will this be a separate program for EAL students or will it be integrated?)?
   e) What downsides to this approach and possible additional forms of support that will need to be established.
   f) What professional development needs you might be able to imagine.

10. Work with a colleague and observe a class. Note examples of each of the feedback types described on page 122. Discuss with each other afterwards and identify how these instances may have contributed to students' learning.

Feedback type	Example	Benefit for learning
Clarification request		
Explicit correction		
Recast		
Elicitation		
Repetition		
Metalinguistic feedback		

References and further reading

Alexander, R. 2008. *Towards Dialogic Teaching: Rethinking Classroom Talk*. North Yorkshire: Dialogos.

Brinton, D. M. 2007. Content-based instruction: reflecting on its applicability to the teaching of Korean. Paper presented at the 12th annual conference of American Association of Teachers of Korean. Chicago 2007.

Brinton, D. M., M. A. Snow, and M. B. Wesche. 1989. *Content-Based Second Language Instruction*. New York: Newbury House.

CLIL Compendium. n.d. *CLIL Dimensions and Focuses*. Available at: http://www.clilcompendium.com; accessed May 6, 2013.

Coxhead, A. 2000. A new academic word list. *TESOL Quarterly* 34: 213–38.

Coxhead, A. 2011. The academic word list 10 years on: research and teaching. *TESOL Quarterly* 45: 355–62.

Coyle, D. 2006. Developing CLIL: towards a theory of practice. In *Monograph 6*. APAC Barcelona. 5–29.

Coyle, D., P. Hood, and D. Marsh. 2010. *Content and Language Integrated Learning*. Cambridge: Cambridge University Press.

Crandall, J. 2012. Content-based language teaching. In A. Burns and J. C. Richards (eds.), *The Cambridge Guide to Pedagogy and Practice in Language Teaching*. New York: Cambridge University Press. 140–60.

Cummins, J. 1984. *Bilingualism and Special Education: Issues in Assessment and Pedagogy*. Clevedon, UK: Multilingual Matters.

Dalton-Puffer, C. 2007. *Discourse in Content and Language Integrated Learning (CLIL) Classrooms*. Amsterdam and Philadelphia. John Benjamins.

Dalton-Puffer. C. 2011. Content-and-language integrated learning: from practice to principles. *Annual Review of Applied Linguistics*, 31: 182–204.

Dalton-Puffer, C., and U. Smith 2007. *Empirical Perspectives on CLIL Classroom Discourse*. Frankfurt and Vienna: Peter Lang.

Davies, S. 2003. Content based instruction in EFL contexts. *The Internet TESL Journal* 9(2), February. Available at: http://iteslj.org/Articles/Davies-CBI.html

Duff, P. 2001. Language, literacy, content, and (pop) culture: challenges for ESL students in mainstream courses. *The Canadian Modern Language Review* 58: 103–32.

EURYDICE. 2013. http://www.eurydice.org/index.shmtl; accessed May 6, 2013. No longer available.

Gibbons, P. 2002. *Scaffolding Language, Scaffolding Learning: Teaching Second Language Learners in the Mainstream Classroom*. Sydney: Heinemann.

Graddol. D. 2006. *English Next*. London: British Council.

Llinares, A., T. Morton, and R. Whittaker 2012. *The Role of Languages in CLIL*. Cambridge: Cambridge University Press.

Lyster, R. 2007. *Learning and Teaching Languages through Content: A Counterbalanced Approach*. Amsterdam: John Benjamins.

Lyster, R. 2011. Content-based second language teaching. In E. Hinkley (ed.), *Handbook of Research in Second Language Teaching and Learning*, Vol II. New York: Routledge. 611–30.

Lyster, R., and L. Ranta. 1997. Corrective feedback and learner uptake: negotiation of form in communicative classrooms. *Studies in Second Language Acquisition* 19: 37–66.

Lyster, R., L. Collins, and S. Ballinger. 2009. Linking languages: a bilingual read-aloud project. *Language Awareness* 18(3/4): 366–83.

Maljers, A., D. Marsh, and D. Wolff (eds.). 2007. *Windows on CLIL: Content and Integrated Learning in the Spotlight.* The Hague: European Platform for Dutch Education.

Mehisto, P., D. Marsh, and M. J. Frigolos. 2008. *Uncovering CLIL: Content and Language Integrated Learning in Bilingual and Multilingual Education.* Oxford: Macmillan.

Met, M. 1999. *Content-Based Instruction: Defining Terms, Making Decisions.* NLFC Reports. Washington, DC: The National Foreign Language Centre.

Paron, A. 2013. Review of Coyle, Hood and March, *Content and Language Integrated Learning. ELT Journal* 67(1): 137–40.

Stoller, F., and W. Grabe. 1997. A Six-T's Approach to Content-Based Instruction. In M. Snow and D. Brinton (eds.), *The Content-Based Classroom: Perspectives on Integrating Language and Content.* White Plains, NY: Longman. 78–94.

Swain, M., P. Kinnear, and L. Steinmann 2010. *Sociocultural Theory in Second Language Education.* Bristol: Multilingual Matters.

Stryker, S., and B. Leaver. 1993. *Content-Based Instruction in Foreign Language Education.* Washington, DC: Georgetown University Press.

Appendix: A CLIL lesson

4 GROUPING LIVING THINGS

> Living things are related to each other.
> Let's study how they live together.

1 In groups, match the living things that belong to the same species.
Justify your answers.

2 Look at the diagram. Use the internet link and write the words in the correct boxes.

| COMMUNITY | SPECIES | ECOSYSTEM | POPULATION |

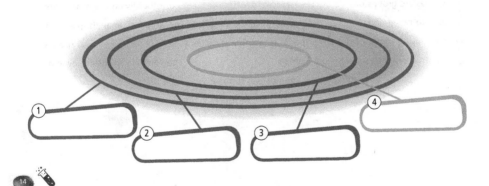

14

3 Justify your answers. Use the following sentences.

> **LANGUAGE HELP**
> - The orange group represents the ... because ...
> - The next group is the ... because ...
> - The brown group ...
> - The ...

4 Watch the video and complete the text.

We can see different _____ _____ such as horses, sheep, vultures and grass in this habitat. A group of horses is called a herd. All the horses in an area are called a _____ of horses. The animals we see all live in the same _____ , a high mountain area, so they all form a _____ .

> ╭─────────── **WE HAVE LEARNED THAT...** ───────────╮
>
> Species are groups of _____ , _____ or other living things that are able to breed and _____ fertile offspring. The group of animals, plants or other living things of the same species in an area is called a _____ . All species which live in the same area are called a _____ . The community and the type of _____ where this community lives form an _____ .
>
> ╰──╯

7 Whole Language

Introduction

While directions in language teaching are generally initiated from within the field of language teaching itself, sometimes trends and movements in general education impact language teaching practices as well. Such is the case with the Whole Language movement – the focus of this chapter – as well as with the notion of multiple intelligences which we turn to in Chapter 12. While the term *Whole Language* as used in second language teaching came to encompass the four skills, the term was created in the 1980s by a group of US educators concerned with the teaching of what is referred to as language arts, that is, the teaching of reading and writing for first language learners. The development of reading and writing in the first language (often termed the teaching of *literacy*) is a very active educational enterprise worldwide, and, like the field of second language teaching, has led to a number of different and at times competing approaches and methodologies. Traditionally, a widespread approach to the teaching of both reading and writing focused on a "decoding" approach to language. By this is meant a focus on teaching the separate components of language such as grammar, vocabulary, and word recognition, and in particular the teaching of phonics. Phonics is based on the theory that reading involves identifying letters and turning them into sounds. Other reading theories approach reading through a focus on the individual skills or micro-skills that are believed to be involved in fluent reading. The Whole Language movement was developed as a reaction to teaching methods such as these. It emerged when "top-down" reading theories were being promoted (the use readers make of context, background knowledge, and inferencing to enable them to avoid word-by-word or "bottom-up" reading strategies) by influential reading specialists such as Kenneth Goodman, Marie Clay, and Frank Smith. The Whole Language movement was strongly opposed to approaches to teaching reading and writing that focused on isolated and discrete features of language and argued that language should be taught as a "whole": "If language isn't kept whole, it isn't language anymore" (Rigg 1991: 522).

Whole Language emphasized learning to read and write naturally with a focus on real communication and reading and writing for pleasure. In the 1990s this approach became popular in the United States as a motivating and innovative way of teaching language arts skills to primary school children. It soon attracted the interest of specialists in second language teaching since it appeared compatible with the principles of both Communicative Language Teaching (CLT) and the Natural Approach (Chapter 14), which were also dominant methodologies during the 1990s. It shares a philosophical and instructional perspective with CLT (Chapter 5) since it emphasizes the importance of meaning and meaning making in teaching and learning as well as the emphasis on experiential learning, the integration of skills, and the role of authentic language. It also relates to "natural approaches" to language learning (see Chapter 14) since it is designed to help children and adults learn a second language in the same way that children are believed to learn their first language. A Whole Language approach was widely used in first language reading programs from the 1990s and has also been used in a number of basic and family literacy programs as well as in some workplace literacy programs in Canada, the United States, and elsewhere. "What began as a holistic way to teach reading has become a movement for change, key aspects of which are respect for each student as a member of a culture and as a creator of knowledge, and respect for each teacher as a professional" (Rigg 1991: 521). However, in both first-language reading instruction and language teaching, interest in the Whole Language movement has waned in recent years. In both fields it has been overtaken by a movement toward skills-based or competency-based approaches and by the adoption of standards that are linked to the mastery of discrete skills and competencies (Chapter 8).

In the 1990s considerable discussion was devoted to whether Whole Language is an approach, a method, a philosophy, or a belief. In a survey of sixty-four articles on Whole Language, Bergeron (1990) found Whole Language treated as an approach (34.4% of the articles), as a philosophy (23.4%), as a belief (14.1%), or as a method (6.3%). Watson (1989) commented: "Whole language is not a program, set of materials, method, practice, or technique; rather, it is a perspective on language and learning that leads to the acceptance of certain strategies, methods, materials and techniques." We see it as an approach based on key principles about language (language is whole) and learning (writing, reading, listening, and speaking should be integrated in learning). Each Whole Language teacher was encouraged to implement the theories of Whole Language as he or she interprets them and according to the kinds of classes and learners he or she is teaching.

Approach

Theory of language

Whole Language views language organization from what we have earlier called an interactional perspective. This perspective is most obviously a social one that views language as a vehicle for human communication and in which there is an interactional relationship between readers and writers. "Language use is always in a social context, and this applies to both oral and written language, to both first and second language use" (Rigg 1991: 523). Heavy emphasis in Whole Language is placed on "authenticity," on engagement with the authors of written texts, and also on conversation. For example, in mastering the sociolinguistic signals for "apologizing," "A whole language perspective requires an authentic, 'real' situation in which one truly needs to apologize to another" (Rigg 1991: 524).

Whole Language also views language cognitively as a vehicle for internal "interaction," for egocentric speech, for thinking. "We use language to think: In order to discover what we know, we sometimes write, perhaps talk to a friend, or mutter to ourselves silently" (Rigg 1991: 323). A functional model of language is also referred to in many articles on Whole Language. Language is always seen as something that is used for meaningful purposes and to carry out authentic functions.

Whole Language also rejects the view that language can be broken down into separate skills. Language is always linked to authentic contexts for its use, which typically involve an integration of skills. Grammar is not taught in isolation but is linked to situations where learners need to use it, such as in editing a piece of written text.

Theory of learning

The learning theory underlying Whole Language is in the humanistic and constructivist schools. The descriptions of Whole Language classrooms recall terms familiar to humanistic approaches to education and to language learning: Whole Language is said to be authentic, personalized, self-directed, collaborative, pluralistic. Such characteristics are believed to focus learner attention and to motivate mastery. Constructivist learning theory holds that knowledge is socially constructed, rather than received or discovered. Thus, constructivist learners "create meaning," "learn by doing," and work collaboratively "in mixed groups on common projects." Rather than transmitting knowledge to students, teachers collaborate with them to create knowledge and understanding in their mutual social context. As Bomengen (2010) puts it:

> Whole language is a constructivist approach to education; constructivist teachers emphasize that students create (construct) their own knowledge from what they encounter. Using a holistic approach to teaching, constructivist teachers do not believe that students learn effectively by analyzing small chunks of a system, such as learning the letters of the alphabet in order to learn language. Constructivist instructors see learning as a cognitive experience unique to each learner's own experience and prior knowledge, which forms the framework for new knowledge.

Rather than seeking to "cover the curriculum," learning focuses on the learners' experience, needs, interests, and aspirations. In this sense, Whole Language does not seek to offer a complete integration of language and content, as do approaches more widely used today, such as Content-Based Instruction (CBI) and CLIL (Chapter 6). However, sociocultural perspectives on learning are also used to support Whole Language, particularly the notion of scaffolded learning, equally important in CBI and CLIL. Students provide scaffolding for each other when they work collaboratively on tasks and projects.

Design

Objectives

The major principles and goals underlying the design of Whole Language instruction are as follows:

- The use of authentic literature rather than artificial, specially prepared texts and exercises designed to practice individual reading skills
- A focus on real and natural events rather than on specially written stories that do not relate to the students' experience
- The reading of real texts of high interest, particularly literature
- Reading for the sake of comprehension and for a real purpose
- Writing for a real audience and not simply to practice writing skills
- Writing as a process through which learners explore and discover meaning
- The use of student-produced texts rather than teacher-generated or other-generated texts
- Integration of reading, writing, and other skills
- Student-centered learning: students have choice over what they read and write, giving them power and understanding of their world
- Reading and writing in partnership with other learners
- Encouragement of risk taking and exploration and the acceptance of errors as signs of learning rather than of failure.

Types of learning and teaching activities

Lyons and Beaver emphasize "flexibility within structure" as the guiding principle for the design and selection of teaching activities.

> Instead of having children do one brief activity or worksheet after another, whole language teachers organize the day in larger blocks of time, so that children can engage in meaningful pursuits. Thus they engage in fewer different tasks, but larger and more satisfying projects. They may have a readers' and writers' workshop, for instance, when the children read books and perhaps use them as models for their own writing. They may study a theme or topic at least part of the day for several days or weeks, using oral and written language and research skills to pursue learning in the realm of social studies and/or science and math, and using language and the arts to demonstrate and share what they have learned. Together and individually, the students have many choices as to what they will do and learn, which enables them to take significant responsibility for their learning. However, the teacher guides, supports, and structures the children's learning as needed. Flexibility within the larger time blocks offers the time that learners need (especially the less proficient) in order to accomplish something meaningful and significant.

> (Lyons and Beaver 1995: 127)

Learner roles

The learner is a collaborator, collaborating with fellow students, with the teacher, and with writers of texts. Students are also evaluators, evaluating their own and others' learning, with the help of the teacher. The learner is self-directed; his or her own learning experiences are used as resources for learning. Students are also selectors of learning materials and activities. "Choice is vital in a whole language class, because without the ability to select activities, materials, and conversational partners, the students cannot use language for their own purposes" (Rigg 1991: 526).

Teacher roles

The teacher is seen as a facilitator and an active participant in the learning community rather than an expert passing on knowledge. The teacher teaches students and not the subject matter and looks for the occurrence of teachable moments rather than following a preplanned lesson plan or script. The teacher creates a climate that will support collaborative learning. The teacher has the responsibility of negotiating a plan of work with the learners and providing support throughout the learning process by "help[ing] children develop skills for interacting with each other, solving interpersonal conflicts and problems, supporting one and other in learning, and taking substantial responsibility for their own behavior and learning" (Weaver 1995).

Role of instructional materials

Whole Language instruction advocates the use of real-world materials rather than commercial texts. A piece of literature is an example of "real-world" materials in that its creation was not instructionally motivated but resulted from the author's wish to communicate with the reader. Other real-world materials are brought to class by the students in the form of newspapers, signs, handbills, storybooks, and printed materials from the workplace in the case of adults. Students also produce their own materials. Rather than purchase pedagogically prepared textbooks and "basal readers," schools make use of class sets of literature, both fictional and nonfictional.

Certainly an interest in and suggestions for the engagement of literature in the teaching of second languages is not unique to Whole Language proposals Many language teachers enter the language teaching field with literature training as their primary background and maintain an interest in literature and its teaching throughout a career in language teaching. Prominent researchers and applied linguists in the field bring with them a strong literary background and maintain that interest in application to second language pedagogy. Maley (2001), for example, overviews the field of literature in the language classroom and outlines approaches to using literature, citing authors and exercise types in his overview.

Procedure

The issue of what instructional characteristics are specific to Whole Language is somewhat problematic. Bergeron (1990) found that Whole Language was described differently in each article of the sixty-four articles she surveyed (except those written by the same author). She found only four classroom features mentioned in more than 50% of the articles. These included:

- the use of literature
- the use of process writing
- encouragement of cooperative learning among students
- concern for students' attitude.

Activities that are often used in Whole Language instruction are:

- individual and small-group reading and writing
- ungraded dialogue journals
- writing portfolios
- writing conferences
- student-made books
- story writing.

Many of these activities are also common in other instructional approaches, such as CLT (Chapter 5), CBI (Chapter 6), and Task-Based Language Teaching (Chapter 9). Perhaps the only feature of Whole Language that does not also appear centrally in discussions of communicative approaches to language teaching is the focus on literature, although this has obviously been of concern to other writers on ELT methodology. Suggestions for exploitation of literary resources in the Whole Language classroom will be familiar to language teachers with a similar interest in the use of literature in support of second language learning. What differs in Whole Language teaching is not the incidental use of such activities based on the topic of the lesson or an item in the syllabus but their use as part of an overall philosophy of teaching and learning that gives a new meaning and purpose to such activities.

The following is an example of the use of literary pieces in a Whole Language workshop and involves activities built around the use of "Parallel Texts." Two English translations of the same short story is an example of parallel texts. Study of the two translations highlights the range of linguistic choices open to the writer (and translator) in the contrast of linguistic choices made by the translators and the responses made to these choices by the students as readers. In pairs, one student acts as presenter/interpreter of one of the two short-story translations and a partner acts as presenter/interpreter of the other.

Parallel Texts: Opening sentences from two translations of a Korean short story

1a. "Cranes" by Hwang Sun-Won (translated by Kevin O'Rourke)

"The village on the northern side of the 38th parallel frontier was ever so quiet and desolate beneath the high, clear autumn sky. White gourds leaned on white gourds as they swayed in the yard of an empty house."

1b. "The Crane" by Hwang Sun-Won (translated by Kim Se-young)

"The northern village at the border of the 38th Parallel was ever so snug under the bright high autumn sky. In the space between the two main rooms of the empty farm house a white empty gourd was lying against another white empty gourd."

Examples of student activities based on parallel texts:

1. Think of the village as described in 1a and 1b as two different villages. Which one would you choose to live in? Why?
2. Do the contrasting opening sentences set up any different expectations in the reader as to what kind of story will follow and what the tone of the story will be?
3. On a map of Korea, each partner should indicate where he/she thinks the village is located. Are the locations the same? If not, why not?
4. Write an opening sentence of a short story in which you briefly introduce the village of 1a as it might appear in winter rather than autumn.
5. Write two parallel text opening sentences in which you describe in different words a village you know. Ask a partner which village he/she prefers.
6. Discuss what different kinds of stories might follow on the basis of the opening sentences. Write an original first sentence of this story thinking of yourself as "translator" and drawing on both translations as your resources.

(Rodgers 1993)

Conclusion

The Whole Language movement was advocated not as a teaching method but as an approach to learning that sees language as a whole entity. In language teaching, each language teacher was free to implement the approach according to the needs of particular classes. Advantages claimed for Whole Language are that it focuses on experiences and activities that are relevant to learners' lives and needs, that it uses authentic materials, and that it can be used to facilitate the development of all aspects of a second language. Critics, however, see it as a rejection of the whole ESL approach in language teaching and one that seeks to apply native-language principles to ESL. Whole Language proposals are seen as anti-direct teaching, anti-skills, and anti-materials, assuming that authentic texts are sufficient to support second language learning and that skill development will follow without special attention (Aaron 1991). Likewise, since the 1990s those reading specialists opposed to the Whole Language approach as it is used with first language learners have criticized it on both theoretical and practical grounds. The Thomas B. Fordham Foundation in 2000 commented:

> The whole-language approach to reading instruction continues to be widely used in the primary grades in U.S. schools, despite having been disproven time and again by careful research and evaluation. Whole language still pervades textbooks for teachers, instructional materials for classroom use, some states' language-arts standards and other policy documents, teacher licensing requirements and preparation programs,

and the professional context in which teachers work. Yet reading science is clear: young children need instruction in systematic, synthetic phonics in which they are taught sound-symbol correspondences singly, directly, and explicitly. Although most state education agencies, school districts, and federal agencies claim to embrace "balanced" reading instruction – implying that worthy ideas and practices from both whole-language and code-emphasis approaches have been successfully integrated – many who pledge allegiance to balanced reading continue to misunderstand reading development and to deliver poorly conceived, ineffective instruction.

Almost every premise advanced by whole language about how reading is learned has been contradicted by scientific investigations that have established the following facts:

- Learning to read is not a natural process. Most children must be taught to read through a structured and protracted process in which they are made aware of sounds and the symbols that represent them, and then learn to apply these skills automatically and attend to meaning.
- Our alphabetic writing system is not learned simply from exposure to print. Phonological awareness is primarily responsible for the ability to sound words out. The ability to use phonics and to sound words out, in turn, is primarily responsible for the development of context-free word-recognition ability, which in turn is primarily responsible for the development of the ability to read and comprehend connected text.
- Spoken language and written language are very different; mastery of each requires unique skills.
- The most important skill in early reading is the ability to read single words completely, accurately, and fluently.
- Context is not the primary factor in word recognition.

The writer then goes on to suggest how Whole Language can be "rooted out" from reading classrooms, and lists several recommendations including the following:

1. Every state should have language-arts content standards and curricular frameworks for each grade from kindergarten through third grade that are explicitly based on solid reading-research findings.
2. State assessments should be calibrated to show the effects of reading instruction as delineated in well-written state standards.
3. State accountability systems should emphasize the attainment of grade-appropriate reading, spelling, and writing skills by third grade.

(Thomas B. Fordham Foundation 2000)

In comparison to the heated discussion that Whole Language aroused in the field of reading instruction, the second language teaching profession has perhaps been kinder to Whole Language, since it never prompted the same level of debate and controversy. It was generally not promoted as a replacement for other approaches to language teaching and could presumably be used in conjunction with other approaches, such as communicative, task-based and text-based approaches (see Chapters 9 and 10). Whole Language advocates make use of a rich array of materials that offer an integrated approach to ESL instruction and that could be adapted for use in a wide variety of contexts (e.g., Whiteson 1998). Whole Language activities may prove useful particularly for younger learners in ESL environments. Many of the activities for older learners in other environments are similar to those recommended in other instructional approaches, for example, Communicative Language Teaching and Cooperative Language Learning (Chapter 13), which can also serve as resources to support a Whole Language approach.

Discussion questions

1. What was the goal of the Whole Language movement as it applied to second language learning? How does Whole Language differ from Content-Based Instruction and CLIL?

2. Rigg comments, "If language isn't kept whole, it isn't language anymore" (p. 139). Do you agree with this statement? Can you find examples of this thinking in materials you are familiar with?

3. Whole Language emphasizes the importance of authenticity. For example, in the case of practicing apologizing, Rigg states that creating this authenticity "requires an authentic, 'real' situation in which one truly needs to apologize to another" (p. 141). What challenges can you see in this, especially with beginner learners?

4. Whole Language is based on a constructivist approach to learning. Explain to a colleague what impact this has on the language classroom, and in particular on the roles of the teacher and the learner.

5. In Whole Language, writing is done for a real audience and not simply to practice writing skills. How can technology support this type of activity?

6. Authentic materials take precedence over commercial texts. In particular, Whole Language teachers use newspapers, literature, signs, and other forms of non-instructional texts. What are some of the possible downsides of such materials?

7. Whole Language does not simply attempt to "cover the curriculum" in terms of teaching a fixed set of skills or language content. Instead, it focuses on the learners' experience, needs, interests, and aspirations. Read the paragraph again by Beaver about "flexibility within structure" on page 142 for some ideas of how this is done in practice. Now take a lesson plan (from your own school curriculum, the Internet, or a textbook) and use the questions below to help you redesign it so that it is based on Whole Language principles.

	Current lesson plan	Changes
Length of lessons		
List of topics for each lesson		

(Continued)

	Current lesson plan	Changes
Frequency and types of feedback		
Opportunities for students to collaborate		
Opportunities for students to self-direct their learning		
Opportunities for students to select content and activities		
Type of assessment		

Did you have to make many changes to your lesson plan? What areas of overlap existed between the two plans? And what differences? Do you think some of the changes you would have to make might be beneficial?

8. A colleague whose classes are based on the Whole Language approach suggests you try to use literature in your classes and recommends a particular book. You think the book is interesting and relevant to your learners, but you are not sure that they will be willing to read a whole book. Think of activities you could use to introduce the book to the class and engage your learners with it.

References and further reading

Aaron, P. 1991. Is there a hole in whole language? *Contemporary Education* 62 (Winter): 127.

Adunyarittigun, D. 1996. *Whole Language: A Whole New World for ESL Programs.* ERIC document (ED386024).

Bergeron, B. S. 1990. What does the term Whole Language mean? *Journal of Reading Behavior* 22(4): 6–7.

Bomengen M. 2010. What is the whole language approach to teaching reading? [blog post] *Reading Horizons.* http://www.readinghorizons.com/blog/post/2010/09/23/What-is-the-Whole-Language-Approach-to-Teaching-Reading.aspx; accessed January 23, 2013.

Brockman, B. 1994. *Whole Language: A Philosophy of Literacy Teaching for Adults Too!* ERIC document (ED376428).

Chitrapu, D. 1996. Whole Language: adapting the approach for large classes. *Forum Magazine* 34(2): 28–9.

Freeman, D., and Y. Freeman. 1993. *Whole Language: How Does It Support Second Language Learners?* ERIC document (ED360875).

Goodman, K. 1986. *What's Whole in Whole Language?* Portsmouth, NH: Heinemann.

Hao, R. N. 1991. Whole Language: some thoughts. *Kamehameha Journal of Education* (March): 16–18.

Heymsfeld, C. R. 1989. Filling the hole in Whole Language. *Educational Leadership* 46(6).

Krashen, S. 1998. *Has Whole Language Failed?* ERIC document (ED586010).

Lems, K. 1995. *Whole Language and the ESL/EFL Classroom.* ERIC document (ED384210).

Lyons, C. A., and J. M. Beaver. 1995. Reducing retention and learning disability placement through reading recovery: an educationally sound, cost-effective choice. In R. L. Allington and S. A. Walmsley (eds.), *No Quick Fix: Rethinking Literacy Programs in America's Elementary Schools*. Language and Literacy Series. New York: Teachers College Press. 116–36.

Maley, A. 2001. Literature in the language classroom. In R. Carter and D. Nunan (eds.), *Teaching English to Speakers of Other Languages*. Cambridge: Cambridge University Press. 180–5.

Manzo, K. K. 2007. Whole Language, *Education Week*, February 6, 2007.

Patzelt, K. E. 1993. *Principles of Whole Language and Implications for ESL Learners*. ERIC document (ED400526).

Rigg, P. 1991. Whole Language in TESOL. *TESOL Quarterly* 25(3): 521–54.

Rodgers, T. S. 1993. Teacher training for Whole Language in ELT. Paper given at City University of Hong Kong Seminar on Teacher in Education in Language Teaching, April 1993.

Shao, X. 1996. *A Bibliography of Whole Language Materials*. Biblio. Series 1993, No. 1. ERIC document (ED393093).

Stahl, S. A. 1994. *The Effects of Whole Language Instruction: An Update and a Reappraisal*. ERIC document (ED364830).

Thomas B. Fordham Foundation. 2000. Whole language lives on: the illusion of balanced reading instruction. Washington DC. Available at: http://www.LDonline.org/article/6394/

Watson, D. 1989. Defining and describing whole language. *Elementary School Journal* 90(2): 129–42.

Weaver, C. 1995. On the nature of whole language education. In C. Weaver, L. Gillmeister-Krause, and G. Vento-Zogby (eds.), *Creating Support for Effective Literacy Education*. New York: Heinemann. Available at: http://www.heinemann.com/shared/onlineresources/08894/08894f6.html

Whiteson, V. 1998. *Play's the Thing: A Whole Language Approach*. New York: St. Martin's Press.

8 Competency-Based Language Teaching, standards, and the Common European Framework of Reference

Introduction

A common way of developing language courses is to first make decisions about *what* to teach, then to determine *how* to teach it, and finally to assess *what* was learned. With this process, what is learned is assumed to be the result of what is taught and how well it is taught. This approach to course planning is referred to as *forward design* in Chapter 21 of this book and often reflects the assumption that the learning outcomes of a course are dependent upon a well-designed syllabus and effective teaching methods. Consequently, we see throughout this book that discussion of the most appropriate form for a syllabus as well as the most appropriate teaching methods have been a recurring focus in language teaching for over a hundred years. However, there is another tradition in educational planning that appears to reverse the typical sequence of activities in which a course is developed. This approach *begins* with a description of learning outcomes, or what the learner should be able to do at the end of the course, and issues related to methodology and syllabus *follow* from the statements of learning outcomes. This approach is referred to as *backward design*, and has had a considerable impact on educational planning in general as well as in language teaching since the 1970s (Wiggins and McTighe 2006). It is discussed in more detail in Chapter 21. Leung (2012: 161–2) comments that "outcomes-based teaching in the past thirty years or so can be associated with the wider public policy environments in which the twin doctrines of corporatist management (whereas the activities in different segments of society are subordinated to the goals of the state) and public accountability (which requires professionals to justify their activiites in relation to declared public policy goals) have predominated." They represent attempts to set standards against which student performance and achievement can be judged and compared at any given stage of a teaching program. Leung further notes that the terms used to designate outcomes-based approaches include attainment targets, benchmarks, core skills, essential learnings/skills, outcomes-based education, performance profiles, and target competencies. Figueras similarly observes (2012: 479): "Curricula and language programmes today are often outcomes-based, drawn up with much more attention to real-life uses, and focused on what students will be able or should be able to do at the end of a course."

In language teaching a focus on learning outcomes characterizes the three approaches that will be described in this chapter: *Competency-Based Language Teaching, the standards movement* (encompassing other standards-based frameworks), and the *Common European Framework of Reference.*

1 Competency-Based Language Teaching (CBLT)

Introduction

CBLT is an example of an approach known as Competency-Based Education (CBE) – an educational movement that focuses on the outcomes or outputs of learning in the development of language programs. CBE addresses what the learners are expected to do with the language, however they learned to do it. The focus on outputs rather than on inputs to learning is central to the competencies perspective. CBE emerged in the United States in the 1970s and advocated defining educational goals in terms of precise measurable descriptions of the knowledge, skills, and behaviors students should possess at the end of a course of study. The characteristics of CBE are described by Schenck (1978: vi):

> Competency-based education has much in common with such approaches to learning as performance-based instruction, mastery learning and individualized instruction. It is outcome-based and is adaptive to the changing needs of students, teachers and the community ... Competencies differ from other student goals and objectives in that they describe the student's ability to apply basic and other skills in situations that are commonly encountered in everyday life. Thus CBE is based on a set of outcomes that are derived from an analysis of tasks typically required of students in life role situations.

CBLT, as mentioned, is an application of the principles of CBE to language teaching. Such an approach had been widely adopted by the end of the 1970s, particularly as the basis for the design of work-related and survival-oriented language teaching programs for adults. It has also been widely used since. Indeed, in many large-scale language programs of different types and at all levels, competency-based curricula are now a common strand. In work-related programs it is no longer the assumption that employees will develop competence through work experience: educational institutions are expected to deliver professionals with the competencies expected (Hoogveld 2003; Baines and Stanley 2006). The Center for Applied Linguistics called competency-based ESL curricula "the most important breakthrough in adult ESL" (1983). By the 1990s, CBLT had come to be accepted as "the state-of-the-art approach to adult ESL by national policymakers and leaders in curriculum development as well" (Auerbach 1986: 411), and any refugee in the United States who wished to receive federal assistance had to be enrolled in a competency-based program (Auerbach 1986: 412). Typically, such programs were based on "a performance outline of language tasks that lead to a demonstrated mastery of language associated with specific skills that are necessary for individuals to function proficiently in the society in which they live" (Grognet and Crandall 1982: 3).

Advocates of CBLT see it as a powerful and positive agent of change:

Competency-based approaches to teaching and assessment offer teachers an opportunity to revitalize their education and training programs. Not only will the quality of assessment improve, but the quality of teaching and student learning will be enhanced by the clear specification of expected outcomes and the continuous feedback that competency-based assessment can offer. These beneficial effects have been observed at all levels and kinds of education and training, from primary school to university, and from academic studies to workplace training.

(Docking 1994: 15)

Comments such as Docking's above are still common today. Mendenhall (2012), the president of an American university – thus reports:

Implemented effectively, competency-based education can improve quality and consistency, reduce costs, shorten the time required to graduate, and provide us with true measures of student learning. We must:

1. Measure student learning rather than time.
2. Harness the power of technology for teaching and learning. Computer-mediated instruction gives us the ability to individualize learning for each student. Because each student learns at a different pace and comes to college knowing different things, this is a fundamental requirement of competency-based education.
3. Fundamentally change the faculty role. When faculty serve as lecturers, holding scheduled classes for a prescribed number of weeks, the instruction takes place at the lecturers' pace. For most students, this will be the wrong pace. Some will need to go more slowly; others will be able to move much faster. Competency-based learning shifts the role of the faculty from that of "a sage on the stage" to a "guide on the side." Faculty members work with students, guiding learning, answering questions, leading discussions, and helping students synthesize and apply knowledge.
4. Define competencies and develop valid, reliable assessments. The fundamental premise of competency-based education is that we define what students should know and be able to do, and they graduate when they have demonstrated their competency. This means that we have to define the competencies very clearly. Getting industry input is essential to make sure that we've identified relevant competencies. Once the competencies are established, we need experts in assessment to ensure that we're measuring the right things.

The benefits of this competency-based approach have been recognized by policy makers and influencers in higher education. The Center for American Progress recently released a white paper that found, "Competency-based education could be the key to providing quality postsecondary education to millions of Americans at lower cost." In a speech in the fall of 2012, U.S. Secretary of Education Arne Duncan, referred to

Western Governors University's competency-based degree programs, saying, "While such programs are now the exception, I want them to be the norm."

Auerbach (1986: 414–15) provided a useful review of factors involved in the implementation of CBLT programs and identified eight key features:

1. *A focus on successful functioning in society.* The goal is to enable students to become autonomous individuals capable of coping with the demands of the world.
2. *A focus on life skills.* Rather than teaching language in isolation, CBLT teaches language as a function of communication about concrete tasks. Students are taught just those language forms/skills required by the situations in which they will function. These forms are determined by "empirical assessment of language required" (Findley and Nathan 1980: 224).
3. *Task or performance-centered orientation.* What counts is what students can do as a result of instruction. The emphasis is on overt behaviors rather than on knowledge or the ability to talk about language and skills.
4. *Modularized instruction.* "Language learning is broken down into manageable and immediately meaningful chunks" (Center for Applied Linguistics 1983: 2). Objectives are broken into narrowly focused sub-objectives so that both teachers and students can get a clear sense of progress.
5. *Outcomes that are made explicit a priori.* Outcomes are public knowledge, known and agreed upon by both learner and teacher. They are specified in terms of behavioral objectives so that students know exactly what behaviors are expected of them.
6. *Continuous and ongoing assessment.* Students are pretested to determine what skills they lack and post-tested after instruction in that skill. If they do not achieve the desired level of mastery, they continue to work on the objective and are retested. Program evaluation is based on test results and, as such, is considered objectively quantifiable.
7. *Demonstrated mastery of performance objectives.* Rather than the traditional paper-and-pencil tests, assessment is based on the ability to demonstrate pre-specified behaviors.
8. *Individualized, student-centered instruction.* In content, level, and pace, objectives are defined in terms of individual needs; prior learning and achievement are taken into account in developing curricula. Instruction is not time-based; students progress at their own rates and concentrate on just those areas in which they lack competence.

There are said to be several advantages of a competencies approach from the learner's point of view:

1. The competencies are specific and practical and can be seen to relate to the learner's needs and interests.
2. The learner can judge whether the competencies seem relevant and useful.
3. The competencies that will be taught and tested are specific and public – hence, the learner knows exactly what needs to be learned.
4. Competencies can be mastered one at a time so the learner can see what has been learned and what still remains to be learned.

Let us now examine the assumptions and practices associated with CBLT at the levels of approach, design, and procedure.

Approach

Theory of language

CBLT is based on a functional and interactional perspective on the nature of language. It seeks to teach language in relation to the social contexts in which it is used. The following understandings of the nature of language are assumed in CBLT.

- *Language is a means of achieving personal and social needs.* In CBLT language always occurs as a medium of interaction and communication between people for the achievement of specific goals and purposes. CBLT has for this reason often been used as a framework for language teaching in situations where learners have specific needs and are in particular roles and where the language skills they need can be fairly accurately predicted or determined. However, it has also been used in developing courses with much more general aims.
- *Language links forms and functions.* CBLT reflects the notion that language form can be inferred from language function; that is, certain life encounters call for certain kinds of language. This assumes that designers of CBLT competencies can accurately predict the vocabulary and structures likely to be encountered in those particular situations that are central to the life of the learner and can state these in ways that can be used to organize teaching/learning units.
- *Language can be broken down into its component parts.* Central to both language and learning theory is the view that language can be functionally analyzed into appropriate parts and subparts: that such parts and subparts can be taught (and tested) incrementally. CBLT thus takes a "mosaic" approach to language learning in that the "whole" (communicative competence) is constructed from smaller components correctly assembled.

Theory of learning

CBLT has several assumptions in terms of learning theory.

- *Language learning is skill-based.* CBLT reflects a skill-based view of learning. Skills are integrated sets of behaviors that are learned through practice. They are made up of individual components that may be learned separately and that come together as a whole to constitute skilled performance.

    The basic claim of skill acquisition theory is that learning of a wide variety of skills shows a remarkable similarity in development from initial representation of knowledge through initial changes in behaviour to eventual fluent, largely spontaneous, and highly skilled behaviour, and that this set of phenomena can be accounted for by a set of basic principles common to the acquisition of all skills.

    (DeKeyser 2007: 97)

Skill learning theory suggests that complex behaviors are made up of a hierarchy of skills.

- *Successful language performance depends upon practice.* Central to the notion of skill-based learning that underlies CBLT is the notion of practice. Practice refers to repeated opportunities to use language over time. Practice is normally accompanied by feedback, allowing the learner to gradually improve his or her performance (DeKeyser 2007). Cook (2008) comments:

> Processing models … see language as the gradual development of preferred ways of doing things. Much language teaching has insisted on the value of incremental practice, whether it is the audio-lingual structure drill or the communicative information gap game … The processing models remind us that language is behaviour and skills as well as mental knowledge. Some skills are learnt by doing them over and over again. These ideas are support for the long-held teaching views about the value of practice – and more practice.

Design
Objectives

Since CBLT courses are developed as a response to perceived learners' specific goals and needs, needs analysis (the process of determining learners' needs) is the starting point in developing the objectives for a CBLT-based course. Needs analysis procedures may include interviews, questionnaires, observations, tests, and other means that can be used to determine appropriate course objectives. (Needs analysis is discussed further in Chapter 21.)

The syllabus

The syllabus for a CBLT language course consists of a description of learning outcomes in terms of "competencies," so it is important to understand how these differ from other syllabus frameworks. Docking (1994) points out that the traditional approach to developing a syllabus involves using one's understanding of subject matter as the basis for syllabus planning. One starts with the field of knowledge that one is going to teach (e.g., contemporary European history, marketing, listening comprehension, or French literature) and then selects concepts, knowledge, and skills that constitute that field of knowledge. A syllabus and the course content are then developed around the subject. Objectives may also be specified, but these usually have little role in the teaching or assessing of the subject. Assessment of students is usually based on norm referencing, that is, students will be graded on a single scale with the expectation either that they will be spread across a wide range of scores or that they conform to a preset distribution. A student receives a set of marks for his or her performance relative to other students, from which it is very difficult to make any form of judgment about the specific knowledge or skills a student has acquired. Indeed, two students may receive the same marks on a test but in fact have widely different capacities and knowledge in the subject:

> CBT by comparison is designed not around the notion of subject knowledge but around the notion of competency. The focus moves from what students know about language to what they can do with it. The focus on competencies or learning outcomes underpins the curriculum framework and syllabus specification, teaching strategies, assessment and reporting. Instead of norm-referenced assessment, criterion-based assessment procedures are used in which learners are assessed according to how well they can perform on specific learning tasks.
>
> (Docking 1994: 16)

Competencies consist of a description of the essential skills, knowledge, attitudes, and behaviors required for effective performance of a real-world task or activity. These activities may be related to any domain of life though have typically been linked to the field of work and to social survival in a new environment. For example, areas for which competencies have been developed in a vocationally oriented ESL curriculum for immigrants and refugees include (Mrowicki 1986):

Task performance
Safety
General word-related
Work schedules, time sheets, paychecks
Social language job application job interview

For the area of "Retaining a Job" the following competencies are described:

- Follow instructions to carry out a simple task.
- Respond appropriately to supervisor's comments about quality of work on the job, including mistakes, working too slowly, and incomplete work.
- Request supervisor to check work.
- Report completion of task to supervisor.
- Request supplies.
- Ask where object is located: Follow oral directions to locate an object.
- Follow simple oral directions to locate a place.
- Read charts, labels, forms, or written instructions to perform a task.
- State problem and ask for help if necessary.
- Respond to inquiry as to nature or progress of current task; state amount and type of work already competed.
- Respond appropriately to work interruption or modification.

(Mrowicki 1986: 26–7)

Competencies for the listening and speaking component of the adult ESL course referred to above are described as follows (Mrowicki 1986: 28):

Students will demonstrate the following language skill proficiencies upon exit from ESL Beginning High:

Listening
- Demonstrate understanding of simple words and phrases drawn from learned topics.
- Identify the main topic of conversation in familiar material.
- Demonstrate understanding of non-face-to-face speech in familiar contexts, such as simple phone conversations and routine announcements.
- Recognize words that signal differences between present, past, and future events.
- Respond appropriately to short emergency warnings.
- Respond to commands and short directions through physical actions.
- Demonstrate strategies to check for understanding – by asking for repetition for example.
- Listen and identify specific information in the context of previously learned language.

Speaking
- Answer simple questions related to basic needs using previously learned phrases or simple sentences.
- Make statements in the present, past, or future tenses relating to basic needs and common activities, using previously learned phrases or simple sentences.
- Ask questions related to basic needs using previously learned utterances.
- Communicate simple personal information on the telephone.
- Give simple commands, warnings, and directions.
- Ask for and give clarification.

Docking (1994: 11) points out the relationship between competencies and job performance:

A qualification or a job can be described as a collection of units of competency, each of which is composed of a number of elements of competency. A unit of competency might be a task, a role, a function, or a learning module. These will change over time, and will vary from context to context. An element of competency can be defined as any attribute of an individual that contributes to the successful performance of a task, job, function, or activity in an academic setting and/or a work setting. This includes specific knowledge, thinking processes, attitudes, and perceptual and physical skills. Nothing is excluded that can be shown to contribute to performance. An element of competency has meaning independent of context and time. It is the building block for competency specifications for education, training, assessment, qualifications, tasks, and jobs.

Tollefson (1986) observes that the analysis of jobs in terms of their constituent functional competencies in order to develop teaching objectives goes back to the mid-nineteenth century. In the 1860s, Spencer (cited in Tollefson) outlined the major areas of human activity he believed should be the basis for curricular objectives. Similarly, in 1926 Bobbitt developed curricular objectives according to his analysis of the functional competencies required for adults living in the United States. This approach has been picked up and refined as the basis for the development of CBLT since the 1960s. Northrup (1977) reports on a study commissioned by the US Office of Education in which a wide variety of tasks performed by adults in American society were analyzed and the behaviors needed to carry out the tasks were classified into five knowledge areas and four basic skill areas. From this analysis, 65 competencies were identified. Docking (1994) describes how he was involved in a project in Australia in 1968 that involved specifying the competencies of more than a hundred trades.

Types of learning and teaching activities

CBLT is an approach to designing courses but does not imply any particular methodology of teaching. The teacher is free to choose any set of activities or to make use of any methods that will enable the learning outcomes to be achieved and the individual competencies to be acquired. In the case of the adult ESL program previously referred to, guidelines for the choice of learning activities are based on a description of standards for adult ESL instruction in California (California Department of Education 1992: 5–8):

1. Instructional activities integrate the four language skills (listening, speaking, reading, and writing) to emphasize the holistic nature of language.
2. Language tasks in the classroom consist of meaningful interchanges that enhance students' communicative competence.
3. Instructional activities focus on the acquisition of communication skills necessary for students to function in real-life situations.
4. Instruction focuses on the development of the receptive skills (listening and reading) before the development of the productive skills (speaking and writing).
5. A variety of grouping activities are used in the classroom to facilitate student-centered instruction.
6. Instructional activities are varied to address different learning styles (aural, oral, visual, kinesthetic) of the students.
7. Instructional activities integrate language and culture so that students learn about the US culture in terms of significant and subtle characteristics that compare and contrast with those of their own cultures.
8. Learning activities develop the language necessary for students to access higher level thought processes (analysis, synthesis, and evaluation).
9. Instructional activities require students to take active roles in the learning process, transferring critical thinking to real problem-solving situations in their everyday lives.

Learner roles

Learners are active participants in the learning process in CBLT. Primary roles assumed for learners are as follows:

- *To monitor their learning in reference to the target competencies.* Learners need to develop skills in self-assessment to monitor their learning in relation to the learning targets.
- *To develop a range of learning strategies.* Successful mastery of target competencies depends upon the ability to use strategies to achieve communication. For example, Rubin (1975: 45–8) identified seven characteristics of "good language learners" that are applicable to learning within a CBLT framework:
  - They are willing and accurate guessers who are comfortable with uncertainty.
  - They have a strong drive to communicate, or to learn from communication, and are willing to do many things to get their message across.
  - They are often not inhibited and are willing to appear foolish if reasonable communication results.
  - They are prepared to attend to form, constantly looking for patterns in the language.
  - They practice, and also seek out opportunities to practice.
  - They monitor their own speech and the speech of others, constantly attending to how well their speech is being received and whether their performance meets the standards they have learned.
  - They attend to meaning, knowing that in order to understand a message, it is not sufficient to attend only to the grammar or surface form of a language.
- *To be able to transfer knowledge and skills to new situations.* Learners must be prepared to apply skills learned in the classroom to situations outside of the classroom and hence be prepared to take risks as they seek to apply what they have learned.

Teacher roles

Teachers too have an active role in CBLT, although the role of the teacher will depend on the extent to which the teacher is primarily implementing a CBLT course design that has been developed by others, or developing a course for a specific group of learners.

- *Needs analyst.* The teacher may be required to conduct a needs analysis of his or her students and is able to select suitable competencies based on the learners' needs.
- *Materials developer and materials resource assembler.* The teacher may be required to assemble suitable materials – including technology-supported materials – as well as to develop materials to address specific target competencies.
- *Assessor.* The teacher is engaged in ongoing assessment of students' learning and may need to re-teach skills that have not been adequately mastered.
- *Coach.* The teacher is also expected to guide students toward use of appropriate learning strategies and to provide the necessary guidance and support for this purpose.

The role of instructional materials

Since CBLT is built around specific learning targets, these can form the basis for the design of published courses as well as teacher-developed materials and technology-supported materials. A wide range of published courses are available based on CBLT, particularly those intended for work-related or social-survival courses, such as the *Ventures* series (Cambridge University Press), that are linked to competency-based standards.

Procedure

Examples of how many of these principles apply in practice are seen in the work of the Australian Migrant Education Program, one of the largest providers of language training to immigrants in the world. The program has undergone a number of philosophical reorientations since the mid-1970s, moving from "centralised curriculum planning with its content-based and structural curriculum in the late 1970s, to decentralised learner-centred, needs-based planning with its multiplicity of methodologies and materials in the 1980s and yet more recently, to the introduction of competency-based curriculum frameworks" (Burns and Hood 1994: 76). In 1993, a competency-based curriculum, the Certificate in Spoken and Written English, was introduced as the framework for its programs. Learning outcomes are specified at three stages in the framework, leading to an Advanced Certificate in Spoken and Written English at Stage 4 of the framework. Hagan (1994: 22) describes how the framework operates:

> After an initial assessment, students are placed within the framework on the basis of their current English proficiency level, their learning pace, their needs, and their social goals for learning English. The twelve core competencies at Stages 1 and 2 relate to general language development ... At Stage 3, learners are more often grouped according to their goal focus and competencies are defined according to the three syllabus strands of Further Study, Vocational English, and Community Access ... The competency descriptions at each stage are divided into four domains ... :
>
> 1. Knowledge and learning competencies
> 2. Oral competencies
> 3. Reading competencies
> 4. Writing competencies
>
> All competencies are described in terms of:
> - elements that break down the competency into smaller components and refer to the essential linguistic features of the text
> - performance criteria that specify the minimal performance required to achieve a competency
> - range of variables that sets limits for the performance of the competency

3 The Common European Framework of Reference

The most influential example of an outcomes-and competency-based approach in language teaching is the Common European Framework of Reference (CEFR) – a framework for language teaching and assessment developed by the European Council of Europe (2001). The outcomes statements contained in the CEFR (known as the "can do" statements) in many cases are simply a restatement of some of the "language functions" contained in the earlier Threshold Level syllabus (Chapter 5). Thus, the CEFR is often combined with Communicative Language Teaching.

The Council of Europe has been actively involved in promoting reform and innovation in language teaching in Europe for many years and, as we saw in Chapter 5, developed one of the first models of a communicative syllabus in the 1970s (the Threshold Level syllabus – Van Ek 1975) which was a key document in the development of Communicative Language Teaching. CEFR was conceived not simply as a framework for the teaching of English but in order to promote successful learning of languages within the European community. It was part of a strategy "To ensure, as far as possible, that all sections of their populations have access to effective means of acquiring a knowledge of the languages of other member states" (CEFR Appendix to Recommendation R(82)18 of the Committee of Ministers of the Council of Europe). The CEFR framework is built around statements of learning outcomes at different levels of proficiency in relation to the skills of listening, speaking, reading, and writing. "It describes in a comprehensive way what language learners have to learn to do in order to use a language for communication and what knowledge and skills they have to develop so as to be able to act effectively" (Council of Europe 2001: 1).

What the CEFR descriptors seek to do is to operationalize what is normally understood by a basic, intermediate, or advanced level of language proficiency. It describes six levels of achievement divided into three broad categories, from lowest (A1) to highest (C2), which describe what a learner should be able to do in listening, speaking, reading, and writing at each level.

Basic user – A1, A2
Independent user – B1, B2
Proficient user – C1, C2

More popularly these six levels have been given the labels

Mastery	C2
Effective Operational Proficiency	C1
Vantage	B2
Threshold	B1
Waystage	A2
Breakthrough	A1

An example of the outcomes for "conversation" is given below (Council of Europe 2001).

Characteristics of conversation in the CEFR	
C2	Can converse comfortably and appropriately, unhampered by any linguistic limitations in conducting a full social and personal life.
C1	Can use language flexibly and effectively for social purposes, including emotional, allusive and joking usage.
B2	Can engage in extended conversation on most general topics in a clearly participatory fashion, even in a noisy environment. Can sustain relationships with native speakers without unintentionally amusing or irritating them or requiring them to behave other than they would with a native speaker. Can convey degrees of emotion and highlight the personal significance of events and experiences.
B1	Can enter unprepared into conversations on familiar topics. Can follow clearly articulated speech directed at him/her in everyday conversations, though will sometimes have to ask for repetition of particular words and phrases. Can maintain a conversation or discussion but may sometimes be difficult to follow when trying to say exactly what he/she would like to. Can express and respond to feelings such as surprise, happiness, sadness, interest and indifference.
A2+	Can establish social contact: greetings and farewells; introductions; giving thanks. Can generally understand clear, standard speech on familiar matters directed at him/her, provided he/she can ask for repetition or reformulations from time to time. Can participate in short conversations in routine contexts on topics of interest. Can express how he/she feels in simple terms, and express thanks.
A2	Can handle very short social exchanges but is rarely able to understand enough to keep conversation going on his/her own accord, though he/she can be made to understand if the speaker will take the trouble. Can use simple everyday polite forms of greeting and address. Can make and respond to invitations, suggestions and apologies. Can say what he/she likes and dislikes.
A1	Can make an introduction and use basic greeting and leave-taking expressions. Can ask how people are and react to news. Can understand everyday expressions aimed at the satisfaction of simple needs of a concrete type, delivered directly to him/her in clear, slow and repeated speech by a sympathetic speaker.

The CEFR is now referred to in many widely used language examinations, which are referenced to the proficiency level they assess on the CEFR. For example, the BULATS (Business Language Testing Service) test published by Cambridge English Language

Appendix: A competency-based lesson

LESSON F Another view

1 Life-skills reading

Appointment Confirmation
Here is your appointment information.

Patient: _J. D. Avona_

Medical record number: _9999999_

Date: _Monday, October 23_

Time: _9:10 a.m._

Doctor: _William Goldman, MD_

Address: _Eye Care Clinic_
2025 Morse Avenue

Cancellation Information
To cancel only: (973) 555-5645   7 days / 24 hours
To cancel and reschedule: (973) 555-5210   Mon-Fri 8:30 a.m. to 5:00 p.m.

A **Read** the questions. Look at the appointment confirmation card.
Fill in the answer.

1. What is the doctor's last name?

   Ⓐ Avona

   Ⓑ Goldman

   Ⓒ Morse

   Ⓓ William

2. What is the appointment for?

   Ⓐ ears

   Ⓑ eyes

   Ⓒ nose

   Ⓓ throat

3. What is the address?

   Ⓐ Monday

   Ⓑ MD

   Ⓒ 2025 Morse Avenue

   Ⓓ 2025 Morris Avenue

4. What do you do to reschedule?

   Ⓐ call J. D. Avona

   Ⓑ call (973) 555-5645

   Ⓒ call (973) 555-5210

   Ⓓ go to the Eye Care Clinic

B **Talk** with your classmates. Ask and answer the questions.

1. Do you have a doctor?
2. Do you get appointment cards?
3. What information is on your appointment cards?

54 UNIT 4

9 Task-Based Language Teaching

Introduction

Task-Based Language Teaching (TBLT) refers to the use of tasks as the core unit of planning and instruction in language teaching. It has been defined as "an approach to language education in which students are given functional tasks that invite them to focus primarily on meaning exchange and to use language for real-world, non-linguistic purposes" (Van den Branden 2006). Some of its proponents (e.g., Willis 1996; Willis and Willis 2007) present it as a logical development of Communicative Language Teaching (Chapter 5) since it draws on several principles that formed part of the CLT movement from the 1980s. For example:

- Activities that involve real communication are essential for language learning.
- Activities in which language is used for carrying out meaningful tasks promote learning.
- Language that is meaningful to the learner supports the learning process.

TBLT is usually characterized as an approach, rather than a method. According to Leaver and Willis (2004: 3), "TBI [task-based instruction] is not monolithic; it does not constitute one single methodology. It is a multifaced approach, which can be used creatively with different syllabus types and for different purposes." Thus, it can be linked with other approaches and methods, such as content-based and text-based teaching (Leaver and Willis 2004). Proponents of TBLT contrast it with earlier grammar-focused approaches to teaching, such as Audiolingualism, that they characterize as "teacher-dominated, form-oriented classroom practice" (Van den Branden 2006).

> A key distinction can be made between curricula/syllabuses that formulate lower-level goals in terms of linguistic content (i.e. elements of the linguistic system to be acquired) and curricula/syllabuses that formulate lower-level goals in terms of language use (i.e. the specific kinds of things that people will be able to do with the target language). Task-based curricula/syllabuses belong to the second category: they formulate operational language learning goals not so much in terms of which particular words or grammar rules the learners will need to acquire, but rather in terms of the purposes for which people are learning a language, i.e. the tasks that earners will need to be able to perform.
>
> (Van den Branden 2006: 3)

3. The cognitive operations required and the resources available
4. The accountability system involved.

These early definitions of tasks and the questions (and proposed answers) relating to their successful classroom implementation as well as the training required to facilitate such implementation mirror similar discussions still taking place today in relation to TBLT. In this chapter, we will outline the principles underlying TBLT and provide examples of the practices that derive from them.

Approach

Theory of language

TBLT is motivated primarily by a theory of learning rather than a theory of language. However, several assumptions about the nature of language can be said to underlie current approaches to TBLT. These are:

- *Language is primarily a means of making meaning.* TBLT emphasizes the central role of meaning in language use. Skehan notes that in task-based instruction, "meaning is primary ... the assessment of the task is in terms of outcome" and that task-based instruction is not "concerned with language display" (1998: 98).
- *Language is a means of achieving real-world goals.* TBLT emphasizes that developing language proficiency is not an end in itself but a means to an end, and that language teaching courses must center on the learners' communicative needs and prepare them for relevant domains and situations of language use (Van Avermaet and Gysen 2006).
- *Lexical units are central in language used and language learning.* In recent years, vocabulary has been considered to play a more central role in second language learning than was traditionally assumed. Vocabulary is here used to include the consideration of lexical phrases, sentence stems, prefabricated routines, and collocations, and not only words as significant units of linguistic lexical analysis and language pedagogy. To carry out communicative tasks, a large vocabulary may be needed; therefore, TBLT and strategies for learning vocabulary are often seen as complementary, and many task-based proposals incorporate this perspective. Skehan, for example (1996b: 21–22), comments:

> Although much of language teaching has operated under the assumption that language is essentially structural, with vocabulary elements slotting in to fill structural patterns, many linguists and psycholinguists have argued that native language speech processing is very frequently lexical in nature. This means that speech processing is based on the production and reception of whole phrase units larger than the word (although analyzable by linguists into words) which do not require any internal processing when they are "reeled off" ... Fluency concerns the learner's capacity to produce language in real time without undue pausing for hesitation. It is likely to rely upon more lexicalized modes of communication, as the pressures of real-time speech production are met only by avoiding excessive rule-based computation.

Thus Ellis (2003) recommends that TBLT courses start with a heavy vocabulary input. As summarized by Leaver and Willis (2004):

> Ellis (2003) argues strongly that syllabuses should begin with a communicative task-based module with an emphasis on rapid vocabulary gain, and then later, at an intermediate level, incorporate a code-based module. By this time learners will already have acquired a rich vocabulary along with many basic structures and patterns.

- *Spoken interaction is the central focus of language and the keystone of language acquisition.* Speaking and trying to communicate with others through the spoken language drawing on the learner's available linguistic and communicative resources is considered the basis for second language acquisition in TBLT; hence, many of the tasks that are proposed within TBLT involve conversation or dialogic interaction based on a text or task.
- *Language use involves integration of skills.* TBLT assumes a holistic view of language – one where language use draws on different skills being used together. Tasks in TBLT hence typically require students to use two or more skills at the same time, thus better reflecting real-world uses of language.

Theory of learning

TBLT shares the general assumptions about the nature of language learning underlying Communicative Language Teaching; however, it draws more centrally on SLA theory, and many of its proponents describe it from a cognitive perspective (see Chapter 2):

- *Language learning is determined by learner internal, rather than external, factors. Learning is promoted by activating internal acquisition processes.* Learning is not the mirror image of teaching but is determined by internal mental processes. Hence, meaning needs to be constructed by the learner, and the creative-construction theory of learning (Chapter 2) may be said to apply. Skehan (1996a: 18) comments:

> The contemporary view of language development is that learning is constrained by internal processes. Learners do not simply acquire the language to which they are exposed, however carefully that the exposure may be orchestrated by the teacher. It is not simply a matter of converting input into output.

The goal of teaching is to activate these processes.

- *Language learning is an organic process.* Language learning develops gradually and learners pass through several stages as they restructure their language system over time. This principle reflects SLA research and the notion of a learner's developing "interlanguage": a language system in its own right and not simply a malformed version of the native speaker's linguistic system.
- *A focus on form can facilitate language learning.* TBLT does not preclude drawing learners' attention to form; however, grammar is not taught as an isolated feature of language but as it arises from, its role in meaningful communication. This can be done through

activities that involve "noticing" or "consciousness-raising" while maintaining emphasis on meaning. Such activities draw learners' attention to forms they might otherwise not have noticed in the input or their output.

- *Negotiation of meaning provides learners with opportunities for provision of comprehensible input and modified output.* This draws on an interactional view of learning (see Chapter 2) that sees language development as resulting from attempts to create meaning through dialogic interaction. In the process the learner receives different forms of feedback such as confirmation checks, comprehension checks, clarification requests, repetition requests, and repetition that support learning and language development. As learners engage in communication, their output is "stretched" and they acquire new linguistic resources. Comprehensible input as well as output are needed for learning.

- *Tasks provide opportunities for learners to "notice the gap."* TBLT also draws on two principles that have had an important impact on SLA theories – the "noticing hypothesis" and "noticing the gap." Schmidt (1990) proposed that for learners to acquire new forms from input (language they hear), it is necessary for them to notice such forms in the input (the noticing hypothesis). Consciousness of features of the input can serve as a trigger which activates the first stage in the process of incorporating new linguistic features into the learner's language competence. In his own study of his acquisition of Portuguese (Schmidt and Frota 1986), Schmidt found that there was a close connection between noticing features of the input and their later emergence in his own speech. Swain suggested (2000) that when learners have to make efforts to ensure that their messages are communicated (pushed output), this puts them in a better position to notice the gap between their productions and those of proficient speakers, thus fostering second language development. This is the "notice the gap" hypothesis. Carefully structured and managed output is essential if learners are to acquire new language. Managed output here refers to tasks and activities that require the use of certain target-language forms, that is, which "stretch" the learner's language knowledge and that consequently require a "restructuring" of that knowledge. Van Gorp and Bogaert (2006: 89) comment:

  > In task-based language education ... learners learn by confronting the gaps in their linguistic repertoire while performing tasks and being interactionally supported ... In fact, for each individual pupil who is performing a task, the actual "gap" will probably be different. This implies that each learner will run into different difficulties when dealing with the same task and, consequently, may learn different things.

- *Interaction and communication through tasks provides opportunities for scaffolded learning.* This refers to the sociocultural perspective on learning (see Chapter 2). The social activities in which the learner participates support learning through a process in which a knower guides and supports the learning of the other, providing a kind of scaffold.

In order for the experienced knower to communicate with the learner, a process of mediation occurs. Learning is a process of participation mediated through the guidance of a more knowledgeable other. Through repeated participation in a variety of joint activities, the novice gradually develops new knowledge and skills. The process of mediation involved is often referred to as scaffolding (see Chapter 2 for more detail). Initially, learners depend on others with more experience than themselves and gradually take on more responsibility over time for their own learning in joint activity (Lave and Wenger 1991; Lee 2008).

In the classroom, scaffolding is the process of interaction between two or more people as they carry out a classroom task and where one person (e.g., the teacher or another learner) has more advanced knowledge than the other (the learner). During the process, discourse is jointly created through the process of assisted or mediated performance and interaction proceeds as a kind of joint problem-solving between teacher and student. For example, in a classroom setting the teacher assists the learners in completing learning activities by observing what they are capable of, and providing a series of guided stages through the task. Wells (1999: 221) identifies three qualities for a learning event to qualify as an example of scaffolding:

- Learners should be enabled to do something they could not do before the event;
- Learners should be brought to a state of competence which enables them to complete the task on their own;
- Be followed by evidence of learners having achieved a greater level of independent competence as a result of the scaffolding experience.

Van Gorp and Bogaert (2006: 101–2) describe how this principle applies in TBLT:

> The cognitive and interactional activity that the students develop at this stage is crucial in terms of intended learning outcomes. After all, task-based language learning is highly dependent on the basic premises of social-constructivism, stating that learners acquire complex skills by actively tackling holistic tasks, calling for an integrated use of the target skills, and by collaborating with peers and more knowledgeable partners while doing so.

- *Task activity and achievement are motivational.* Tasks are also said to improve learner motivation and therefore promote learning. This is because they require the learners to use authentic language, they have well-defined dimensions and closure, they are varied in format and operation, they typically include physical activity, they involve partnership and collaboration, they may call on the learner's past experience, and they tolerate and encourage a variety of communication styles. One teacher trainee, commenting on an experience involving listening tasks, noted that such tasks are "genuinely authentic, easy to understand because of natural repetition; students are motivated to listen because they have just done the same task and want to compare how they did it"

5. Many tasks require the learners' main focus to be on meaning. However, TBLT does see an important role for a focus on form. Read the quote by Van Gorp and Bogaert on page 181. What strategies would you use as a teacher to encourage learners to "notice the gap" between themselves and more proficient speakers while performing tasks?

6. Skehan recommends using "channelling" of learners' attention to particular aspects of the language to make tasks easier or harder. In addition to a focus on form, what other aspects of language might a teacher channel a learner's attention to?

7. This chapter makes a distinction between pedagogical and real-world tasks. Give two examples of each.

   Pedagogical   *Real-world*
   1   1
   2   2

8. Read the description of the tasks and subtasks on page 185 for the tour guides course. Then choose another profession. What do you think are the main tasks and subtasks required? Create a chart similar to the one on page 185.

9. Using a current textbook or your own teaching materials, give an example of each of the five task types mentioned on page 186 of the chapter.

10. Supporting task performance (p. 187) is an important part of the classroom procedures a teacher uses in TBLT. Refer to activities in a textbook or ones you use in class, and give an example of how teachers could do each of the following:

    a) Provide interactional support in which the teacher mediates between task demands and the learner's current abilities.

    b) Offer supportive interventions focusing on clarifying meaning or guiding the choice of language.

    c) Combine focus on meaning with focus on form.

11. TBLT, when not combined with more traditional approaches, places considerable demands on teachers and, as mentioned in the conclusion, "is likely to appeal to teachers who have considerable experience and professional training, as well as a high-level competence in English or the language they teach." What might be some of the drawbacks of using TBLT with less experienced teachers or those less proficient in the target language?

12. On page 183, you read about task complexity and Skehan's suggestions for varying this. Work with a colleague who has experience in teaching students at the same level as you. Select two tasks from a coursebook you both know and each grade the tasks in terms of their complexity for your target students. Were your answers similar? How can you determine task complexity?

13. Read the following description of a task for intermediate level learners. Next, select (where possible) which of the characteristics below (described on pp. 186–7) best describe this task.

> *You are members of a medical team working with organ transplants. You have one heart available but three patients who need one. A decision needs to be made right now. Which of the following patients would you give the heart to? Discuss this with the team. You must come to a unanimous agreement.*

1. Male, 38 years old, married, father of three children. Heavy smoker. Despite warnings in the past has not quit.
2. Male, 72 years old. Widowed. Healthy for his age. He is forgetful which may cause a problem when taking his daily medications after the operation.
3. Female, 18 years old. Currently in prison for two years for having injured someone in a fight.

one-way or two-way	
convergent or divergent	
collaborative or competitive	
concrete or abstract language	
simple or complex processing	
simple or complex language	
reality-based or not reality-based	

References and further reading

Astika, G. 2004. A task-based approach to syllabus design. *ACELT Journal*: 6–19.

Beglar, D., and A. Hunt. 2002. Implementing task-based language teaching. In J. C. Richards and W. Renandya (eds.), *Methodology in Language Teaching: An Anthology of Current Practice*. New York: Cambridge University Press. 96–106.

Beretta, A. 1990. Implementation of the Bangalore Project. *Applied Linguistics* 11(4): 321–37.

Beretta, A., and A. Davies. 1985. Evaluation of the Bangalore Project. *English Language Teaching Journal* 30(2): 121–7.

Burns, A., and J. C. Richards (eds.). 2012. *The Cambridge Guide to Pedagogy and Practice in Language Teaching*. New York: Cambridge University Press.

Cameron, L. 2001. *Teaching Languages to Young Children*. Cambridge: Cambridge University Press.

Cook, G. IATEFL. 2003 debate with Martin Bygate in Brighton, 2003.

Doyle, W. 1983. Adademic work. *Review of Educational Research* 53(2): 159–99.

Edwards, C., and J. Willis (eds.). 2005. *Teachers Exploring Tasks in English Language Teaching*. Hampshire: Palgrave Macmillan.

Ellis, R. 1992. *Second Language Acquisition and Language Pedagogy*. Clevedon: Multilingual Matters.

Ellis, R. 2003. *Task-Based Language Teaching and Learning*. Oxford: Oxford University Press.

English Language Syllabus in Malaysian Schools, Tingkatan 4–5. 1975. Kuala Lumpur: Dewan Bahasa Dan Pustaka.

Feez, S. 1998. *Text-Based Syllabus Design*. Sydney: National Centre for English Teaching and Research.

Frost, R. 2004. (26 April) *A Task-Based Approach*. Available at: http://www.teachingenglish.org.uk/articles/a-task-based-approach; accessed May 9, 2013.

Lave, J., and E. Wenger. 1991. *Situated Learning: Legitimate Peripheral Participation*. Cambridge: Cambridge University Press.

Leaver, B. L., and J. R. Willis (eds.). 2004. *Task-Based Instruction in Foreign Language Education*. Washington, DC: Georgeotwn University Press.

Leaver, B. L., and M. A. Kaplan. 2004. Task-based instruction in US Government Slavic Language Programs. In Leaver and Willis (eds.), 47–66.

Lee, L. 2008. Focus-on-form through collaborative scaffolding in expert-to-novice online interaction. *Language, Learning and Technology* 12(3): 53–72.

Long, M., and G. Crookes. 1993. Units of analysis in course design – the case for task. In G. Crookes and S. Gass (eds.), *Tasks in a Pedagogical Context: Integrating Theory and Practice*. Clevedon: Multilingual Matters. 9–54.

Nunan, D. 1989. *Designing Tasks for the Communicative Classroom*. Cambridge: Cambridge University Press.

Nunan, D. 2004. *Task-Based Language Teaching*. Cambridge: Cambridge University Press.

Oliveira, C. P. 2004. Implementing task-based assessment in a TEFL environment. In Leaver and Willis (eds.), 253–79.

Pica, T., R. Kanagy, and J. Falodun. 1993. Choosing and using communicative tasks for second language instruction. In G. Crookes and S. Gass (eds.), *Tasks and Language Learning: Integrating Theory and Practice*. Clevedon: Multilingual Matters. 9–34.

Prabhu, N. S. 1987. *Second Language Pedagogy*. Oxford: Oxford University Press.

Richards, J. C. Forthcoming. *Key Issues in Language Teaching*, Cambridge: Cambridge University Press.

Schmidt, R., and S. Frota. 1986. Developing basic conversational ability in a second language: a case study of an adult learner of Portuguese. In R. Day (ed.), *Talking to Learn: Conversation in Second Language Acquisition*. Rowley, MA: Newbury House. 237–326.

Schmidt, R. 1990. The role of consciousness in second language learning. *Applied Linguistics* 11: 129–59.

Shehadeh, Ali. 2005. Task-based learning and teaching: theories and application. In Edwards and Willis (eds.), 13–30.

Skehan, P. 1996a. A framework for the implementation of task-based instruction. *Applied Linguistics* 17(1): 38–61.

Skehan, P. 1996b. Second language acquisition research and task-based instruction. In J. Willis and D. Willis (eds.), *Challenge and Change in Language Teaching*. Oxford: Heinemann. 17–30.

Skehan, P. 1998. *A Cognitive Approach to Language Learning*. Oxford: Oxford University Press.

Smith, D. 1971. Task training. In *AMA Encyclopedia of Supervisory Training*. New York: American Management Association. 581–6.

Stark, P. P. 2005. Integrating task-based learning into a business English program. In Edwards and Willis (eds.), 40–9.

Swain, M. 1985. Communicative competence: some roles of comprehensible input and comprehensible output in development. In S. Gass and C. Madden (eds.), *Input in Second Language Acquisition*. Rowley, MA: Newbury House. 235–56.

Swain, M. 2000. The output hypothesis and beyond: mediating acquisition through collaborative dialogue. In J. P. Lantolf (ed.), *Sociocultural Theory and Second Language Learning*. Oxford: Oxford University Press. 97–114.

Thomas, M. and Reinders, H. (eds.). 2010. *Task-Based Language Teaching and Technology*. New York: Continuum.

Van Avermaet, P., and S. Gysen. 2006. From needs to tasks: language learning needs in a task-based approach. In Van den Branden (ed.), 17–46.

Van den Branden, K. (ed.). 2006. *Task-Based Language Education: From Theory to Practice*. New York: Cambridge University Press.

Van den Branden, K. 2012. Task-based language education. In Burns and Richards (eds.), 140–8.

Van den Branden, K., M. Bygate, and J. Norris (eds.) 2009. *Task-Based Language Teaching: A Reader*. Amsterdam: John Benjamins.

Van Gorp, K., and N. Bogaert 2006. Developing language tasks for primary and secondary education. In Van den Branden (ed.), 76–105.

Wang, W., and A. Lam 2009. The English language curriculum for secondary schools in China: its evolution from 1949. *RELC Journal* 40(1): 65–82.

Wells, G. 1999. *Dialogic Inquiry: Towards a Sociocultural Practice and Theory of Education*. New York: Cambridge University Press.

Willis, D., and J. Wiliis 2007. *Doing Task-Based Teaching*. Oxford: Oxford University Press.

Willis, J. 1996. A flexible framework for task-based learning. In Willis and Willis (eds.), 235–56.

Willis, J., and D. Willis (eds.). 1996. *Challenge and Change in Language Teaching*. Oxford: Heinemann.

Appendix: A task-based lesson plan

Review and Homework

1. Teacher greets class and conducts a quick review of the content dealt with in the previous class.
2. Teacher checks homework orally with students.

Listening Tasks

3. Teacher elicits information from students (using realia, games, flashcards etc.), aiming at the listening activity (in the textbook) that is to come.
4. Teacher sets a pretask (questions, gap-filling, exercise, tick the words you hear, etc.) for the listening.
5. Tape is played a number of times as more challenging comprehension tasks are presented to learners. Learners get both teacher and peer feedback (pair work) during the process.

Dialogue Practice

6. Teacher reads aloud follow-up dialogue in the textbook (intended for pair work) and drills it with students.
7. Learners are then asked to practice it in pairs.
8. Teacher walks around providing learners with feedback on pronunciation.

Speaking Task

9. Learners are given a handout with an oral information-gap task based on the information dealt with so far, in which they have to talk to several peers and gather information.
10. Teacher monitors learners' work to help out and to try to minimize the use of Portuguese.
11. Learners are called on to share some of the date collected with the rest of the class.

Grammar Focus

12. Teacher explains some of the grammar in the unit and asks them to do a written exercise (in the textbook) on that, either individually or in pairs.
13. Teacher corrects exercise orally.

Reading and Writing Task

14. Teacher brainstorms following topic on the board, eliciting information from learners.
15. Teacher gives learners strips of paper with parts of an authentic reading excerpt related to the topic of the book unit and asks them to, in groups, put the pieces together.
16. Learners are then asked to devise comprehension questions about the reading to be assigned to other groups. Teacher monitors learners' work to help out and to try to minimize the use of Portuguese.
17. Groups get the questions devised by the other groups and answer them. Questions are then returned to the groups that initially devised them for correction.
18. Teacher visits groups to check their corrections.

Homework Assignment

19. Teacher assigns a piece of writing related to the work done in class.

10 Text-Based Instruction

Introduction

Text-Based Instruction (TBI) is an approach that is based on the following principles:

- Teaching explicitly about the structures and grammatical features of spoken and written texts
- Linking spoken and written texts to the social and cultural contexts of their use
- Designing units of work which focus on developing skills in relation to whole texts
- Providing students with guided practice as they develop language skills for meaningful communication through whole texts.

(Feez 1998: v)

While developed originally in Australia through the work of educationalists and applied linguists working in the area of literacy and drawing on the work of Halliday (1989), Derewianka (1990), Christie (2002), and others, it has also been influential in developing approaches to language teaching at all levels in countries such as New Zealand, Singapore, and Canada, as well as in a number of European countries, such as Sweden. The Common European Framework of Reference (Chapter 8) also specifies outcomes for what students can do with texts. TBI shares many assumptions with a genre-based approach to course design, often used in the development of courses in English for Academic Purposes (Paltridge 2006). Unlike Task-Based Language Teaching (Chapter 9), which is motivated by a creative-construction theory of second language learning, TBI, while compatible with theories of learning, derives from a genre theory of the nature of language (see below) and the role that texts play in social contexts. Communicative competence is seen to involve the mastery of different types of texts, or genres. *Text* here is used in a special sense to refer to structured sequences of language that are used in specific contexts in specific ways. For example, in the course of a day a speaker of English may use spoken English in many different ways including the following:

- Casual conversational exchange with a friend
- Conversational exchange with a stranger in an elevator
- Telephone call to arrange an appointment at a hair salon
- An account to friends of an unusual experience
- Discussion of a personal problem with a friend to seek advice.

Each of these uses of language can be regarded as a text in that it exists as a unified whole with a beginning, middle, and end, it conforms to norms of organization and content, and it draws on appropriate grammar and vocabulary. Second language learning thus involves being able to use different kinds of spoken and written texts in the specific contexts in which they are used. According to this view learners in different contexts have to master the use of the text-types occurring most frequently in these contexts. These contexts might include studying in an English-medium university, studying in an English-medium primary or secondary school, working in a restaurant, working in an office, working in a store, or socializing with neighbors in a housing complex.

Approach

Theory of language

A number of assumptions about the nature of language inform TBI.

Texts occur in relation to different genres of discourse

As mentioned earlier, the notion of genre also plays an important part in the theory of language underlying TBI. The situations, contexts, purposes, audiences, and relationships that are involved when we use language account for patterns and norms of language use and result in different genres of discourse. Examples of genres are scientific writing, fiction, conversation, news broadcasts, songs, poems, interviews, sports commentaries, letters. *Genre* refers to spoken and written contexts for language use, in which our expectations for the kinds of discourse that occur are shaped by our knowledge of the types of conventions in place for that type of discourse, that is, genre conventions (Dean 2008). Within a given genre, different types of texts may occur. For example, the genre of conversation may include such text-types as *small talk, anecdotes, jokes, personal recounts* (or narratives). Members of a culture or "discourse community" have a shared knowledge of the kinds of texts that occur in different genres and of the features of different text-types. The Common European Framework of Reference for Languages (CEFR; Council of Europe 2001) lists the following examples of genres and text-types that learners may need to understand, produce, or participate in:

Spoken discourse	Written discourse
Public announcements and instructions	Books, fiction and non-fiction
Public speeches, lectures, presentations, sermons	Magazines
	Newspapers
Rituals (ceremonies, formal religious services)	Instructions (e.g. cookbooks, etc.)
	Textbooks
Entertainment (drama, shows, readings, songs)	Comic strips
	Brochures, prospectuses
Sports commentaries (football, cricket, etc.)	Leaflets
	Advertising material
	Public signs and notices

(Continued)

Spoken discourse	Written discourse
News broadcasts	Supermarket, shop, market stall signs
Public debates and discussion	Packaging and labelling on goods
Interpersonal dialogues and	Tickets, etc.
conversations	Forms and questionnaires
Telephone conversations	Dictionaries (monolingual and bilingual), thesauri
Job interviews	Business and professional letters, faxes
	Personal letters
	Essays and exercises
	Memoranda, reports, and papers
	Notes and messages, etc.
	Database (news, literature, general information, etc.)

Language is a social process

This view was described by Halliday (1978: 1): "Language arises in the life of the individual through an ongoing exchange of meanings with significant others." According to Feez (Chapter 2), the implications of this view of language include, on the one hand, the fact that texts are shaped by the social context in which they are used and, on the other hand, that the social context is simultaneously shaped by people using language.

Texts have distinctive patterns of organization and distinctive linguistic features

Texts are constructed of words and sentences, but they function in communication as units. They may consist of a single word, a sentence, or much longer constructions, and they reflect recognizable and conventional patterns of organization. There have been a number of classifications of text-types. The following text-types were originally proposed for genre-based instruction in schools in Australia by the Sydney Group (Johns 2002):

- *Recounts*: Relate an event that happened in the past.
- *Procedures*: Outline a process, system or procedure.
- *Descriptions*: Classify, describe, and give characteristics of a group of things.
- *Reports*: Tell a story or report information to entertain or educate.
- *Explanations*: Present instructions that explain how something should be done.
- *Expositions*: Take a position and argue a case.

Others have amplified this list. For example, two different kinds of text-types are commonly used in describing past experiences: *recounts* and *narratives* (Eggins and Slade 1997; Thornbury and Slade 2006).

The purpose of a recount is to list and describe past personal experiences by retelling events in the order they happened. They have the purpose of either informing the listener or entertaining him or her or both. There are two main types of recounts (Thornbury and Slade 2006):

- *Personal recounts* usually retell an event the speaker was personally involved in (e.g., a traffic accident).
- *Factual recounts* describe an incident the speaker is familiar with (e.g., a school fair).

Each genre type has its own internal complexity. For example, recounts typically have three parts:

- The *setting or orientation*, providing background information concerning who, when where and why
- *Events* described in a chronological order
- *Concluding comments,* usually expressing a personal opinion regarding the events described.

Linguistic features include past tense, verbs, and adverbs. Personal recounts are common in casual conversation and in email communication, blogs, etc. Narratives are similar to recounts and share many of the linguistic features of recounts, except that rather than simply recounting events, they tell a story. Students will have come across many different forms of narratives in their reading, and common to many of them is a structure that consists of:

- *orientation* (in which the setting is presented and the characters in the story are introduced);
- *complication* (that part in the story in which the character or characters experience some kind of problem);
- *resolution* where a solution is found to the problem or complication.

Language use reflects the contexts in which it occurs

Another assumption of TBI is that language is shaped by the situations in which it is used and the nature of the interactions in which it occurs. An important principle that derives from this assumption is that spoken and written language have different functions and use different grammatical resources. The teaching of spoken and written texts should be informed by research on authentic language use, drawing on such traditions as discourse and conversation analysis and corpus research. The availability of corpora presenting large samples of spoken and written language in different genres enables proponents of TBI to focus on the unique characteristics of spoken and written texts in ways that would not have been possible in the past.

Theory of learning

Several assumptions about the nature of second language learning are used to support TBI.

Learning is facilitated by explicit knowledge of language

Explicit learning is conscious learning and results in knowledge that can be described and explained, as compared with implicit learning which is learning that takes place without conscious awareness and results in knowledge that the learner may not be able to verbalize or explain. In teaching from the perspective of texts, students study the discourse and linguistic features of texts and how texts reflect the contexts of their use. This information is presented directly, and students are expected to understand and learn organizational features underlying the organization of different text-types. This view of learning contrasts with implicit models of learning found in the Natural Approach (Chapter 14) and Community Language Learning (Chapter 17).

Learning is facilitated by the study of authentic models and examples
Students are presented with authentic examples of different text-types, and these are used to display and model the features of different kinds of texts.

Learning depends upon the scaffolded support of the teacher
The notion of scaffolded learning, an essential component of the sociocultural model of learning (see Chapter 2), is central to TBI, and learning is viewed as "the outcome of a joint collaboration between teacher and learner" (Feez 1998: 12). In learning how to create texts, the teacher first presents an example of the text-type, leads students through an analysis of the text to identify its distinguishing features, and then works with the students to jointly create a similar text or texts before the students create their own texts. (See below under *procedure.*) Burns (2012: 145–6) comments:

> This approach views the teacher as the "expert" who has the skills to monitor and diagnose learner progress and to guide learners toward the aspects of language they need to practice at various points as their skills develop ... Thus, scaffolding involves temporary, and gradually withdrawn support, where learning is assisted in two ways (Hammond and Gibbons 2001); *designed-in scaffolding* (the content, strategies and learning experiences the teacher plans to build into the syllabus) and *contingent scaffolding* (the moment-by-moment classroom interactions that support learners at the point of need).

Design

Objectives

The objectives of a text-based course are linked to the contexts in which the learner will use English and the type of texts he or she will encounter in those contexts. Hence, the starting point in developing course objectives is an analysis of learner needs and of the learning context in order to identify the genres of discourse and the associated text-types the course will focus on. Thus Feez (1998: 23) comments: "The objectives of a course based on a text-based syllabus are always related to the use of whole texts in context."

Feez (1998: 23) gives the following examples of course objectives for a unit of work in a text-based course on "casual conversation."

Goal

To enable learners to participate in casual conversation in a workplace.

Objectives

The learners will:
- understand the purpose of casual conversation in Australian workplace culture
- know which conversation topics are appropriate in Australian workplaces
- recognize and use the elements of a casual conversation, i.e., greetings and closures, feedback, topic shifts

---

- recognize and use conversational chunks such as comments, descriptions, or recounts
- take turns appropriately within simple exchanges, i.e., question/answer, statement/agreement, statement/disagreement
- use language appropriate to casual conversation, including politeness strategies, informal language, idiom
- build pronunciation and paralinguistic skills and strategies, specifically in the areas of intonation and gesture

The syllabus

Feez suggests that the syllabus in a text-based approach can be initiated from a number of different perspectives and that one unit might be designed around a topic, while the next is designed around a particular text-type. In other words, any of the units of organization below could be used:

- Topics and related contexts of use
- Text-types and related language features (discourse features at the level of the whole text, grammatical and lexical features at the level of the clause)
- Skills and strategies
- Activities.

Burns comments (2012: 145):

> Based on the concepts of scaffolding and support built up over time, it follows that texts and tasks presented to learners need to be logically sequenced with both short-term and long-term learning goals in mind. Teachers will have in mind the "macro-framework" of what they want learners to achieve by the end of the course, as well as the "micro-framework" of how a specific lesson focussing on a specific text contributes to the larger plan. They can also consider what kind of spoken and written texts logically relate and connect in authentic communicative situations.

The following text-types are included in the *Certificates in Spoken and Written English*, which are widely taught language qualifications in Australia.

Exchanges	Simple exchanges relating to information and goods and services
	Complex or problematic exchanges
	Casual conversation
Forms	Simple formatted texts
	Complex formatted texts
Procedures	Instructions
	Procedures
	Protocols
Information texts	Descriptions
	Explanations

	Reports
	Directives
	Texts which combine one or more of these text-types
Story texts	Recounts
	Narratives
Persuasive texts	Opinion texts
	Expositions
	Discussions

A text-based approach formed a key component of the 2001 syllabus for primary and secondary schools in Singapore, where the text-types that are identified can be understood as forming the communicative building blocks Singapore children need in order to perform in an English-medium school setting (Singapore Ministry of Education 2001). The text-types are as follows:

- Explanations, e.g., reference books, dictionaries
- Expositions, e.g., discussions, assembly talks
- Factual recount, e.g., news stories, eye-witness accounts
- Information reports, e.g., brochures, advertisements, documentaries
- Procedures, e.g., how to do kits
- Conversations and short functional texts, e.g., making arrangements, thank-you notes
- Narratives and personal recounts, e.g., oral anecdotes, diary entries.

The Singapore syllabus also identifies the grammatical items that are needed in order to master different text-types. For example, the following items are identified in relation to the text-types of narratives and personal recounts at Secondary 2 level:

- Adjectives, adjectival phrases, and clauses
- Adverbs and adverbials
- Connectors to do with time and sequence
- Direct and indirect speech
- Nouns, noun phrases, and clauses
- Prepositions and prepositional phrases
- Pronouns
- Tenses to express past time
- Verbs and verb phrases.

Types of learning and teaching activities

Activities used in TBI are varied and relate to the different stages of a text-based unit of work as well as the type of text in focus, which could be either a spoken or a written text. Activities typically focus on building the context for a text, modeling and deconstructing the text, joint construction of a text, and independent construction of a text. Teacher-led activities as well as pair and group-based activities will all be used, but central to all of them is a focus on the nature of an authentic text, what its purpose and features are, and how it reflects the context of its use.

Learner roles

Learners learn in TBI both through the support and guidance of the teacher and through the use of rules and patterns to creating texts related to their needs. They use teacher-provided models to create texts of their own. They learn through a process of collaboration and guidance until they reach a level where they can function independently without the teacher's support. Learners are also expected to develop skills that enable them to monitor their own learning and to compare their own performance and those of others against models.

Teacher roles

The teacher has a somewhat demanding role in TBI, since a text-based course is typically not a pre-packed course but one developed by a teacher or group of teachers for a specific group of learners. This will often involve:

- developing a syllabus based on learners' needs;
- selecting suitable texts as the basis for the course;
- sequencing elements of the course;
- modeling processes of deconstructing and constructing appropriate texts;
- assessing students' progress in understanding and mastering different text-types.

In addition the teacher is expected to have a sound knowledge of the nature of different kinds of texts, and the ability to analyze texts and guide students' awareness and mastery of text conventions. The ability to scaffold learning is a key part of the teacher's role.

The role of instructional materials

Materials play an important role in TBI since examples of authentic spoken and written texts provide the basis for teaching and learning. Texts can be obtained from a variety of sources: from the real world (i.e., texts from everyday life such as forms, documents, reports), from the Internet, from the media (e.g., YouTube), or from students themselves, that is, from their work, study, and other non-pedagogical contexts. However, teachers may also prepare model texts (adapted from authentic texts) to highlight the discourse and language features of particular text-types. Student-generated texts (either spoken or written) are also used as a basis for assessing student learning. A text-based approach can also be used as the basis for designing textbooks (see appendix to this chapter).

Procedure

Feez (1998: 28–31) gives the following description of procedures used in a text-based lesson or series of lessons. Recall that texts may be spoken or written and differ according to the discourse context in which they are used. Hence, these phases given by Feez would be modified accordingly, depending on the type of text being presented. While TBI may advocate going through all of these phases systematically in any one lesson, it is possible to combine aspects of this procedure with other approaches.

Phase 1 Building the context

In this stage students:
- Are introduced to the social context of an authentic model of the text-type being studied
- Explore features of the general cultural context in which the text-type is used and the social purposes the text-type achieves
- Explore the immediate context of situation by investigating the register of a model text which has been selected on the basis of the course objectives and learner needs

An exploration of register involves:
- Building knowledge of the topic of the model text and knowledge of the social activity in which the text is used, e.g. *job seeking*
- Understanding the roles and relationships of the people using the text and how these are established and maintained, e.g. the relationship between a job seeker and a prospective employer
- Understanding requirements of the channel of communication being used, e.g. using the telephone, speaking face-to-face with members of an interview panel

Context-building activities include:
- Presenting the context through pictures, audiovisual materials, realia, excursions, field-trips, guest speakers, etc.
- Establishing the social purpose through discussions or surveys etc
- Cross-cultural activities such as comparing differences in the use of the text in two cultures
- Comparing the model text with other texts of the same or contrasting type, e.g comparing a job interview with a complex spoken exchange involving close friends, a work colleague, or a stranger in a service encounter.

*Phase 2 Modelling and deconstructing the text**

In this stage students:
- Investigate the structural pattern and language features of the model
- Compare the model with other examples of the same text-type

Phase 3 Joint construction of the text

In this stage:
- Students begin to contribute to the construction of whole examples of the text-type
- The teacher gradually reduces the contribution to text construction, as the students move closer to being able to control text-type independently

* Feez (1998: 29) comments that "modeling and deconstruction are undertaken at both the whole text, clause and expression levels. It is at this stage that many traditional ESL language teaching activities come into their own."

Joint construction activities include:

- Teacher questioning, discussing and editing whole class construction, then scribing onto board or OHT
- Skeleton texts
- Jigsaw and information gap activities
- Small-group construction of tests
- Dictogloss
- Self-assessment and peer assessment activities

Phase 4 Independent construction of the text

In this stage:

- Students work independently with the text
- Learner performances are used for achievement assessment

Independent construction activities include:

- Listening tasks, e.g. comprehension activities in response to live or recorded material, such as performing a task, sequencing pictures, numbering, ticking or underlining material on a worksheet, answering questions
- Listening and speaking tasks, e.g. role plays, simulated or authentic dialogues
- Speaking tasks, e.g. spoken presentation to class, community organization, workplace
- Reading tasks, e.g. comprehension activities in response to written material such as performing a task, sequencing pictures, numbering, ticking or underlining material on a worksheet, answering questions
- Writing tasks which demand that students draft and present whole texts

Phase 5 Linking to related texts

In this stage students investigate how what they have learned in this teaching/learning cycle can be related to:

- Other texts in the same or similar context
- Future or past cycles of teaching and learning

Activities which link the text-type to related texts include:

- Comparing the use of the text-type across different fields
- Researching other text-types used in the same field
- Role playing what happens if the same text-type is used by people with different roles and relationships
- Comparing spoken and written modes of the same text-type
- Researching how a key language feature used in this text-type is used in other text-types

Conclusion

As can be seen from the above summary, a text-based approach focuses especially on the products of learning rather than the processes involved. Advocates of the approach argue that it "provides for the basis for coherent syllabus design drawing on tasks that are based on understandings of how people actually communicate in a wide range of social situations. It is an approach where teachers can incorporate many of the resources and activities they already use within the broader framework of assisting learners to gain greater knowledge of relevant texts" (Burns 2012: 146). Critics have pointed out that, when a TBI model is used exclusively, an emphasis on individual creativity and personal expression is sometimes missing from the TBI model, which is heavily wedded to a methodology based on the study of model texts and the creation of texts based on models. Likewise, critics point out that there is a danger that the approach becomes repetitive over time since the five-phase cycle described above is applied to the teaching of all four skills.

Discussion questions

1. Explain to a colleague how the term *text* is used in TBI.

2. How are the terms *text* and *genre* related?

3. Which academic discourse communities are you a member of? Consider the types of discourse used in both speech and writing in your given profession.

4. Look at the following isolated sentences. For each one:

   - decide if it is probably spoken or written English;
   - think about what language would come before and after it;
   - give further relevant details of the context;
   - state the communicative function;
   - analyze the form.

   1. She's been here for years.
   2. He must have forgotten about it.
   3. Having a great time here in Bali.
   4. I'll get you another one.

5. Look at the following pairs of sentences. For each pair:

   - discuss the likely text-type each utterance is taken from;
   - discuss the possible context of each;
   - compare and contrast them in terms of function and form.

   1. You must see the latest Tom Cruise movie.
   2. You must have a visa to enter Australia.
   3. I wish I had a car.
   4. I wish I had known.
   5. I'm having a good time in the States.
   6. I'm working tonight.
   7. PS. We're out of milk.

6. Which of the following are "texts"? For the ones that aren't, why don't they work as texts?

A	This box contains, on average, 100 large paper clips. Did you watch the news? Yes, please.
B	Playback. Raymond Chandler. Penguin Books in association with Hamish Hamilton. To Jean and Helga, without whom this book could not have been written. One. The voice on the phone sounded sharp and ...
C	Which one of you is the fish? That's me.
D	Phone. I'm in the shower. OK.

7. Match the following text-types with the descriptions of their purposes below:

   1. Narratives
   2. Recounts
   3. Procedures
   4. Expositions
   5. Information reports
   6. Explanations

   - Classify, describe, and give characteristics of a group of things.
   - Outline a process, system, or procedure.
   - Tell a story or report information to entertain or educate.
   - Relate an event that happened in the past.
   - Take a position and argue a case.
   - Present instructions that explain how something should be done.

8. Select a language teaching textbook.

   a) Find examples of each of the text-types in the list below from the book. Are other text-types included?
   b) What is the approximate distribution of the text-types (which ones are more frequent)? (You do not need to count all instances in the book – a general impression is sufficient.)
   c) Are any not covered? Should they be?

   - Explanations, e.g., grammar paradigms, dictionary entries
   - Expositions, e.g., discussions, public meetings
   - Factual recount, e.g., news stories, eye-witness accounts
   - Information reports, e.g., brochures, advertisements, documentaries
   - Procedures, e.g., "how to do" kits

- Conversations and short functional texts, e.g., making arrangements, thank-you notes
- Narratives and personal recounts, e.g., oral anecdotes, diary entries

References and further reading

Burns, A. 2005. Teaching speaking: a text-based syllabus approach. In E. Uso-Juan and A. Martinez-Flor (eds.), *Current Trends in the Development and Teaching of the Four Language Skills* Amsterdam: Mouton de Gruyter. 235–58.

Burns, A. 2012. Text-based teaching. In A. Burns and J. C. Richards (eds.), *The Cambridge Guide to Pedagogy and Practice in Language Teaching*. New York: Cambridge University Press. 132–9.

Carter, R., A. Goddard, D. Reah, K. Sanger, N. Swift, and A. Beard. 2008. *Working with Texts*. 3rd edn. London: Routledge.

Christie, F. 2002. *Classroom Discourse Analysis: A Functional Perspective*. London: Continuum.

Council of Europe. 2001. *Common European Framework of Reference for Languages: Learning, Teaching, Assessment*. Cambridge: Cambridge University Press.

Dean, S. T. 2008. *Discourse and Practice: New Tools for Critical Analysis*. Oxford: Oxford University Press.

Derewianka, B. 1990. *Exploring How Texts Work*. Sydney: Primary English Teachers' Association.

Eggins, S., and D. Slade. 1997. *Analysing Casual Conversation*. London: Cassell.

Feez, S. 1998. *Text-Based Syllabus Design*. Sydney: National Centre for English Language Teaching and Research.

Gibbons, P. 2006. *Bridging Discourses in the ESL Classroom*. London: Continuum.

Halliday, M. A. K. 1978. *Language as Social Semiotic: The Social Interpretation of Language and Meaning*. London: Edward Arnold.

Halliday, M. A. K. 1989. *Spoken and Written Language*. Oxford: Oxford University Press.

Hammond, J., and B. Derewianka. 2001. Genre. In R. Carter and D. Nunan (eds.), *The Cambridge Guide to Teaching English to Speakers of Other Languages*. New York: Cambridge. 194–200.

Hammond, J., and Gibbons, P. 2001. What is scaffolding? In J. Hammond (ed.), *Scaffolding Teaching and Learning in Language and Literacy Education*. Sydney: Primary English Teachers' Association. 1–14.

Johns. A. (ed.). 2002. *Genres in the Classroom*. Mahwah, NJ: Lawrence Erlbaum.

McCarthy, M., and R. Carter. 1994. *Language as Discourse: Perspectives for Language Teaching*. London: Longman.

Macken-Horarik, M. 2002. "Something to short for": a systemic functional approach to teaching genre in secondary school science. In A. Johns (ed.), *Genres in the Classroom*. Mahwah, NJ: Lawrence Erlbaum. 17–42.

Maybin, J., N. Mercer, and B. Stierer. 1992. "Scaffolding" learning in the classroom. In K. Norman (ed.), *Thinking Voices: The Work of the National Oracy Project*. London: Hodder and Stoughton for the National Curriculum Council. 186–95.

O'Keefe, A., M. McCarthy, and R. Carter. 2007. *From Corpus to Classroom*. Cambridge: Cambridge University Press.

Paltridge, B. 2006. *Discourse Analysis*. London: Continuum.

Singapore Ministry of Education 2001. *English Language Syllabus 2001 for Primary and Secondary Schools*. Singapore: Ministry of Education,.

Thornbury, S., and D. Slade. 2006. *Conversation: From Description to Pedagogy*. Cambridge: Cambridge University Press.

Appendix: Text-based activities

The Information Report Text Type

Features of an Information Report

An information report presents facts about a topic. These facts are organised in different paragraphs. An information report has four main parts: **Title, Introduction, Paragraphs about the Topic** and **Conclusion.** Examples of information reports include news reports, science reports and weather reports.

Text Features

Language Features

Title [*The Paralympics — Games for the Disabled*

Introduction
A general statement about the topic

The Paralympics or 'Parallel Olympics' are the Olympic Games for the disabled. They take place alongside the Olympics in the same host country every four years. …

Simple present tense

Origins of the Paralympics
Ludwig Guttmann, who was a doctor in England, founded the Paralympics. In 1948, he organised sports competitions for his disabled patients. He believed in using sports to help them …

Relative pronouns

The Paralympics Today
Today, the Games emphasise athletic ability rather than physical disability. The participants compete like able-bodied athletes even though they have an artificial leg or arm, or are wheelchair users. The visually impaired athletes team up …

Paragraphs about the Topic
• Sub-headings
• Main ideas
• Details

Some Outstanding Paralympians
There are many great athletes who have competed at the Paralympics.

An outstanding athlete is Yip Pin Xiu from Singapore. She has muscular dystrophy which prevents her from walking. …

Present perfect tense

Benefits of the Paralympics
The Paralympics have changed the way we treat the disabled. Many countries have made changes to their sports buildings. They build ramps so that the disabled can move around easily. …

Conclusion
Key points

The Paralympics have inspired millions of people around the world. Through sports, the disabled have gained a sense of pride and dignity in themselves. …

Celebrating the Olympic Spirit 35

Try This!

1. Write a paragraph on the topic: *Popular Sports in My Country*.
   Write a main idea at the beginning of the paragraph. The main idea
   should sum up what the paragraph is about. Provide details in the rest of
   the paragraph.

2. Write an information report on the topic: *Popular Sports in My Country*.
   Write a suitable introduction, paragraphs about the topic and a conclusion.
   For every paragraph, include a sub-heading, a main idea and supporting
   details. Add pictures and captions to your report.

Introduction
A general
statement
about the topic

**Paragraphs
about the
Topic**
• Sub-headings
• Main ideas
• Details

Conclusion
Key points

Check!

I have used:
☐ Simple present tense
☐ Relative pronouns
☐ Present perfect tense

Celebrating the Olympic Spirit   37

11 The Lexical Approach

Introduction

We have seen throughout this book that central to an approach or method in language teaching is a view of the nature of language, and this shapes teaching goals, the type of syllabus that is adopted, and the emphasis given in classroom teaching. The syllabuses that were reflected in language courses in the first half of the twentieth century viewed vocabulary (particularly single-word lexical items) and grammar as the building blocks of language. Changed views of language that emerged with the concept of communicative competence prompted a search for alternative syllabus conceptions (see Chapter 5). One type of syllabus and teaching proposal that appeared in the 1990s and that has been refined and developed since that time was termed the Lexical Approach (Lewis 1993, 1997, 2000a; Boers and Lindstromberg 2009). A lexical approach in language teaching refers to one derived from the belief that the building blocks of language learning and communication are not grammar, functions, notions, or some other unit of planning and teaching but lexis, that is, words and particularly multi-word combinations. The Lexical Approach reflects a belief in the centrality of the lexicon to language structure, second language learning, and language use, and in particular to multi-word lexical units or "chunks" that are learned and used as single items. While early discussions of the Lexical Approach (e.g., Lewis 1993) emphasized the important role of vocabulary in general in language learning, subsequent discussion of this approach has focused mainly on the role of multi-word units, or "chunks," which is the focus taken in this chapter. The role of vocabulary in language teaching per se is not central to current formulations of the Lexical Approach but is dealt with extensively in the literature (e.g., Bogaards and Laufer-Dvorkin 2004; Schmitt 2008; Meara 2009; Nation 2013).

Schmitt (n.d.) comments, clarifying that chunks may consist of either collocations, a term that refers to the regular occurrence together of words, or fixed phrases:

> The Lexical Approach can be summarized in a few words: language consists not of traditional grammar and vocabulary but often of multi-word prefabricated chunks. The lexical approach is a way of analysing and teaching language based on the idea that it is made up of lexical units rather than grammatical structures. The units are words and chunks formed by collocations and fixed phrases.

An interest in the role of chunks in language learning goes back at least to Palmer (1925), but their status in language theory has undergone reassessment, beginning with a classic paper by Pawley and Syder (1983), by the development of corpus-based studies of language use (drawing on large-scale computer databases of authentic language use, e.g., O'Keefe, McCarthy, and Carter 2007), as well as by research in psycholinguistics (e.g., Wray 2002). Boers and Lindstromberg (2009: 23) observe:

> The relevance of chunks for second and foreign language learners has meanwhile stimulated dictionary makers to include more information about collocation in learners dictionaries generally and to produce dictionaries of collocations in particular. Concrete proposals for instructional methods targeting chunks have also been launched and resource books for teachers are becoming available.

A lexical approach in language teaching thus seeks to develop proposals for syllabus design and language teaching founded on a view of language in which multi-word units, or chunks, play the central role.

Approach

Theory of language

The Lexical Approach reflects what we have termed a structural view of language (Chapter 2). This views language as a system of structurally related elements for the coding of meaning. Traditionally, the elements of the system included lexical items as well as grammatical units. The Lexical Approach adds another level of "structure," namely multi-word units. Whereas Chomsky's influential theory of language emphasized the capacity of speakers to create and interpret sentences that are unique and have never been produced or heard previously, in contrast, the lexical view holds that only a minority of spoken sentences are entirely novel creations and that multi-word units functioning as "chunks" or memorized patterns form a high proportion of the fluent stretches of speech heard in everyday conversation (Pawley and Syder 1983; O'Keefe et al. 2007). The role of collocation is also important in lexically based theories of language. For example, compare the following collocations of verbs with nouns:

do	my hair / the cooking / the laundry / my work
make	my bed / a promise / coffee / a meal

Many other multi-word units also occur frequently in language. For example:

binomials	clean and tidy, back to front
trinomials	cool, calm, and collected
idioms	dead drunk, to run up a bill
similes	as old as the hills
connectives	finally, to conclude
social-routine formulae	Nice to meet you.
discourse markers	on the other hand
compounds	fast forward
proverbs	Too many cooks spoil the broth.
exclamations	You must be kidding!

Multi-word lexical units such as these are thought by some to play a central role in learning and in communication. Studies based on extensive language corpora have examined patterns of phrase and clause sequences as they appear in samples of various kinds of texts, including both written and spoken samples. For example, the Cambridge English Corpus (formerly the Cambridge International Corpus; http://cambridge.org/corpus) is a corpus of several billion words based on samples of written and spoken English from many different sources. This and other corpora are important sources of information about collocations and other multi-word units in English.

The Lexical Approach holds that chunks are a central feature of naturalistic language use. From the perspective of language production, there are advantages in constructing utterances from ready-made chunks rather than from single lexical items; the ability to call on chunks is an important factor that contributes to fluent speech. O'Keefe et al. (2007: 63) comment: "an over-emphasis in language teaching on single words out of context may leave second language learners ill-prepared in both the processing of heavily chunked input such as casual conversation, and of their own productive fluency." However, this does not downplay the importance of grammar in language use or in language teaching. Rather, the point is that language ability requires not only the ability to produce language through syntactic generation (via grammatical competence) but also the ability to use lexical chunks in appropriate situations. This is especially true if learners hope to gain the pragmatic fluency that comes from knowing the right lexical phrase for the right functional situation. Ultimately, language learners need mastery of both abilities to use language well.

Drawing on research on first language learning, chunks are also believed to play a role in language acquisition. They constitute a significant proportion of the data which learners use to develop their grammatical competence. As Lewis put it, language should be recognized as grammaticalized lexis instead of lexicalized grammar (1993: iv). Chunks are hence understood not only to be an important feature of language structure and language use but also to play a key role in second language learning. Nattinger (1980: 341) commented:

> Perhaps we should base our teaching on the assumption that, for a great deal of the time anyway, language production consists of piecing together the ready-made units appropriate for a particular situation and that comprehension relies on knowing which of these patterns to predict in these situations. Our teaching, therefore, would center on these patterns and the ways they can be pieced together, along with the ways they vary and the situations in which they occur.

Theory of learning

Lewis (2000a: 184) proposed the following account of the learning theory assumed in his initial proposal for a lexical approach:

- Encountering new learning items on several occasions is a necessary but sufficient condition for learning to occur.
- Noticing lexical chunks or collocations is a necessary but not sufficient condition for "input" to become "intake."

- Noticing similarities, differences, restrictions, and examples contributes to turning input into intake, although formal description of rules probably does not help.
- Acquisition is based not on the application of formal rules but on an accumulation of examples from which learners make provisional generalizations. Language production is the product of previously met examples, not formal rules. No linear syllabus can adequately reflect the nonlinear nature of acquisition.

Learning of chunks is assumed to take place both through incidental learning and through direct instruction. Incidental learning is dependent upon the frequency with which chunks are encountered and noticed in normal language use. Procedures for direct instruction will be discussed later in this chapter. Boers and Lindstromberg (2009) elaborate an account of chunk-based learning from the perspective of cognitive theory, which we have referred to as cognitive-code theory in Chapter 2. The goal of learning is that "chunks that are met, noticed and learned must then be adequately entrenched in the learners' long-term memory" (2009: 10). The learning of chunks is facilitated in a number of ways:

- *Through noticing*: targeted chunks must first be noticed in the input learners receive.
- *Through cognitive processing*: chunks must be processed through different forms of elaboration, which will increase the level of cognitive involvement needed to foster retention (Boers and Lindstromberg 2009).
- *Through exposure*: repeated encounters with chunks are likely to increase the likelihood of them being learned. Krashen, in elaborating the Natural Approach (Chapter 14), suggested that massive amounts of "language input," especially through reading, is the only effective approach to such learning. Others propose making the language class a laboratory in which learners can explore, via computer concordance databases, the contexts of lexical use that occur in different kinds of texts and language data.
- *Through comparisons with L1*: another approach to learning lexical chunks has been a "contrastive" one (an example of "elaboration" referred to above). Some applied linguists have suggested that for a number of languages there is an appreciable degree of overlap within a given language in the form and meaning of lexical collocations, collocations that may not exist in the language being studied. Bahns (1993: 58) suggests that "the teaching of lexical collocations in EFL should concentrate on items for which there is no direct translational equivalence between English and the learners' respective mother tongues."

Design

Objectives

Unlike other teaching proposals in this book, the Lexical Approach is not conceptualized as a comprehensive plan for a language program (i.e., one that provides a complete framework for the design of a language course). Rather, it can be understood as providing one strand of a language course for students, thought by some educators to be appropriate at intermediate level and above, and one that can be used in conjunction with other approaches and methods. Stengers et al. (2010: 101) comment:

> Given its reliance on incidental acquisition through independent reading and listening, we take it that the Lexical Approach is intended for learners above lower-intermediate level. The level of proficiency of the students who participated in our experiments was generally estimated by their teachers to be around B2 according to the descriptors of the Common European Framework of Reference (CEFR).

The goal of the Lexical Approach is to develop learners' awareness and use of lexical chunks as an important feature of naturalistic language use. A related goal is for learners to develop strategies for identifying and learning the chunks that they encounter in spoken and written texts. Stengers et al. (2010: 101) continue:

> The advice given by Lewis and his colleagues is therefore to help students develop *strategies* for the recognition and the recording of chunks they encounter not just in, but outside the classroom too: What is essential is that the teacher equips the students with search skills which will enable them to discover significant collocations for themselves, in both the language they meet in the classroom and, more importantly, in the language they meet outside the classroom. In other words, Lexical Approach advocates are hopeful that students will transfer their heightened awareness of the ubiquity of chunks to their dealings with the L2 samples they encounter outside the classroom, and that this will then accelerate the students' incidental uptake in long-term memory of lexical phrases.

The Lexical Approach may, however, be used with lower-level students when the chunks are provided, rather than acquired through independent reading and listening.

The syllabus

As with lexis in general, proponents of the Lexical Approach recommend, for lower-level students, direct teaching of the chunks that occur most frequently in the kinds of texts students engage with in their learning, and that language corpora can be a source of information for this strategy. Shin and Nation (2008), for example, provide a list of the most frequent chunks that occur in spoken English. However, for intermediate and advanced-level learners, similar information is not readily available. Since there are potentially many thousands of multi-word units that students may encounter in their exposure to English and that cannot be predicted in advance, some advocates of the Lexical Approach argue that the goal for learners at higher levels is not to teach a core set of lexical units but rather to develop students' awareness of the nature of lexical units and to provide them with strategies for recognizing, learning, structuring, storing, and using chunks which they encounter. The "syllabus" will therefore consist of an organized record of the chunks learners have encountered in different written and spoken texts – i.e., it is a retrospective syllabus.

A lexical approach was used in the COBUILD English Course (Willis and Willis 1989), the rationale and design for which was described in *The Lexical Syllabus* (Willis 1990). This was the first published coursebook to be built around a lexical rather than a conventional grammatical syllabus (albeit a syllabus mainly consisting of single-word lexical items rather than chunks). Willis notes that the COBUILD computer analyses of texts indicate that "the 700 most frequent words of English account for around 70% of all English text." This "fact" led to the decision that "word frequency would determine the contents of our course. Level 1 would aim to cover the most frequent 700 words together with their common patterns and uses" (Willis 1990: vi). In one respect, this work resembled the earlier frequency-based analyses of vocabulary by West (1953) and others. The difference in the COBUILD course was the attention to word patterns derived from the computer analysis. Willis stresses, however, that "the lexical syllabus not only subsumes a structural syllabus, it also indicates how the structures which make up a syllabus should be exemplified" since the computer corpus reveals the commonest structural patterns in which words are used (1990: vi). The *Touchstone* series (McCarthy, McCarten, and Sandiford 2005) is another example of a coursebook series that incorporates a corpus-based lexical syllabus including both single-word units and chunks. The lexical syllabus is based on the most common words and phrases in the North American spoken segment of the Cambridge English Corpus.

Other proposals have been put forward as to how lexical material might be organized for instruction. Nation (1999) reviews criteria for classifying collocations and chunks and suggests approaches to instructional sequencing and treatment for different types of collocations. Nattinger and DeCarrico (1992: 185) propose using a functional schema for organizing instruction:

> Distinguishing lexical phrases as social interactions, necessary topics, and discourse devices seems to us the most effective distinction for pedagogical purposes, but that is not to say that a more effective way of grouping might not be found necessary in the wake of further research.

Types of learning and teaching activities

Activities used with the Lexical Approach include awareness activities, training in text chunking, as well as activities designed to enhance the remembering of chunks. Such activities can be included in any course and not necessarily one based on the Lexical Approach.

Awareness activities

These are activities that facilitate the noticing of chunks. An example is the use of corpora, a resource that is particularly useful in revealing collocation restrictions. An example of the kinds of displays that appear in text materials and in the concordancing displays from which the printout materials derive is illustrated below. The difference between how the vocabulary items "predict" and "forecast" are used and how they collocate is not easy to explain. However, access to these items in context in the computer corpus allows students (and their teachers) to see how these words actually behave in authentic texts.

SOME CONTEXTS OF *PREDICT*

1.	... in copper binding. Our findings *predict* that the results will show ...
2.	... the stratosphere. The present models *predict* that a warming of the winter polar ...
3.	... after an analysis of the DNA, we are able to *predict* the complete amino ...
4.	... this survey data is then used to *predict* values on the vertical profile; ...
5.	... the natural order hypothesis would *predict* an increase in frequency of use, ...

SOME CONTEXTS OF *FORECAST*

1.	... a second analysis. The center makes *forecasts* seven days ahead for all regions ...
2.	... action whose success depends on a *forecast* being accurate. They might end ...
3.	... the difficulties of attempting to *forecast* Britain's economic performance ...
4.	... labor of its people. This gloomy *forecast* can be better explained if ...
5.	... But three months earlier the detailed *forecast* published by the Treasury ...

Many different kinds of corpora are available and O'Keefe et al. (2007) give detailed information on how teachers can create and use their own corpora, such as through the use of free online corpus tools that show how language is used in real situations. Another application of corpora that is relevant to the study of chunks is known as data-driven learning, which O'Keefe et al. (2007: 24) describe as directive activities "where learners get hands-on experience of using a corpus through guided tasks or through materials based on corpus evidence ... an inductive approach [that] relies on an ability to see patterning in the target language and to form generalisations about language form and use." In other words, teachers may ask students to do online corpus searches of the target item directly, or may provide handouts showing the results of a search.

Training in text chunking

Chunking exercises seek to raise awareness of chunks and how they operate. Boers and Lindstromberg (2009: 89) describe an activity as follows:

> This involves asking students to highlight or underline word strings in an authentic text that they consider to be multiword units (e.g., strong collocations). Their selections are subsequently compared to those of peers or checked against the teacher's selection. Alternatively, dictionaries or online sources (e.g., concordance tools or search engines such as Google) can be accessed to in order to verify the chunk status of selected word strings.

Memory-enhancing activities

One type of memory-enhancing activity is what Boers and Lindstromberg (2009) have termed *elaboration*. They give this account of elaboration (2009: 35).

> This is an umbrella term for diverse mental operations, beyond mere noticing, that a learner may perform with regard to the meaning and/or the form of words and phrases.

Elaboration can, for instance, consist in thinking about a term's spelling, pronunciation, grammatical category, meaning, and associations with other words as well as thinking which involves the formation of visual and motoric images related to the meaning of the term. The more of these dimensions that are involved, the more likely it is that the term will be entrenched in long-term memory.

Retelling

After studying a text with a particular focus on the chunks that appear in it, students take part in retelling activities, where they summarize or retell what they have read but attempt to use the same chunks that appeared in the text.

Teacher roles

Teachers have several roles in the Lexical Approach. The teacher is assumed to be a language analyst, capable of recognizing multi-word units in texts, able to assess which ones are important enough to justify sustained attention in class, and able to use texts in such a way as to exploit their potential for the learning of chunks. The teacher may be expected to be familiar with the use of computer software and corpora and to use data-driven learning activities as the basis for both deductive and inductive learning. Lewis (1993) supports Krashen's Natural Approach procedures (Chapter 14) and suggests that teacher talk is a major source of learner input in demonstrating how lexical phrases are used for different functional purposes. Willis (1990) proposes that teachers need to understand and manage a classroom methodology based on stages composed of Task, Planning, and Report, the task cycle recommended for Task-Based Language Teaching (Chapter 9). In general terms, Willis views the teacher's role as one of creating an environment in which learners can operate effectively and then helping learners manage their own learning, particularly in respect to lexicality. This requires that teachers "abandon the idea of the teacher as 'knower' and concentrate instead on the idea of the learner as 'discoverer'" (Willis 1990: 131).

Learner roles

Learners assume an active role in chunk-based approaches to learning. As language analysts they may be expected to work with computers to analyze text data previously collected or made available "free-form" on the Internet. Here the learner assumes the role of data analyst constructing his or her own linguistic generalizations based on examination of large corpora of language samples taken from "real life." In such schemes, teachers have a major responsibility for organizing the technological system and providing scaffolding to help learners build autonomy in use of the system. The most popular computer-based applications using corpora are built on the presentation of what are known as *concordance lines* (see p. 221), where the target word, structure, or chunk appears in the middle of a line of text, with the remaining text showing the context in which the item has been used. These lines of text are generated by a computer program, or concordancer, explained in more detail below. However, learners need training in how to use the concordancer effectively.

Teaching assistance will be necessary to lead the learner, by example, through the different stages of lexical analysis such as observation, classification, and generalization.

Learners are also encouraged to monitor their own learning of chunks and to review chunks they have encountered – for example, through the use of a vocabulary notebook or electronic journal – as a way of helping remember them.

The role of instructional materials

Materials and teaching resources to support lexical approaches in language teaching include (a) coursebooks that include a focus on multi-word units in the syllabus, such as the *Touchstone* series; (b) corpus-informed materials such as McCarthy and O'Dell (2004); (c) corpora that can be accessed by teachers and students in which a corpus of texts can be used with concordancing software to explore how words and multi-word units are used. As described by Allan (2008: 23):

> The learner inputs the target word or words into the software and all examples from the corpus are returned, usually in a keyword in context (KWIC) format, with the target word in the middle of the line. These lines can be sorted in a variety of ways that may help to reveal patterns in meaning and usage … Learners then interact with the concordance and find answers to their questions about the target words by looking for patterns in it, categorizing them and deriving their own hypotheses, rather than relying on a teacher's intuition or research.

An example of a useful corpus is the Bank of English, which forms part of the Collins Corpus – a 650 million word corpus used in the preparation of the COBUILD dictionaries. However, despite the pleas from advocates of a lexically based approach for a greater use of corpus-based lexus in coursebooks, this appeal is influencing the design of certain coursebooks, but not others. Burton (2012: 98) observes:

> The reason why many course books do not currently make much reference to corpus findings is simply that the students who buy the books – or perhaps more likely the teachers, school administrators and policy makers who instruct students to buy the books, or buy them on their behalf – do not demand it, and there is, therefore, no motivation for publishers to innovate in this way. This remains true even though in many ways the use of corpus data would perhaps be one of the simplest innovations that could be envisaged course book production, as many findings do not necessitate fundamentally new pedagogical approaches, but, simply, modified descriptions and presentations of language – arguably closer to the "minimally evolutionary" rather than "revolutionary" noted by Littlejohn (1992: 206). I have also seen little evidence to suggest that corpus-based or corpus-informed coursebooks will emerge, despite a lack of demand, in the way that corpus-based dictionaries did in the 1980s.

Some corpus-informed coursebooks (a modified approach, where the raw corpus-based data is simplified to be accessible to students) have emerged, but as the process of doing extensive corpus searches and analyzing the data can be time consuming, it is unclear to what extent the practice will extend beyond coursebooks intended for very large numbers of students.

Procedure

Procedural sequences for lexically based language teaching reflect whether the focus is on awareness raising or remembering multi-word units for later use, in other words, the classic distinction between reception and production. Boers and Lindstromberg (2009: 19), drawing on Lewis (1997), summarize the current status of classroom procedures with the Lexical Approach:

> The LA [Lexical Approach] in its present form proposes classroom activities and exercises that raise learners' awareness of the importance of chunks. The central strategy is pedagogical chunking; its essence is the encouragement of learners to notice chunks. That is, students should first of all be alerted to lexical phrases encountered in authentic texts and then encouraged to make records of these chunks in vocabulary notebooks adapted to accommodate this kind of lexis. Lewis recognizes that the quantity of lexical phrases that qualify as good targets for learning far exceeds what can be acquired on a normal, non-intensive language course. His advice is to help students develop strategies for the recognition and recording of chunks in samples of L2 they encounter not just in the classroom, but outside it too. In more detail, his recommendation is to expose students to substantial quantities of listening and reading materials in the classroom, make them conscious of the chunks that occur in these materials by helping them "chunk" texts "correctly," that is, notice the authentic chunks they contain.

With these activities the learner must take on the role of "discourse analyst," with the discourse being either packaged data (delivered by the teacher for lower-level learners) or data "found" via one of the text search computer programs (in higher-level classes). Classroom procedures typically involve the use of activities that draw students' attention to lexical collocations (as mentioned, one of the major categories of chunks) and seek to enhance their retention and use of collocations. Woolard (2000) suggests that teachers should reexamine their coursebooks for collocations, adding exercises that focus explicitly on lexical phrases. They should also develop activities that enable learners to discover collocations themselves, both in the classroom and in the language they encounter outside of the classroom. Woolard (2000: 35) comments:

> The learning of collocations is one aspect of language development which is ideally suited to independent language learning. In a very real sense, we can teach students to teach themselves. Collocation is mostly a matter of noticing and recording, and trained students should be able to explore texts for themselves. Not only should they notice common collocations in the texts they meet, but more importantly, they should select those collocations which are crucial to their particular needs.

Hill (2000) suggests that classroom procedures involve (a) teaching individual collocations, (b) making students aware of collocation, (c) extending what students already know by adding knowledge of collocation restrictions to known vocabulary, and (d) storing collocations through encouraging students to keep a lexical notebook.

Little of the classroom practice Lewis (1997) proposes goes beyond variants of matching and gap-filling exercises, however. Neither does he suggest ways of helping students remember the chunks they have been exposed to. Nonetheless, in recent years extensive research into the learning of vocabulary, mainly focusing on repeated exposure, has helped teachers develop suitable activities for the learning of chunks.

Conclusion

The status of lexis in language teaching has been considerably enhanced by developments in lexical and linguistic theory, by work in corpus analysis, and by recognition of the role of multi-word units in language learning and communication. However, lexis still refers to only one component of communicative competence. Lewis and others have coined the term *lexical approach* to characterize their proposals for a lexis-based approach to language teaching, and this chapter has examined what is meant by that term. However, such proposals lack the full characterization of an approach or method as described in this book. Since Lewis's original proposal for a lexical approach and a lexically based syllabus as an alternative to more traditional syllabus models, the concept has not been further developed to show how linguistic competence could develop only through the grammaticalization of lexus, as opposed to presenting a lexical approach as a valid, but single, component of a broader language syllabus. Nor do activity types and teaching procedures advocated for use with lexus lead further in this direction. Rather than a broadening of the scope of a lexical approach since its conception, subsequent years have seen a narrowing of its application, limiting it largely to techniques for developing an awareness of the nature of chunks. While a focus on multi-word units or chunks is doubtless an important dimension of second language learning and of communicative performance, little has been done to show how such a focus can be used to develop either linguistic or communicative competence. Hence, it remains to be convincingly demonstrated how a lexically based theory of language and language learning can be applied at the levels of design and procedure in language teaching, suggesting that it is still an idea in search of an approach and a methodology. Nevertheless, the Lexical Approach, as described in this chapter, may be merged effectively with other approaches, such as Communicative Language Teaching, and an understanding of how chunks are learned has been facilitated by the advent of corpora.

Discussion questions

1. When teaching greetings, what would be some examples of "chunks" that would be helpful?

2. In the terminology of this chapter, explain why the following two sentences don't "work":
   Sorry I am late, I had to make my hair.
   Your room is a mess, go and do your bed.

3. Match the following terms with the examples. (Review other examples of these terms on p. 216, as necessary.)

binomials	Lovely to see you again.
trinomials	tall as a mountain
idioms	in summary,
similes	For crying out loud!
connectives	Blood is thicker than water.
social-routine formulae	a piece of cake
discourse markers	fast forward
compounds	ready, willing and able
proverbs	having said that,
exclamations	cheap and cheerful

4. Using the above as examples, explain to a colleague the role of chunks in language use and language acquisition.

5. Learning of chunks involves (a) noticing, (b) cognitive processing, and (c) exposure. Give examples of how teachers can facilitate chunk learning at all these three levels.

6. Do you think the Lexical Approach can be useful when you are designing a syllabus? A colleague says she read somewhere that the Lexical Approach is a "retrospective syllabus." Explain to her what this means. Do you agree?

7. During class you tell students to look up words using a concordancer and identify the different ways and contexts in which they can be used. After class a student comes to you and says he doesn't see the point: it is time-consuming and it would better if you just explained the vocabulary. How would you respond?

8. The selection of the language in many textbooks is done based on the authors' intuition. Corpora can give more accurate information in terms of the frequency and distribution of specific language, as used by native speakers. Let's investigate the extent to which the language in your textbook matches that used by L1 speakers. Take one lesson from a textbook, preferably at intermediate level. Select a longer text from this lesson. Next you will follow steps to analyze this language using several free, online corpus tools:

   1) Copy and paste the text into the corpus tool, Vocabulary Profilers, part of the website for Compleat Lexical Tutor, a search engine developed by the University of Quebec (http://www.lextutor.ca/vp/eng/) to get insight into the distribution of the vocabulary in the text. How many of the words are in the first 1,000, second 1,000 or academic word lists? Do you think this is reasonable for the target students?
   2) Next, copy the same text into the frequency section of Compleat Lexical Tutor (http://www.lextutor.ca/freq/). What is the distribution of the vocabulary in your text?
   3) Next, identify three lexical phrases from the text and type these into the British National Corpus website, a 100-million-word collection of samples of modern British English, at http://www.natcorp.ox.ac.uk.

4) Now also select one binomial, one simile, and one connective and do the same.

5) How are these words most commonly used in the corpus? Is this different to the way the words are used in the textbook? If so, can you think of reasons why this might be?

9. There is a close connection between lexis and grammar. Take a random unit from a course you are familiar with and identify three new words introduced in that unit.

1) Copy every word in to one of the free corpora available online, mentioned earlier (such as the British National Corpus at http://www.natcorp.ox.ac.uk). How are the words most commonly used? For example, what prepositions do they take? Are they normally used in present or past tense? Plural or singular? Which words commonly precede or follow them?

2) Having identified the most common usages, can you identify any "chunks" of language that it would be useful to present to students?

References and further reading

Allan, R. 2008. Can a graded reader corpus provide "authentic" input? *ELT Journal* 63(1): 23–32.

Bahns, J. 1993. Lexical collocations: a contrastive view. *ELT Journal* 7(1): 56–63.

Boers, F., and S. Lindstromberg. 2005. Finding ways to make phrase-learning feasible: the mnemonic effect of alliteration. *System* 33: 225–38.

Boers, F., and S. Lindstromberg. 2008a. Structural elaboration by the sound (and feel) of it. In F. Boers and S. Lindstromberg (eds.), *Cognitive Linguistic Approaches to Teaching Vocabulary and Phraseology*. Berlin and New York: Mouton de Gruyter. 330–53.

Boers, F., and S. Lindstromberg. 2008b. From empirical findings to pedagogical Practice. In F. Boers and S. Lindstromberg (eds.), *Cognitive Linguistic Approaches to Teaching Vocabulary and Phraseology*. Berlin and New York: Mouton de Gruyter. 375–93.

Boers, F., and S. Lindstromberg. 2008c. How cognitive linguistics can foster effective vocabulary teaching. In F. Boers and S. Lindstromberg (eds.), *Cognitive Linguistic Approaches to Teaching Vocabulary and Phraseology*. Berlin and New York: Mouton de Gruyter. 1–61.

Boers, F., and S. Lindstromberg. 2009. *Optimizing a Lexical Approach to Instructed Second Language Acquisition*. Basingstoke, UK: Palgrave Macmillan.

Boers, F., and S. Lindstromberg. 2012. Experimental and intervention studies on formulaic sequences in a second language. *Annual Review of Applied Linguistics* 32: 83–110.

Boers, F., J. Eyckmans, J. Kappel, H. Stengers, and M. Demecheleer. 2006. Formulaic sequences and perceived oral proficiency: putting a lexical approach to the test. *Language Teaching Research* 10: 245–61.

Bogaards, P., and B. Laufer-Dvorkin. 2004. *Vocabulary in a Second Language: Selection, Acquisition, and Testing*. Amsterdam: John Benjamins.

British National Corpus. 2010. http://www.natcorp.ox.ac.uk; accessed May 9, 2013.

Burton, G. 2012. Corpora and coursebooks: destined to be strangers forever? *Corpora* 7(1): 69–90.

Compleat Lexical Tutor. University of Quebec. http://www.lextutor.ca/vp/eng/; accessed May 9, 2013.

De Knop, S., F. Boers, and A. De Rycker. 2010. *Fostering Language Teaching Efficiency through Cognitive Linguistics*. Berlin: Mouton de Gruyter.

Ellis, N. C., R. Simpson-Vlach, and C. Maynard. 2008. Formulaic language in native and second language speakers: psycholinguistics, corpus linguistics, and TESOL. *TESOL Quarterly* 42: 375–96.

Hill, J. 2000. Revising priorities: from grammatical failure to collocational success. In Lewis (ed.), 47–69.

Lewis, M. 1993. *The Lexical Approach*. London: Language Teaching Publications.

Lewis, M. 1997. *Implementing the Lexical Approach*. London: Language Teaching Publications.

Lewis, M. (ed.). 2000a. *Teaching Collocation: Further Developments in the Lexical Approach*. London: Language Teaching Publications.

Lewis, M. 2000b. Learning in the lexical approach. In Lewis (ed.), 155–84.

Lewis, M. 2000c. There is nothing as practical as a good theory. In Lewis (ed.), 10–27.

Lindstromberg, S., and F. Boers. 2008. *Teaching Chunks of Language: From Noticing to Remembering*. Innsbruck: Helbling Languages.

McCarthy, M. J., and F. O'Dell. 2004. *English Phrasal Verbs in Use: Intermediate Level*. Cambridge: Cambridge University Press.

McCarthy, M. J., J. McCarten, and H. Sandiford, H. 2005. *Touchstone: Student's Book 1*. Cambridge: Cambridge University Press.

Meara, P. 2009. *Connected Words: Word Associations and Second Language Vocabulary Acquisition*. Amsterdam: John Benjamins.

Milton, J. 2011. *Measuring Second Language Vocabulary Acquisition*. Bristol: Channel View Publications.

Nation, I. S. P. 1999. *Learning Vocabulary in Another Language*. New York: Cambridge University Press.

Nation, I. S. P. 2013. *Learning Vocabulary in a Second Language*. 2nd edn. Cambridge: Cambridge University Press.

Nattinger, J. 1980. A lexical phrase grammar for ESL. *TESOL Quarterly* 14: 337–44.

Nattinger, J., and J. DeCarrico. 1992. *Lexical Phrases and Language Teaching*. Oxford: Oxford University Press.

O'Keefe, A., M. McCarthy, and R. Carter. 2007. *From Corpus to Classroom*. Cambridge: Cambridge University Press.

Palmer, H. E. [1925] 1999. Conversation. Repr. in R. C. Smith (ed.), *The Writings of Harold E. Palmer*. Tokyo: Hon-no-Tomosha. 185–91.

Pawley, A., and F. Syder. 1983. Two puzzles for linguistic theory: native-like selection and native-like fluency. In J. Richards and R. Schmidt (eds.), *Language and Communication*. London: Longman. 191–226.

Peters, A. 1983. *The Units of Language Acquisition*. Cambridge: Cambridge University Press.

Phillips, M. 1989. *Lexical Structure of Text*. Discourse Analysis Monograph No. 12. Birmingham: University of Birmingham.

Schmitt, N. (ed.). 2004. *Formulaic Sequences: Acquisition, Processing and Use*. Amsterdam: John Benjamins.

Schmitt, N. 2008. Instructed second language vocabulary learning. *Language Teaching Research* 12(3): 329–63.

Schmitt, N. n.d. *Lexical Approach: A Very Brief Overview*. Available at: http://www.esoluk.co.uk/calling/pdf/Lexical_approach.pdf; accessed May 28, 2013.

Shin, D., and P. Nation. 2008. Beyond single words: the most frequent collocations in spoken English. *ELT Journal* 62: 339–48.

Siyanova, A., and N. Schmitt. 2007. Native and nonnative use of multiword versus one-word verbs. *International Review of Applied Linguistics in Language Teaching* 45(2): 119–39.

Stengers, H. 2007. Is English exceptionally idiomatic? Testing the waters for a lexical approach to Spanish. In F. Boers, J. Darquennes, and R. Temmerman (eds.), *Multilingualism and Applied Comparative Linguistics*, Vol. I: *Pedagogical Perspectives*. Cambridge: Cambridge Scholars Publishing. 107–25.

Stengers H., F. Boers, A, Housen, and J. Eyckman. 2010. Does chunking foster chunk uptake? In De Knop et al. 99–120.

West, M. 1953. *A General Service List of English Words*. London: Longman.

Willis, J. D. 1990. *The Lexical Syllabus*. London: Collins COBUILD.

Willis, J. D., and D. Willis. 1989. *Collins COBUILD English Course*. London: Collins.

Wood, M. 1981. *A Definition of Idiom*. Manchester, UK: Centre for Computational Linguistics, University of Manchester.

Woolard, G. 2000. Collocation-encouraging learner independence. In M. Lewis (ed.), *Teaching Collocation: Further Developments in the Lexical Approach*. London: Language Teaching Publications. 28–46.

Wray, A. 2002. *Formulaic Language and the Lexicon*. Cambridge: Cambridge University Press.

Wray, A. 2008. *Formulaic Language: Pushing the Boundaries*. Oxford: Oxford University Press.

12 Multiple Intelligences

Introduction

A feature of language learning classrooms is the diversity of learners who are often studying in the same class. Diversity refers to the many ways in which learners may differ from one another. They may differ in their motivations for learning English, their beliefs about how best to learn a language, the kinds of strategies they favor, and their preference for different kinds of teaching methods and classroom activities. Language teaching has often been based on the assumption that "one size fits all," and some of the teaching approaches and methods described in this book reflect this view of learners. The learner's role in learning has been predetermined and planned in advance, and the learner's role is to adapt him- or herself to the method. Such is the case with methods such as the Silent Way (Chapter 16) and Suggestopedia (Chapter 18). More recent approaches to language teaching seek to acknowledge the differences learners bring to learning. Learners are viewed as possessing individual learning styles, preferences, and strategies, and these influence how they approach classroom learning and the kinds of learning activities they favor or learn most effectively from. Pedagogy is hence assumed to be more successful when these learner differences are acknowledged, analyzed for particular groups of learners, and accommodated in teaching. In both general education and language teaching, a focus on individual differences has been a recurring theme in the last 40 years or so, as seen in such movements or approaches as individualized instruction, autonomous learning, learner training, and learner strategies (see Chapter 19). The theory of Multiple Intelligences shares a number of commonalities with these earlier proposals.

Multiple Intelligences (MI) refers to a learner-based philosophy that characterizes human intelligence as having multiple dimensions that must be acknowledged and developed in education. Traditional intelligence or IQ (Intelligence Quotient) tests are based on a test called the Stanford–Binet, founded on the idea that intelligence is a single, unchanged, inborn capacity. However, traditional IQ tests, while still given to most schoolchildren, are increasingly being challenged by the MI movement. MI is based on the work of Howard Gardner of the Harvard Graduate School of Education (Gardner 1993). Gardner notes that traditional IQ tests measure only logic and language, yet the brain has other equally important types of intelligence. Gardner argues that all humans have these intelligences, but people differ in the strengths and combinations of intelligences. He believes that all of them can be enhanced through training and practice. MI thus belongs to a group of instructional perspectives that focus on differences between learners and the need to recognize learner differences in teaching.

Gardner (1993) proposed a view of natural human talents that is labeled the "Multiple Intelligences Model." This model is one of a variety of learning style models that have been proposed in general education and have subsequently been applied to language teaching (see, e.g., Christison 1998; Palmberg 2011). (Gardner himself was not convinced that his theory had any application to language teaching – Gardner 2006.) Gardner claims that his view of intelligence(s) is culture-free and avoids the conceptual narrowness usually associated with traditional models of intelligence (e.g., the Intelligent Quotient [IQ] testing model). Gardner originally posited eight native "intelligences," which are described as follows:

1. *Linguistic*: the ability to use language in special and creative ways, which is something lawyers, writers, editors, and interpreters are strong in.
2. *Logical/mathematical*: the ability to think rationally, often found with doctors, engineers, programmers, and scientists.
3. *Spatial*: the ability to form mental models of the world, something architects, decorators, sculptors, and painters are good at.
4. *Musical*: having a good ear for music, as is strong in singers and composers.
5. *Bodily/kinesthetic*: having a well-coordinated body, something found in athletes and craftspersons.
6. *Interpersonal*: the ability to be able to work well with people, which is strong in salespeople, politicians, and teachers.
7. *Intrapersonal*: the ability to understand oneself and apply one's talent successfully, which leads to happy and well-adjusted people in all areas of life.
8. *Naturalist*: the ability to understand and organize the patterns of nature.

He later suggested a ninth intelligence – existential intelligence – "a concern with philosophical issues such as the status of mankind in relation to universal existence. In learning situations, the need to see 'the big picture' in order to understand minor learning points and details" (Palmberg 2011: 8). Armstrong (1999) introduced the following convenient memory tags for each intelligence:

- *Linguistic intelligence*: "word smart"
- *Logical/mathematical intelligence*: "number/reasoning smart"
- *Visual/spatial intelligence*: "picture smart"
- *Bodily/kinesthetic intelligence*: "body smart"
- *Musical intelligence*: "music smart"
- *Interpersonal intelligence*: "people smart"
- *Intrapersonal intelligence*: "self smart"
- *Naturalist intelligence*: "nature smart"
- *Existentialist intelligence*: "existence smart"

All learners are believed to have personal intelligence profiles – so-called "MI profiles" – that consist of combinations of different intelligence types and for some intelligences to be more highly developed than others, hence favoring a particular approach to learning.

Christison (2005) suggested that most people are believed to have a few intelligences that are highly developed, most modestly developed, and one or two underdeveloped. Several checklists have been developed to enable people to "identify" their personal MI profile, such as McKenzie's "Multiple Intelligences Survey" (1999), which requires potential test-takers to tick statements they agree with out of a total of 90 statements which are grouped into nine sections (ten statements for each section), each representing one of Gardner's nine intelligence types. Skeptics might question the reliability of such a crude measure of these complex qualities of human cognition.

When it was first proposed, the idea of Multiple Intelligences attracted the interest of many educators as well as the general public. Schools began to use MI theory to encourage learning that goes beyond traditional books, pens, and pencils. Teachers and parents were encouraged to recognize their learners'/children's particular gifts and talents and to provide learning activities that build on those inherent gifts. As a result of strengthening such differences, individuals would be free to be intelligent in their own ways.

Approach

Theory of language

MI theory was originally proposed by Gardner (1993) as a contribution to cognitive science. Fairly early on, it was interpreted by some general educators, such as Armstrong (1994), as a framework for rethinking school education. Some schools in the United States have indeed remade their educational programs around the MI model. Applications of MI in language teaching have been more recent, so it is not surprising that MI theory lacks some of the basic elements that might link it more directly to language education. One issue is the lack of a concrete view of how MI theory relates to any existing language and/or language learning theories, though attempts have been made to establish such links (e.g., Reid 1997; Christison 1998). It certainly is fair to say that MI proposals look at the language of an individual, including one or more second languages, not as an "added on" and somewhat peripheral skill but as central to the whole life of the language learner and user. In this sense, language is held to be integrated with music, bodily activity, interpersonal relationships, and so on. Language is not seen as limited to a "linguistics" perspective but encompasses all aspects of communication.

Theory of learning

Language learning and use are obviously closely linked to what MI theorists label "Linguistic Intelligence." However, MI proponents believe there is more to language than what is usually subsumed under the rubric linguistics. There are aspects of language such as rhythm, tone, volume, and pitch that are more closely linked, say, to a theory of music than to a theory of linguistics. Other intelligences enrich the tapestry of communication we call "language." In addition, language has its ties to life through the senses. The senses provide the accompaniment and context for the linguistic message that give it meaning and purpose. A multisensory view of language is necessary, it seems, to construct an adequate theory of language as well as an effective design for language learning. Therefore, the theory of learning might be termed holistic, since we learn through all of our senses.

A widely accepted, but divergent, view of intelligence is that intelligence – however measured and in whatever circumstance – comprises a single factor, usually called the "g" factor. From this point of view, "Intelligence (g) can be described as the ability to deal with cognitive complexity ... The vast majority of intelligence researchers take these findings for granted" (Gottfredson 1998: 24). One popular explication of this view sees intelligence as a hierarchy with g at the apex of the hierarchy:

> More specific aptitudes are arrayed at successively lower levels: the so-called group factors, such as verbal ability, mathematical reasoning, spatial visualization and memory, are just below g, and below these are skills that are more dependent on knowledge or experience, such as the principles and practices of a particular job or profession.
>
> (Gottfredson 1998: 3)

The view of Gardner (and some other cognitive scientists) "contrasts markedly with the view that intelligence is based on a unitary or 'general' ability for problem solving" (Teele 2000: 27). In the Gardner view, there exists a cluster of mental abilities that are separate but equal and that share the pinnacle at the top of the hierarchy called intelligence – thus, the eight Multiple Intelligences that Gardner has described. One way of looking at the learning theoretical argument is to apply the logic of the single factor (g) model to the Multiple Intelligences model. The single factor model correlates higher intelligence (+g) with greater speed and efficiency of neural processing; that is, the higher the g factor in the individual, the greater the speed and efficiency of that individual's brain in performing cognitive operations (Gottfredson 1998: 3). If there is not just one I (that is, not one "intelligence") but several I's, then one can assume that the speed and efficiency of neural processing will be greatest when a particular I is most fully exercised; that is, if a language learner has a high musical intelligence, that person will learn most quickly (e.g., a new language) when that content is embedded in a musical frame.

Palmberg (2011: 17) describes the influence of particular intelligences on language learning – an account that seems to identify differences in intelligences as differences in learning styles (see Chapter 19):

> Depending on their personal MI profiles, people tend to develop their own favorite way (or ways) of learning foreign languages. For vocabulary learning, for example, some prefer traditional rote learning. Others divide the foreign words into parts or components and concentrate on memorizing these instead. Some look for similarities between the foreign-language words and grammatical structures and the corresponding words and structures in their mother tongue or other languages they may know. Some people find mnemonic devices helpful, at least occasionally. Others have adopted accelerated learning techniques and use them on a more or less permanent basis.

Design

Objectives

There are no goals stated for MI instruction in linguistic terms. MI pedagogy focuses on the language class as the setting for a series of educational support systems aimed at making the language learner a better designer of his or her own learning experiences. Such a learner is both better empowered and more fulfilled than a learner in traditional classrooms. A more goal-directed learner and happier person is held to be a likely candidate for being a better second language learner and user.

The syllabus

Also, there is no syllabus as such, either prescribed or recommended, in respect to MI-based language teaching, although an MI perspective can combine with virtually any approach or method. However, there is a basic developmental sequence that has been proposed (Lazear 1991) as an alternative to what we have elsewhere considered as a type of "syllabus" design. The sequence consists of four stages:

- *Stage 1*: Awaken the Intelligence. Through multisensory experiences – touching, smelling, tasting, seeing, and so on – learners can be sensitized to the many-faceted properties of objects and events in the world that surrounds them.
- *Stage 2*: Amplify the Intelligence. Students strengthen and improve the intelligence by volunteering objects and events of their own choosing and defining with others the properties and contexts of experience of these objects and events.
- *Stage 3*: Teach with/for the Intelligence. At this stage the intelligence is linked to the focus of the class, that is, to some aspect of language learning. This is done via worksheets and small-group projects and discussion.
- *Stage 4*: Transfer of the Intelligence. Students reflect on the learning experiences of the previous three stages and relate these to issues and challenges in the out-of-class world.

Types of learning and teaching activities

MI has been applied in many different types of classrooms. In some, there are eight self-access activity corners, each corner built around one of the eight or nine intelligences. Students work alone or in pairs on intelligence foci of their own choosing. Nicholson-Nelson (1988: 73) describes how MI can be used to individualize learning through project work. She lists five types of projects:

1. *Multiple intelligence projects.* These are based on one or more of the intelligences and are designed to stimulate particular intelligences.
2. *Curriculum-based projects.* These are based on curriculum content areas but are categorized according to the particular intelligences they make use of.
3. *Thematic-based projects.* These are based on a theme from the curriculum or classroom but are divided into different intelligences.

4. *Resource-based projects.* These are designed to provide students with opportunities to research a topic using multiple intelligences.

5. *Student-choice projects.* These are designed by students and draw on particular intelligences.

In other, more fully teacher-fronted classrooms, the students move through a cycle of activities highlighting use of different intelligences in the activities that the teacher has chosen and orchestrated.

Some suggest that the use of MI profiles enables teachers to select activities that match learners' profiles. For example (Berman 2002):

- *Linguistic intelligence*: word-building games
- *Logical/mathematical intelligence*: logical-sequential presentations
- *Visual/spatial intelligence*: mind maps
- *Bodily/kinesthetic intelligence*: relaxation exercises
- *Musical intelligence*: jazz chants
- *Interpersonal intelligence*: brainstorming
- *Intrapersonal intelligence*: learner diaries
- *Naturalist intelligence*: background music in the form of sounds created in the natural world

Learning activities are often shown or suggested in tables in which a particular intelligence is paired with possible activities useful for working with this intelligence in class. Such a table is reproduced in Table 12.1.

Table 12.1 Taxonomy of language learning activities for Multiple Intelligences (Christison 1997: 7-8)

Linguistic Intelligence	
lectures	student speeches
small- and large-group discussions	storytelling
books	debates
worksheets	journal keeping
word games	memorizing
listening to cassettes or talking books	using word processors
publishing (creating class newspapers or collections of writing)	
Logical/Mathematical Intelligence	
scientific demonstrations	creating codes
logic problems and puzzles	story problems
science thinking	calculations
logical-sequential presentation of subject matter	

(Continued)

Spatial Intelligence

charts, maps, diagrams	visualization
videos, slides, movies	photography
art and other pictures	using mind maps
imaginative storytelling	painting or collage
graphic organizers	optical illusions
telescopes, microscopes	student drawings
visual awareness activities	

Bodily/Kinesthetic Intelligence

creative movement	hands on activities
Mother-may-I?	field trips
cooking and other "mess" activities	mime
role plays	

Musical Intelligence

playing recorded music	singing
playing live music (piano, guitar)	group singing
music appreciation	mood music
student-made instruments	jazz chants

Interpersonal Intelligence

cooperative groups	conflict mediation
peer teaching	board games
group brainstorming	pair work

Intrapersonal Intelligence

independent student work	reflective learning
individualized projects	journal keeping
options for homework	interest centers
inventories and checklists	self-esteem journals
personal journal keeping	goal setting
self-teaching/programmed instruction	

The following list summarizes several alternative views as to how the MI model can be used to serve the needs of language learners within a classroom setting, and may serve as an aid in choosing appropriate learning activities:

- *Play to strength.* If you want an athlete or a musician (or a student having some of these talents) to be an involved and successful language learner, structure the learning material for each individual (or similar group of individuals) around these strengths.
- *Variety is the spice.* Providing a teacher-directed rich mix of learning activities variously calling upon the eight different intelligences makes for an interesting, lively, and effective classroom for all students.
- *Pick a tool to suit the job.* Language has a variety of dimensions, levels, and functions. These different facets of language are best served instructionally by linking their learning to the most appropriate kind of MI activity.

- *All sizes fit one.* Every individual exercises all intelligences even though some of these may be out of awareness or undervalued. Pedagogy that appeals to all the intelligences speaks to the "whole person" in ways that more unifaceted approaches do not. An MI approach helps to develop the Whole Person within each learner, which best serves the person's language learning requirements as well.
- *Me and my people.* IQ testing is held to be badly biased in favor of Western views of intelligence. Other cultures may value other intelligences more than the one measured in IQ testing. Since language learning involves culture learning as well, it is useful for the language learner to study language in a context that recognizes and honors a range of diversely valued intelligences.

Each of these views has strengths and weaknesses, some of a theoretical, some of a pedagogical, and some of a practical nature. It seems that potential MI teachers need to consider each of these possible applications of MI theory in light of their individual teaching situations.

Learner roles

Learners need to see themselves engaged in a process of personality development above and beyond that of being successful language learners. The MI classroom is one designed to support development of the "whole person," and the environment and its activities are intended to enable students to become more well-rounded individuals and more success-ful learners in general. Learners are encouraged to see their goals in these broader terms. Learners are typically expected to take an MI inventory and to develop their own MI pro-files based on the inventory. "The more awareness students have of their own intelligences and how they work, the more they will know how to use that intelligence [*sic*] to access the necessary information and knowledge from a lesson" (Christison 1997: 9). All of this is to enable learners to benefit from instructional approaches by reflecting on their own learning.

Teacher roles

Campbell (1997: 19) notes that MI theory "is not prescriptive. Rather, it gives teachers a complex mental model from which to construct curriculum and improve themselves as educators." In this view, teachers are expected to understand, master, and be committed to the MI model. Teachers are encouraged to administer an MI inventory on themselves and thereby be able to "connect your life's experiences to your concept of Multiple Intelligences" (Christison 1997: 7). Teachers then become curriculum developers, lesson designers and analysts, activity finders or inventors, and, most critically, orchestrators of a rich array of multisensory activities within the realistic constraints of time, space, and resources of the classroom. Teachers are encouraged not to think of themselves merely as language teachers. They have a role that is not only to improve the second language abilities of their students but also to become major "contributors to the overall development of students' intelli-gences" (Christison 1999: 12).

The role of instructional materials

Where MI is richest is in proposals for lesson organization, multisensory activity planning, and in using realia. There are also now a number of reports of actual teaching experiences from an MI perspective that are both teacher-friendly and candid in their reportage. Activities and the materials that support them resemble the taxonomy from Christison shown in Table 12.1 above. Because MI requires significant creativity on the part of the teacher, it may not always be possible to find appropriate activities in published materials. Thus, one of the challenges of MI is extensive planning and the time necessary to prepare appropriate classroom activities.

Procedure

MI-based lessons may vary a great deal, but several examples are offered of how one might be prepared. Palmberg (2011: 29) describes the following procedures that can be used:

> Assume that you are going to teach a given topic to a group of foreign-language learners. Select the topic to be taught (such as shopping, at the zoo, flowers, etc.) and make sure that you have a specific learner group in mind (for example beginners, intermediate-level learners, or advanced learners). Write down the topic on a large sheet of paper and draw a circle around it. If possible, set up detailed teaching goals. Make notes of all tasks, texts, exercises, visual aids, classroom activities, and songs that relate to the given topic (and teaching goals) that you come to think of. It does not matter at this stage whether some of them appear unrealistic or impractical.

> Arrange your ideas according to the intelligence type that, in your opinion, each task, text, exercise, visual aid, classroom activity, song, etc. will be most suitable for. If you are a visual-spatial person, you may want to draw nine new circles around the central circle and draw lines from the central circle to each of the new circles. Label the new circles according to each intelligence, and write down each task, text, exercise, visual aid, classroom activity, and song into the appropriate circles;

> If you feel that you have no more fresh ideas, read through the very practical teaching suggestions listed on the Literacyworks® website "Multiple Intelligences for Adult Literacy and Education" for the various intelligences [http://www.literacyworks.org/mi/intro/about.html]. Make notes of the ones that appeal to you and might fit into your lesson. After a while, take an overall look at your sheet of paper. Are there any activities that can be combined? Are there activities that can be modified to fulfil the teaching goals more efficiently? Are there activities that do not seem at all suitable for the present purpose?

> To wrap things up, arrange, and, if needed, rearrange the (remaining) ideas and activities into a lesson outline that is logical and fulfils the teaching goals of the proposed lesson. Make sure that your lesson caters for all of the nine multiple intelligences.

Christison (1997: 6) describes a low-level language lesson dealing with description of physical objects. As explained below, the lesson plan recapitulates the sequence described earlier in the "syllabus" section. This particular lesson is seen as giving students opportunities to "develop their linguistic intelligence (for example, describing objects), logical intelligence (for example, determining which object is being described), visual/spatial intelligence (for example, determining how to describe things), interpersonal intelligence (for example, working in groups), and intrapersonal intelligence (for example, reflecting on one's own involvement in the lesson)."

- *Stage 1*: Awaken the Intelligence. The teacher brings many different objects to class. Students experience feeling things that are soft, rough, cold, smooth, and so on. They might taste things that are sweet, salty, sour, spicy, and so on. Experiences like this help activate and make learners aware of the sensory bases of experience.
- *Stage 2*: Amplify the Intelligence. Students are asked to bring objects to class or to use something in their possession. Teams of students describe each object attending to the five physical senses. They complete a worksheet including the information they have observed and discussed (Table 12.2).
- *Stage 3*: Teach with/for the Intelligence. At this stage, the teacher structures larger sections of lesson(s) so as to reinforce and emphasize sensory experiences and the language that accompanies these experiences. Students work in groups, perhaps completing a worksheet such as that shown in Table 12.3.
- *Stage 4*: Transfer of the Intelligence. This stage is concerned with application of the intelligence to daily living. Students are asked to reflect on both the content of the lesson and its operational procedures (working in groups, completing tables, etc.).

Table 12.2 The sensory handout (Christison 1997: 10)

Name of team _____

Team members _____

Sight _____

Sound _____

Feel _____

Smell _____

Size _____

What it's used for _____

Name of the object _____

Table 12.3 Multiple Intelligences description exercise (Christison 1997: 10–12)

> *What am I describing?*
> Directions: Work with your group. Listen as the teacher reads the description of the object. Discuss what you hear with your group. Together, decide which object in the class is being described.

Name of the object

Object 1 _____

Object 2 _____

Object 3 _____

Object 4 _____

Object 5 _____

Next have each group describe an object in the classroom using the formula given in Stage 2. Then, collect the papers and read them, one at a time. Ask each group to work together to write down the name of the object in the classroom that you are describing.

Conclusion

Multiple Intelligences was one of a number of learner-centered initiatives which attracted considerable interest from educators as well as language teachers when it was first proposed in the early 1990s. It was seen as an approach to characterizing the ways in which learners are unique and to developing instruction to respond to this uniqueness. MI is one of a set of such perspectives dealing with learner differences and borrows heavily from these in its recommendations and designs for lesson planning. It offers a new rationale both for the selection of existing language teaching activities and for the design of activities to reflect particular intelligences in the MI inventory. The literature on MI provides a rich source of classroom ideas regardless of one's theoretical perspective and can help teachers think about instruction in their classes in unique ways. Some teachers may see the assumptions of identifying and responding to the variety of ways in which students differ to be unrealistic in their own settings and antithetical to the expectations of their students and administrators. There have been, however, entire schools as well as language programs that were restructured around the MI perspective. In order to justify the claims of MI in education and in second language teaching, the success of these innovations will need to be more fully evaluated.

Discussion questions

1. Gardner (p. 231) lists eight native intelligences that describe the ways in which learners differ from each other. Rank them in order of importance. Which have the greatest impact on the way students learn in class?

2. Do the same for the impact Gardner's native intelligences have on the teaching in class. Do you feel the MI model is an effective way to address these differences?

3. Look at the four stages (on p. 234) of the basic developmental sequence of a syllabus based on a Multiple Intelligences view of learning. How would this sequence work at a practical level? In other words, when teaching, for example, the past perfect tense, how would you introduce and teach this subject in this sequence? How difficult would these stages be to implement in class?

4. A colleague experienced in using a Multiple Intelligences approach in teaching suggests using the school's self-access center as a way to individualize the learning experience. Consider a specific skill (e.g., reading or listening) and a particular language level. In order to use the self-access center effectively:

   - What kind of preparation would the students need to successfully learn in the center?
   - What kinds of materials would need to be provided?
   - What kinds of activities could be used?
   - What kinds of teacher support might be needed?

   In what other ways does self-access learning (potentially) support individualization of learning?

5. One claim made by proponents of Multiple Intelligences is that "Pedagogy that appeals to all the intelligences speaks to the 'whole person'" (p. 237). Explain to a colleague how this is helpful for learning.

6. Multiple Intelligences emphasizes that traditional views of intelligence (such as measurement of "IQ") are biased towards Western views of education. Can you think of an example of ways in which a non-Western culture you are familiar with might give more weight to one or more intelligences than Western culture? Do you think there are any problems with considering questions of this sort about non-Western cultures?

7. Look again at the taxonomy of activity types for Multiple Intelligences in Table 12.1 on page 235. Which of these do you use in your teaching? Which of those you could you incorporate in your classes?

8. Refer again to Gardner's Multiple Intelligences Model on page 231. This includes the "intelligences" listed in the table below. Using classroom materials you are familiar with, identify, or create, an activity that would allow students to practice each of these, in the context of language learning.

Intelligence	Activity	Contribution to language learning
Linguistic		
Logical/mathematical		
Spatial		

(Continued)

Intelligence	Activity	Contribution to language learning
Musical		
Bodily/kinesthetic		
Interpersonal		
Intrapersonal		
Naturalist		
Existential		

After completing the table, (a) consider to what extent activities like these feature in materials you are familiar with, and (b) consider what contribution having each of these intelligences can make to language learning.

References and further reading

Armstrong, T. 1994. *Multiple Intelligences in the Classroom*. Alexandria, VA: Association for Supervision and Curriculum Development.

Armstrong, T. 1999. *7 Kinds of Smart: Identifying and Developing Your Multiple Intelligences*. New York: Plume Books.

Atkinson, R. C. 1975. Mnemotechniques in second-language learning. *American Psychologist* 30: 821–8.

Berman, M. 2001. *Intelligence Reframed for ELT*. London: Golem Press.

Berman, M. 2002. *A Multiple Intelligences Road to an ELT Classroom*. 2nd edn. Carmarthen: Crown House Publishing.

Berman, M. 2010. *In a Faraway Land*. Ropley, Hampshire: O-Books.

Campbell, L. 1997. How teachers interpret MI theory. *Educational Leadership* 55(1): 15–19.

Christison, M. 1997. An introduction to multiple intelligences theory and second language learning. In J. Reid (ed.), *Understanding Learning Styles in the Second Language Classroom*. Englewood Cliffs, NJ: Prentice Hall/Regents. 1–14.

Christison, M. 1998. Applying multiple intelligences theory in preservice and inservice TEFL education programs. *English Language Teaching Forum* 36(2) (April–June): 2–13.

Christison, M. 1999. Multiple Intelligences: teaching the whole student. *ESL Magazine* 2(5): 10–13.

Christison, M. 2001. *Applying Multiple Intelligences Theory in the Second and Foreign Language Classroom*. Burlingame, CA: Alta Book Center Publishers.

Christison, M. 2005. *Multiple Intelligences and Language Learning: A Guidebook of Theory, Activities, Inventories, and Resources*. San Francisco: Alta Books.

Gardner, H. 1985. *Frames of Mind: The Theory of Multiple Intelligences.* New York: Basic Books.

Gardner, H. 1993. *Multiple Intelligences: The Theory and Practice.* New York: Basic Books.

Gardner, H. 2006. *Multiple Intelligences: New Horizons.* New York: Basic Books.

Gardner, H. 2008. *The 25th Anniversary of the Publication of Howard* Gardner's Frames of Mind: The Theory of Multiple Intelligences. April 2008. Available at: http://pzweb.harvard.edu/pis/MIat25.pdf; accessed March 2012.

Gottfredson, L. 1998. The general intelligence factor. *Scientific American* 9(4) (Winter): 24–9.

Kerr, P. 2009. Should "Multiple Intelligences Theory" play a role in teacher education programmes? *Newsletter of The Teacher Training and Education Special Interest Group, IATEFL* 2.

Lazear, D. 1991. *Seven Ways of Teaching: The Artistry of Teaching with Multiple Intelligences.* Palatine, IL: IRI Skylight.

Marzano, R., R. Brandt, C. Hughes, B. Jones, B. Presseisen, and S. Rankin. 1988. *Dimensions of Thinking: A Framework for Curriculum and Instruction.* Alexandria, VA: Association for Supervision and Curriculum Development.

McKenzie, W. 1999. *Multiple Intelligences Survey.* Available at: http://surfaquarium.com/MI/inventory.htm

McKenzie, W. 2005. *Multiple Intelligences and Instructional Technology.* 2nd edn. Washington, DC: International Society for Technolgy in Education.

Nicholson-Nelson, K. 1988. *Developing Students' Multiple Intelligences.* New York: Scholastic.

Palmberg, R. 2011. *Multiple Intelligences Revisited* [Ebook]. Available at: http://www.esldepot.com/PDF/EnglishClub-Multiple-Intelligences-Revisited.pdf

Reid, J. 1997. *Understanding Learning Styles in the Second Language Classroom.* Englewood Cliffs, NJ: Prentice Hall/Regents.

Teele, S. 2000. *Rainbows of Intelligence: Exploring How Students Learn.* Thousand Oaks, CA: Corwin Press.

Weinreich-Haste, H. 1985. The varieties of intelligence: an interview with Howard Gardner. *New Ideas in Psychology* 3(4): 47–65.

13 Cooperative Language Learning

Introduction

Language teaching is sometimes discussed as if it existed independently of the teaching of other subjects and of trends in teaching generally. However, like teachers in other areas of a school curriculum, language teachers too have to to create a positive environment for learning in the classroom. They have to find ways of engaging students in their lessons, to use learning arrangements that encourage active student participation in lessons, to acknowledge the diversity of motivations and interests learners bring to the classroom, and to use strategies that enable the class to function as a cohesive group that collaborates to help make the lesson a positive learning experience. In dealing with issues such as these, language teachers can learn much from considering approaches that have been used in mainstream education. Cooperative Language Learning (CLL) is one such example. CLL is part of a more general instructional approach, known as Collaborative or Cooperative Learning (CL), which originated in mainstream education and emphasizes peer support and coaching. CL is an approach to teaching that makes maximum use of cooperative activities involving pairs and small groups of learners in the classroom. It has been defined as follows:

> Cooperative learning is group learning activity organized so that learning is dependent on the socially structured exchange of information between learners in groups and in which each learner is held accountable for his or her own learning and is motivated to increase the learning of others.

> (Olsen and Kagan 1992: 8)

Cooperative Learning has antecedents in proposals for peer-tutoring and peer-monitoring that go back hundreds of years and longer. The early-twentieth-century US educator John Dewey is usually credited with promoting the idea of building cooperation in learning into regular classrooms on a regular and systematic basis (Rodgers 1988). It was more generally promoted and developed in the United States in the 1960s and 1970s as a response to the forced integration of public schools and has been substantially refined and developed since then. Educators were concerned that traditional models of classroom learning were teacher-fronted, fostered competition rather than cooperation, and favored majority students. They believed that minority students might fall behind higher-achieving students in this kind of learning environment. CL in this context sought to do the following:

- raise the achievement of all students, including those who are gifted or academically handicapped
- help the teacher build positive relationships among students
- give students the experiences they need for healthy social, psychological, and cognitive development
- replace the competitive organizational structure of most classrooms and schools with a team-based, high-performance organizational structure

(Johnson, Johnson, and Holubec 1994: 2)

In second language teaching, CL (where, as noted above, it is often referred to as Cooperative Language Learning – CLL) has been embraced as a way of promoting communicative interaction in the classroom and is seen as an extension of the principles of Communicative Language Teaching (Chapter 5). It is viewed as a learner-centered approach to teaching that is held to offer advantages over teacher-fronted classroom methods. In language teaching its goals are:

- to provide opportunities for naturalistic second language acquisition through the use of interactive pair and group activities;
- to provide teachers with a methodology to enable them to achieve this goal and one that can be applied in a variety of curriculum settings (e.g., content-based, foreign language classrooms; mainstreaming);
- to enable focused attention to particular lexical items, language structures, and communicative functions through the use of interactive tasks;
- to provide opportunities for learners to develop successful learning and communication strategies;
- to enhance learner motivation and reduce learner stress and to create a positive affective classroom climate.

CLL is thus an approach that crosses both mainstream education and second and foreign language teaching. CLL also seeks to develop learners' critical thinking skills, which are seen as central to learning of any sort. Some authors have even elevated critical thinking to the same level of focus as that of the basic language skills of reading, writing, listening, and speaking (Kagan 1992). One approach to integrating the teaching of critical thinking adopted by CLL advocates is called the *Question Matrix* (Wiederhold 1995). Wiederhold has developed a battery of cooperative activities built on the matrix that encourages learners to ask and respond to a deeper array of alternative question types. Activities of this kind are believed to foster the development of critical thinking. (The matrix is based on the well-known Taxonomy of Educational Objectives devised by Bloom [1956], which assumes a hierarchy of learning objectives ranging from simple recall of information to forming conceptual judgments.) Kagan and other CL theorists have adopted this framework as an underlying learning theory for Cooperative Learning. The word *cooperative* in Cooperative Learning emphasizes another important dimension of CLL: it seeks to develop classrooms that foster cooperation rather than competition in learning. Advocates of CLL in general education stress the benefits of cooperation in promoting learning:

> Cooperation is working together to accomplish shared goals. Within cooperative situations, individuals seek outcomes beneficial to themselves and all other group members. Cooperative learning is the instructional use of small groups through which students work together to maximize their own and each other's learning. It may be contrasted with competitive learning in which students work against each other to achieve an academic goal such as a grade of "A."
>
> (Johnson et al. 1994: 4)

From the perspective of second language teaching, McGroarty (1989) offers six learning advantages for ESL students in CLL classrooms:

1. Increased frequency and variety of second language practice through different types of interaction
2. Possibility for development or use of language in ways that support cognitive development and increased language skills
3. Opportunities to integrate language with Content-Based Instruction
4. Opportunities to include a greater variety of curricular materials to stimulate language as well as concept learning
5. Freedom for teachers to master new professional skills, particularly those emphasizing communication
6. Opportunities for students to act as resources for each other, thus assuming a more active role in their learning.

Approach

Theory of language

Although CLL supports an interactional theory of language, it is not linked directly to any specific theory and is compatible with several theories of language that inform approaches to language teaching.

- *Language is a resource for expressing meaning.* Language is not something that is acquired for its own sake but serves the goal of making meaning. Meaning is often realized through a joint process of collaboration.
- *Language is a means of expressing different communicative functions.* CLL shares with Communicative Language Teaching the notion that communicative competence

depends on the ability to express and understand functions or speech acts, such as those used to express personal, interpersonal, directive, referential, and imaginative meanings. CLL activities can be used to develop fluency in expressing categories of functional meaning.

- *Language is a means of interpersonal and social interaction.* In CLL learners are required to interact through the use of both spoken and written language, and language is the means by which interaction is achieved and develops through the results of such interaction.
- *Language is a resource for carrying out tasks.* The focus of many CLL activities is collaborating to complete different kinds of tasks. Language thus serves to achieve practical goals that relate to the learners' needs.

Theory of learning

Learning theory that supports CLL draws on SLA-related theory as well as sociocultural learning theory (Chapter 2).

Learning results from conversational interaction

This strand of theory is central to some theories of second language acquisition. It is based on the assumption that as learners seek to achieve meaning, they engage in a joint process of negotiation of meaning, during which various communication strategies are used to maintain the flow of communication. These are such things as "repetitions, confirmations, reformulations, comprehension checks, clarification requests etc." (Long 1996: 418), and it is these aspects of conversational interaction that serve as the basis for learning. CLL activities provide an optimal context for negotiation of meaning and hence should be beneficial to second language development. Abdullah and Jacobs (2004) suggest that CL promotes interaction in the following ways:

1. The literature on Cooperative Learning recommends that students who are different from each other according to the variable of proficiency become groupmates. This heterogeneity increases the likelihood that negotiation for meaning will be necessary. Furthermore, teachers often use the variable of second language proficiency when creating heterogeneous groups. This means that more proficient students will be available to facilitate comprehension of their less proficient peers.
2. In Cooperative Learning, teachers can encourage more negotiation for meaning by allowing groups to try to sort out their own communication difficulties without teacher intervention, although teachers do stand ready to help, if, after trying, groups remain deadlocked or confused.
3. Cooperative Learning activities provide a context in which students may be more likely to interact than in a whole class setting.
4. SLA researchers propose that group activities can encourage students to interact with each other in a way that promotes a focus on form ... Such a focus on form can be

encouraged when grammar constitutes at least one aspect of group tasks. Examples of making grammar an aspect of groups' tasks include:

- noticing tasks in which students analyze how a grammar point functions and formulate their own rule;
- peer assessment in which students check each other's writing or speaking for particular grammatical features, for example, in an English L2 class, the presence of plural -*s*.

The teaching of collaborative skills can play a crucial role in promoting peer interaction, because the skills provide students with strategies for effective interaction. Examples include collaborative skills that second language learners can use to repair communication breakdowns, such as asking for repetition, slower speed of speaking, louder volume, and explanation of words. Collaborative skills also prove useful when students understand the input they have received but wish to disagree or ask for further information.

Language learning is a sociocultural process

This theory of learning, derived initially from the work of the Soviet psychologist Vygotsky ([1935] 1978) but elaborated considerably since its original formulation, makes use particularly of the notions of the zone of proximal development (ZPD) and scaffolding (Chapter 2). Scaffolding refers to the assistance a more advanced learner or language user gives to a less advanced learner in completing a task and makes use of collaborative dialogue (Swain 2000: 102) – a form of discourse in which new knowledge or skill is the outcome of interaction. CLL tasks provide extended opportunities for these processes to take place. Abdullah and Jacobs (2004) cite sociocultural learning theory as support for CLL.

CLL overlaps with sociocultural learning theory by attempting to build an environment that fosters mutual aid. As Newman and Holtzman (1993: 77) note: "Vygotsky's strategy was essentially a cooperative learning strategy. He created heterogeneous groups of children (he called them a collective), providing them not only with the opportunity but the need for cooperation and joint activity by giving them tasks that were beyond the development level of some, if not all, of them."

Design

Objectives

Since CLL is an approach designed to foster cooperation rather than competition, to develop critical thinking skills, and to develop communicative competence through socially structured interaction activities, these can be regarded as the overall objectives of CLL. More specific objectives will derive from the context in which CLL is used.

The syllabus

CLL does not assume any particular form of language syllabus, since activities from a wide variety of curriculum orientations can be taught via this approach. Thus, we find CLL used in teaching content classes, ESP, the four skills, grammar, pronunciation, and vocabulary. What defines CLL is the systematic and carefully planned use of group-based procedures in teaching as an alternative to teacher-fronted teaching. A sense of what a whole course design looks like organized around CLL, and the ways in which it promotes a focus on critical and creative thinking, can be found in Jacobs, Lee, and Ball (1995).

Types of learning and teaching activities

Johnson et al. (1994: 4–5) describe three types of CLL groups.

1. *Formal CLL groups.* These last from one class period to several weeks. These are established for a specific task and involve students working together to achieve shared learning goals.
2. *Informal CLL groups.* These are ad-hoc groups that last from a few minutes to a class period and are used to focus student attention or to facilitate learning during direct teaching.
3. *Cooperative base groups.* These are long-term, lasting for at least a year, and consist of heterogeneous learning groups with stable membership whose primary purpose is to allow members to give each other the support, help, encouragement, and assistance they need to succeed academically.

The success of CLL is crucially dependent on the nature and organization of group work. This requires a structured program of learning carefully designed so that learners interact with each other and are motivated to increase each other's learning. Olsen and Kagan (1992) propose the following key elements of successful group-based learning in CL:

- Positive interdependence
- Group formation
- Individual accountability
- Social skills
- Structuring and structures

Positive interdependence occurs when group members feel that what helps one member helps all and what hurts one member hurts all. It is created by the structure of CLL tasks and by building a spirit of mutual support within the group. For example, a group may produce a single product, such as an essay, or the scores for members of a group may be averaged.

Group formation is an important factor in creating positive interdependence. Factors involved in setting up groups include the following:

- Deciding on the size of the group. This will depend on the tasks they have to carry out, the age of the learners, and time limits for the lesson. Typical group size is from two to four.
- Assigning students to groups. Groups can be teacher-selected, random, or student-selected, although teacher-selected is recommended as the usual mode so as to create groups that are heterogeneous on such variables as past achievement, ethnicity, or sex.
- Student roles in groups. Each group member has a specific role to play in a group, such as noise monitor, turn-taker monitor, recorder, or summarizer.

Individual accountability involves both group and individual performance, for example, by assigning each student a grade on his or her portion of a team project or by calling on a student at random to share with the whole class, with group members, or with another group.

Social skills determine the way students interact with each other as teammates. Usually some explicit instruction in social skills is needed to ensure successful interaction.

Structuring and Structures refer to ways of organizing student interaction and different ways in which students are to interact, such as Three-step interview or Round Robin (discussed later in this section).

Numerous descriptions exist of activity types that can be used when transferring the above elements of cooperative learning to a language environment. Coelho (1992b: 132) describes three major kinds of CL tasks and their learning focus, each of which has many variations.

1. *Team practice from common input – skills development and mastery of facts*
   - All students work on the same material.
   - Practice could follow a traditional teacher-directed presentation of new material and for that reason is a good starting point for teachers and/or students new to group work.
   - The task is to make sure that everyone in the group knows the answer to a question and can explain how the answer was obtained or understands the material. Because students want their team to do well, they coach and tutor each other to make sure that any member of the group could answer for all of them and explain their team's answer.
   - When the teacher takes up the question or assignment, anyone in a group may be called on to answer for the team.
   - This technique is good for review and for practice tests; the group takes the practice test together, but each student will eventually do an assignment or take a test individually.
   - This technique is effective in situations where the composition of the groups is unstable (e.g., in adult programs). Students can form new groups every day.

2. *Jigsaw: differentiated but predetermined input – evaluation and synthesis of facts and opinions*

- Each group member receives a different piece of the information.
- Students regroup in topic groups (expert groups) composed of people with the same piece to master the material and prepare to teach it.
- Students return to home groups (Jigsaw groups) to share their information with each other.
- Students synthesize the information through discussion.
- Each student produces an assignment of part of a group project, or takes a test, to demonstrate synthesis of all the information presented by all group members.
- This method of organization may require team-building activities for both home groups and topic groups, long-term group involvement, and rehearsal of presentation methods.
- This method is very useful in the multilevel class, allowing for both homogeneous and heterogeneous grouping in terms of English proficiency.
- Information gap activities in language teaching are jigsaw activities in the form of pair work. Partners have data (in the form of text, tables, charts, etc.) with missing information to be supplied during interaction with another partner.

3. *Cooperative projects: topics/resources selected by students – discovery learning*

- Topics may be different for each group.
- Students identify subtopics for each group member.
- Steering committee may coordinate the work of the class as a whole.
- Students research the information using resources such as library reference, interviews, visual media.
- Students synthesize their information for a group presentation: oral and/or written. Each group member plays a part in the presentation.
- Each group presents to the whole class.
- This method places greater emphasis on individualization and students' interests. Each student's assignment is unique.
- Students need plenty of previous experience with more structured group work for this to be effective.

Olsen and Kagan (1992: 88) describe the following examples of CLL activities:

- *Three-step interview.* (1) Students are in pairs; one is interviewer and the other is interviewee. (2) Students reverse roles. (3) Each shares with his or her partner what was learned during the two interviews.
- *Roundtable.* There is one piece of paper and one pen for each team. (1) One student makes a contribution and (2) passes the paper and pen to the student on his or her left. (3) Each student makes contributions in turn. If done orally, the structure is called Round Robin.

- *Think-Pair-Share.* (1) Teacher poses a question (usually a low-consensus question). (2) Students think of a response. (3) Students discuss their responses with a partner. (4) Students share his or her partner's response with the class.
- *Solve-Pair-Share.* (1) Teacher poses a problem (a low-consensus or high-consensus item that may be resolved with different strategies). (2) Students work out solutions individually. (3) Students explain how they solved the problem in Interview or Round Robin structures.
- *Numbered heads.* (1) Students number off in teams. (2) Teacher asks a question (usually high-consensus). (3) Heads Together – students literally put their heads together and make sure everyone knows and can explain the answer. (4) Teacher calls a number and students with that number raise their hands to be called on, as in a traditional classroom.

Learner roles

The primary role of the learner is as a member of a group who must work collaboratively on tasks with other group members. Learners have to learn teamwork skills. Learners are also directors of their own learning. They are taught to plan, monitor, and evaluate their own learning, which is viewed as a compilation of lifelong learning skills. Thus, learning is something that requires students' direct and active involvement and participation. Pair grouping is the most typical CLL format, ensuring the maximum amount of time both learners spend engaged on learning tasks. Pair tasks in which learners alternate roles involve partners in the role of tutors, checkers, recorders, and information sharers.

Teacher roles

The role of the teacher in CLL differs considerably from the role of teachers in traditional teacher-fronted lessons. The teacher has to create a highly structured and well-organized learning environment in the classroom, setting goals, planning and structuring tasks, establishing the physical arrangement of the classroom, assigning students to groups and roles, and selecting materials and time (Johnson et al. 1994). An important role for the teacher is that of facilitator of learning. In his or her role as facilitator, the teacher must move around the class helping students and groups as needs arise:

> During this time the teacher interacts, teaches, refocuses, questions, clarifies, supports, expands, celebrates, empathizes. Depending on what problems evolve, the following supportive behaviors are utilized. Facilitators are giving feedback, redirecting the group with questions, encouraging the group to solve its own problems, extending activity, encouraging thinking, managing conflict, observing students, and supplying resources.
>
> (Harel 1992: 169)

Teachers speak less than in teacher-fronted classes. They provide broad questions to challenge thinking, they prepare students for the tasks they will carry out, they assist students with the learning tasks, and they give few commands, imposing less disciplinary control (Harel 1992). The teacher may also have the task of restructuring lessons so that students can work on them cooperatively. This involves the following steps, according to Johnson et al. (1994: 9):

1. Take your existing lessons, curriculum, and sources and structure them cooperatively.
2. Tailor cooperative learning lessons to your unique instructional needs, circumstances, curricula, subject areas, and students.
3. Diagnose the problems some students may have in working together and intervene to increase learning groups' effectiveness.

The role of instructional materials

Materials play an important part in creating opportunities for students to work cooperatively. The same materials can be used as are used in other types of lessons, but variations are required in how the materials are used. For example, if students are working in groups, each might have one set of materials (or groups might have different sets of materials), or each group member might need a copy of a text to read and refer to. Materials may be specially designed for CLL learning (such as commercially sold jigsaw and information gap activities), modified from existing materials, or borrowed from other disciplines.

Comparison of Cooperative Language Learning and traditional approaches

Zhang compares CLL and traditional approaches in Table 13.1. In practice, many classrooms may fall somewhere between CLL and traditional approaches, where teaching is not necessarily teacher-fronted and elements of CLL are incorporated, but where the approach does not form the basis for the organization of the course.

Table 13.1 Comparison of Cooperative Language Learning and traditional language teaching (from Yan Zhang 2010)

	Traditional language teaching	**Cooperative Language Learning**
Independence	None or negative	Positive
Learner roles	Passive receiver and performer	Active participator, autonomous learners
Teacher roles	The center of the classroom, controller of teaching pace and direction, judge of students' right or wrong, the major source of assistance, feedback, reinforcement and support	Organizer and counselor of group work, facilitator of the communication tasks, intervener to teach collaborative skills

(Continued)

	Traditional language teaching	Cooperative Language Learning
Materials	Complete set of materials for each student	Materials are arranged according to purpose of lesson. Usually one group shares a complete set of materials.
Types of activities	Knowledge recall and review, phrasal or sentence pattern practice, role play, translation, listening, etc.	Any instructional activity, mainly group work to engage learners in communication, involving processes like information sharing, negotiation of meaning, and interaction
Interaction	Some talking among students, mainly teacher–student interaction	Intense interaction among students, a few teacher–student interactions
Room arrangement	Separate desks or students placed in pairs	Collaborative small groups
Student expectations	Take a major part in evaluating own progress and the quality of own efforts toward learning. Be a winner or loser.	All members in some way contribute to success of group. The one who makes progress is the winner.
Teacher–student relationship	Superior, inferior or equal	Cooperating and equal

Procedure

The procedure for a CLL lesson follows from going through the steps involved in determining the lesson objective and choosing appropriate cooperative activity types for teaching and learning. Johnson et al. (1994: 67–8) give the following example of how a collaborative learning lesson would be carried out when students are required to write an essay, report, poem, or story, or review something that they have read. A cooperative writing and editing pair arrangement is used. Pairs verify that each member's composition matches the criteria that have been established by the teacher; they then receive an individual score on the quality of their compositions. They can also be given a group score based on the total number of errors made by the pair in their individual compositions. The procedure works in the following way:

1. The teacher assigns students to pairs with at least one good reader in each pair.
2. Student A describes what he or she is planning to write to Student B, who listens carefully, probes with a set of questions, and outlines Student A's ideas. Student B gives the written outline to Student A.
3. This procedure is reversed, with Student B describing what he or she is going to write and Student A listening and completing an outline of Student B's ideas, which is then given to Student B.

4. The students individually research the material they need for their compositions, each keeping an eye out for material useful to their partner.
5. The students work together to write the first paragraph of each composition to ensure that they both have a clear start on their compositions.
6. The students write their compositions individually.
7. When the students have completed their compositions, they proofread each other's compositions, making corrections in capitalization, punctuation, spelling, language usage, and other aspects of writing the teacher specifies. Students also give each other suggestions for revision.
8. The students revise their compositions.
9. The students then reread each other's compositions and sign their names to indicate that each composition is error-free.

During this process, the teacher monitors the pairs, intervening when appropriate to help students master the needed writing and cooperative skills.

Conclusion

This chapter has reviewed the principles underlying Cooperative Language Learning and some ways in which the approach can be implemented. The use of discussion groups, group work, and pair work has often been advocated in teaching both languages and other subjects. Typically, such groups are used to provide a change from the normal pace of class-room events and to increase the amount of student participation in lessons. Such activities, however, are not necessarily cooperative. In CLL, group activities are the major mode of learning and are part of a comprehensive theory and system for the use of group work in teaching. Group activities are carefully planned to maximize students' interaction and to facilitate students' contributions to each other's learning. CLL activities can also be used in collaboration with other teaching methods and approaches, for example, Communicative Language Teaching, as mentioned earlier.

Unlike most language teaching proposals, CLL has been extensively researched and evaluated, and research findings are generally supportive (see Slavin 1995; Baloche 1998; Crandall 2000; Jia 2003; McGafferty and Jacobs 2006), although little of this research was conducted in L2 classrooms. CLL is not without its critics, however. Some have questioned its use with learners of different proficiency levels, suggesting that some groups of students (e.g., intermediate and advanced learners) may obtain more benefits from it than others. In addition, it places considerable demands on teachers, who may have difficulty adapting to the new roles required of them. Proponents of CLL stress that it enhances both learning and learners' interaction skills.

Discussion questions

1. CLL emphasizes pair and group work and extensive collaboration and learning through interaction. Do you think that the benefits of this are age-related? For example, might such an approach work better with younger learners? Why (not)?

2. By promoting interaction, CLL activities may encourage the following (p. 247):
   - Negotiation of meaning
   - Focus on form
   - (Repairing) communication breakdowns

   For each of these, think of one classroom activity (from this chapter or elsewhere) that would be likely to lead to these.

3. In the chapter you have read about *positive interdependence*, which occurs when group members feel that what helps one member helps all and what hurts one member hurts all. One way of encouraging it is by building a spirit of mutual support within the group; for example, by asking a group to produce a single product such as an essay on which the scores for all members are averaged. Can you think of other ways to encourage positive interdependence? Compare your answer with a colleague's.

4. Jigsaw tasks with differentiated input are "very useful in the multilevel class, allowing for … heterogeneous grouping in terms of English proficiency" (p. 251) as it will encourage interaction between learners. Give an example of a *language* outcome of such a task.

5. Read the description of the essay writing task on page 254. If you teach essay writing, is this different from the way you conduct your classes? If so, how?

6. Some research has suggested that CLL, with its focus on heterogeneous groups, may work better with intermediate and advanced learners. Why would this be so?

7. Together with a colleague, select a classroom task you are both familiar with and redesign it using the principles of CLL. Try to include:

   - ample opportunities for interaction;
   - a focus on collaboration (not competition);
   - activities that are student rather than teacher-managed;
   - (where appropriate) a focus on critical thinking skills.

   Now try out the task with a group of students. One of you teaches it in its original form, the other in its revised form. Observe each other. Which task worked better? What were some of the (dis)advantages of each?

8. One of the benefits given for CLL is that it provides "opportunities for students to act as resources for each other, thus assuming a more active role in their learning" (p. 246). A colleague comes to you and says he is concerned that this will not work with his class which has very mixed abilities. How will you respond to this teacher? Now reread point 1 on page 248, which suggests that students who are different from each other according to the variable of proficiency become groupmates. Do you agree with this? Can you think of disadvantages to creating such heterogeneous groups?

9. On page 252 you have read a description of the roles of the teacher in CLL. Your school is looking for a new teacher who is familiar with this approach. Write a short job announcement (maximum 200 words) describing the teaching style and experience the successful candidate should have.

References and further reading

Abdullah, M., and G. Jacobs 2004. Promoting cooperative learning at primary school. *TESOL-EJ* 7(4).

Baloche, L. 1998. *The Cooperative Classroom*. Englewood Cliffs, NJ: Prentice Hall.

Bloom, S. 1956. *Taxonomy of Educational Objectives*. New York: David McKay.

Brody, C., and N. Davidson (eds.). 1998. *Professional Development for Cooperative Learning*. New York: State University of New York Press.

Christison, M., and S. Bassano. 1981. *Look Who's Talking*. San Francisco: Alemany Press.

Coelho, E. 1992a. Cooperative learning: foundation for a communicative curriculum. In Kessler (ed.), 31–51.

Coelho, E. 1992b. Jigsaw: integrating language and content. In Kessler (ed.), 129–52.

Coelho, E. 1994. *Learning Together in the Multicultural Classroom*. Scarborough, Ont.: Pippin.

Crandall, J. 1999. Cooperative language learning and affective factors. In J. Arnold (ed.), *Affect in Language Learning*. Cambridge: Cambridge University Press, 226–45.

Dishon, D., and P. W. O'Leary. 1998. *A Guidebook for Cooperative Learning*. Holmes Beach, FL: Learning Publications.

Fathman, A., and C. Kessler. 1992. Cooperative language learning in school contexts. *Annual Review of Applied Linguistics* 13: 127–40.

Grice, H. P. 1975. Logic and conversation. In P. Cole and J. Morgan (eds.), *Syntax and Semantics*, Vol. III: *Speech Acts*. New York: Academic Press. 41–58.

Harel, Y. 1992. Teacher talk in the cooperative learning classroom. In Kessler (ed.), 153–62.

Jacobs, G. M., G. Lee, and J. Ball. 1995. *Learning Cooperative Learning via Cooperative Learning*. Singapore: Regional Language Centre.

Jacobs, G. M., and C. M. C. Goh. 2007. *Cooperative Learning in the Language Classroom*. Singapore: SEAMEO Regional Language Centre.

Jacobs, G. M., and D. Hannah. 2004. Combining cooperative learning with reading aloud by teachers. *International Journal of English Studies* 4: 97–118.

Jia, G. 2003. *Psychology of Foreign Language Education*. 2nd edn. Nanning: Guangxi Education Press.

Johnson, D., R. Johnson, and E. Holubec. 1994. *Cooperative Learning in the Classroom*. Alexandria, VA: Association for Supervision and Curriculum Development.

Johnson, D. W., and R. T. Johnson. 1991. *Learning Together and Alone: Cooperative, Competitive, and Individualistic*. 3rd edn. Englewood Cliffs, NJ: Prentice Hall.

Kagan, S. 1992. *Cooperative Learning*. San Juan Capistrano, CA: Kagan Cooperative Learning.

Kessler, C. (ed.). 1992. *Cooperative Language Learning: A Teacher's Resource Book*. New York: Prentice Hall.

Long, M. H. 1996. The role of the linguistic environment in second language acquisition. In W. C. Ritchie and T. K. Bhatia (eds.), *Handbook of Second Language Acquisition*. New York: Academic Press. 413–68.

McGafferty, S. G., and G. M. Jacobs. 2006. *Cooperative Learning and Second Language Teaching*. New York: Cambridge University Press.

McGroarty, M. 1989. The benefits of cooperative learning arrangements in second language instruction. *NABE Journal* 13(2) (Winter): 127–43.

Newman, F., and L. Holzman. 1993. *Lev Vygotsky: Revolutionary Scientist*. London: Routledge.

Olsen, J. W. B. 1978. *Communication Starters and Other Activities for the ESL Classroom*. San Francisco: Alemany Press.

Olsen, R., and S. Kagan. 1992. About cooperative learning. In Kessler (ed.), 1–30.

Palmer, A., and T. Rodgers. 1986. *Back and Forth: Pair Activities for Language Development.* San Francisco: Alemany Press.

Piaget, J. 1965. *The Language and Thought of the Child.* New York: World Publishing Co.

Richards, J., and R. Schmidt. 1983. *Language and Communication.* London: Longman.

Rodgers, T. 1988. Cooperative language learning: What's new? *PASAA: A Journal of Language Teaching and Learning* 18(2): 12–23.

Sharan, S. (ed.). 1994. *Handbook of Cooperative Learning Methods.* Westport, CT: Greenwood Press.

Skehan, P. 1998. *A Cognitive Approach to Language Learning.* Oxford: Oxford University Press.

Slavin, R. 1995. *Cooperative Learning: Theory, Research and Practice.* 2nd edn. New York: Prentice Hall.

Swain, M. 2000.The output hypothesis and beyond: Mediating acquisition through collaborative dialogue. In J. P. Lantolf (ed.), *Sociocultural Theory and Second Language Learning*. Oxford: Oxford University Press. 97–114.

Vygotsky, L. 1962. *Thought and Language.* Cambridge, MA: MIT Press.

Vygotsky, L. S. [1935] 1978. *Mind in Society: The Development of Higher Psychological Processes.* Cambridge, MA: Harvard University Press.

Weeks, T. 1979. *Born to Talk.* Rowley, MA: Newbury House.

Wiederhold, C. 1995. *The Question Matrix.* San Juan Capistrano, CA: Kagan Cooperative Learning.

Zhang, Y. 2010. Cooperative language learning and foreign language learning and teaching. *Journal of Language Teaching and Research* 1(1): 81–3.

Part III *Alternative twentieth-century approaches and methods*

The period from the 1970s to the 1980s witnessed a major paradigm shift in language teaching. The quest for alternatives to grammar-based approaches and methods led in several different directions. Mainstream language teaching embraced the growing interest in communicative approaches to language teaching, as we saw in Part II. The communicative movement sought to move the focus away from grammar as the core component of language, to a different view of language, of language learning, of teachers, and of learners, one that focused on language as communication. Other directions in language teaching, also quests for alternatives, appeared during this period and are the focus of this part of the book.

Whereas Audiolingualism and Situational Language Teaching were mainstream teaching methods developed by linguists and applied linguists, the approaches and methods described in this section were either developed outside of mainstream language teaching or represent an application in language teaching of educational principles developed elsewhere. They are represented by such innovative methods of the 1970s as the Natural Approach (Chapter 14), Total Physical Response (Chapter 15), the Silent Way (Chapter 16), Community Language Learning (Chapter 17), and Suggestopedia (Chapter 18). Rather than starting from a theory of language and drawing on research and theory in applied linguistics, the majority of these methods are developed around particular theories of learners and learning, sometimes the theories of a single theorizer or educator. Many of these methods are consequently relatively underdeveloped in the domain of language theory, and the learning principles they reflect are generally different from theories found in second language acquisition (SLA) textbooks. The one exception in this group is the Natural Approach, as explained below.

Alternative approaches and methods of the 1970s and 1980s have had a somewhat varied history. Although Total Physical Response, the Silent Way, Community Language Learning, and Suggestopedia did not succeed in attracting the support of mainstream language teaching, each can be seen as expressing important dimensions of the teaching/learning process. They can be seen as offering particular insights that have attracted the attention and/or allegiance of some teachers and educators, but they have each seen their popularity rise and fall since the 1970s. Today, in most places, they are of little more than historical interest. The Natural Approach, on the other hand, was based on Krashen's interpretation of SLA research and his distinction between acquisition, learning, and the role of the monitor attracted widespread interest for many years.

14 The Natural Approach

Introduction

In 1977, Tracy Terrell, a teacher of Spanish in California, outlined "a proposal for a 'new' philosophy of language teaching which [he] called the Natural Approach" (1977; 1982: 121). This was an attempt to develop a language teaching proposal that incorporated the "naturalistic" principles researchers had identified in studies of second language acquisition. In the Natural Approach there is an emphasis on exposure, or *input*, rather than practice; optimizing emotional preparedness for learning; a prolonged period of attention to what the language learners hear before they try to produce language; and a willingness to use written and other materials as a source of input.

The Natural Approach grew out of Terrell's experiences of teaching Spanish classes, although it has also been used in elementary to advanced-level classes and with several other languages. At the same time, he joined forces with Stephen Krashen, an applied linguist at the University of Southern California, in elaborating a theoretical rationale for the Natural Approach, drawing on Krashen's understanding of the findings of the emerging field of second language acquisition. Krashen and Terrell's combined statement of the principles and practices of the Natural Approach appeared in their book *The Natural Approach*, published in 1983. At the time the Natural Approach attracted a wide interest because of the accessibility of the principles on which it was based, the ease with which it confirmed many teachers' common sense understandings of second language learning, the fact it appeared to be supported by state-of-the-art theory and research, and the fact that Krashen himself is a charismatic presenter and persuasive advocate of his own views – as is evident from the numerous examples of his presentations available on the Internet. Krashen and Terrell's book contains theoretical sections prepared by Krashen that outline his views on second language acquisition (Krashen 1981, 1982), and sections on implementation and classroom procedures, prepared largely by Terrell.

Krashen and Terrell identified the Natural Approach with what they call "traditional" approaches to language teaching. Traditional approaches are defined as "based on the use of language in communicative situations without recourse to the native language" – and, perhaps, needless to say, without reference to grammatical analysis, grammatical drilling, or a particular theory of grammar. Hence, traditional approaches, as defined by Krashen and Terrell, have much in common with the Direct Method (Chapter 1). Krashen and Terrell noted that such "approaches have been called natural, psychological, phonetic, new, reform, direct, analytic, imitative and so forth" (1983: 9). The fact that the authors of the Natural

Approach relate their approach to the Natural Method, a precursor of the Direct Method has led some people to assume that *Natural Approach* and *Natural Method* are synonymous terms. Although the tradition is a common one, there are important differences between the Natural Approach and the older Natural Method, which it will be useful to consider at the outset.

The Natural Method (see Chapter 1) is another term for what by 1900 had become known as the Direct Method. It is described in a report on the state of the art in language teaching commissioned by the Modern Language Association in 1901 (the report of the "Committee of 12"):

> In its extreme form the method consisted of a series of monologues by the teacher interspersed with exchanges of question and answer between the instructor and the pupil – all in the foreign language ... A great deal of pantomime accompanied the talk. With the aid of this gesticulation, by attentive listening and by dint of much repetition, the learner came to associate certain acts and objects with certain combinations of the sounds and finally reached the point of reproducing the foreign words or phrase ... Not until a considerable familiarity with the spoken word was attained was the scholar allowed to see the foreign language in print. The study of grammar was reserved for a still later period.
>
> (Cole 1931: 58)

The term *natural*, used in reference to the Direct Method, merely emphasized that the principles underlying the method were believed to conform to the principles of naturalistic language learning in young children. Similarly, the Natural Approach, as defined by Krashen and Terrell, is believed to conform to the naturalistic principles found in successful second language acquisition. Unlike the Direct Method, however, it places less emphasis on teacher monologues, direct repetition, and formal questions and answers, and less focus on accurate production of target-language sentences. It is, in fact, an example of a cognitive approach to language learning, as described in Chapter 2. Language learning is believed to emerge naturally given appropriate exposure and conditions – a result of the innate properties of the human mind (see below). The emphasis on the central role of comprehension in the Natural Approach links it to other comprehension-based approaches in language teaching, such as the Lexical Approach (see Chapter 11).

Approach

Theory of language

The Natural Approach is primarily developed from a theory of language learning rather than a theory of language – something it has in common with Task-Based Language Teaching and which distinguishes it from methods such as Text-Based Instruction, which are based primarily around a theory of language. Krashen and Terrell see communication as the primary function of language, and since their approach focuses on teaching communicative abilities, they refer to the Natural Approach as an example of a communicative approach. The Natural Approach "is similar to other communicative approaches being developed today" (Krashen and Terrell 1983: 17). They reject earlier methods of language teaching, such as the Audiolingual Method (Chapter 4), which viewed grammar as the central component of language. According to Krashen and Terrell, the major problem with these methods was that they were built not around "actual theories of language acquisition, but theories of something else; for example, the structure of language" (1983: 1). Unlike proponents of Communicative Language Teaching (Chapter 5), however, Krashen and Terrell give little attention to a theory of language. Indeed, a critic of Krashen suggested that he has no theory of language at all (Gregg 1984). What Krashen and Terrell do describe about the nature of language emphasizes the primacy of meaning. The importance of the vocabulary is stressed, for example, suggesting the view that a language is essentially its lexicon and only inconsequently the grammar that determines how the lexicon is exploited to produce messages, where the term *message* refers essentially to what the speaker intends to communicate. Terrell quotes Dwight Bolinger to support this view:

> The quantity of information in the lexicon far outweighs that in any other part of the language, and if there is anything to the notion of redundancy it should be easier to reconstruct a message containing just words than one containing just the syntactic relations. The significant fact is the subordinate role of grammar. The most important thing is to get the words in.
>
> (Bolinger, in Terrell 1977: 333)

Language is viewed as a vehicle for communicating meanings and messages. Hence, Krashen and Terrell stated that "acquisition can take place only when people understand messages in the target language" (1983: 19). Yet despite their avowed communicative approach to language, they view language learning, as do audiolingualists, as mastery of structures by stages. "The input hypothesis states that in order for acquirers to progress to the next stage in the acquisition of the target language, they need to understand input language that includes a structure that is part of the next stage" (Krashen and Terrell 1983: 32). Krashen refers to this with the formula "i + 1" (i.e., input that contains structures slightly above the learner's present level). We assume that Krashen means by *structures* something at least in the tradition of what such linguists as Charles Fries meant by *structures*. For Fries, grammar or "structure" referred to the basic sentence patterns of a language, and oral drilling formed the core of language teaching (see Chapter 4). The Natural Approach thus assumes a linguistic hierarchy of structural complexity that one masters through encounters with "input" containing structures at the "i + 1" level.

We are left, then, with a view of language that consists of lexical items, structures, and messages, or the communicative goal. Obviously, there is no particular novelty in this view as such, except that messages are considered of primary importance in the Natural Approach. The lexicon for both perception and production is considered critical in the construction and interpretation of messages. Lexical items in messages are necessarily grammatically structured, and more complex messages involve more complex grammatical structure. Although they acknowledge such grammatical structuring, Krashen and Terrell feel that grammatical structure does not require explicit analysis or attention by the language teacher, by the language learner, or in language teaching materials.

Theory of learning

In order to understand the origins of the theoretical assumptions underlying the Natural Approach, it is necessary to go back to the emergence of cognitive approaches to language and language learning that were prompted by Chomsky's claim that the potential to learn a language was an innate property of the human mind – a theory that later was phrased in terms of universal grammar (Chapter 2). All that was needed was exposure to language and the need to communicate, and the brain would take care of the rest. The psychologist Roger Brown investigated how this process occurred in first language learning in his influential book *A First Language* (1973), which documented the common stages of development evidenced in children's initial learning of their first language. Prompted by this research, applied linguists turned their attention to second language acquisition and sought to demonstrate that second language development could not be explained by behaviorist learning theory. It was not dependent upon imitation and repetition of utterances the learner was exposed to but – as with first language learning – was dependent upon universal principles of learning. These accounted for the common patterns of development that were observed in second language learners and that could not be explained simply through interference from the first language. Krashen argued that there was a natural sequence of development for many features of English (Bailey, Madden, and Krashen 1974), and this theory was elaborated as part of a more comprehensive account of second language learning in a book that echoes the title of Brown's book – *Language Two* (Dulay, Burt, and Krashen 1982). The Natural Approach can be seen as an attempt to develop a pedagogical application of the theory Krashen and other researchers were developing in their applied linguistics research in the 1970s and 1980s.

Krashen and Terrell hence make continuing reference to the theoretical and research base claimed to underlie the Natural Approach and to the fact that the method is unique in having such a base. "It is based on an empirically grounded theory of second language acquisition, which has been supported by a large number of scientific studies in a wide variety of language acquisition and learning contexts" (Krashen and Terrell 1983: 1). The theory and research are grounded in Krashen's views of language acquisition, which we will collectively refer to as *Krashen's language acquisition theory*. Krashen's views have been presented and discussed extensively elsewhere (e.g., Krashen 1982), so we will not try to present or critique his arguments here. (For a detailed critical review, see Gregg 1984 and McLaughlin 1978.) It is necessary, however, to outline the principal tenets of the theory, since it is on these that the design and procedures in the Natural Approach are based.

The Acquisition/Learning Hypothesis

The Acquisition/Learning Hypothesis claims that there are two distinctive ways of developing competence in a second or foreign language. *Acquisition* is the "natural" way, paralleling first language development in children. Acquisition refers to an unconscious process that involves the naturalistic development of language proficiency through understanding language and through using language for meaningful communication. *Learning*, by contrast, refers to a process in which conscious rules about a language are developed. It results in explicit knowledge about the forms of a language and the ability to verbalize this knowledge. Formal teaching is necessary for "learning" to occur, and correction of errors helps with the development of learned rules. Learning, according to the theory, cannot lead to acquisition, as will be explained below.

The Monitor Hypothesis

The acquired linguistic system is said to initiate utterances when we communicate in a second or foreign language. Conscious learning can function only as a monitor or editor that checks and repairs the output of the acquired system. The Monitor Hypothesis claims that we may call upon learned knowledge to correct ourselves when we communicate, but that conscious learning (i.e., the *learned* system) has *only* this function. Three conditions limit the successful use of the monitor:

1. *Time.* There must be sufficient time for a learner to choose and apply a learned rule.
2. *Focus on form.* The language user must be focused on correctness or on the form of the output.
3. *Knowledge of rules.* The performer must know the rules. The monitor does best with rules that are simple in two ways. They must be simple to describe and they must not require complex movements and rearrangements.

The Natural Order Hypothesis

According to the Natural Order Hypothesis, the acquisition of grammatical structures proceeds in a predictable order. Research is said to have shown that certain grammatical structures or morphemes are acquired before others in first language acquisition of English, and a similar natural order is found in second language acquisition. Errors are signs of naturalistic developmental processes, and during acquisition (but not during learning), similar developmental errors occur in learners no matter what their native language is.

The Input Hypothesis

The Input Hypothesis claims to explain the relationship between what the learner is exposed to of a language (the input) and language acquisition. It involves four main issues.

1. The hypothesis relates to acquisition, and not to learning.
2. As mentioned earlier, people acquire language best by understanding input that is slightly beyond their current level of competence: "An acquirer can 'move' from a stage i (where i is the acquirer's level of competence) to a stage i + 1 (where i + 1 is the

stage immediately following i along some natural order) by understanding language containing i + 1" (Krashen and Terrell 1983: 32). Clues based on the situation and the context, extralinguistic information, and knowledge of the world make comprehension possible.

3. The ability to speak fluently cannot be taught directly; rather, it "emerges" independently in time, after the acquirer has built up linguistic competence by understanding input.

4. If there is a sufficient quantity of comprehensible input, i + 1 will usually be provided automatically. Comprehensible input refers to utterances that the learner understands based on the context in which they are used as well as the language in which they are phrased. When a speaker uses language so that the acquirer understands the message, the speaker "casts a net" of structure around the acquirer's current level of competence, and this will include many instances of i + 1. Thus, input need not be finely tuned to a learner's current level of linguistic competence, and in fact cannot be so finely tuned in a language class, where learners will be at many different levels of competence. Just as child acquirers of a first language are provided with samples of "caretaker speech," rough-tuned to their present level of understanding, so adult acquirers of a second language are provided with simple codes that facilitate second language comprehension. One such code is "foreigner talk," which refers to the speech native speakers use to simplify communication with foreigners. Foreigner talk is characterized by a slower rate of speech, repetition, restating, use of Yes/No instead of *Wh*-questions, and other changes that make messages more comprehensible to persons of limited language proficiency.

The Affective Filter Hypothesis

Krashen sees the learner's emotional state or attitudes as an adjustable filter that freely passes, impedes, or blocks input necessary to acquisition. A low affective filter is desirable, since it impedes or blocks less of this necessary input. The hypothesis is built on research in second language acquisition, which has identified three kinds of affective or attitudinal variables related to second language acquisition:

1. *Motivation.* Learners with high motivation generally do better.
2. *Self-confidence.* Learners with self-confidence and a good self-image tend to be more successful.
3. *Anxiety.* Low personal anxiety and low classroom anxiety are more conducive to second language acquisition.

The Affective Filter Hypothesis states that acquirers with a low affective filter seek and receive more input, interact with confidence, and are more receptive to the input they receive. Anxious acquirers have a high affective filter, which prevents acquisition from taking place. It is believed that the affective filter (e.g., fear or embarrassment) rises in early adolescence, and this may account for the apparent ease with which children acquire new languages compared to older acquirers of a second language.

These five hypotheses have obvious implications for language teaching. In sum, these are as follows:

1. As much comprehensible input as possible must be presented.
2. Whatever helps comprehension is important. Visual aids are useful, as is exposure to a wide range of vocabulary rather than study of syntactic structure.
3. The focus in the classroom should be on listening and reading; speaking should be allowed to "emerge."
4. In order to lower the affective filter, student work should center on meaningful communication rather than on form; input should be interesting and so contribute to a relaxed classroom atmosphere.

Design

Objectives

The Natural Approach "is for beginners and is designed to help them become intermediates." It has the expectation that students

> will be able to function adequately in the target situation. They will understand the speaker of the target language (perhaps with requests for clarification), and will be able to convey (in a non-insulting manner) their requests and ideas. They need not know every word in a particular semantic domain, nor is it necessary that the syntax and vocabulary be flawless – but their production does need to be understood. They should be able to make the meaning clear but not necessarily be accurate in all details of grammar.
>
> (Krashen and Terrell 1983: 71)

However, since the Natural Approach is offered as a general set of principles applicable to a wide variety of situations, as in Communicative Language Teaching, specific objectives depend on learner needs and the skill (listening, speaking, reading, or writing) and level being taught. Krashen and Terrell believe that it is important to communicate to learners what they can expect of a course as well as what they should not expect. They offer as an example a possible goal and non-goal statement for a beginning Natural Approach Spanish class:

> After 100–150 hours of Natural Approach Spanish, you will be able to: "get around" in Spanish; you will be able to communicate with a monolingual native speaker of Spanish without difficulty; read most ordinary texts in Spanish with some use of a dictionary; know enough Spanish to continue to improve on your own.
>
> After 100–150 hours of Natural Approach Spanish you will not be able to: pass for a native speaker, use Spanish as easily as you use English, understand native speakers when they talk to each other (you will probably not be able to eavesdrop successfully); use Spanish on the telephone with great comfort; participate easily in a conversation with several other native speakers on unfamiliar topics.
>
> (Krashen and Terrell 1983: 74)

The syllabus

Krashen and Terrell (1983) approach course organization from two points of view. First, they list some typical goals for language courses and suggest which of these goals are the ones at which the Natural Approach aims. They list such goals under four areas:

1. Basic personal communication skills: oral (e.g., listening to announcements in public places)
2. Basic personal communication skills: written (e.g., reading and writing personal letters)
3. Academic learning skills: oral (e.g., listening to a lecture)
4. Academic learning skills: written (e.g., taking notes in class)

Of these, they note that the Natural Approach is primarily "designed to develop basic communication skills – both oral and written" (1983: 67). They then observe that communication goals "may be expressed in terms of situations, functions and topics" and proceed to order four pages of topics and situations "which are likely to be most useful to beginning students" (ibid.). The order in which the functions are presented are not specified or suggested but are felt to derive naturally from the topics and situations. This approach to syllabus design would appear to reflect Threshold Level specifications (see Chapter 5).

The second point of view holds that "the purpose of a language course will vary according to the needs of the students and their particular interests" (Krashen and Terrell 1983: 65):

> The goals of a Natural Approach class are based on an assessment of student needs. We determine the situations in which they will use the target language and the sorts of topics they will have to communicate information about. In setting communication goals, we do not expect the students at the end of a particular course to have acquired a certain group of structures or forms. Instead we expect them to deal with a particular set of topics in a given situation. We do not organize the activities of the class about a grammatical syllabus.
>
> (Krashen and Terrell 1983: 71)

From this point of view, it is difficult to specify communicative goals that necessarily fit the needs of all students. Thus, any list of topics and situations must be understood as syllabus suggestions rather than as specifications.

As well as fitting the needs and interests of students, content selection should aim to create a low affective filter by being interesting and fostering a friendly, relaxed atmosphere, should provide a wide exposure to vocabulary that may be useful to basic personal communication, and should resist any focus on grammatical structures, since if input is provided "over a wider variety of topics while pursuing communicative goals, the necessary grammatical structures are automatically provided in the input" (Krashen and Terrell 1983: 71).

Types of learning and teaching activities

From the beginning of a class taught according to the Natural Approach, emphasis is on presenting comprehensible input in the target language. Teacher talk focuses on objects in the classroom and on the content of pictures, as with the Direct Method. To minimize stress, learners are not required to say anything until they feel ready, but they are expected to respond to teacher commands and questions in other ways.

When learners are ready to begin talking in the new language, the teacher provides comprehensible language and simple response opportunities. The teacher talks slowly and distinctly, asking questions and eliciting one-word answers. There is a gradual progression from Yes/No questions, through either/or questions, to questions that students can answer using words they have heard used by the teacher. Students are not expected to use a word actively until they have heard it many times. Charts, pictures, advertisements, and other realia serve as the focal point for questions, and when the students' competence permits, talk moves to class members. "Acquisition activities" – those that focus on meaningful communication rather than language form – are emphasized. Pair or group work may be employed, followed by whole-class discussion led by the teacher.

Techniques recommended by Krashen and Terrell are often borrowed from other methods and adapted to meet the requirements of Natural Approach theory. These include command-based activities from Total Physical Response (Chapter 15); Direct Method activities in which mime, gesture, and context are used to elicit questions and answers (Chapter 1); and even situation-based practice of structures and patterns (Chapter 3). Group-work activities are often identical to those used in Communicative Language Teaching (Chapter 5), where sharing information in order to complete a task is emphasized. There is nothing novel about the procedures and techniques advocated for use with the Natural Approach. A casual observer might not be aware of the philosophy underlying the classroom techniques he or she observes. What characterizes Natural Approach learning and teaching activities is the use of familiar techniques within the framework of a method that focuses on providing comprehensible input and a classroom environment that provides comprehension of input, minimizes learner anxiety, and maximizes learner self-confidence.

Learner roles

There is a basic assumption in the Natural Approach that learners should not try to learn a language in the usual sense. The extent to which they can lose themselves in activities involving meaningful communication will determine the amount and kind of acquisition they will experience and the fluency they will ultimately demonstrate. The language acquirer is seen as a processor of comprehensible input. When the acquirer is challenged by input that is slightly beyond his or her current level of competence, he or she is able to assign meaning to this input through active use of context and extralinguistic information.

Learners' roles are seen to change according to their stage of linguistic development. Central to these changing roles are learner decisions on when to speak, what to speak about, and what linguistic expressions to use in speaking.

In the *pre-production stage*, students "participate in the language activity without having to respond in the target language" (Krashen and Terrell 1983: 76). For example, students can act out physical commands, identify student colleagues from teacher description, point to pictures, and so forth.

In the *early-production stage*, students respond to either/or questions, use single words and short phrases, fill in charts, and use fixed conversational patterns (e.g., How are you? What's your name?).

In the *speech-emergent phase*, students involve themselves in role play and games, contribute personal information and opinions, and participate in group problem-solving.

Learners have four kinds of responsibilities in the Natural Approach classroom:

1. To provide information about their specific goals so that acquisition activities can focus on the topics and situations most relevant to their needs.
2. To take an active role in ensuring comprehensible input. They should learn and use conversational management techniques to regulate input.
3. To decide when to start producing speech and when to upgrade it.
4. Where learning exercises (i.e., grammar study) are to be a part of the program, to decide with the teacher the relative amount of time to be devoted to them and perhaps even complete and correct them independently.

Learners are expected to participate in communication activities with other learners. Although communication activities are seen to provide naturalistic practice and to create a sense of camaraderie, which lowers the affective filter, they may fail to provide learners with well-formed and comprehensible input at the i + 1 level. Krashen and Terrell warn of these shortcomings but do not suggest means for their amelioration.

Teacher roles

The Natural Approach teacher has three central roles. First, the teacher is the primary source of comprehensible input in the target language. "Class time is devoted primarily to providing input for acquisition" (Krashen and Terrell 1983: 35) and the teacher is the primary generator of that input. In this role, the teacher is required to generate a constant flow of language input while providing a multiplicity of nonlinguistic clues to assist students in interpreting the input. The Natural Approach demands a much more center-stage role for the teacher than do many methods.

Second, the Natural Approach teacher creates a classroom atmosphere that is interesting, friendly, and in which there is a low affective filter for learning. This is achieved in part through such Natural Approach techniques as not demanding speech from the students before they are ready for it, not correcting student errors, and providing subject matter of high interest to students.

Finally, the teacher must choose and orchestrate a rich mix of classroom activities, involving a variety of group sizes, content, and contexts. The teacher is seen as responsible for collecting materials and designing their use. These materials, according to Krashen and Terrell, are based not just on teacher perceptions but on elicited student needs and interests. As with other unconventional teaching systems, the Natural Approach teacher has a particular responsibility to communicate clearly and compellingly to students the assumptions, organization, and expectations of the method, since in many cases these will violate student views of what language learning and teaching are supposed to be.

The role of instructional materials

The primary goal of materials in the Natural Approach is to make classroom activities as meaningful as possible by supplying "the extralinguistic context that helps the acquirer to understand and thereby to acquire" (Krashen and Terrell 1983: 55), by relating classroom activities to the real world, and by fostering real communication among the learners. Materials come from the world of realia rather than from textbooks. The primary aim of materials is to promote comprehension and communication. Pictures and other visual aids are essential, because they supply the content for communication. As the pictures prompt the teacher to provide the vocabulary necessary to describe what is contained in them, they facilitate the acquisition of a large vocabulary within the classroom. Other recommended materials include schedules, brochures, advertisements, maps, and books at levels appropriate to the students, if a reading component is included in the course. Games, in general, are seen as useful classroom materials, since "games by their very nature, focus the students on what it is they are doing and use the language as a tool for reaching the goal rather than as a goal in itself" (Terrell 1982: 121). The selection, reproduction, and collection of materials place a considerable burden on the Natural Approach teacher.

Procedure

We have seen that the Natural Approach adopts techniques and activities freely from various method sources and can be regarded as innovative only with respect to the purposes for which they are recommended and the ways they are used. Krashen and Terrell (1983) provide suggestions for the use of a wide range of activities, all of which are familiar components of Situational Language Teaching (Chapter 3), Communicative Language Teaching, and other methods discussed in this book. To illustrate procedural aspects of the Natural Approach, we will cite examples of how such activities are to be used in the Natural Approach classroom to provide comprehensible input, without requiring production of responses or minimal responses in the target language. The first steps rely on the Total Physical Response (TPR) method (Chapter 15), which attempts to teach language through physical or motor activity.

1. Start with TPR commands. At first the commands are quite simple: "Stand up. Turn around. Raise your right hand."
2. Use TPR to teach names of body parts and to introduce numbers and sequence. "Lay your right hand on your head, put both hands on your shoulder, first touch your nose, then stand up and turn to the right three times" and so forth.
3. Introduce classroom terms and props into commands. "Pick up a pencil and put it under the book, touch a wall, go to the door and knock three times." Any item which can be brought to the class can be incorporated. "Pick up the record and place it in the tray. Take the green blanket to Larry. Pick up the soap and take it to the woman wearing the green blouse."
4. Use names of physical characteristics and clothing to identify members of the class by name. The instructor uses context and the items themselves to make the meanings of the key words clear: hair, long, short, etc. Then a student is described. "What is your name?" (selecting a student). "Class. Look at Barbara. She has long brown hair. Her hair is long and brown. Her hair is not short. It is long." (Using mime, pointing and context to ensure comprehension.) "What's the name of the student with long brown hair?" (Barbara). Questions such as "What is the name of the woman with the short blond hair?" or "What is the name of the student sitting next to the man with short brown hair and glasses?" are very simple to understand by attending to key words, gestures and context. And they require the students only to remember and produce the name of a fellow student. The same can be done with articles of clothing and colors. "Who is wearing a yellow shirt? Who is wearing a brown dress?"
5. Use visuals, typically magazine pictures, to introduce new vocabulary and to continue with activities requiring only student names as response. The instructor introduces the pictures to the entire class one at a time focusing usually on one single item or activity in the picture. He may introduce one to five new words while talking about the picture. He then passes the picture to a particular student in the class. The students' task is to remember the name of the student with a particular picture. For example, "Tom has the picture of the sailboat. Joan has the picture of the family watching television" and so forth. The instructor will ask questions like "Who has the picture with the sailboat? Does Susan or Tom have the picture of the people on the beach?" Again the students need only produce a name in response.
6. Combine use of pictures with TPR. "Jim, find the picture of the little girl with her dog and give it to the woman with the pink blouse."
7. Combine observations about the pictures with commands and conditionals. "If there is a woman in your picture, stand up. If there is something blue in your picture, touch your right shoulder."
8. Using several pictures, ask students to point to the picture being described.
9. Picture 1. "There are several people in this picture. One appears to be a father, the other a daughter. What are they doing? Cooking. They are cooking a hamburger." Picture 2. "There are two men in this picture. They are young. They are boxing." Picture 3 ...

(Krashen and Terrell 1983: 75–7)

In all these activities, the instructor maintains a constant flow of "comprehensible input," using key vocabulary items, appropriate gestures, context, repetition, and paraphrase to ensure the comprehensibility of the input.

Conclusion

The Natural Approach belongs to a tradition of language teaching methods based on observation and interpretation of how learners acquire both first and second languages in nonformal settings. Such methods reject the formal (grammatical) organization of language as a prerequisite to teaching. They hold with Newmark and Reibel that "an adult can effectively be taught by grammatically unordered materials" (even if, in practice, there is generally an intuitive attempt on the part of the teacher to provide a basic order) and that such an approach is, indeed, "the *only* learning process which we know for certain will produce mastery of the language at a native level" (1968: 153). In the Natural Approach, a focus on comprehension and meaningful communication as well as the provision of the right kinds of comprehensible input provide the necessary and sufficient conditions for successful classroom second and foreign language acquisition. This has led to a rationale for the integration and adaptation of techniques drawn from a wide variety of existing sources. Like Communicative Language Teaching, the Natural Approach is hence evolutionary rather than revolutionary in its procedures. Its greatest claim to originality lies not in the techniques it employs but in their use in a method that emphasizes comprehensible and meaningful practice activities, rather than production of grammatically perfect utterances and sentences.

The Natural Approach is very much a product of the 1980s and attracted a great deal of interest at that time. It was particularly influential in Krashen's home state of California where it helped frame an approach to the teaching of language minority students (Krashen 1981). Krashen himself for many years has been a powerful advocate for bilingual education in the face of growing pressure to limit its role in Californian schools. However, numerous articles as well as full-length books since that time have been devoted to rejecting both the theory and research Krashen used in support of the principles of the Natural Approach (e.g., Gregg 1984; McLaughlin 1978) as well as its practical applications. In California at least, policy changes in recent years have made the Natural Approach largely irrelevant to the needs of teachers in public schools. As with public education in many other countries, teachers are now required to teach to standards (Chapter 8) that specify the language skills learners need to develop at different stages in the school curriculum. However, the Natural Approach still has its advocates elsewhere. A leading language institute in Thailand (AUA), for example, offers a Natural Approach course for the learning of Thai as an option students can choose when studying Thai. As a general approach in other contexts, the Natural Approach is unlikely to prove attractive to many teachers today. Although, as noted earlier in this chapter, the principles on which it is based, such as exposing learners to extensive input slightly above their level before production is required, seem to confirm what many people would describe as common sense – whether or not they are supported by current research – practical limitations would not make the Natural Approach an option for many teachers. In particular:

- There are no published materials or coursebooks to support the approach.
- It requires a high level of training and language proficiency for its implementation.
- English may be assigned as little as three or four hours a week in some countries, requiring an accelerated rather than a gradual approach to English teaching.
- The English curriculum may be linked to national standards and tests, giving teachers little choice over what to teach.

Although Krashen and Terrell published the Natural Approach several decades ago, the principles behind the approach continue to be debated today, in particular the value of a considerable amount of comprehensible input. More recently, Krashen has been an advocate of extensive reading, an approach advocating free reading for pleasure, which bears much in common with his earlier research.

Discussion questions

1. Explain to a colleague what the word *natural* in the Natural Approach refers to.

2. The Natural Approach makes a distinction between *acquisition* and *learning* of a second language. Explain to a colleague how these are different and how this impacts the way an L2 is taught.

3. "Learning, according to the theory, cannot lead to acquisition" (p. 265). What is your view on this? Can you think of examples (perhaps from your own learning or teaching) where learning did lead to acquisition?

4. The Monitor Hypothesis states that learners can only call upon learned knowledge if they (a) have sufficient time, (b) are focused on form, and (c) have knowledge of the rules. Can you think of examples of real-world language tasks that meet these requirements?

5. "Input need not be finely tuned to a learner's current level of linguistic competence" (p. 266). What characteristics *does* input need to have according to the Natural Approach?

6. "The Affective Filter Hypothesis states that acquirers with a low affective filter seek and receive more input, interact with confidence, and are more receptive to the input they receive" (p. 266). What can teachers do to lower students' affective filter? Talk to a colleague and exchange techniques you both use with students.

7. Now review the five basic principles of the Natural Approach again: The Acquisition/ Learning Hypothesis, the Monitor Hypothesis, the Natural Order Hypothesis, the Input Hypothesis, and the Affective Filter Hypothesis. Which of these areas do you think are most important? Do you use any of these principles in your own teaching?

8. The Natural Approach does not prescribe a well-defined syllabus or order in which topics or structures need to be presented. How do you think teachers using this approach decide on course content and sequencing?

9. The Natural Approach makes considerable use of realia as source for comprehensible input. Can you think of downsides to the use of realia to this degree?

10. Below are some of the key characteristics of the Natural Approach. Work with a colleague and do the following:

   1) Select (a) one conversational skill (e.g., interrupting someone), and (b) one grammatical structure (e.g., the passive).
   2) Create a classroom activity using the principles below.
   3) Find an example from a textbook you are familiar with.
   4) Complete the table and compare your activities with those from the textbook. How are they different? Which do you think would be more successful for your learners and why? Does either your activity or the textbook activity work better for either the conversational skill or the grammar point? Why?

	Natural Approach	Textbook
Conversational skill		
Input		
Practice		
Emotional preparation		
Opportunities to listen		
Grammar point		
Input		
Practice		
Emotional preparation		
Opportunities to listen		

11. "Learners' roles are seen to change according to their stage of linguistic development. Central to these changing roles are learner decisions on when to speak, what to speak about, and what linguistic expressions to use in speaking" (p. 270). How does this compare with your own classes? Can you think of (a) some advantages, and (b) some drawbacks to not specifying when learners will speak nor telling them which linguistic expressions to use?

References and further reading

Bailey, N., C. Madden, and S. Krashen. 1974. Is there a "natural sequence" in adult second language learning? *Language Learning* 21: 235–43.

Baltra, A. 1992. On breaking with tradition: the significance of Terrell's Natural Approach. *Canadian Modern Language Review* 49(3): 565–93.

Berne, J. 1990. A comparison of teaching for proficiency with the natural approach: procedure, design and approach. *Hispania* 73(4): 147–53.

Brown, J. M., and A. Palmer. 1988. *Listening Approach: Methods and Materials for Applying Krashen's Input Hypothesis.* Harlow, UK: Longman.

Brown, R. 1973. *A First Language: The Early Stages.* Boston: Harvard University Press.

Cole, R. 1931. *Modern Foreign Languages and Their Teaching.* New York: Appleton-Century-Crofts.

Dulay, H., M. Burt, and S. Krashen. *Language Two.* New York: Oxford University Press.

Ellis, R. 1997. *Second Language Acquisition.* Oxford: Oxford University Press.

Gregg, K. 1984. Krashen's monitor and Occam's razor. *Applied Linguistics* 5(2): 79–100.

Hashemipor, P., R. Maldonado, and M. van Naerssen (eds.). 1995. *Studies in Language Learning and Spanish Linguistics: Festschrift in Honor of Tracy D. Terrell.* New York: McGraw-Hill.

Krashen, S. 1981. *Second Language Acquisition and Second Language Learning.* Oxford: Pergamon.

Krashen, S. 1982. *Principles and Practices in Second Language Acquisition.* Oxford: Pergamon.

Krashen, S. 1985. *The Input Hypothesis: Issues and Implications.* London: Longman.

Krashen, S. 1989. We acquire vocabulary and spelling by reading: additional evidence for the input hypothesis. *Modern Language Journal* 73(4): 440–64.

Krashen, S. 1992. *Fundamentals of Language Education.* Beverley Hills, CA: Laredo.

Krashen, S. 1993. The case for free voluntary reading. *Canadian Modern Language Review* 50(1): 72–82.

Krashen, S. 1996a. The case for narrow listening. *System* 24(1): 97–100.

Krashen, S. 1996b. Principles of English as a foreign language. *English Teachers' Journal* (Israel) 49: 11–19.

Krashen, S. 1997. The comprehension hypothesis: recent evidence. *English Teachers' Journal* (Israel) 51: 17–29.

Krashen, S., and T. Terrell. 1983. *The Natural Approach: Language Acquisition in the Classroom.* Oxford: Pergamon.

McLaughlin, B. 1978. The Monitor Model: some methodological considerations. *Language Learning* 28(2): 309–32.

Newmark, L., and D. A. Reibel. 1968. Necessity and sufficiency in language learning. *International Review of Applied Linguistics* 6(2): 145–64.

Rivers, W. 1981. *Teaching Foreign-Language Skills.* 2nd edn. Chicago: University of Chicago Press.

Skehan, P. 1998. *A Cognitive Approach to Language Learning.* Oxford: Oxford University Press.

Stevick, E. W. 1976. *Memory, Meaning and Method: Some Psychological Perspectives on Language Learning.* Rowley, MA: Newbury House.

Terrell, T. D. 1977. A natural approach to second language acquisition and learning. *Modern Language Journal* 61: 325–36.

Terrell, T. D. 1981. The natural approach in bilingual education. Ms. California Office of Bilingual Education.

Terrell, T. D. 1982. The natural approach to language teaching: an update. *Modern Language Journal* 66: 121–32.

15 Total Physical Response

Introduction

We saw in Chapter 2 that major approaches and methods throughout the twentieth century were generally influenced by theories of language and language learning drawn from the disciplines of linguistics and applied linguistics – and from the 1960s onwards, often from the discipline of second language acquisition. However, some methods were based on learning theories not specific to language learning; for example, Audiolingualism (Chapter 4) drew on behaviorism. Total Physical Response (TPR) is another example of a teaching method that goes outside mainstream applied linguistics for its theoretical basis. It is a language teaching method built around the coordination of speech and action; it attempts to teach language through physical (motor) activity. Developed by James Asher, who was a professor of psychology at San Jose State University, California, it draws on several traditions, including developmental psychology, learning theory, and humanistic pedagogy, as well as on language teaching procedures proposed by Harold and Dorothy Palmer in 1925. Let us briefly consider these precedents to TPR.

TPR is linked to the "trace theory" of memory in psychology (e.g., Katona 1940), which holds that the more often or more intensively a memory connection is traced, the stronger the memory association will be and the more likely it will be recalled. Retracing can be done verbally (e.g., by rote repetition) and/or in association with motor activity. Combined tracing activities, such as verbal rehearsal accompanied by motor activity, hence increase the probability of successful recall.

In a development sense, Asher sees successful adult second language learning as a parallel process to child first language acquisition. He claims that speech directed to young children consists primarily of commands which children respond to physically before they begin to produce verbal responses. Asher feels adults should recapitulate the processes by which children acquire their mother tongue.

Asher shares with the school of humanistic psychology a concern for the role of affective (emotional) factors in language learning. A method that is undemanding in terms of linguistic production and that involves gamelike movements reduces learner stress, he believes, and creates a positive mood in the learner, which facilitates learning.

Asher's emphasis on developing comprehension skills before the learner is taught to speak links him to a movement in foreign language teaching sometimes referred to as the Comprehension Approach (Winitz 1981). This refers to several different comprehension-based language teaching proposals which share the belief that (a) comprehension abilities precede productive skills in learning a language; (b) the teaching of speaking should be delayed until comprehension skills are established; (c) skills acquired through listening transfer to other skills; (d) teaching should emphasize meaning rather than form; and (e) teaching should minimize learner stress. These principles are also compatible with the tenets of the Natural Approach (Chapter 14).

The emphasis on comprehension and the use of physical actions to teach a foreign language at an introductory level has a long tradition in language teaching. We saw in Chapter 1 that in the nineteenth century Gouin had advocated a situationally based teaching strategy in which a chain of action verbs served as the basis for introducing and practicing new language items. Palmer experimented with an action-based teaching strategy in his book *English through Actions* (first published in Tokyo in 1925 and ultimately reissued as Palmer and Palmer in 1959), which claimed that "no method of teaching foreign speech is likely to be economical or successful which does not include in the first period a very considerable proportion of that type of classroom work which consists of the carrying out by the pupil of orders issued by the teacher" (Palmer and Palmer 1959: 39).

Approach

Theory of language

Asher does not directly discuss the nature of language or how languages are organized. However, the labeling and ordering of TPR classroom drills seem to be built on assumptions that owe much to structuralist or grammar-based views of languages. Asher states that "most of the grammatical structure of the target language and hundreds of vocabulary items can be learned from the skilful use of the imperative by the instructor" (1977: 4). He views the verb in the imperative as the central linguistic motif around which language use and learning are organized.

Asher sees language as being composed of abstractions and non-abstractions, with non-abstractions being most specifically represented by concrete nouns and imperative verbs. He believes that learners can acquire a "detailed cognitive map" as well as "the grammatical structure of a language" without recourse to abstractions. Abstractions should be delayed until students have internalized a detailed cognitive map of the target language. Abstractions are not necessary for people to decode the grammatical structure of a language. Once students have internalized the code, abstractions can be introduced and explained in the target language (Asher 1977: 11–12).

Despite Asher's belief in the central role of comprehension in language learning, he does not elaborate on the relation between comprehension, production, and communication (e.g., he has no theory of speech acts, or functions [Chapter 5] or their equivalents), although in advanced TPR lessons imperatives are used to initiate different speech acts, such as requests ("John, ask Mary to walk to the door"), and apologies ("Ned, tell Jack you're sorry"). Asher also refers in passing to the fact that language can be internalized as wholes or chunks, as defined in the Lexical Approach (Chapter 11), rather than as single lexical items, and, as such, links are possible to more theoretical proposals of this kind as well as to work on the role of prefabricated patterns in language learning and language use (e.g., Pawley and Syder 1983: Boers et al. 2006).

Theory of learning

Asher's language learning theories are reminiscent of the views of other behavioral views of learning. Although psychologists have abandoned such simple stimulus–response models of language acquisition and development, and although SLA theory has long rejected them as incapable of accounting for the fundamental features of second language learning and use (see Chapters 2 and 4), Asher still sees a stimulus–response view as providing the learning theory underlying language teaching pedagogy. In addition, Asher has an elaborate account of what he feels facilitates or inhibits foreign language learning. For this dimension of his learning theory, he draws on three rather influential learning hypotheses:

1. There exists a specific innate bio-program for language learning, which defines an optimal path for first and second language development.
2. Brain lateralization defines different learning functions in the left- and right-brain hemispheres.
3. Stress (an affective filter) intervenes between the act of learning and what is to be learned; the lower the stress, the greater the learning.

Let us consider how Asher views each of these in turn.

The bio program

Asher's TPR is a "Natural Method" (see Chapters 1 and 14), in as much as Asher sees first and second language learning as parallel processes. Second language teaching and learning should reflect the naturalistic processes of first language learning. Asher sees three processes as central. (a) Children develop listening competence before they develop the ability to speak. At the early stages of first language acquisition, they can understand complex utterances that they cannot spontaneously produce or imitate. Asher speculates that during this period of listening, the learner may be making a mental "blueprint" of the language that will make it possible to produce spoken language later. (b) Children's ability in listening comprehension is acquired because children are required to respond physically to spoken language in the form of parental commands. (c) Once a foundation in listening comprehension has been established, speech evolves naturally and effortlessly out of it. As we noted earlier, these principles are held by proponents of a number of other method proposals and are referred to collectively as a Comprehension Approach.

Parallel to the processes of first language learning, the foreign language learner should first internalize a "cognitive map" of the target language through listening exercises. Listening should be accompanied by physical movement. Speech and other productive skills should come later. The speech-production mechanisms will begin to function spontaneously when the basic foundations of language are established through listening training. Asher bases these assumptions on his belief in the human brain of a bio-program for language, which defines an optimal order for first and second language learning.

A reasonable hypothesis is that the brain and nervous system are biologically programmed to acquire language … in a particular sequence and in a particular mode. The sequence is listening before speaking and the mode is to synchronize language with the individual's body.

(Asher 1977: 4)

Brain lateralization

Asher sees TPR as directed to right-brain learning, whereas most second learning teaching methods are directed to left-brain learning. Asher refers to neurological studies of the brains of cats and studies of a boy with a seizure disorder whose corpus callosum, connecting the left and right hemispheres of the brain, was surgically divided, at which point the boy's language function appeared to move from the left to the right hemisphere. Asher interprets these studies as demonstrating that the brain is divided into hemispheres according to function, with language activities centralized in the right hemispheres. Drawing on work by Jean Piaget, Asher holds that the child language learner acquires language through motor movement – a right-hemisphere activity. Right-hemisphere activities must occur before the left hemisphere can process language for production.

Similarly, the adult should proceed to language mastery through right-hemisphere motor activities, while the left hemisphere watches and learns. When a sufficient amount of right-hemisphere learning has taken place, the left hemisphere will be triggered to produce language and to initiate other, more abstract language processes.

Reduction of stress

An important condition for successful language learning is the absence of stress. First language acquisition takes place in a stress-free environment, according to Asher, whereas the adult language learning environment often causes considerable stress and anxiety. The key to stress-free learning is to tap into the natural bio-program for language development and thus to recapture the relaxed and pleasurable experiences that accompany first language learning. By focusing on meaning interpreted through movement, rather than on language forms studied in the abstract, the learner is said to be liberated from self-conscious and stressful situations and is able to devote full energy to learning.

Design

Objectives

The general objectives of TPR are to teach oral proficiency at a beginning level. Comprehension is a means to an end, and the ultimate aim is to teach basic speaking skills. A TPR course aims to produce learners who are capable of an uninhibited communication that is intelligible to a native speaker. Specific instructional objectives are not elaborated, for these will depend on the particular needs of the learners. Whatever goals are set, however, must be attainable through the use of action-based drills in the imperative form. Conversational dialogues are delayed until after about 120 hours of instruction.

The syllabus

The type of syllabus Asher uses can be inferred from an analysis of the exercise types employed in TPR classes. This analysis reveals the use of a sentence-based syllabus, with grammatical and lexical criteria being primary in selecting teaching items. Unlike methods that operate from a grammar-based or structural view of the core elements of language, TPR requires initial attention to meaning rather than to the form of items. Grammar is thus taught inductively. Grammatical features and vocabulary items are selected not according to their frequency of need or use in target-language situations, but according to the situations in which they can be used in the classroom and the ease with which they can be learned.

The criterion for including a vocabulary item or grammatical feature at a particular point in training is ease of assimilation by students. If an item is not learned rapidly, this means that the students are not ready for that item. Withdraw it and try again at a future time in the training program (Asher 1977: 42). Asher also suggests that a fixed number of items be introduced at a time, to facilitate ease of differentiation and assimilation. "In an hour, it is possible for students to assimilate 12 to 36 new lexical items depending upon the size of the group and the stage of training" (ibid.). Asher sees a need for attention to both the global meaning of language, or the overall communicative purpose, and to the finer details of its organization, that is, its grammatical structure.

The movement of the body seems to be a powerful mediator for the understanding, organization, and storage of macro-details of linguistic input. Language can be internalized in chunks, but alternative strategies must be developed for fine-tuning to macro-details, such as the grammar of these chunks or the function of individual words within them (Asher, Kusodo, and de la Torre 1974: 28).

A course designed around TPR principles, however, would not be expected to follow a TPR syllabus exclusively.

> We are not advocating only one strategy of learning. Even if the imperative is the major or minor format of training, variety is critical for maintaining continued student interest. The imperative is a powerful facilitator of learning, but it should be used in combination with many other techniques. The optimal combination will vary from instructor to instructor and class to class.
>
> (Asher 1977: 28)

Types of learning and teaching activities

Imperative drills are the major classroom activity in TPR, for the first 120 hours of instruction, as mentioned. They are typically used to elicit physical actions and activity on the part of the learners. Asher's rationale for this is that "everyday conversations are highly abstract and disconnected; therefore to understand them requires a rather advanced internalization of the target language" (1977: 95). Other class activities include role plays and slide presentations. Role plays center on everyday situations, such as at the restaurant, supermarket, or gas station. Slide presentations are used to provide a visual center for teacher narration, which is followed by commands, and for questions to students, such as "Which person in the picture is the salesperson?" Reading and writing activities may also be employed to further consolidate structures and vocabulary, and as follow-ups to oral imperative drills.

Learner roles

Learners in TPR have the primary roles of listener and performer. They listen attentively and respond physically to commands given by the teacher. Learners are required to respond both individually and collectively. Learners have little influence over the content of learning, since content is determined by the teacher, who must follow the imperative-based format for lessons. Learners are also expected to recognize and respond to novel combinations of previously taught items:

> Novel utterances are recombinations of constituents you have used directly in training. For instance, you directed students with "Walk to the table!" and "Sit on the chair!" These are familiar to students since they have practiced responding to them. Now, will a student understand if you surprise the individual with an unfamiliar utterance that you created by recombining familiar elements (e.g. "Sit on the table!").
>
> (Asher 1977: 31)

Learners are also required to produce novel combinations of their own.

Learners monitor and evaluate their own progress. They are encouraged to speak when they feel ready to speak – that is, when a sufficient basis in the language has been internalized.

Teacher roles

The teacher plays an active and direct role in TPR: "The instructor is the director of a stage play in which the students are the actors" (Asher 1977: 43). It is the teacher who decides what to teach, who models and presents the new materials, and who selects supporting materials for classroom use. The teacher is encouraged to be well prepared and well organized so that the lesson flows smoothly and predictably. Asher recommends detailed lesson plans: "It is wise to write out the exact utterances you will be using and especially the novel commands because the action is so fast-moving there is usually not time for you to create spontaneously" (1977: 47). Classroom interaction and turn taking is teacher-directed rather than learner-directed. Even when learners interact with other learners, it is usually the teacher who initiates the interaction:

> Teacher: Maria, pick up the box of rice and hand it to Miguel and ask Miguel to read the price.

Asher stresses, however, that the teacher's role is not so much to teach as to provide opportunities for learning. The teacher has the responsibility of providing the best kind of exposure to language so that the learner can internalize the basic rules of the target language. Thus, the teacher controls the language input the learners receive, providing the raw material for the "cognitive map" that the learners will construct in their own minds. The teacher should also allow speaking abilities to develop in learners at the learners' own natural pace.

In giving feedback to learners, the teacher should follow the example of parents giving feedback to their children. At first, parents correct very little, but as the child grows older, parents are said to tolerate fewer mistakes in speech. Similarly teachers should refrain from too much correction in the early stages and should not interrupt to correct errors, since this will inhibit learners. As time goes on, however, more teacher intervention is expected, as the learners' speech becomes "fine-tuned."

Asher cautions teachers about preconceptions that he feels could hinder the successful implementation of TPR principles. First, he cautions against the "illusion of simplicity," where the teacher underestimates the difficulties involved in learning a foreign language. This results in progressing at too fast a pace and failing to provide a gradual transition from one teaching stage to another. The teacher should also avoid having too narrow a tolerance for errors in speaking.

> You begin with a wide tolerance for student speech errors, but as training progresses, the tolerance narrows ... Remember that as students progress in their training, more and more attention units are freed to process feedback from the instructor. In the beginning, almost no attention units are available to hear the instructor's attempts to correct distortions in speech. All attention is directed to producing utterances. Therefore the student cannot attend efficiently to the instructor's corrections.
>
> (Asher 1977: 27)

The role of instructional materials

There is generally no basic text in a TPR course. Materials and realia play an increasing role, however, in later learning stages and a number of published resources are now available to support TPR-based teaching. For absolute beginners, lessons may not require the use of materials, since the teacher's voice, actions, and gestures may be a sufficient basis for classroom activities. Later the teacher may use common classroom objects, such as books, pens, cups, furniture. As the course develops, the teacher will need to make or collect supporting materials to support teaching points. These may include pictures, realia, slides, and word charts. Asher has developed TPR student kits that focus on specific situations, such as the home, the supermarket, the beach. Students may use the kits to construct scenes (e.g., "Put the stove in the kitchen").

Procedure

A typical procedure for students in the early phase of a new course, before conversational dialogues are introduced, is presented below and serves as a source of information on the procedures used in the TPR classroom. Asher (1977) provides a lesson-by-lesson account of a course taught according to TPR principles. The course was for adult immigrants and consisted of 159 hours of classroom instruction. The sixth class in the course proceeded in the following way:

Review. This was a fast-moving warm-up in which individual students were moved with commands such as:

Pablo, drive your car around Miako and honk your horn.
Jeffe, throw the red flower to Maria.
Maria, scream.
Rita, pick up the knife and spoon and put them in the cup.
Eduardo, take a drink of water and give the cup to Elaine.

New commands. These verbs were introduced.

Wash	your hands.
	your face.
	your hair.
Look for	a towel.
	the soap.
	a comb.
Hold	the book.
	the cup.
	the soap.
Comb	your hair.
	Maria's hair.
	Shirou's hair.
Brush	your teeth.
	your pants.
	the table.

Other items introduced were:

Rectangle	Draw a rectangle on the chalkboard.
	Pick up a rectangle from the table and give it to me.
	Put the rectangle next to the square.
Triangle	Pick up the triangle from the table and give it to me.
	Catch the triangle and put it next to the rectangle.
Quickly	Walk quickly to the door and hit it.
	Quickly, run to the table and touch the square.
	Sit down quickly and laugh.
Slowly	Walk slowly to the window and jump.
	Slowly, stand up.
	Slowly walk to me and hit me on the arm.
Toothpaste	Look for the toothpaste.
	Throw the toothpaste to Wing.
	Wing, unscrew the top of the toothpaste.

Toothbrush	Take out your toothbrush.
	Brush your teeth.
	Put your toothbrush in your book.
Teeth	Touch your teeth.
	Show your teeth to Dolores.
	Dolores, point to Eduardo's teeth.
Soap	Look for the soap.
	Give the soap to Elaine.
	Elaine, put the soap in Ramiro's ear.
Towel	Put the towel on Juan's arm.
	Juan, put the towel on your head and laugh.
	Maria, wipe your hands on the towel.

Next, the instructor asked simple questions which the student could answer with a gesture such as pointing. Examples would be:

Where is the towel? [Eduardo, point to the towel!]
Where is the toothbrush? [Miako, point to the toothbrush!]
Where is Dolores?

Role reversal. Students readily volunteered to utter commands that manipulated the behavior of the instructor and other students …

Reading and writing. The instructor wrote on the chalkboard each new vocabulary item and a sentence to illustrate the item. Then she spoke each item and acted out the sentence. The students listened as she read the material. Some copied the information in their notebooks.

(Asher 1977: 54–6)

Conclusion

Total Physical Response is in a sense a revival and extension of the language teaching procedures proposed in Palmer and Palmer's *English through Actions*, updated with references to more recent psychological theories. It enjoyed some popularity when it was first introduced because of its support by those who emphasized the role of comprehension in second language acquisition. Krashen (1981), for example, regards provision of comprehensible input and reduction of stress as keys to successful language acquisition, and he sees performing physical actions in the target language as a means of making input comprehensible and minimizing stress (see Chapter 14). Asher continues to be the primary advocate of TPR. In 2007 he published an article entitled "TPR after 40 Years: Still a Good Idea," and he continues to promote his book and related publications on the TPR website (http://www.tpr-world.com/). Nevertheless, Asher himself has stressed that TPR should be used in association with other methods and techniques. The experimental support for the effectiveness of TPR is sketchy (as it is for most methods) and typically deals with only the very beginning stages of learning. Proponents of Communicative Language Teaching would question the relevance to real-world learner needs of the TPR syllabus and the utterances and sentences used within it. Therefore, as Asher has recommended in more recent years, practitioners of TPR typically follow his suggestion that TPR represents a useful set of techniques and is compatible with other approaches to teaching. Today TPR activities are often included in training courses for teachers of young learners, though not usually Asher's theoretical justifications for them. TPR practices, therefore, may be effective for reasons other than those proposed by Asher and do not necessarily demand commitment to the theories used to justify them.

Discussion questions

1. Asher claims that adults should copy the processes by which children acquire their mother tongue (p. 277). What do you think are some of the ways in which adults learn differently from children?

2. One of the tenets of TPR (and several other comprehension-based approaches) is the practice of receptive before productive skills. Can you think of reasons or situations in which it may be preferable to start with spoken language?

3. In TPR, grammar is taught inductively, and initial attention is paid to meaning rather than form. Can you think of other language teaching methods or approaches that do the same?

4. "Grammatical features and vocabulary items are selected not according to their frequency of need or use in target-language situations, but according to the situations in which they can be used in the classroom and the ease with which they can be learned" (p. 281). What is the reason for this?

5. TPR uses mainly imperatives to teach language at the early stages. Consider the following three situations and give examples of how appropriate language for them could be introduced in this way:

   - Buying a train ticket
   - Watching the news on TV
   - Participating in a classroom discussion with other learners about rising food prices.

   Did you find this easier to do for some tasks than others? Why?

6. *Discovery task.* Several claims are made by proponents of TPR. Let's test these out in a mini experiment.

   1) Find two learners who are willing to assist you and choose a topic you are comfortable teaching (i.e., that you are familiar with and have taught before).
   2) Plan a TPR activity in great detail, deciding beforehand how you will introduce the topic, how you will handle new words, and what responses you expect from your students.

3) Both you and the students answer the questions in the table below.

Questions	Teacher	Students
How much did you enjoy the lesson compared to a normal lesson? (1 = not at all, 5 = very much)		
How stressful was the class?		
How much did you / the students learn? (1 = nothing, 5 = very much)		
How useful do you think what you / the students have learned will be outside the class? (1 = not at all, 5 = very much)		
For the teacher only		
How much preparation time did the class involve compared to your normal classes? (1 = much less, 5 = much more)		

References and further reading

Asher, J. 1965. The strategy of the total physical response: an application to learning Russian. *International Review of Applied Linguistics* 3: 291–300.

Asher, J. 1966. The learning strategy of the total physical response: a review. *Modern Language Journal* 50: 79–84.

Asher, J. 1969. The total physical response approach to second language learning. *Modern Language Journal* 53: 3–17.

Asher, J. 1972. Children's first language as a model of second language learning. *Modern Language Journal* 56: 133–9.

Asher, J. 1977. *Learning Another Language through Actions: The Complete Teacher's Guide Book.* Los Gatos, CA: Sky Oaks Productions. 2nd edn. 1982.

Asher, J. 1981a. The extinction of second language learning in American schools: an intervention model. In H. Winitz (ed.), *The Comprehension Approach to Foreign Language Instruction.* Rowley, MA: Newbury House. 49–68.

Asher, J. 1981b. The fear of foreign languages. *Psychology Today* 15(8): 52–9.

Asher, J., J. A. Kusodo, and R. de la Torre. 1974. Learning a second language through commands: the second field test. *Modern Language Journal* 58: 24 –32.

Asher, J., and B. S. Price. 1967. The learning strategy of the total physical response: some age differences. *Child Development* 38: 1219–27.

Boers, F., J. Eyckmans, J. Kappel, H. Stengers, and M. Demecheleer. 2006. Formulaic sequences and perceived oral proficiency: putting a lexical approach to the test. *Language Teaching Research* 10: 245–61.

DeCecco, J. P. 1968. *The Psychology of Learning and Instruction: Educational Psychology.* Englewood Cliffs, NJ: Prentice Hall.

Katona, G. 1940. *Organizing and Memorizing: Studies in the Psychology of Learning and Teaching.* New York: Columbia University Press.

Krashen, S. D. 1981. *Second Language Acquisition and Second Language Learning.* Oxford: Pergamon.

Kunihira, S., and J. Asher. 1965. The strategy of the total physical response: an application to learning Japanese. *International Review of Applied Linguistics* 3: 277–89.

Miller, G. A., E. Galanter, and K. H. Pribram. 1960. *Plans and the Structure of Behavior.* New York: Henry Holt.

Palmer, H., and D. Palmer. 1925. *English through Actions.* Repr. London: Longman Green, 1959.

Pawley, A., and F. Syder. 1983. Two puzzles for linguistic theory: native-like selection and native-like fluency. In J. Richards and R. Schmidt (eds.), *Language and Communication.* London: Longman. 191–226.

Winitz, H. (ed.). 1981. *The Comprehension Approach to Foreign Language Instruction.* Rowley, MA: Newbury House.

Winitz, H., and J. Reeds. 1975. *Comprehension and Problem Solving as Strategies for Language Training.* The Hague: Mouton.

Yorio, C. 1980. Conventionalized language forms and the development of communicative competence. *TESOL Quarterly* 14(4): 433–42.

16 The Silent Way

Introduction

While some of the teaching methods that have gained prominence at different times represented the consensus of academics, language teaching specialists, and educational institutions and hence were often widely adopted, others have been the product of individual educators advocating a personal view of teaching and learning. Such is the case with the Silent Way. The Silent Way is the name of a method of language teaching devised by Caleb Gattegno (1911–1988). Gattegno's name is well known for his revival of interest in the use of colored wooden sticks called Cuisenaire rods and for his series *Words in Color*, an approach to the teaching of initial reading in which sounds are coded by specific colors. His reading materials are copyrighted and continue to be marketed through Educational Solutions Inc., in New York. The Silent Way represents Gattegno's venture into the field of foreign language teaching. As applied to language teaching, a Silent Way lesson progresses through a number of stages, beginning in a similar way with pronunciation practice and then moving to practice of simple sentence patterns, structure, and vocabulary. It is based on the premise that the teacher should be silent as much as possible in the classroom and the learner should be encouraged to produce as much language as possible. Elements of the Silent Way, particularly the use of color charts and the colored Cuisenaire rods, grew out of Gattegno's previous experience as an educational designer of reading and mathematics programs. (Cuisenaire rods were first developed by Georges Cuisenaire, a European educator who used them for the teaching of math. Gattegno had observed Cuisenaire rods and this gave him the idea for their use in language teaching.) Working from what is a rather traditional structural and lexical syllabus, the Silent Way method exemplifies many of the features that characterize more traditional methods, such as Situational Language Teaching (Chapter 3) and Audiolingualism (Chapter 4), with a strong focus on accurate repetition of sentences, modeled initially by the teacher, and a movement through guided elicitation exercises to freer communication.

It is interesting to speculate that one of the reasons for the early popularity of the Silent Way in the United States and its use in official US Foreign Officer and Peace Corps training programs is that silence has been noted to be a stronger inducement to verbalization among Americans than for many other cultural groups. Americans are said to think of communication as essentially a verbal activity (Langer 1942; Knapp 1978). Hence, they are uncomfortable with long periods of silence (Mehrabian 1981). Within the media industries, for example, merchants buy time for advertising and the metaphor of "time is money" becomes a central concern. Dead time (long periods of silence) in radio and television is seen as a critical problem of miscommunication. Periods of silence are avoided among individuals engaged in conversations with others. Silence is seen, in this context, as a moment of awkwardness (St. Clair 2003). Second language teachers typically encourage their students to "speak out" as an essential way of learning. Silence in the Silent Way may have been seen by its American practitioners as a way to lever participation in the foreign language class – that is, have the teacher take responsibility for most of the speaking – so students could avoid "moments of awkwardness."

Approach

Theory of language

Gattegno takes an openly skeptical view of the role of linguistic theory in language teaching methodology. He feels that linguistic studies "may be a specialization, [that] carry with them a narrow opening of one's sensitivity and perhaps serve very little towards the broad end in mind" (Gattegno 1972: 84). In other words, linguistic studies, according to Gattegno, may increase one's sensitivity toward language only slightly and does not contribute in a meaningful way to teaching methodology. Gattegno views language itself "as a substitute for experience, so experience is what gives meaning to language" (1972: 8). We are not surprised, then, to see simulated experiences using tokens and picture charts as central elements in Silent Way teaching.

Considerable discussion is devoted to the importance of grasping the "spirit" of the language, and not just its component forms. By the "spirit" of the language, Gattegno is referring to the way each language is composed of phonological and suprasegmental elements that combine to give the language its unique sound system and melody. The learner must gain a "feel" for this aspect of the target language as soon as possible, though how the learner is to do this is not altogether clear.

By looking at the material chosen and the sequence in which it is presented in a Silent Way classroom, it is clear that the Silent Way takes a structural approach to the organization of language to be taught. Language is seen as groups of sounds arbitrarily associated with specific meanings and organized into sentences or strings of meaningful units by grammar rules. Language is separated from its social context and taught through artificial situations, usually represented by rods. Lessons follow a sequence based on grammatical complexity, and new lexical and structural material is meticulously broken down into its elements, with one element presented at a time. The sentence is the basic unit of teaching, and the teacher focuses on propositional meaning (i.e., complete sentences that generally have a "yes or no" truth value), rather than communicative value. Students are presented with the structural patterns of the target language and learn the grammar rules of the language through largely inductive processes.

Gattegno sees vocabulary as a central dimension of language learning and the choice of vocabulary as crucial. He distinguishes between several classes of vocabulary items. The "semi-luxury vocabulary" consists of expressions common in the daily life of the target language culture; this refers to food, clothing, travel, family life, and so on. "Luxury vocabulary" is used in communicating more specialized ideas, such as political or philosophical opinions. The most important vocabulary for the learner deals with the most functional and versatile words of the language, many of which may not have direct equivalents in the learner's native language. "Functional vocabulary" includes such areas as pronouns, numbers, and comparison words that refer to oneself and to others. This functional vocabulary provides a key, says Gattegno, to comprehending the "spirit" of the language.

Theory of learning

The Silent Way draws on Gattegno's understanding of a cognitive-code theory of learning (see Chapter 2; Atkinson 2011). In cognitively based approaches, language learning is understood as a mental activity – one in which the learner is a lone scientist or explorer, building up his or her understanding of language from exposure to and experience of it. Cognitive approaches to learning are an established approach in psychology and are based on the view that learning reflects properties of the mind and the processes involved in acquiring, storing and retrieving knowledge.

The learning hypotheses underlying Gattegno's work could be stated as follows:

- Learning is facilitated if the learner discovers or creates rather than remembers and repeats what is to be learned.
- Learning is facilitated by accompanying (mediating) physical objects.
- Learning is facilitated by problem-solving involving the material to be learned.

Let us consider each of these issues in turn.

1. The educational psychologist and philosopher Jerome Bruner distinguishes two traditions of teaching – that which takes place in the expository mode and that which takes place in the hypothetical mode. In the expository mode "decisions covering the mode and pace and style of exposition are principally determined by the teacher as expositor: the student is the listener." In the hypothetical mode "the teacher and the student are in a more cooperative position. The student is not a bench-bound listener but is taking part in the formulation and at times may play the principal role in it" (Bruner 1966: 83). The Silent Way belongs to the latter tradition, which views learning as a problem-solving, creative, discovering activity, in which the learner is a principal actor rather than a bench-bound listener. Bruner discusses the benefits derived from "discovery learning" under four headings: (a) the increase in intellectual potency, (b) the shift from extrinsic to intrinsic rewards, (c) the learning of heuristics by discovering, and (d) the aid to conserving memory (Bruner 1966: 83). In other words, this type of learning enhances intellect, is more rewarding, develops the individual's ability to make discoveries, and helps the learner to retain what is learned. As we shall see, Gattegno claims similar benefits from learners taught via the Silent Way.
2. The rods and the color-coded pronunciation charts (called Fidel charts) provide physical foci for student learning and also create memorable images to facilitate student recall. In psychological terms, these visual devices serve as associative mediators for student

learning and recall. The psychological literature on mediation in learning and recall is voluminous but, for our purposes, can be briefly summarized in a quote from Earl Stevick: "If the use of associative mediators produces better retention than repetition does, it seems to be the case that the quality of the mediators and the student's personal investment in them may also have a powerful effect on memory" (1976: 25).

3. The Silent Way is also related to a set of premises that we have called "problem-solving approaches to learning." These premises are succinctly represented in the words of Benjamin Franklin:

> *Tell me and I forget,*
> *teach me and I remember,*
> *involve me and I learn.*

In the languages of experimental psychology, the kind of subject involvement that promotes greatest learning and recall involves processing of material to be learned at the "greatest cognitive depth" (Craik 1973) or, for our purposes, involving the greatest amount of problem-solving activity. Memory research has demonstrated that the learner's "memory benefits from creatively searching out, discovering and depicting" (Bower and Winzenz 1970). In the Silent Way, "the teacher's strict avoidance of repetition forces alertness and concentration on the part of the learners (Gattegno 1972: 80). Similarly, the learner's grappling with the problem of forming an appropriate and meaningful utterance in a new language leads the learner to realization of the language "through his own perceptual and analytical powers" (Selman 1977). The Silent Way student is expected to become "independent, autonomous and responsible" (Gattegno 1976) – in other words, a good problem-solver in language.

Like many other method proponents, Gattegno also makes extensive use of his understanding of first language learning processes as a basis for deriving principles for teaching foreign languages to adults. Gattegno recommends, for example, that the learner needs to "return to the state of mind that characterizes a baby's learning – surrender" (Scott and Page 1982: 273)

Having referred to these processes, however, Gattegno states that the processes of learning a second language are "radically different" from those involved in learning a first language. The second language learner is unlike the first language learner and "cannot learn another language in the same way because of what he now knows" (Gattegno 1972: 11). The "natural" or "direct" approaches to acquiring a second language are thus misguided, says Gattegno, and a successful second language approach will "replace a 'natural' approach by one that is very 'artificial' and, for some purposes, strictly controlled" (1972: 12). The "artificial approach" that Gattegno proposes is based on the principle that successful learning involves commitment of the self to language acquisition through the use of silent awareness and then active trial. Gattegno's repeated emphasis on the primacy of learning over teaching places a focus on the self of the learner, on the learner's priorities and commitments.

Awareness is educable. As one learns "in awareness," one's powers of awareness and one's capacity to learn become greater. Again, the process chain that develops awareness proceeds from attention, production, self-correction, and absorption. Silent Way learners acquire "inner criteria," which play a central role "in one's education throughout all of one's life" (Gattegno 1976: 29). These inner criteria allow learners to monitor and self-correct their own production. It is in the activity of self-correction through self-awareness that the Silent Way claims to differ most notably from other ways of language learning. It is this capacity for self-awareness that the Silent Way calls upon, a capacity said to be little appreciated or exercised by first language learners.

However, the Silent Way is not merely a language teaching method. Gattegno sees language learning through the Silent Way as a recovery of innocence – "a return to our full powers and potential." Gattegno's aim is not just second language learning; it is nothing less than the education of the spiritual powers and of the sensitivity of the individual. Mastery of linguistic skills are seen in the light of an emotional inner peace resulting from the sense of power and control brought about by new levels of awareness.

Design

Objectives

The general objective of the Silent Way is to give beginning-level students oral and aural facility in basic elements of the target language. The general goal set for language learning is near-native fluency in the target language, and correct pronunciation and mastery of the prosodic elements (variations of pitch, stress, and rhythm) of the target language are emphasized. An immediate objective is to provide the learner with a basic practical knowledge of the grammar of the language. This forms the basis for independent learning on the learner's part. Gattegno discusses the following kinds of objectives as appropriate for a language course at an elementary level (1972: 81–3). Students should be able to:

- correctly and easily answer questions about themselves, their education, their family, travel, and daily events;
- speak with a good accent;
- give either a written or an oral description of a picture, "including the existing relationships that concern space, time and numbers";
- answer general questions about the culture and the literature of the native speakers of the target language;
- perform adequately in the following areas: spelling, grammar (production rather than explanation), reading comprehension, and writing.

Gattegno states that the Silent Way teaches learners *how* to learn a language, and the skills developed through the process of learning a foreign or second language can be employed in dealing with "unknowns" of every type. The method, we are told, can also be used to teach reading and writing, and its usefulness is not restricted to beginning-level students. Most of the examples Gattegno describes, however, as well as the classes we have observed, deal primarily with a basic level of aural/oral proficiency.

The syllabus

The Silent Way adopts a basically structural syllabus, with lessons planned around grammatical items and related vocabulary. Gattegno does not, however, provide details as to the precise selection and arrangement of grammatical and lexical items to be covered. There is no general Silent Way syllabus. But from observation of Silent Way programs developed by the Peace Corps to teach a variety of languages at a basic level of proficiency, it is clear that language items are introduced according to their grammatical complexity, their relationship to what has been taught previously, and the ease with which items can be presented visually. Typically, the imperative is the initial structure introduced, because of the ease with which action verbs may be demonstrated using Silent Way materials. New elements, such as the plural form of nouns, are taught within a structure already familiar. Numeration occurs early in a course, because of the importance of numbers in everyday life and the ease with which they can be demonstrated. Prepositions of location also appear early in the syllabus for similar reasons.

Vocabulary is selected according to the degree to which it can be manipulated within a given structure and according to its productivity within the classroom setting. In addition to prepositions and numbers, pronouns, quantifiers, words dealing with temporal relations, and words of comparison are introduced early in the course, because they "refer to oneself and to others in the numerous relations of everyday life" (Stevick 1976). These kinds of words, as mentioned earlier, are referred to as the "functional vocabulary" of a language because of their high utility.

The following is a section of a Peace Corps Silent Way Syllabus for the first ten hours of instruction in Thai. It was used to teach American Peace Corps volunteers being trained to teach in Thailand. At least 15 minutes of every hour of instruction would be spent on pronunciation. A word that is italicized can be substituted for by another word having the same part of speech or purpose. (The English represents translations of the Thai sentences.)

Lesson	*Vocabulary*
1. Wood color *red*.	wood, red, green, yellow, brown, pink, white, orange, black, color
2. Using the numbers 1–10.	one, two, … ten
3. Wood color *red* two pieces.	
4. Take (pick up) wood color *red* two pieces.	take (pick up)
5. Take wood color *red* two pieces give *him*.	give, object pronouns
6. Wood *red* where? Wood *red* on table.	where, on, under, near, far, over, next to, here, there
7. Wood color red on table, *is it*? Yes, on. Not on.	Question-forming rules. Yes, No.

8. Wood color *red long*.
   Wood color *green longer*.
   Wood color orange *longest*.
9. Wood color green *taller*.
   Wood color *red*, is it?
10. Review. Students use structures taught
    in new situations, such as comparing the
    heights of students in the class.

adjectives of comparison

(Joel Wiskin, personal communication)

Types of learning and teaching activities

Learning tasks and activities in the Silent Way have the function of encouraging and shaping student oral response without direct oral instruction from or unnecessary modeling by the teacher. Basic to the method are simple linguistic tasks in which the teacher models a word, phrase, or sentence and then elicits learner responses, initially by having learners silently carry out their commands containing these words, phrases, or sentences. Learners then go on to create their own utterances by putting together old and new information. Charts, rods, and other aids may be used to elicit learner responses, and much of the activity may be teacher-directed. However, after the initial presentation of language, teacher modeling is minimal. Responses to commands, questions, and visual cues thus constitute the basis for classroom activities.

Learner roles

Gattegno sees language learning as a process of personal growth resulting from growing student awareness and self-challenge. The learner first experiences a "random or almost random feeling of the area of activity in question until one finds one or more cornerstones to build on. Then starts a systematic analysis, first by trial and error, later by directed experiment with practice of the acquired subareas until mastery follows" (Gattegno 1972: 79). Learners are expected to develop independence, autonomy, and responsibility. Independent learners are those who are aware that they must depend on their own resources and realize that they can use "the knowledge of their own language to open up some things in a new language" or that they can "take their knowledge of the first few words in the new language and figure out additional words by using that knowledge" (Stevick 1980: 42). The autonomous learner chooses proper expressions in a given set of circumstances and situations. "The teacher cultivates the student's 'autonomy' by deliberately building choices into situations" (Stevick 1980: 42). Responsible learners know that they have free will to choose among any set of linguistic choices. The ability to choose intelligently and carefully is said to be evidence of responsibility. The absence of correction and repeated modeling from the teacher requires the students to develop "inner criteria" and to correct themselves. The absence of explanations requires learners to make generalizations, come to their own conclusions, and formulate whatever rules they themselves feel they need.

Learners exert a strong influence over each other's learning and, to a lesser degree, over the linguistic content taught. They are expected to interact with each other and suggest alternatives to each other. Learners have only themselves as individuals and the group to rely on, and so must learn to work cooperatively rather than competitively. They need to feel comfortable both correcting each other and being corrected by each other.

In order to be productive members of the learning group, learners thus have to play varying roles. At times one is an independent individual, at other times a group member. A learner also must be a teacher, a student, part of a support system, a problem-solver, and a self-evaluator. And it is the student who is usually expected to decide on what roles are most appropriate to a given situation.

Teacher roles

Teacher silence is, perhaps, the unique and, for many traditionally trained language teachers, the most demanding aspect of the Silent Way. Teachers are exhorted to resist their long-standing commitment to model, remodel, assist, and direct desired student responses. Silent Way teachers have remarked upon the arduousness of self-restraint to which early experience of the Silent Way has subjected them. Gattegno talks of subordinating "teaching to learning," but that is not to suggest that the teacher's role in Silent Way is not critical and demanding. Gattegno anticipates that using the Silent Way would require most teachers to change their perception of their role. Stevick (1980: 56) defines the Silent Way teacher's tasks as (a) to teach, (b) to test, and (c) to get out of the way. Although this may not seem to constitute a radical alternative to standard teaching practice, the details of the steps the teacher is expected to follow are unique to the Silent Way.

By "teaching" is meant the presentation of an item once, typically using nonverbal clues to get across meanings. Testing follows immediately and might better be termed elicitation and shaping of student production, which, again, is done in as silent a way as possible. Finally, the teacher silently monitors learners' interactions with each other and may even leave the room while learners struggle with their new linguistic tools. For the most part, Silent Way teacher's manuals are unavailable (however, see Arnold 1981), and teachers are responsible for designing teaching sequences and creating individual lessons and lesson elements. Gattegno emphasized the importance of teacher-defined learning goals that are clear and attainable. Sequence and timing in Silent Way classes are more important than in many kinds of language teaching classes, and the teacher's sensitivity to and management of them is critical.

More generally, the teacher is responsible for creating an environment that encourages student risk-taking and that facilitates learning. This is not to say that the Silent Way teacher becomes "one of the group." In fact, observers have noted that Silent Way teachers often appear aloof or even gruff with their students. The teacher's role is one of neutral observer, neither elated by correct performance nor discouraged by error. Students are expected to come to see the teacher as a disinterested judge, supportive but emotionally uninvolved. The teacher uses gestures, charts, and manipulatives in order to elicit and shape student responses and so must be both facile and creative as a pantomimist and puppeteer. In sum, the Silent Way teacher, like the complete dramatist, writes the script, chooses the props, sets the mood, models the action, designates the players, and is critic for the performance.

The role of instructional materials

The Silent Way is perhaps as well known for the unique nature of its teaching materials as for the silence of its teachers. The materials consist mainly of a set of colored rods, color-coded pronunciation and vocabulary wall charts, a pointer, and reading/writing exercises, all of which are used to illustrate the relationships between sound and meaning in the target language. The materials are designed for manipulation by the students as well as by the teacher, independently and cooperatively, in promoting language learning by direct association.

The pronunciation charts, called "Fidels," have been devised for a number of languages and contain symbols in the target language for all of the vowel and consonant sounds of the language. The symbols are color-coded according to pronunciation; thus, if a language possesses two different symbols for the same sound, they will be colored alike. Classes often begin by using Fidel charts in the native language, color-coded in an analogous manner, so that students learn to pair sounds with its associated color. There may be from one to eight of such charts, depending upon the language. The teacher uses the pointer to indicate a sound symbol for the students to produce. Where native-language Fidels are used, the teacher will point to a symbol on one chart and then to its analogues on the Fidel in the other language. In the absence of native-language charts, or when introducing a sound not present in the native language, the teacher will give one clear, audible model after indicating the proper Fidel symbol in the target language. The charts are hung on the wall and serve to aid in remembering pronunciation and in building new words by sounding out sequences of symbols as they are pointed to by the teacher or student.

Just as the Fidel charts are used to visually illustrate pronunciation, the colored Cuisenaire rods are used to directly link words and structures with their meanings in the target language, thereby avoiding translation into the native language. The rods vary in length from 1 to 10 centimeters, and each length has a specific color. The rods may be used for naming colors, for size comparisons, to represent people, build floor plans, constitute a road map, and so on. Use of the rods is intended to promote inventiveness, creativity, and interest in forming communicative utterances on the part of the students, as they move from simple to more complex structures. Gattegno and his proponents believe that the range of structures that can be illustrated and learned through skillful use of the rods is as limitless as the human imagination. When the teacher or student has difficulty expressing a desired word or concept, the rods can be supplemented by referring to the Fidel charts, or to the third major visual aid used in the Silent Way, the vocabulary charts.

The vocabulary or word charts are likewise color-coded, although the colors of the symbols will not correspond to the phonetics of the Fidels, but rather to conceptual groupings of words. There are typically twelve such charts containing 500 to 800 words in the native language and script. These words are selected according to their ease of application in teaching, their relative significance in the "functional" or "luxury" vocabulary, their flexibility in terms of generalization and use with other words, and their importance in illustrating basic grammatical structures. The content of word charts will vary from language to language, but the general content of the vocabulary charts (Gattegno 1972) is paraphrased below:

Chart 1:	the word rod, colors of the rods, plural markers, simple imperative verbs, personal pronouns, some adjectives and question words
Charts 2, 3:	remaining pronouns, words for "here" and "there," *of, for,* and *name*
Chart 4:	numbers
Charts 5, 6:	words illustrating size, space, and temporal relationships as well as some concepts difficult to illustrate with rods, such as order, causality, condition, similarity, and difference
Chart 7:	words that qualify, such as adverbs
Charts 8, 9:	verbs, with cultural references where possible
Chart 10:	family relationships
Charts 11, 12:	words expressing time, calendar elements, seasons, days, week, month, year, etc.

Other materials that may be used include books and worksheets for practicing reading and writing skills, picture books, tapes, videotapes, films, and other visual aids. Reading and writing are sometimes taught from the beginning, and students are given assignments to do outside the classroom at their own pace. These materials are of secondary importance and are used to supplement the classroom use of rods and charts. Choice and implementation depends upon need as assessed by teachers and/or students.

Procedure

A Silent Way lesson typically follows a standard format. The first part of the lesson focuses on pronunciation. Depending on student level, the class might work on sounds, phrases, even sentences designated on the Fidel chart. At the beginning stage, the teacher will model the appropriate sound after pointing to a symbol on the chart. Later, the teacher will silently point to individual symbols and combinations of utterances, and monitor student utterances. The teacher may say a word and have students guess what word the sequence of symbols represents. The pointer is used to indicate stress, phrasing, and intonation. Stress can be shown by touching certain symbols more forcibly than others when pointing out a word. Intonation and phrasing can be demonstrated by tapping on the chart to the rhythm of the utterance.

After practice with the sounds of the language, sentence patterns, structure, and vocabulary are practiced. The teacher models an utterance while creating a visual realization of it with the colored rods. After modeling the utterance, the teacher will have a student attempt to produce the utterance and will indicate its acceptability. If a response is incorrect, the teacher will attempt to reshape the utterance or have another student present the correct model. After a structure is introduced and understood, the teacher will create a situation in which the students can practice the structure through the manipulation of the rods. Variations on the structural theme will be elicited from the class using the rods and charts.

The sample lesson that follows illustrates a typical lesson format. The language being taught is Thai, for which this is the first lesson.

1. Teacher empties rods onto the table.
2. Teacher picks up two or three rods of different colors, and after each rod is picked up says: [mai].
3. Teacher holds up one rod of any color and indicates to a student that a response is required. Student says: [mai]. If response is incorrect, teacher elicits response from another student, who then models for the first student.
4. Teacher next picks up a red rod and says: [mai sii daeng].
5. Teacher picks up a green rod and says: [mai sii khiaw].
6. Teacher picks up either a red or green rod and elicits response from student. If response is incorrect, procedure in step 3 is followed (student modeling).
7. Teacher introduces two or three other colors in the same manner.
8. Teacher shows any of the rods whose forms were taught previously and elicits student response. Correction technique is through student modeling, or the teacher may help student isolate error and self-correct.
9. When mastery is achieved, teacher puts one red rod in plain view and says: [mai sii daeng nung an].
10. Teacher then puts two red rods in plain view and says: [mai sii daeng song an].
11. Teacher places two green rods in view and says: [mai sii khiaw song an].
12. Teacher holds up two rods of a different color and elicits student response.
13. Teacher introduces additional numbers, based on what the class can comfortably retain. Other colors might also be introduced.
14. Rods are put in a pile. Teacher indicates, through his or her own actions, that rods should be picked up, and the correct utterance made. All the students in the group pick up rods and make utterances. Peer-group correction is encouraged.
15. Teacher then says: [kep mai sii daeng song an].
16. Teacher indicates that a student should give the teacher the rods called for. Teacher asks other students in the class to give him or her the rods that he or she asks for. This is all done in the target language through unambiguous actions on the part of the teacher.
17. Teacher now indicates that the students should give each other commands regarding the calling for of rods. Rods are put at the disposal of the class.
18. Experimentation is encouraged. Teacher speaks only to correct an incorrect utterance, if no peer-group correction is forthcoming.

(Joel Wiskin, personal communication)

Conclusion

Despite the philosophical and sometimes almost metaphysical quality of much of Gattegno's writings, the actual practices of the Silent Way are much less revolutionary than might be expected. As noted earlier, the Silent Way follows a traditional grammatical and lexical syllabus and moves from guided repetition to freer practice. The innovations in Gattegno's method derive primarily from the manner in which classroom activities are organized, the indirect role the teacher is required to assume in directing and monitoring learner performance, the responsibility placed on learners to figure out and test their hypotheses about how the language works, and the materials used to elicit and practice language. Although the Silent Way has been viewed as outside the mainstream of language teaching since its inception, it continues to be promoted with enthusiasm by small numbers of users in different parts of the word. In 2011 a commemorative volume was published on the occasion of the 100th anniversary of Gattegno's birth, containing accounts of teachers' successful use of the method as the basis for introductory courses in many different languages and in many different countries (Educational Solutions Inc. 2011). However, because of its status as a "fringe" method, it has not attracted the attention of researchers in language acquisition or of the applied linguistic community; hence, there is little research available to enable its claims to be seriously evaluated. For many of its practitioners, little further evidence is needed apart from the success they report in using it.

Discussion questions

1. The Silent Way makes extensive use of Cuisenaire rods to teach aspects of the language. Do you see a value in this approach? What kinds of realia do you use in your classes, and for what purpose?

2. Related to this, Stevick says that rods and pronunciation charts create memory aids, and that these physical aids are "associative mediators": "If the use of associative mediators produces better retention than repetition does, it seems to be the case that the quality of the mediators and the student's personal investment in them may also have a powerful effect on memory" (p. 292). How can teachers improve the quality of the mediators (i.e., what would be an example of a good mediator) and students' investment in them?

3. By the "spirit" of the language, Gattegno is referring to the way in which each language is composed of phonological and suprasegmental elements that combine to give the language its unique sound system and melody. To some people this may sound rather vague. Have you noticed examples in your own language study where phonological and suprasegmental elements (such as its intonation and rhythm) give languages a special, recognizable voice quality or tone?

4. Language that is processed more deeply (Craik 1973), or that involves the greatest amount of problem-solving, is likely to lead to better learning outcomes. How would you measure how deeply something was processed by a learner, or how much problem-solving it involves?

5. In the Silent Way, mastery of linguistic skills is seen in the light of an emotional inner peace resulting from the sense of power and control brought about by new levels of awareness. It is perhaps understandable that this aspect of the Silent Way did not become part of mainstream language teaching. Keeping an open mind, however, what do you think the benefits for learning of "an emotional inner peace" and "awareness" are? How might the Silent Way, in this respect, be similar to some of the elements of Cooperative Language Learning (Chapter 13) or the Natural Approach (Chapter 14)?

6. The first part of a Silent Way lesson is usually dedicated to pronunciation. Why do you think there is such a strong focus on pronunciation?

7. Search on the Internet for a video of a Silent Way lesson. One is currently available on YouTube (http://bit.ly/ZqwC5S). As you watch the video, answer the following questions.

How is new language introduced?	
What kind of language is used?	
Who does most of the talking?	
What kind of feedback do learners receive?	
Can you identify aspects of the lesson that reflect the "spirit" of the language? Give examples.	

References and further reading

Arnold, F. 1981. *College English: A Silent-Way Approach.* Nara, Japan: Dawn Press.

Atkinson, D. (ed.). 2011. *Alternative Approaches to Second Language Acquisition.* London: Routledge.

Blair, R. W. (ed.). 1982. *Innovative Approaches to Language Teaching.* Rowley, MA: Newbury House.

Bower, G. H., and D. Winzenz. 1970. Comparison of associative learning strategies. *Psychonomic Sciences* 20: 119–20.

Bruner, J. 1966. *On Knowing: Essays for the Left Hand.* New York: Atheneum.

Cheery, D. 1994. Learning with rods: one account. Master's thesis, School for International Training, Brattleboro, Vermont.

Craik, F. I. M. 1973. A levels of analysis view of memory. In P. Pliner, L. Krames, and T. Alloway (eds.), *Communication and Affect: Language and Thought.* New York: Academic Press. 112–19.

Diller, C. 1978. *The Language Teaching Controversy.* Rowley, MA: Newbury House.

Gattegno, C. 1972. *Teaching Foreign Languages in Schools: The Silent Way.* 2nd edn. New York: Educational Solutions.

Gattegno, C. 1976. *The Common Sense of Teaching Foreign Languages*. New York: Educational Solutions.

Educational Solutions Inc 2011. *The Gattegno Effect*. http://www.educationalsolutions.com

Knapp, M. L. 1978. *Nonverbal Communication in Human Interaction*. 2nd edn. New York: Holt, Rinehart and Winston.

Langer, S. K. 1942. *Philosophy in a New Key*. Cambridge, MA: Harvard University Press.

Mehrabian, A. 1981. *Silent Messages: Implicit Communication of Emotions and Attitudes*. Belmont, CA: Wadsworth Publishing Company.

Mataira, K. 1980. The effectiveness of the Silent Way method in the teaching of Maori as a second language. Master's thesis, University of Waikato, New Zealand.

Rossner, R. 1982. Talking shop: a conversation with Caleb Gattegno, inventor of the Silent Way. *ELT Journal* 36(4): 237–41.

Scott, R., and M. Page. 1982. The subordination of teaching to learning: a seminar conducted by Dr. Caleb Gattegno. *ELT Journal* 36(4): 273–4.

Selman, M. 1977. The Silent Way: insights for ESL. *TESL Talk* 8: 33–6.

St. Clair, R. N. 2003. The social and cultural construction of silence. *Intercultural Communication Studies* 12(3): 87–91.

Stevick, E. W. 1976. *Memory, Meaning and Method: Some Psychological Perspectives on Language Learning*. Rowley, MA: Newbury House.

Stevick, E. W. 1980. *Teaching Languages: A Way and Ways*. Rowley, MA: Newbury House.

Thompson, G. J. 1980. The Silent Way: interpretation and application. Master's thesis, University of Hawaii.

Varvel, T. 1979. The Silent Way: panacea or pipedream? *TESOL Quarterly* 13(4): 483–94.

17 Community Language Learning

Introduction

Community Language Learning (CLL[1]) is the name of a method developed by Charles A. Curran and his associates. Curran was a specialist in counseling and a professor of psychology at Loyola University, Chicago. His application of psychological counseling techniques to learning is known as Counseling-Learning. CLL represents the use of Counseling-Learning theory to teach languages. As the name indicates, CLL derives its primary insights, and indeed its organizing rationale, from Rogerian counseling. Counseling, as Rogerians see it, consists of one individual (the counselor) assuming, insofar as he or she is able, the internal frame of reference of the client, perceiving the world as that person sees it and communicating something of this empathetic understanding (Rogers 1951). In lay terms, counseling is one person giving advice, assistance, and support to another who has a problem or is in some way in need. CLL draws on the counseling metaphor to redefine the roles of the teacher (the *counselor*) and learners (the *clients*) in the language classroom.

Within the language teaching tradition, CLL is sometimes cited as an example of a "humanistic approach." The content of the language class stems from topics learners want to talk about, and the teacher translates their requests into an appropriate syllabus. Links can also be made between CLL procedures and those of bilingual education, particularly the set of bilingual procedures referred to as *language alternation* or *code switching*. Let us discuss briefly the debt of CLL to these two traditions.

Because of the humanistic approach of CLL, the basic procedures can thus be seen as derived from the counselor–client relationship. Consider the following CLL procedures: A group of learners sit in a circle with the teacher standing outside the circle: a student whispers a message in the native language (L1); the teacher translates it into the foreign language (L2); the student repeats the message in the foreign language into an audio recorder; students compose further messages in the foreign language with the teacher's help; students reflect about their feelings. We can compare the client–counselor relationship in psychological counseling with the learner–knower relationship in CLL (Table 17.1).

---

[1] The abbreviation CLL is also used for Cooperative Language Learning (Chapter 13).

Table 17.1 Comparison of client–counselor relationships in psychological counseling and CLL

Psychological counseling (client–counselor)	Community Language Learning (learner–knower)
1. Client and counselor agree [contract] to counseling.	1. Learner and knower agree to language learning.
2. Client articulates his or her problem in language of affect.	2. Learner presents to the knower (in L1) a message he or she wishes to deliver to another.
3. Counselor listens carefully.	3. Knower listens and other learners overhear.
4. Counselor restates client message in language of cognition.	4. Knower restates learner's message in L2.
5. Client evaluates the accuracy of counselor's message restatement.	5. Learner repeats the L2 message form to its addressee.
6. Client reflects on the interaction of the counseling session.	6. Learner replays (from tape or memory) and reflects upon the messages exchanged during the language class.

The term *humanistic approach* is often associated with Moskowitz (1978). CLL techniques, as the chart above demonstrates, belong to a larger set of foreign language teaching practices that are seen as humanistic. Moskowitz defines the techniques within this approach as those that

> blend what the student feels, thinks and knows with what he is learning in the target language. Rather than self-denial being the acceptable way of life, self-actualization and self-esteem are the ideals the exercises pursue. [The techniques] help build rapport, cohesiveness, and caring that far transcend what is already there ... help students to be themselves, to accept themselves, and be proud of themselves ... help foster a climate of caring and sharing in the foreign language class.
>
> (Moskowitz 1978: 2)

In sum, humanistic techniques engage the whole person, including the emotions and feelings (the affective realm) as well as linguistic knowledge and behavioral skills.

Another language teaching tradition with which CLL is linked is a set of practices used in certain kinds of bilingual education programs and referred to by Mackey (1972) as "language alternation." In language alternation, a message/lesson/class is presented first in the native language and then again in the second language. Students know the meaning and flow of an L2 message from their recall of the parallel meaning and flow of an L1 message. They begin to holistically piece together a view of the language out of these message sets. In CLL, a learner presents a message in L1 to the knower. The message is translated into L2 by the knower. The learner then repeats the message in L2, addressing it to another learner with whom he or she wishes to communicate. CLL learners are encouraged to attend to the "overhears" they experience between other learners and their knowers. The result of the "overhear" is that every member of the group can understand what any given learner is trying to communicate (La Forge 1983: 45). In view of the reported success of language alternation procedures in several well-studied bilingual education settings (e.g., Lim 1968; Mackey 1972), it may be that this little-discussed aspect of CLL accounts for more of the informally reported successes of CLL students than is usually acknowledged.

Approach

Theory of language

Curran himself wrote little about his theory of language. His student La Forge (1983) has attempted to be more explicit about this dimension of CLL theory, and we draw on his account for the language theory underlying the method. La Forge reviews linguistic theory as a prelude to presenting the CLL model of language. He seems to accept that language theory must start, though not end, with criteria for sound features, the sentence, and abstract models of language (La Forge 1983: 4). The foreign language learners' tasks are "to apprehend the sound system, assign fundamental meanings, and to construct a basic grammar of the foreign language." He cites with pride that "after several months a small group of students was able to learn the basic sounds and grammatical patterns of German" (1983: 47).

A theory of language built on "basic sound and grammatical patterns" does not appear to suggest any departures from traditional structuralist positions on the nature of language. However, the writings of CLL proponents deal at great length with what they call an alternative theory of language, which is referred to as *Language as Social Process*. La Forge (1983) begins by suggesting that language as social process is "different from language as communication." We are led to infer that the concept of communication that La Forge rejects is the classic sender-message-received model in information theory, which considers the transfer of information in only one direction. The social-process model is different from earlier information-transmitting models, La Forge (1983: 3) suggests, because

> communication is more than just a message being transmitted from a speaker to a listener. The speaker is at the same time both subject and object of his own message ... communication involves not just the unidirectional transfer of information to the other, but the very constitution of the speaking subject in relation to its other ... Communication is an exchange which is incomplete without a feedback reaction from the destinee of the message.

The information-transmission model and the social-process model of communication are compared in Figure 17.1.

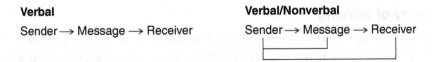

Figure 17.1 Comparison of the information-transmission model (**left**) and the social-process model (**right**) of communication

The social-process view of language is then elaborated in terms of six qualities or sub-processes that include verbal and nonverbal messages:

1. The whole-person process
2. The educational process
3. The interpersonal process
4. The developmental process
5. The communicative process
6. The cultural process

Explanation of these is beyond the scope of this chapter, which focuses on the communicative process and, indeed, appears to involve elements outside a theory of language.

La Forge also elaborates on the interactional view of language underlying CLL (see Chapter 2): "Language is people; language is persons in contact; language is persons in response" (1983: 9). CLL interactions are of two distinct and fundamental kinds: interactions between learners and interactions between learners and knowers. Interactions between learners are unpredictable in content but typically are said to involve exchanges of affect or emotional content, which includes such areas as motivation, self-confidence, and the level of anxiety. Learner exchanges deepen in intimacy as the class becomes a community of learners. The desire to be part of this growing intimacy pushes learners to keep pace with the learning of their peers. Tranel (1968: 159) notes that "the students of the experimental group were highly motivated to learn in order to avoid isolation from the groups." *Intimacy*, then, appears to be defined here as the desire to avoid isolation.

Interaction between learners and knowers involves five stages. The first is initially dependent (stage 1). The learner tells the knower what he or she wishes to say in the target language, and the knower tells the learner how to say it. In later stages, interactions between learner and knower are characterized as self-assertive (stage 2), resentful and indignant (stage 3), tolerant (stage 4), and independent (stage 5). These changes of interactive relationship are paralleled, therefore, not only by five stages of language learning, but also five stages of affective conflicts (La Forge 1983: 50).

The changes that occur between learners and knowers may be said to be microcosmically equivalent to the two major classes of human interactions – interaction between equals (symmetrical) and interactions between unequals (asymmetrical) (Munby 1978). They also appear to represent examples of (a) interaction that changes in degree (learner to learner) and (b) interaction that changes in kind (learner to knower). That is, learner–learner interaction is held to change in the direction of increasing intimacy and trust, whereas learner–knower interaction is held to change in its very nature from dependent to resentful to tolerant to independent.

Theory of learning

Curran's counseling experience led him to conclude that the techniques of counseling could be applied to learning in general (this became Counseling-Learning) and to language teaching in particular (CLL). The CLL view of learning is contrasted with two other types of learning, which Curran saw as widespread and undesirable. The first of these describes a putative learning view long popular in Western culture. In this view, "the intellectual and factual, or cognitive, processes alone are regarded as the main intent of learning, to the neglect of engagement and involvement of the self" (Curran 1972: 58). The second view of learning is the behavioral view. Curran refers to this kind of learning as "animal learning," in which learners are "passive" and their involvement limited (Curran 1976: 84).

In contrast, CLL advocates a holistic approach to language learning, since "true" human learning is both cognitive and affective. This is termed whole-person learning. Such learning takes place in a communicative situation where teachers and learners are involved in "an interaction … in which both experience a sense of their own wholeness" (Curran 1972: 90). Within this, the development of the learner's relationship with the teacher is central. The process is divided into five stages and compared to the ontogenetic development of the child from birth to maturity.

In the first, "birth," stage, feelings of security and belonging are established. In the second, as the learner's abilities improve, the learner, as child, begins to achieve a measure of independence from the parent. By the third, the learner "speaks independently" and may need to assert his or her own identity, often rejecting unasked-for advice. The fourth stage sees the learner as secure enough to take criticism, and by the last stage, the learner merely works on improving style and knowledge of linguistic appropriateness. By the end of the process, the child has become adult. The learner knows everything the teacher does and can become knower for a new learner. The process of learning a new language, then, is like being reborn and developing a new persona, with all the trials and challenges that are associated with birth and maturation. Insofar as language learning is thought to develop through creating social relationships, success in language learning follows from a successful relationship between learner and teacher, and learner and learner. "Learning is viewed as a unified, personal and social experience." The learner "is no longer seen as learning in isolation and in competition with others" (Curran 1972: 11–12).

Curran in many places discusses what he calls "consensual validation," or "convalidation," in which mutual warmth, understanding, and a positive evaluation of the other person's worth develop between the teacher and the learner. A relationship characterized by convalidation is considered essential to the learning process and is a key element of CLL classroom procedures. A group of ideas concerning the psychological requirements for successful learning are collected under the acronym SARD (Curran 1976: 6), which can be explained as follows, again using some analogies from child development:

S   stands for security. Unless learners feel secure, they will find it difficult to enter into a successful learning experience.

A   stands for attention and aggression. CLL recognizes that a loss of attention should be taken as an indication of the learner's lack of involvement in learning, the implication being that variety in the choice of learner tasks will increase attention and therefore promote learning. Aggression applies to the way in which a child, having learned something, seeks an opportunity to show his or her strength by taking over and demonstrating what has been learned, using the new knowledge as a tool for self-assertion.

R   stands for retention and reflection. If the whole person is involved in the learning process, what is retained is internalized and becomes a part of the learner's new persona in the foreign language. Reflection is a consciously identified period of silence within the framework of the lesson for the student "to focus on the learning forces of the last hour, to assess his present stage of development, and to re-evaluate future goals" (La Forge 1983: 68).

D   denotes discrimination. When learners "have retained a body of material, they are ready to sort it out and see how one thing relates to another" (La Forge 1983: 69). This discrimination process becomes more refined and ultimately "enables the students to use the language for purposes of communication outside the classroom" (La Forge 1983: 69).

These central aspects of Curran's learning philosophy address not the psycholinguistic and cognitive processes involved in second language acquisition, but rather the personal commitments that learners need to make before language acquisition processes can operate. CLL learning theory hence stands in marked contrast to linguistically or psycholinguistically based learning theories, such as those informing Audiolingualism (Chapter 4) or the Natural Approach (Chapter 14).

Design

Objectives

Since linguistic or communicative competence is specified only in social terms, explicit linguistic or communicative objectives are not defined in the literature on CLL. Most of what has been written about CLL describes its use in introductory conversation courses in a foreign language. The assumption seems to be that through the method, the teacher can successfully transfer his or her knowledge and proficiency in the target language to the learners, which implies that attaining near-native mastery of the target language is set as a goal. Specific objectives are not addressed.

The syllabus

CLL is most often used in the teaching of oral proficiency, but with some modifications it may be used in the teaching of writing, as Tranel (1968) has demonstrated. CLL does not use a conventional language syllabus, which sets out in advance the grammar, vocabulary, and other language items to be taught and the order in which they will be covered. If a course is based on Curran's recommended procedures, the course progression is topic-based, with learners nominating things they wish to talk about, as mentioned earlier, and messages they wish to communicate to other learners. The teacher's responsibility is to provide a conveyance for these meanings in a way appropriate to the learners' proficiency level. Although CLL is not explicit about this, skilled CLL teachers seem to sift the learners' intentions through the teacher's implicit syllabus, providing lessons that match what learners can be expected to do and say at that level. In this sense, then, a CLL syllabus emerges from the interaction between the learner's expressed communicative intentions and the teacher's reformulations of these into suitable target-language utterances. Specific grammatical points, lexical patterns, and generalizations will sometimes be isolated by the teacher for more detailed study and analysis, and subsequent specification of these as a retrospective account of what the course covered could be a way of deriving a CLL language syllabus. Each CLL course would evolve its own syllabus, however, since what develops out of teacher–learner interactions in one course will be different from what happens in another.

Types of learning and teaching activities

As with most methods, CLL combines innovative learning tasks and activities with conventional ones. They include the following:

- *Translation.* Learners form a small circle. A learner whispers a message or meaning he or she wants to express, the teacher translates it into (and may interpret it in) the target language, and the learner repeats the teacher's translation.
- *Group work.* Learners may engage in various group tasks, such as small-group discussion of a topic, preparing a conversation, preparing a summary of a topic for presentation to another group, preparing a story that will be presented to the teacher and the rest of the class.
- *Recording.* Students record conversations in the target language.
- *Transcription.* Students transcribe utterances and conversations they have recorded for practice and analysis of linguistic forms.
- *Analysis.* Students analyze and study transcriptions of target-language sentences in order to focus on particular lexical usage or on the application of particular grammar rules.
- *Reflection and observation.* Learners reflect and report on their experience of the class, as a class or in groups. This usually consists of expressions of feelings – sense of one another, reactions to silence, concern for something to say, and so on.
- *Listening.* Students listen to a monologue by the teacher involving elements they might have elicited or overheard in class interactions.
- *Free conversation.* Students engage in free conversation with the teacher or with other learners. This might include discussion of what they learned as well as feelings they had about how they learned.

Learner roles

In CLL, learners become members of a community – their fellow learners and the teacher – and learn through interacting within the community. Learning is not viewed as an individual accomplishment but as something that is achieved collaboratively. Learners are expected to listen attentively to the knower, to freely provide meanings they wish to express, to repeat target utterances without hesitation, to support fellow members of the community, to report deep inner feelings and frustrations as well as joy and pleasure, and to become counselors of other learners. CLL learners are typically grouped in a circle of six to twelve learners, with the number of knowers varying from one per group to one per student. CLL has also been used in larger school classes where special grouping arrangements are necessary, such as organizing learners in temporary pairs in facing parallel lines.

Learner roles are keyed to the five stages of language learning by La Forge, outlined earlier (see p. 308). The view of the learner is an organic one, with each new role growing developmentally out of the one preceding. These role changes are not easily or automatically achieved. They are in fact seen as outcomes of affective crises: "When faced with a new cognitive task, the learner must solve an affective crisis. With the solution of the five affective crises, one for each CLL stage, the student progresses from a lower to a higher stage of development" (La Forge 1983: 44). Learning is a "whole-person" process, and the learner at each stage is involved not just in the accomplishment of cognitive (language learning) tasks but in the solution of affective conflicts and "the respect for the enactment of values" as well (La Forge 1983: 55). Moreover, as noted above, CLL compares language learning to the stages of human growth.

Teacher roles

At the deepest level, the teacher's role derives from the functions of the counselor in Rogerian psychological counseling, as mentioned earlier. A counselor's clients are people with problems, who in a typical counseling session will often use emotional language to communicate their difficulties to the counselor. The counselor's role is to respond calmly and nonjudgmentally, in a supportive manner, and help the client try to understand his or her problems better by applying order and analysis to them. The counselor is not responsible for paraphrasing the client's problem element for element but rather for capturing the essence of the client's concern, such that the client might say, "Yes, that's exactly what I meant." "One of the functions of the counseling response is to relate affect … to cognition. Understanding the language of 'feeling', the counselor replies in the language of cognition" (Curran 1976: 26). It was the model of teacher as counselor that Curran attempted to bring to language learning.

There is also room for actual counseling in CLL. Explicit recognition is given to the psychological problems that may arise in learning a second language. "Personal learning conflicts … anger, anxiety and similar psychological disturbance – understood and responded to by the teacher's counseling sensitivity – are indicators of deep personal investment" (J. Rardin, in Curran 1976: 103). In this case, the teacher is expected to play a role very close to that of the "regular" counselor. The teacher's response may be of a different order of detachment, consideration, and understanding from that of the average teacher in the same circumstances.

More specific teacher roles are, like those of the students, keyed to the five developmental stages that were indicated by La Forge. In the early stages of learning, the teacher operates in a supportive role, providing target-language translations and a model for imitation on request of the clients. Later, interaction may be initiated by the students, and the teacher monitors learner utterances, providing assistance when requested. As learning progresses, students become increasingly capable of accepting criticism, and the teacher may intervene directly to correct deviant utterances, supply idioms, and advise on usage and fine points of grammar. The teacher's role is initially likened to that of a nurturing parent. The student gradually "grows" in ability, and the nature of the relationship changes so that the teacher's position becomes somewhat dependent upon the learner. The knower derives a sense of self-worth through requests for the knower's assistance.

One continuing role of the teacher is particularly notable in CLL. The teacher is responsible for providing a safe environment in which clients can learn and grow. Learners, feeling secure, are free to direct their energies to the tasks of communication and learning rather than to building and maintaining their defensive positions. Curran (1976: 6) describes the importance of a secure atmosphere as follows:

> As whole persons, we seem to learn best in an atmosphere of personal security. Feeling secure, we are freed to approach the learning situation with the attitude of willing openness. Both the learner's and the knower's level of security determine the psychological tone of the entire learning experience.

Many of the nontraditional language teaching methods we discuss in this book stress teacher responsibility for creating and maintaining a secure environment for learning; probably no method attaches greater importance to this aspect of language learning than does CLL. Thus, it is interesting to note two "asides" in the discussion of learning security in CLL.

First, security is a culturally relative concept. What provides a sense of security in one cultural context may produce anxiety in another. La Forge gives as an example the different patterns of personal introduction and how these are differentially expressed and experienced in early stages of CLL among students of different backgrounds. "Each culture had unique forms which provide for acquaintance upon forming new groups. These must be carefully adopted so as to provide cultural security for the students of the foreign language" (La Forge 1983: 66).

Second, it may be undesirable to create too secure an environment for learners. "The security of the students is never absolute: otherwise no learning would occur" (La Forge 1983: 65). This is reminiscent of the teacher who says, "My students would never learn anything if the fear of examination failure didn't drive them to it." How much insecurity is optimal for language learning in CLL is unfortunately not further discussed in the literature.

The role of instructional materials

Since a CLL course evolves out of the interactions of the community, a textbook is not considered a necessary component. A textbook would impose a particular body of language content on the learners, thereby impeding their growth and interaction. Materials may be developed by the teacher as the course progresses, although these generally consist of little more than summaries on the blackboard or overhead projector of some of the linguistic features of conversations generated by students. Conversations may also be transcribed and distributed for study and analysis, and learners may work in groups to produce their own materials, such as scripts for dialogues and mini-dramas.

In early accounts of CLL, the use of teaching machines for pronunciation and vocabulary, such as the Chromachord® Teaching System, is recommended for necessary "rote-drill and practice" in language learning. "The ... design and use of machines ... now appear to make possible the freeing of the teacher to do what only a human person can do ... become a learning counselor" (Curran 1976: 6). In later CLL descriptions (e.g., La Forge 1983), teaching machines and their accompanying materials are not mentioned, and we assume that contemporary CLL classes do not use teaching machines at all.

Procedure

Since each CLL course is in a sense a unique experience, description of typical CLL procedures in a class period is problematic. Stevick (1976) distinguishes between "classical" CLL (based directly on the model proposed by Curran) and personal interpretations of it, such as those discussed by different advocates of CLL (e.g., La Forge 1983). The following description attempts to capture some typical activities in CLL classes.

Generally, the observer will see a circle of learners all facing one another. The learners are linked in some way to knowers or a single knower as teacher. The first class (and subsequent classes) may begin with a period of silence, in which learners try to determine what is supposed to happen in their language class. In later classes, learners may sit in silence while they decide what to talk about (La Forge 1983: 72). The observer may note that the awkwardness of silence becomes sufficiently agonizing for someone to volunteer to break the silence. The knower may use the volunteered comment as a way of introducing discussion of classroom contacts or as a stimulus for language interaction regarding how learners felt about the period of silence. The knower may encourage learners to address questions to one another or to the knower. These may be questions on any subject a learner is curious enough to enquire about. The questions and answers may be recorded for later use, as a reminder and review of topics discussed and language used.

The teacher might then form the class into facing lines for three-minute pair conversations. These are seen as equivalent to the brief wrestling sessions by which judo students practice. Following this the class might be re-formed into small groups in which a single topic, chosen by the class or the group, is discussed. The summary of the group discussion may be presented to another group, which in turn tries to repeat or paraphrase the summary back to the original group.

In an intermediate or advanced class, a teacher may encourage groups to prepare a paper drama for presentation to the rest of the class. A paper drama group prepares a story that is told or shown to the counselor. The counselor provides or corrects target-language statements and suggests improvements to the story sequence. Students are then given materials with which they prepare large picture cards to accompany their story. After practicing the story dialogue and preparing the accompanying pictures, each group presents its paper drama to the rest of the class. The students accompany their story with music, puppets, and drums as well as with their pictures (La Forge 1983: 81–2).

Finally, the teacher asks learners to reflect on the language class, as a class or in groups. Reflection provides the basis for discussion of contracts (written or oral contracts that learners and teachers have agreed upon and that specify what they agree to accomplish within the course), personal interaction, feelings toward the knower and learner, and the sense of progress and frustration.

Dieter Stroinigg (in Stevick 1980: 185–6) presents a protocol of what a first day's CLL class covered, which is outlined here:

1. Informal greetings and self-introductions were made.
2. The teacher made a statement of the goals and guidelines for the course.
3. A conversation in the foreign language took place.

   a) A circle was formed so that everyone had visual contact with each other.
   b) One student initiated conversation with another student by giving a message in the L1 (English).
   c) The instructor, standing behind the student, whispered a close equivalent of the message in the L2 (German).
   d) The student then repeated the L2 message to its addressee and into the tape recorder as well.
   e) Each student had a chance to compose and record a few messages.
   f) The tape recorder was rewound and replayed at intervals.
   g) Each student repeated the meaning in English of what he or she had said in the L2 and helped to refresh the memory of others.

4. Students then participated in a reflection period, in which they were asked to express their feelings about the previous experience with total frankness.
5. From the materials just recorded the instructor chose sentences to write on the blackboard that highlighted elements of grammar, spelling, and peculiarities of capitalization in the L2.
6. Students were encouraged to ask questions about any of the items above.
7. Students were encouraged to copy sentences from the board with notes on meaning and usage. This became their "textbook" for home study.

This inventory of activities encompasses the major suggestions for classroom practices appearing in the most recent literature on CLL. Other procedures, however, may emerge fortuitously on the basis of learner–knower interactions in the classroom context.

Conclusion

Community Language Learning is the most responsive of the methods we have reviewed in terms of its sensitivity to learner communicative intent. It should be noted, however, that this communicative intent is constrained by the number and knowledge of fellow learners. A learner's desire to understand or express technical terms used in aeronautical engineering is unlikely to receive adequate response in the CLL class. CLL places unusual demands on language teachers. They must be highly proficient and sensitive to nuance in both L1 and L2. They must be familiar with and sympathetic to the role of counselors in psychological counseling. They must resist the pressure "to teach" in the traditional senses. As one CLL teacher notes, "I had to relax completely and to exclude my own will to produce something myself. I had to exclude any function of forming or formulating something within me, not trying to *do* something" (Curran 1976: 33).

The teacher must also be relatively nondirective and must be prepared to accept and even encourage the "adolescent" aggression of the learner as he or she strives for independence. The teacher must operate without conventional materials, depending on student topics to shape and motivate the class. In addition, the teacher must be prepared to deal with potentially hostile learner reactions to the method. The teacher must also be culturally sensitive and prepared to redesign the language class into more culturally compatible organizational forms. And the teacher much attempt to learn these new roles and skills without much specific guidance from CLL texts presently available. Special training in CLL techniques is usually required.

Critics of CLL question the appropriateness of the counseling metaphor on which it is predicated, asking for evidence that language learning in classrooms indeed parallels the process that characterizes psychological counseling. Questions also arise about whether teachers should attempt counseling without special training. CLL procedures were largely developed and tested with groups of college-age Americans. The problems and successes experienced by one or two different client groups may not necessarily represent language learning universals. Other concerns have been expressed regarding the lack of a syllabus, which makes objectives unclear and evaluation difficult to accomplish, and the focus on fluency rather than accuracy, which may lead to inadequate control of the grammatical system of the target language. Supporters of CLL (e.g., Samimy 1989), on the other hand, emphasize the positive benefits of a method that centers on the learner and stresses the humanistic side of language learning, and not merely its linguistic dimensions. While CLL isn't discussed much today, the affective dimension of language learning is widely accepted as relevant to the learner's success in mastering the target language.

Discussion questions

1. CLL is heavily influenced by ideas from psychology, and in particular counseling. As mentioned earlier, motivation, self-confidence, and anxiety are other ideas from psychology that also impact language learning. What impact have such factors had among your own students or in your own language learning?

2. Explain to a colleague what *language alternation* is. What do you think might be some of the benefits of language alternation in a CLL class?

3. CLL emphasizes language as a *social process*, which goes beyond the mechanical aspects of communication to incorporate its relationship to the interlocutors and their identities. Review the six qualities or sub-processes mentioned on page 306 that include verbal and non verbal messages. While the details of these processes were not discussed, can you think of ways in which they are reflected in teaching situations you are familiar with.

4. Look again at the SARD model on page 307 of the chapter. Do you think that *reflection* and *discrimination* are given enough attention in current classrooms and teaching materials?

5. CLL sees learners as progressing through five stages: initially dependent, self-assertive, resentful and indignant, tolerant, and independent. Do you recognize these stages in your learners? Do you think they are particular to language learning?

6. There is a strong emphasis on the affective aspect of learning in CLL. Think of a group of learners you are familiar with. How would they respond to a class such as the one described below?

   Students then participated in a reflection period, in which they were asked to express their feelings about the previous experience with total frankness.

7. "A learner's desire to understand or express technical terms used in aeronautical engineering is unlikely to receive adequate response in the CLL class" (p. 313). Why would this be so?

8. One of the key characteristics of CLL is its emphasis on providing a secure environment for learning. To an extent, this focus on the learner's affective experience is visible in other current approaches to language teaching. However, as described on page 311, interpretations or experiences of "security" differ across cultures. Work with a colleague to do the following:

   - Describe your ideal language learning environment, giving special attention to the ways in which the environment is made to feel comfortable and safe, for example by the teacher, the kinds of activities that take place, or even the furnishings.
   - Now compare your answers with those of your colleague. How are they different? How are they similar?
   - Now describe to what extent your own classrooms match these descriptions.

References and further reading

Brown, H. D. 1977. Some limitations of C-L/CLL models of second language teaching. *TESOL Quarterly* 11(4): 365–72.

Curran, C. A. 1972. *Counseling-Learning: A Whole-Person Model for Education.* New York: Grune and Stratton.

Curran, C. A. 1976. *Counseling-Learning in Second Languages.* Apple River, IL: Apple River Press.

La Forge, P. G. 1971. Community language learning: a pilot study. *Language Learning* 21(1): 45–61.

La Forge, P. G. 1975a. *Research Profiles with Community Language Learning.* Apple River, IL: Apple River Press.

La Forge. P. G. 1975b. Community language learning: the Japanese case. In F. C. C. Peng (ed.), *Language in Japanese Society.* Tokyo: University of Tokyo Press. 215–46.

La Forge, P. G. 1977. Uses of social silence in the interpersonal dynamics of Community Language Learning. *TESOL Quarterly* 11(4): 373–82.

La Forge, P. G. 1983. *Counseling and Culture in Second Language Acquisition.* Oxford: Pergamon.

Lim, K. B. 1968. The unified language project. *RELC Journal* 9(1): 19–27.

Mackey, W. F. 1972. *Bilingual Education in a Binational School.* Rowley, MA: Newbury House.

Moskowitz, G. 1978. *Caring and Sharing in the Foreign Language Class.* Rowley, MA: Newbury House.

Munby, J. 1978. *Communicative Syllabus Design.* Cambridge: Cambridge University Press.

Rardin, J. 1976. A Counseling-Learning model for second language learning. *TESOL Newsletter* 10(2): 21–2.

Rardin, J. 1977. The language teacher as facilitator. *TESOL Quarterly* 11(4): 383–7.

Rardin, J., and D. D. Tranel. 1988. *Education in a New Dimension.* Cliffside Park, NJ: Counseling Learning Institutes.

Rogers, C. R. 1951. *Client-Centered Therapy.* Boston: Houghton Mifflin.

Samimy, K. K. 1989. A comparative study of teaching Japanese in the audiolingual method and the counseling learning approach. *Modern Language Journal* 73(11): 169–77.

Samimy, K. K., and J. Rardin. 1994. Adult language learners' reactions to community language learning: a descriptive study. *Foreign Language Annals* 27(3): 379–90.

Stevick, E. W. 1973. Review article: Charles A. Curran's Counseling-Learning: a whole person model for education. *Language Learning* 23(2): 259–71.

Stevick, E. W. 1976. *Memory, Meaning and Method: Some Psychological Perspectives on Language Learning.* Rowley, MA: Newbury House.

Stevick, E. W. 1980. *Teaching Languages: A Way and Ways.* Rowley, MA: Newbury House.

Stevick, E. W. 1998. *Working with Teaching Methods: What's at Stake.* Boston: Heinle and Heinle.

Taylor, B. P. 1979. Exploring Community Language Learning. In C. Yorio, K. Perkins, and J. Schachter (eds.), *On TESOL '79.* Washington, DC: TESOL. 80–4.

Tranel, D. D. 1968. Teaching Latin with the chromachord. *The Classical Journal* 63: 157–60.

18 Suggestopedia

Introduction

We have seen several instances in this book of language teaching methods that have been developed by educators from outside mainstream language teaching, such as the Silent Way (Chapter 16), and Community Language Learning (Chapter 17). Methods such as these sometimes interest teachers who may be attracted by their novelty and the results they are said to deliver. Many of the "innovative" methods of the 1980s and 1990s are mainly of historical interest today, although they may still have some practitioners in different parts of the world. Suggestopedia is another method of this type and was developed by the Bulgarian psychiatrist-educator Georgi Lozanov. Suggestopedia is a specific set of learning recommendations derived from Suggestology, which Lozanov describes as a "science … concerned with the systematic study of the nonrational and/or nonconscious influences" that human beings are constantly responding to (Stevick 1976: 42). Suggestopedia tries to harness these influences and redirect them so as to optimize learning. The most conspicuous characteristics of Suggestopedia are the decoration, furniture, and arrangement of the classroom, the use of music, and the authoritative behavior of the teacher. Music is an especially important element of Suggestopedia, and both intonation and rhythm are coordinated with a musical background, which helps to induce a relaxed attitude. The method has a somewhat mystical air about it, partially because it has few direct links with established learning or educational theory in the West, and partially because of its arcane terminology and neologisms, which one critic has unkindly called a "package of pseudo-scientific gobbledygook" (Scovel 1979: 258).

Hansen (2011: 403), a current advocate of Suggestopedia, provides this commentary:

> Suggestopedia (SP) … was received with incomprehension when it surfaced in the 1960s because its claims of prodigious learning could not be explained in a way consistent with the science of the time. Nor could it be explained by its founder, psychiatrist Dr Georgi Lozanov working at the University of Sofia during the Communist regime, because as a therapist he worked from intuition, following subtle indications that emerged from interactions. Healing victims of the regime, and obliged to use hypnosis for the worst cases, he sought to find a means to bring profoundly traumatised patients "back to life". What he developed through very delicate suggestion was a way of resuscitating the very essence of life – and it was the polar opposite of hypnosis, which in his experience drains away the life force. To banish the damaging

implication of "sick" people who needed "help," he gave his therapeutic method the new goal of teaching a foreign language, and it was at that point that he discovered its extraordinary efficiency: not only did the trauma vanish but the learners learned English incredibly fast! Word spread, the government rushed in to seize the benefit of his work.

The claims for suggestopedic learning are dramatic. "There is no sector of public life where suggestology would not be useful" (Lozanov 1978: 2). The extraordinary efficiency described by Hansen seems to refer to a claim by Lozanov (1978: 27) that "Memorization in learning by the suggestopedic method seems to be accelerated 25 times over that in learning by conventional methods." Lozanov acknowledges ties in tradition to yoga and Soviet psychology. From raja-yoga Lozanov has borrowed and modified techniques for altering states of consciousness and concentration, and the use of rhythmic breathing. From Soviet psychology Lozanov has taken the notion that all students can be taught a given subject matter at the same level of skill. Lozanov claims that his method works equally well whether or not students spend time on outside study. He promises success through Suggestopedia to the academically gifted and the ungifted alike. Soviet psychology also stresses the learning environment, and Lozanov similarly specifies the requirements of an optimal learning environment in great detail.

A most conspicuous feature of Suggestopedia is the centrality of music and musical rhythm to learning. Suggestopedia thus has a kinship with other functional uses of music, particularly therapy. One of the earliest attested uses of music therapy is recorded in the Old Testament of the Bible: "When the evil spirit from God was upon Saul, David took up his harp and played with his hand; so Saul found relief; and it was well with him, and the evil spirit departed from him" (1 Samuel 12:23). Lozanov might have described this incident as the use of music to assist in the "liberation from discrete micro psychotraumata, for destruction of incompatible ideas about the limits of human capabilities" (1978: 252). In other words, the relief provided by music will vanquish the evil spirit.

Gaston (1968) defines three functions of music in therapy: to facilitate the establishment and maintenance of personal relations; to bring about increased self-esteem through increased self-satisfaction in musical performance; and to use the unique potential of rhythm to energize and bring order. This last function seems to be the one that Lozanov calls upon in his use of music to relax learners as well as to structure, pace, and punctuate the presentation of linguistic material.

Approach

Theory of language

Lozanov does not articulate a theory of language, nor does it seem that he is much concerned with any particular assumptions regarding language elements and their organization. The emphasis on memorization of vocabulary pairs – a target-language item and its native-language translation – suggests a view of language in which lexis is central and in which lexical translation rather than contextualization is stressed. However, Lozanov does occasionally refer to the importance of experiencing language material in "whole meaningful texts" (Lozanov 1978: 268) and notes that the suggestopedic course directs "the student not to vocabulary memorization and acquiring habits of speech, but to acts of communication" (1978: 109).

Lozanov recommends home study of recordings of "whole meaningful texts (not of a fragmentary nature)" that are, "above all, interesting." These are listened to "for the sake of the music of the foreign speech" (1978: 277). The texts should be lighthearted stories with emotional content. Lozanov's recommendation of such stories seems to be entirely motivational, however, and does not represent a commitment to the view that language is preeminently learned for and used in its emotive function. In class, on the other hand, the focus of a lesson is a dialogue, supported by music and other soothing accompaniments, as mentioned.

In describing coursework and text organization, Lozanov refers most often to the language to be learned as "the material" (e.g., "The new material that is to be learned is read or recited by a well-trained teacher": 1978: 270). One feels that the linguistic nature of the material is largely irrelevant and that if the focus of a language course were, say, memorization of grammar rules, Lozanov would feel a suggestopedic approach to be the optimal one. The sample protocol given for an Italian lesson (Lozanov 1978) does not suggest a theory of language markedly different from that which holds a language to be its vocabulary and the grammar rules for organizing vocabulary.

Hansen (2011: 411) highlights the role of grammar in working with texts:

> The major slot for overt grammatical presentation in the Lozanov cycle [of imitation and reading, described below] is in the first elaboration during the choral reading of the text. After the repetition of a certain sentence, there will be a momentary and apparently spontaneous (but carefully planned and prepared) focus on a grammatical item. This must:
> a) come from the text, so that the learner's mind remains focused on the drama rather than on the linguistic structure;
> b) be brief so that the learners do not get a chance to switch into analytical mode. Thus, it is never followed by an exercise or drill, which may occur at a later stage;
> c) be incomplete so that there is still material for the unconscious to puzzle over and work on; the mind is a compulsive pattern maker, positively stimulated by challenge.
> Grammar never appears to be dwelt upon for its own sake, but to arise spontaneously as a textual puzzle.

Theory of learning

Suggestion is at the heart of Suggestopedia. To many, *suggestion* conjures up visions of the penetrating stare, swimming cat's eye, and monotonically repeated injunctions of the hypnotist. Lozanov acknowledges the likelihood of this association to Suggestopedia but claims that his own views separate Suggestopedia from the "narrow clinical concept of hypnosis as a kind of static, sleeplike, altered state of consciousness" (1978: 3). Lozanov further claims that what distinguishes his method from hypnosis and other forms of mind control is that these other forms lack "a desuggestive-suggestive sense," as explained below, and "fail to create a constant set up access to reserves through concentrative psycho-relaxation" (1978: 267). (We interpret *reserves* as being something like human memory banks. *Desuggestion* seems to involve unloading the memory banks, or reserves, of unwanted or blocking memories. *Suggestion*, then, involves loading the memory banks with desired and facilitating memories.) There are six principal theoretical components through which desuggestion and suggestion operate and that set up access to reserves. We will describe these briefly following Bancroft (1972).

Authority

People remember best and are most influenced by information coming from an authoritative source. Lozanov dictates a variety of prescriptions and proscriptions aimed at having Suggestopedia students experience the educational establishment and the teacher as sources having great authority. Lozanov talks of choosing a "ritual placebo system" that is most likely to be perceived of by students as having high authority (1978: 267). The ritual placebo system that Lozanov refers to might be yoga, it might be hypnosis, it might be biofeedback, it might be experimental science. "Ritual placebo systems will change dramatically in accordance with the times" (ibid.). In other words, Lozanov appears to believe that scientific-sounding language, highly positive experimental data, and true-believer teachers constitute a ritual placebo system that is authoritatively appealing to most learners. Well-publicized accounts of learning success lend the method and the institution authority, and commitment to the method, self-confidence, personal distance, acting ability, and a highly positive attitude give an authoritative air to the teacher.

Infantilization

Authority is also used to suggest a teacher–student relation like that of parent to child. In the child's role the learner takes part in role playing, games, songs, and gymnastic exercises that help "the older student regain the self-confidence, spontaneity and receptivity of the child" (Bancroft 1972: 19).

Double-planedness

The learner learns not only from the effect of direct instruction but from the environment in which the instruction takes place. The bright decor of the classroom, the musical background, the shape of the chairs, and the personality of the teacher are considered as important in instruction as the form of the instructional material itself.

Intonation, rhythm, and concert pseudo-passiveness

Varying the tone and rhythm of presented material helps both to avoid boredom through monotony of repetition and to dramatize, emotionalize, and give meaning to linguistic material. In the first presentation of linguistic material, three phrases are read together, each with a different voice level and rhythm. In the second presentation, the linguistic material is given a proper dramatic reading, which helps learners visualize a context for the material and aids in memorization (Bancroft 1972: 19).

Lozanov refers to the relaxed attitude induced by music as concert pseudo-passiveness. This state is felt to be optimal for learning, in that anxieties and tension are relieved and power of concentration for new material is raised. Because the role of music is central in suggestopedic learning, it needs to be considered in somewhat more detail.

The type of music is critical to learning success.

> The idea that music can affect your body and mind certainly isn't new … The key was to find the right kind of music for just the right kind of effect … The music you use in superlearning [the American term for Suggestopedia] is extremely important. If it does not have the required pattern, the desired altered states of consciousness will not be induced and results will be poor … It is specific music – sonic patterns – for a specific purpose.
>
> (Ostrander, Schroeder, and Ostrander 1979: 73–4)

At the institute Lozanov recommends a series of slow movements (sixty beats a minute) in 4/4 time for Baroque concertos strung together into about a half-hour concert. He notes that in such concerts "the body relaxed, the mind became alert" (Ostrander et al. 1979: 74). As a further refinement, "East German researchers of Suggestopedia at Karl Marx University in Leipzig observed that slow movements from Baroque instrumental music featuring string instruments gave the very best results" (Ostrander et al. 1979: 115).

The rate of presentation of material to be learned within the rhythmic pattern is keyed to the rhythm. Superlearning uses an eight-second cycle for pacing out data at slow intervals. During the first four beats of the cycle, there is silence. During the second four beats, the teacher presents the dialogue, known as "the material." Ostrander et al. present a variety of evidence on why this pacing to Baroque largo music is so potent. They note that musical rhythms affect body rhythms, such as heartbeat, and that researchers have noted that "with a slow heartbeat, mind efficiency takes a great leap forward" (1979: 63). They cite experimental data such as those which show disastrous learning results when the music of Wagner was substituted for slow Baroque. They reflect that "the minute is divided into sixty seconds and that perhaps there's more to this than just an arbitrary division of time." They further report that "the Indian vilambita, for instance, has the required rhythms of sixty beats a minute" and suggest that Indian yogis may have built the sixty-beat rhythm into yogic techniques. Finally, they observe that not only human but vegetable subjects thrive under sixty-beat stimulation. "Plants grown in the chambers given Baroque music by Bach and Indian music by Ravi Shankar rapidly grew lush and abundant … The plants in the chamber getting rock music shriveled and died" (1979: 82). Suggestopedic learning is consequently built on a particular type of music and a particular rate of presentation.

Design

Objectives

Suggestopedia aims to deliver advanced conversational proficiency quickly. It apparently bases its learning claims on student mastery of prodigious lists of vocabulary pairs and, indeed, suggests to the students that it is appropriate that they set such goals for themselves.

Lozanov emphasizes, however, that increased memory power is not an isolated skill but a result of "positive, comprehensive stimulation of personality" (1978: 253). Lozanov states categorically, "The main aim of teaching is not memorization, but the understanding and creative solution of problems" (1978: 251). As learner goals, he cites increased access to understanding and creative solutions and problems. However, because students and teachers place a high value on vocabulary recall, memorization of vocabulary pairs continues to be seen as an important goal of the suggestopedic method.

The syllabus

A Suggestopedia course lasts 30 days and consists of ten units of study. Classes are held four hours a day, six days a week. The central focus of each unit is a dialogue consisting of 1,200 words or so, with an accompanying vocabulary list and grammatical commentary. The dialogues are graded by lexis and grammar.

There is a pattern of work within each unit and a pattern of work for the whole course. Unit study is organized around three days: day 1 – half a day, day 2 – full day, day 3 – half a day. On the first day of work on a new unit, the teacher discusses the general content (not structure) of the unit dialogue. The learners then receive the printed dialogue with a native-language translation in a parallel column. The teacher answers any questions of interest or concern about the dialogue. The dialogue then is read a second and third time in ways to be discussed subsequently. This is the work for day 1. Days 2 and 3 are spent in primary and secondary elaboration of the text. Primary elaboration consists of imitation, question and answer, reading, and so on of the dialogue and of working with the 150 new vocabulary items presented in the unit. The secondary elaboration involves encouraging students to make new combinations and productions based on the dialogues. A story or essay paralleling the dialogue is also read. The students engage in conversation and take small roles in response to the text read.

The whole course also has a pattern of presentation and performance. On the first day a test is given to check the level of student knowledge and to provide a basis for dividing students into two groups – one of new beginners and one of modified (false) beginners. The teacher then briefs the students on the course and explains the attitude they should take toward it. This briefing is designed to put them in a positive, relaxed, and confident mood for learning. Students are given a new name in the second language and a new biography in the second culture with which they are to operate for the duration of the course. The new names contain phonemes from the target culture that learners find difficult to pronounce. For example, a student of English might be "the *actress Anne Mackey from Kansas.*"

During the course there are two opportunities for generalization of material. In the middle of the course, students are encouraged to practice the target language in a setting where it might be used, such as hotels or restaurants. The last day of the course is devoted to a performance in which every student participates. The students construct a play built on the material of the course. Rules and parts are planned, but students are expected to speak extempore rather than from memorized lines. Written tests are also given throughout the course, and these and the performance are reviewed on the final day of the course.

Types of learning and teaching activities

We have mentioned a variety of activities in passing in the discussion of the syllabus. These include imitation, question and answer, and role play – which are not activities "that other language teachers would consider to be out of the ordinary" (Stevick 1976: 157). The types of activities that are more original to Suggestopedia are the listening activities, which concern the text and text vocabulary of each unit. These activities are typically part of the "pre-session phase," which takes place on the first day of a new unit. The students first look at and discuss a new text with the teacher, who answers questions about the dialogue. In the second reading, students relax comfortably in reclining chairs and listen to the teacher read the text in a certain way. Stevick (1976) suggests that the exact nature of the "special way" is not clear. Bancroft notes that the material is "presented with varying intonations and a coordination of sound and printed word or illustration" (1972: 17). During the third reading, the material is acted out by the instructor in a dramatic manner over a background of the special musical form described previously. During this phase students lean back in their chairs and breathe deeply and regularly as instructed by the teacher. This is the point at which Lozanov believes the unconscious learning system takes over.

Learner roles

Students volunteer for a Suggestopedia course, but having volunteered, they are expected to be committed to the class and its activities. The mental state of the learners is critical to success; learners must avoid distractions and immerse themselves in the procedures of the method. Learners must not try to figure out, manipulate, or study the material presented but must maintain a pseudo-passive state, in which the material rolls over and through them. Students are expected to tolerate and in fact encourage their own "infantilization." This is accomplished partly by acknowledging the absolute authority of the teacher and partly by giving themselves over to activities and techniques designed to help them regain the self-confidence, spontaneity, and receptivity of the child. Such activities include role playing, games, songs, and gymnastic exercises (Bancroft 1972: 19). To assist them in the role plays and to help them detach themselves from their past learning experiences, students are given a new name and personal history within the target culture, as mentioned.

Groups of learners are ideally socially homogeneous, 12 in number, and divided equally between men and women. Learners sit in a circle, which encourages face-to-face exchange and activity participation.

Teacher roles

The primary role of the teacher is to create situations in which the learner is most suggestible and then to present linguistic material in a way most likely to encourage positive reception and retention by the learner.

Lozanov (1978: 275–6) lists several expected teacher behaviors that contribute to these presentations.

1. Show absolute confidence in the method.
2. Display fastidious conduct in manners and dress.
3. Organize properly and strictly observe the initial stages of the teaching process – this includes choice and play of music, as well as punctuality.
4. Maintain a solemn attitude toward the session.
5. Give tests and respond tactfully to poor papers (if any).
6. Stress global rather than analytical attitudes toward material.
7. Maintain a modest enthusiasm.

As Stevick (1976) points out, there are certain styles of presentation of material that are important, intricate, and inaccessible. It appears that teachers have to be prepared to be initiated into the method by stages and that certain techniques are withheld until such time as the master teacher feels the initiate is ready. In addition, Bancroft (1972) suggests that teachers are expected to be skilled in acting, singing, and psycho-therapeutic techniques and that a Lozanov-taught teacher will spend three to six months training in these fields.

The role of instructional materials

Materials consist of direct support materials, primarily text and audio, and indirect support materials, including classroom fixtures and music.

The text is organized around the ten units described earlier. The textbook should have emotional force, literary quality, and interesting characters. Language problems should be introduced in a way that does not worry or distract students from the content. "Traumatic themes and distasteful lexical material should be avoided" (Lozanov 1978: 278). Each unit should be governed by a single idea featuring a variety of subthemes, "the way it is in life" (ibid.).

Although not language materials per se, the learning environment plays such a central role in Suggestopedia that the important elements of the environment need to be briefly enumerated. The environment (the indirect support materials) comprises the appearance of the classroom (bright and cheery), the furniture (reclining chairs arranged in a circle), and the music (Baroque largo, selected for reasons discussed previously).

Procedure

Hansen (2011: 408) describes a typical lesson cycle in a Suggestopedia course:

> Lessons are considered in terms of a cycle: first comes the presentation, when learners absorb the material in three different ways, carefully orchestrated. The first, an informal, dramatised introduction to the vocabulary of the text, is followed by two formal but very different "concerts," when the teacher reads the text aloud in synchrony with a piece of music. These "input" sessions spark an unconscious "incubation" process in each student that will continue throughout the course. Input can be completed in one long session, depending on circumstances, but it needs to be followed by at least one night's break. Then the "elaboration" of the text begins, at first a

autonomy. The portfolio has three components: a language passport, which prov
means for the learner to summarize his or her linguistic identity; a language biog
which provides an opportunity for the learner to describe and reflect on his or her langu
learning experience with the foreign language; and a dossier, in which the learner docu
ments different forms of evidence of how his or her proficiency in the language is developing. Regular goal setting and self-assessment is also included in the ELP.

Other applications of learner autonomy in language teaching (Reinders 2009) include
the following:

- *Needs analysis.* After consultation and assessment, the teacher may help the learner develop a profile of his or her strengths and weaknesses and suggest independent learn-ing approaches to address the weaknesses identified. Nunan (1995: 145) comments: "Learners who have reached a point where they are able to define their own goals and create their own learning opportunities have, by definition, become autonomous."
- *Learner training.* This can involve short courses or training activities that seek to intro-duce strategies for independent learning.
- *Self-monitoring.* Another aspect of autonomous learning is for learners to develop skills needed to monitor their own learning. A learning diary or portfolio can be used for this purpose, but technology offers many other options. For example, students can video record themselves performing different tasks (e.g., a recount or narrative task) and com-pare their performance on the same tasks over time.
- *Learning-counseling.* This refers to regular meetings between teachers and learners to help learners plan for their own learning.
- *Learning resources.* The institution may provide links to online or print resources such as the ELP referred to above or other resources that foster autonomous learning.
- *Self-access centers.* Many institutions have a facility available online or in a dedicated center where a variety of self-directed learning resources are available, both to comple-ment classroom instruction and for independent self-directed learning. Staff support is often provided to facilitate the choice and use of learning resources.
- *Follow-up and support.* Successful implementation of the development of learner autonomy involves provision of ongoing support and encouragement. This may involve student-directed group discussion sessions as well as opportunities for reflective review involving students and teachers.
- *Self-study.* There are a number of commercial language-learning packages presently intended entirely for self-study. These are in a sense exclusively learner-centered and teacher-free. However, all of these do involve a "Method" and are marketed with a principal focus on "The Method" (e.g., Rosetta Stone®, TELL ME MORE®, the Pimsleur® Method, Language101.com., etc.).

In reviewing strategies for developing learner autonomy, Reinders (2009: 53) comments:

> Although implementing [an approach to learner autonomy] ... will not guarantee students develop autonomy, the activities do involve a shift of focus from you onto the learners.

are valued as individuals and are supported in their learning will mean
...ore likely to develop this mind set, and knowing this, teachers are
...er the importance of student ownership of the learning process.

... autonomy suggests that teachers using a particular approach or
...se of the method to determine if it can be used in conjunction
...velop autonomous learning or whether it limits the learners' capacity
... and direct their own learning. What types of approaches and methods might lend
...emselves best to learner autonomy? Essentially, the more flexibility the approach provides
in terms of ways it may be interpreted and implemented, the more amenable it will be to
encouraging learner autonomy. Therefore, Communicative Language Teaching, an approach
which has persisted because it lends itself to "strong" (less traditional) and "weak" (more
traditional) forms, was cited as early as the 1970s as one that would be particularly suitable
to promoting learner autonomy (Chapter 5). Content-based approaches or CLIL (Chapter 6)
likewise aim to increase motivation and develop an active, autonomous approach to learning.

Learner strategies

Learning strategies represent another approach to considering the learner's role in language
learning. Some methods prescribe the kinds of strategies learners are encouraged to make
use of in learning. Communicative Language Teaching and Cooperative Language Learning
(Chapter 13), for example, encourage the use of communication strategies as a basis for
developing fluency in language use as well as the use of interactional strategies that enable
learners to learn through the negotiation of meaning. The Silent Way (Chapter 16) is based
on the role of cognitive strategies in learning (see below). But what exactly do we mean by
learning strategies? Cohen's (2011: 682) depiction of strategies captures the concept as the
term is commonly understood: "Language learning strategies can be defined as thoughts and
actions, consciously selected by learners, to assist them in learning and using language in
general, and in the completion of specific language tasks." However, learning strategies have
a broader role in language learning and suggest an active role for learners in managing their
own learning – one that may be used in conjunction with, or independently of, the method
or approach the teacher is using (Cohen 2011). The notion of learning strategies is sometimes
viewed as an aspect of learner autonomy; however, it has had an independent history in language teaching since the 1980s and can be conveniently reviewed in its own terms.

Early discussion of the role of strategies in language learning is often linked to the
work of Rubin on characteristics of the good language learner. Rubin (1975: 45–8) identified
seven characteristics that she claimed distinguished good language learners:

1. They are willing and accurate guessers who are comfortable with uncertainty.
2. They have a strong drive to communicate, or to learn from communication, and are willing to do many things to get their message across.
3. They are often not inhibited and are willing to appear foolish if reasonable communication
   results.

4. They are prepared to attend to form, constantly looking for patterns in the language.

5. They practice and also seek out opportunities to practice.

6. They monitor their own speech and the speech of others, constantly attending to how well their speech is being received and whether their performance meets the standards they have learned.

7. They attend to meaning, knowing that in order to understand a message, it is not sufficient to attend only to the grammar or surface form of a language.

The concept of strategies has attracted some degree of controversy since Rubin's work, because some researchers feel it overlaps with other constructs. For example, Cohen and Dörnyei (2002) give the following examples of reading strategies:

a) With regard to reading habits in the target language:
   - Making a real effort to find reading material that is at or near one's level.
b) As basic reading strategies:
   - Planning how to read a text, monitor to see how the reading is going, and then check to see how much of it was understood
   - Making ongoing summaries either in one's mind or in the margins of the text.
c) When encountering unknown words and structures:
   - Guessing the appropriate meaning by using clues from the surrounding context
   - Using a dictionary to get a detailed sense of what individual words mean.

The relevance of strategy theory to teaching is that some strategies are likely to be more effective than others, and by recognizing the differences between the strategies used by expert and novice language learners or between successful and less successful learners, the effectiveness of teaching and learning can be improved. Methods and approaches implicitly or explicitly require the use of specific learning strategies; however, the focus of much strategy research is on self-managed strategies that may be independent of those favored by a particular method.

A well-known classification of strategies distinguishes four different kinds of strategies according to their function (Chamot 1987, 2001; Oxford 1990): cognitive strategies, metacognitive strategies, social strategies, and affective strategies.

- *Cognitive strategies.* These refer to the processes learners make use of in order to better understand or remember learning materials or input and in retrieving it, such as by making mental associations, underlining key phrases in a text, making word lists to review following a lesson, and so on.
- *Metacognitive strategies.* These are ways in which learners "control their language learning by planning what they will do, checking on progress, and then evaluating their performance on a given task" (Cohen 2011: 682). For example, a student might focus on the following kinds of questions in relation to a listening text that a teacher uses during a lesson:

"How should I approach this listening text?" (planning)
"What parts of the text should I pay more attention to?" (planning)

"Am I focusing on the appropriate parts of the text?" (monitoring)

"Did I understand correctly the words the writer used?" (monitoring)

"Did I perform the task well?" (evaluating)

"What caused me to misunderstand part of the text?" (evaluating)

- *Social strategies.* These are "the means employed by learners for interacting with other learners and native speakers, such as through asking questions to clarify social roles and relationships, asking for an explanation or verification, and cooperating with others in order to complete tasks" (Cohen 2011: 682). For example, a learner may prepare a set of questions that he or she could use when meeting speakers of English to enable him or her to have more opportunities to use English.

- *Affective strategies.* These are actions the learner takes to manage the emotions they experience when learning a language or when they try out what they have learned in communication. For example, a learner may find it less stressful to first try out their language skills by talking to more proficient second language users than with native speakers.

Research on learning strategies is useful to the extent that it leads to insights that can be used in teaching or in developing learner autonomy. Cohen (2011: 683) suggests that in order to give learners a better understanding of the nature of strategies and to help them develop effective strategy use, four issues need to be addressed:

1. Raising awareness of the strategies learners are already using
2. Presenting and modeling strategies so that learners become increasingly aware of their own thinking and learning processes
3. Providing multiple practice opportunities to help learners move toward autonomous use of the strategies through gradual withdrawal of teacher scaffolding, and
4. Getting learners to evaluate the effectiveness of the strategies used and any efforts that they have made to transfer these strategies to new tasks.

In teaching strategies, both direct and indirect strategies are used. With a direct approach, strategy training is a feature of a normal language lesson and a training session includes five stages: preparation, presentation, practice, evaluation, and expansion. As described by Gu (2012: 321):

> Strategies are first introduced and modeled by the teacher, before students are given tasks to practice using the taught strategies. Teachers and learners reflect along the way about the reason for choosing and the effectiveness of using the strategy in question. Learners are finally encouraged to extend the use of the taught strategies similar to language learning and language use tasks. In this way, the responsibility for strategic decision-making shifts gradually from the teacher to the learners as classroom instruction moves from stage to stage, resulting in full learner responsibility in strategy choice and use at the end of training.

The concept of learning strategies adds an important dimension to what we understand by "teaching," since while approaches and methods are generally conceptualized as instructional designs for second language *teaching*, in reality they are designs for language *learning*, and appropriate strategy use is often the key to successful language learning. Important questions for teachers to ask in relation to approaches and methods therefore include: What learning strategies does this method develop? What learning strategies do my learners use? What other learning strategies would be useful for my learners to use? Within an approach or method, learning strategies, as illustrated by the examples of reading and listening strategies given above, often combine with the teaching of specific skills. Since learning strategies may be viewed as an aspect of learner autonomy, as mentioned, it stands to reason that here, too, flexible approaches and methods will lend themselves well to the development of learning strategies. In addition, methods such as Cooperative Language Learning that encourage group interaction and success lend themselves naturally to encouraging the use of learning strategies.

Learning styles

Another dimension of learner-centeredness is known as learning styles. Whereas *strategies* refer to specific actions learners take to address particular learning tasks or language use situations, *learning styles* refer to a general predisposition or preference to approach learning in particular ways. Although there are many different ways of conceptualizing and defining learning styles (see, e.g., Griffiths 2008), Reid's characterization of learning styles as "an individual's natural, habitual and preferred ways(s) of absorbing processing, and retaining new information and skills" (1995: viii) is often used in relation to language teaching. Differences in learning styles may be reflected in the preferences learners have for particular kinds of classroom activities, for particular roles for the teacher and for the learners, for particular grouping arrangements, and for particular modes of learning both inside and outside the classroom. The notion of learning styles can help capture the diversity of types of learners we meet in language classrooms and the different ways in which learners respond to teaching methods based on their learning style preferences. These preferences will influence how learners respond to different learning situations. For example:

- Some learners like to work independently, while others prefer working in a group.
- Some learners like to spend a lot of time planning before they complete a task, while others spend little time planning and sort out problems that arise while they are completing a task.
- Some people can focus on only one task at a time, while others seem to be able to do several different tasks at once.
- Some learners feel uncomfortable in situations where there is ambiguity or uncertainly, while others are able to handle situations where there is conflicting information and opinions.
- When solving problems, some people are willing to take risks and to make guesses without worrying about the possibility of being wrong, while others try to avoid situations where there is such a risk.
- Some people learn best when they use visual cues and write notes to help them remember, while others learn better through auditory learning, without writing notes.

These kinds of differences are often observable over time in a teacher's class and can also be revealed through interviews, journal writing, questionnaires, and other activities in which teachers explore their learners' view of learning. Many different research instruments and approaches have been used to investigate the notion of learning styles, and consequently there are many different lists and taxonomies of learning styles. The following are commonly referred to (Reid 1995; Richards and Lockhart 1994):

- *Visual learners.* These learners respond to new information in a visual fashion and prefer visual, pictorial, and graphic representations of experience. They benefit most from reading and learn well by seeing words in books, workbooks, and on the board. They can often learn on their own with a book, and they take notes of lectures to remember the new information.
- *Auditory learners.* These learners learn best from oral explanation and from hearing words spoken. They benefit from listening to recordings, teaching other students, and by conversing with their classmates and teachers.
- *Kinesthetic learners.* Learners of this type learn best when they are physically involved in the experience. They remember new information when they actively participate in activities, such as through field trips or role plays.
- *Tactile learners.* These learners learn best when engaged in "hands on" activities. They like to manipulate materials and like to build, fix, or make things, or put things together.
- *Group learners.* These learners prefer group interaction and classwork with other students and learn best when working with others. Group interaction helps them to learn and understand new material better.
- *Individual learners.* Learners of this type prefer to work on their own. They are capable of learning new information by themselves and remember the material better if they learned it alone.
- *Authority-oriented learners.* These learners relate well to a traditional classroom. They prefer the teacher as an authority figure. They like to have clear instructions and know exactly what they are doing. They are less comfortable with consensus-building discussion.

Learning style preferences also reflect the learner's cultural background since conceptions of both teaching and learning differ from culture to culture (Tsui 2009). In some cultures a good teacher is one who controls and directs learners and who maintains a respectful distance between the teacher and the learners. Learners are the more or less passive recipients of the teacher's expertise. Teaching is viewed as a teacher-controlled and directed process. In other cultures the teacher may be viewed more as a facilitator. The ability to form close interpersonal relations with students is highly valued and there is a strong emphasis on individual learner creativity and independent learning. Students may even be encouraged to question and challenge what the teacher says. Similarly, in some cultures students may be more willing to communicate in front of their peers in the classroom than in other cultures. Wen and Clement (2003) suggest that in China, group cohesiveness and attachment to group members influence Chinese students communication patterns in the classroom. A student may believe that if he or she speaks up in class, this may not be valued by other students since it is judged as "showing off" and an attempt to make other students look weak. Language teaching approaches and methods often have built into them assumptions about preferred learning styles. Some such as Communicative Language Teaching, Community Language Learning (Chapter 17) and Task-Based Language Teaching favor a group-based interactive learning style which, critics have pointed out, reflects a Western-based view of learning (Holliday 1994a, 1994b, 2003, 2009). Students from other educational traditions may prefer teaching that is more teacher-led or which depends more on individual than group-based learning.

However, research has not been able to establish that some learning styles are more effective than others (Griffiths 2012), and some researchers question the notion of learning styles (Cassidy 2004). Griffiths (2012: 162) concludes that "no particular style can be isolated as being important for success in language learning. Instead success rather depends on learners choosing a style which suits their own individual and contextual needs."

The usefulness of the concept of learning styles is in how it can provide a better understanding of the diversity of learners that may be present in a single class. And as we noted above, it also accounts for the fact that learners from different cultural backgrounds may have different learning style preferences because of the type of teaching they have experienced in the past. In terms of how learning styles combine with approaches and methods, the important consideration is the following: students who come from educational backgrounds where the teacher plays a more dominant role and where the individual is not encouraged to stand out in a group, as in the example cited above from China, may prefer more conventional teaching methods, including Audiolingualism (Chapter 4), Situational Language Teaching (Chapter 3), or even Grammar-Translation (Chapter 1). It is very important for the teacher to be sensitive to the cultural environment when choosing an approach or method.

The impact of technology

The movement toward a learner-centered approach to teaching in recent years reflects a philosophical reorientation and change in thinking about the roles of learners as well as a response to changed opportunities for learner-initiated learning through the use of the Internet and other forms of technology. Waters (2012: 448) comments:

> research shows that the use of the interactive whiteboard can have a significant effect on teaching methodology, by making it possible for new kinds of learning opportunities to occur. There is also evidence that the increasing ubiquity of web-based teaching and learning resources has the potential to redistribute the balance between teacher-led and learner-led interaction. In addition, many course books are nowadays already accompanied by an ever-widening range of linked e-resources and these are likely to increase the opportunities for learners to work more independently as well ...

Technology thus provides opportunities for learners to be less dependent on classroom learning and the teacher's approach or method. It does this by:

- *providing a wider exposure to English*, including authentic example of language use;
- *increasing opportunities for interaction* both with other learners and with native-speakers and second language users of English worldwide;

- *supporting different learning styles*, allowing students to find learning resources that match their preferred way of learning (e.g., visual or auditory styles);
- *providing learners with opportunities to focus on particular skills*, such as reading or speaking;
- *providing support that is suitable for learners of different proficiency levels*, enabling learners to choose activities that range in difficulty from beginner to advanced;
- *encouraging more active learning* through changes in the roles of students that technology makes possible: students are no longer the passive recipients of instruction but are actively engaged in furthering their own knowledge and skills and are more in control of the process and the learning outcomes;
- *encouraging learner autonomy* through giving learners a greater level of choice over what they learn and how they learn it, thus developing a greater sense of learner autonomy;
- *providing a stress-reduced environment*, since for some learners technology-based learning is a less stressful way to practice using English than classroom-based activities where they feel they are being compared with their peers;
- *providing a social context for learning* by allowing learners to join a learning community in which they interact socially with other learners; in this way technology encourages collaborative learning (with some activities students provide peer-tutoring, helping each other accomplish tasks);
- *increasing motivation*, since motivation often increases and discipline problems decrease when students are engaged in technology-based learning;
- *providing access to more engaging material*, since through the Internet learners can access content that is often very engaging for them, such as digital games, YouTube content, and so on;
- *supporting learning outside of the classroom*, such as through the use of mobile technologies that can be helpful in supporting learners to use English at the point of need, for example when traveling;
- *offering opportunities for more and alternative types of feedback* as with programs that include immediate or relayed feedback to learners, and collaborative tools such as email and chat that allow learners to work with other learners to get peer-feedback, or to get help from a (remote) teacher.

Technology can also support many of the approaches and methods discussed in this book. For example, it can be used as a component of Communicative Language Teaching, Task-Based Language Teaching, Text-Based Instruction, as well as Cooperative Language Learning, by providing opportunities for authentic interactions during which learners have to employ and expand their communicative resources, supported by the ability to link sound, word, texts, and images in the process. There are many possibilities, such as through chat rooms and discussion boards. Technology also provides easy access to a rich range of authentic materials, and it enables learners in different locations to work together on collaborative tasks and to make use of a variety of different modes of communication – including print, audio, and visual. The classroom textbook can be enriched by making links to topics, functions, and activities that appear in the book. Similarly, students can engage in follow-up work in the media lab or on the computer and work with real examples of the interactions and transactions they practiced in the classroom. Technology similarly offers support for Content-Based Instruction and CLIL (see Chapter 6). Content-focused instruction is content-driven and integrates language learning and content learning. Authentic content can be accessed on the Internet, providing examples of natural language use. Students can also explore websites, watch online videos and news clips, and share their reactions to these with other learners. They may be given specific tasks to carry out (e.g., in the form of webquests), they can prepare their own materials either individually or in groups and record blog posts or podcasts. They can share these with other students, all while using the target language. With task-based and text-based teaching, technology provides many opportunities to create texts or tasks that reflect real-world uses of language, that require them to integrate skills, that engage them in negotiation of meaning with other learners, and that also require a focus on form. Communicative online tasks support second language acquisition through providing opportunities for noticing and for restructuring language as students engage with the production of both spoken and written texts (Pellettieri 2000). Task-Based Language Teaching emphasizes the need for a broad, or holistic, approach to language development and makes use of tasks that require the integration of different skills. Similarly, integrative CALL provides for the integration of skills, and technology is now increasingly seen as a useful medium for the creation and delivery of task-based teaching.

However, regardless of the support for autonomous learning available through technology, it has been pointed out that language learning and language use is primarily a social endeavor. Nielson (2011: 110–11) comments:

> There is no existing empirical research on learning outcomes from foreign language self-study using commercially available, stand-alone CALL materials. There is, however, research from related areas that suggests the most effective learning is not achieved by learners working alone, and that any materials designed as stand-alone, self-study solutions will have to compensate for this lack of interpersonal interaction. For example, researchers investigating learner autonomy, or "the ability to take charge of one's own learning" (Holec, 1981, p. 3), make it clear that achieving autonomy – a condition argued to be beneficial to the language acquisition process – does not necessarily come about as a result of self-study. In fact, according to Benson's (2007) literature review on autonomous learning, "learners do not develop the ability to self-direct their learning simply by being placed in situations where they have no other option" (p. 22). That is, autonomy is learner-internal, and not a situational condition.

Conclusion

While approaches and methods generally contain defined roles for learne
specific assumptions about the strategies and processes learners should make
guage learning, learners' contributions to language learning should not be
the practices of a particular teaching approach or method. A focus on lear
learning strategies, learning styles, and the opportunities for learner-fo

provided by technology expands our understanding of the role of learners in language learning. It reminds us that language teaching is not simply about teaching language. A learner-centered approach to teaching has as its goal to provide learners with learning resources that they can use both in and outside the classroom and ways in which learners can focus and manage their own learning.

Discussion questions

1. Respond to the following statements by saying "yes" or "no" and giving reasons for your answers.

   Learners should always be given a choice about what to learn.
   Learners should always be given a choice about how to learn.
   All language courses should include the flexibility to meet learners' diverse and changing needs.

2. "Learning is not necessarily a mirror image of teaching" (p. 331). Exchange experiences with a colleague about the mismatches you have experienced between what you intended to teach and what learners ended up learning.

3. The European Language Portfolio (ELP) embodies the concept of learner autonomy and is provided by the Council of Europe at the following website: http://www.coe.int/portfolio. Look at this portfolio, or search for a similar one on the Internet, and answer the following questions:

   - Who completes the portfolio?
   - Is it assessed by a teacher?
   - What is the purpose of the portfolio?
   - Do you think using the portfolio might work with your learners? Why (not)?

4. What are some examples of strategies for independent learning and learner autonomy? (Review pp. 332–3.) Which of these do you think might be most effective?

5. How would you respond to a teacher who asks students to set their own goals, only to have students respond that the teacher isn't actually teaching them? Would you encourage the teacher to change his or her teaching style?

6. Many teachers feel that their learners' experiences and beliefs do not predispose them toward learner autonomy and that it may be a concept that works better in some, mostly Western, cultures than others. Do you think your students would be comfortable with taking more responsibility for their learning? If not, how could you gradually accustom them to this idea?

7. Review the four types of strategies: cognitive, metacognitive, social, and affective, mentioned on pages 335–6. What types of strategies are the following examples of?

   Using flashcards to memorize new vocabulary.
   Joining a sports club to meet more target language speakers.
   Keeping a learning diary.
   Creating a relaxing learning environment.

8. The first stage in developing strategy use is raising learners' awareness of the strategies they are already using. How would you go about this? Specifically, how would you create an environment in which learners are most likely to use a cognitive, a metacognitive, a social, and an affective strategy?

9. A good teacher takes account of learners' preferred learning styles. However, these may run counter to the tenets of some of the approaches and methods described in this book. For example, in some countries learners are used to teachers being firmly in control, but the teacher may want to use a more learner-centered approach. What would you do in such a situation?

10. What teachers aim for and what learners actually learn can be two vastly different things. Similarly, what teachers mean and what learners understand are not necessarily the same. As a mini research project, identify one class that you have a detailed lesson plan for with well-worked-out goals. At the end of the lesson give your students a short questionnaire asking them the following:

- What they thought they had to do during one of the main activities
- Why they think they had to do this – i.e., what the learning purpose was
- What they thought the three main purposes of the overall lesson were (you can include a list of options), in order of importance
- Up to three things they learned from the class, in order of importance.

How did these match with your own goals?

11. Work with a colleague and observe each other's class. To what extent do each of you do the following?

	1 (not at all) 5 (all the time)	How is this done?
Take active involvement in student learning		
Provide options and resources		
Offer choices and decision-making opportunities		
Support learners		
Encourage reflection		

12. As you read in the chapter, it is important for teachers to ask the following questions in relation to approaches and methods:

- What learning strategies does this method develop?
- What learning strategies do my learners use?
- What other learning strategies would be useful for my learners to use?

Answer these questions for your own teaching method and learners or for a language class where you have been a student.

References and further reading

Alsagoff, L. 2012. Identity and the EIL Learner. In L. Alsagoff, S. L. McKay, G. Hu, and W. A. Renandya (eds.), *Principles and Practices for Teaching English as an International Language*. New York: Routledge. 104–22.

Atkinson, D. (ed.). 2011. *Alternative Approaches to Second Language Acquisition*. New York: Routledge.

Benson, P. 2001. *Teaching and Researching Autonomy in Language Learning*. London: Longman.

Benson. P., and D. Nunan (eds.). 2005. *Learners' Stories: Difference and Diversity in Language Learning*. Cambridge: Cambridge University Press.

Blumberg, P. 2004. Beginning journey toward a culture of learning centered teaching. *Journal of Student Centered Learning* 2(1): 68–80.

Breen. M. P. (ed.). 2001. *Learner Contributions to Language Learning*. London: Longman.

Cassidy, S. 2004. Learning styles: an overview of theories, models, and measures. *Educational Psychology* 24(4): 419–44.

Chamot, A. U. 1987. The learning strategies of ESL students. In A. Wenden and J. Rubin (eds.), *Learner Strategies in Language Learning*. Englewood Cliffs, NJ: Prentice Hall. 71–84.

Chamot. A. U. 2001. The role of learning strategies in second language acquisition. In Breen (ed.), 25–43.

Cohen, A. D. 2011. Second language learner strategies. In Hinkley (ed.), 681–98.

Cohen, A. D., and Z. Dornyei. 2002. Focus on the language learner: motivation, styles, and strategies. In N. Schmitt (ed.), *An Introduction to Applied Linguistics*. London: Arnold. 170–90.

European Language Portfolio (ELP). http://www.coe.int/portfolio; accessed May 17, 2013.

Griffiths, C. (ed.). 2008. *Lessons From Good Language Learners*. Cambridge: Cambridge University Press.

Gu, Y. P. 2012. Language learning strategies: an EIL perspective. In Alsagoff et al. (eds.), 318–34.

Hinkley, E. (ed.). 2011. *Handbook of Research in Second Language Teaching and Learning*, Vol II. New York: Routledge.

Holliday, A. 1994a. *Appropriate Methodology and Social Context*. Cambridge: Cambridge University Press.

Holliday, A. 1994b. The house of TESEP and the communicative approach: the special needs of state English language education. *ELT Journal* 48(1): 3–11.

Holliday, A. 2003. Social autonomy: addressing the dangers of culturism in TESOL. In D. Palfreyman and R. Smith (eds.), *Learner Autonomy across Cultures: Language Education Perspectives*. Basingstoke: Palgrave Macmillan. 110–26.

Holliday, A. 2009. The role of culture in English language education: key challenges. *Language and Intercultural Communication* 10(2): 165–77.

Little, D. 2002. The European Language Portfolio: structure, origins, implementation and challenges. *Language Teaching* 35(3): 182–9.

Nielson, K. 2011. Self-study with language learning software in the workplace: what happens? *Language Learning & Technology* 15(3): 110–29.

Nunan, D. 1988. *The Learner-Centred Curriculum: A Study in Second Language Teaching*. New York: Cambridge University Press.

Nunan, D. 1995. Closing the gap between learning and instruction. *TESOL Quarterly* 29: 133–58.

Ortega, L. 2009. *Understanding Second Language Acquisition*. London: Hodder Education.

Oxford, R. 1990. *Language Learning Strategies: What Every Teacher Should Know*. Rowley, MA: Newbury House.

Pellettieri, J. 2000. Negotiation in cyberspace. In M. Warschauer and R. L. Kern (eds.), *Network-Based Language Teaching: Concepts and Practice*. New York: Cambridge University Press. 59–86.

Reid, J. (ed.). 1995. *Learning Styles in the ESL/EFL Classroom*. New York: Heinle and Heinle.

Reinders, H., and S. Wattana. 2012. Talk to me! Games and students' willingness to communicate. In H. Reinders (ed.), *Digital Games in Language Learning and Teaching*. Basingstoke: Palgrave Macmillan. 156–88.

Reinders, H. 2009. Technology and second language teacher education. In A. Burns and J. Richards (eds.), *Cambridge Guide to Second Language Teacher Education*. Cambridge: Cambridge University Press. 230–7.

Richards, J. C., and C. Lockhart. 1994. *Reflective Teaching in Second Language Classrooms*. Cambridge: Cambridge University Press.

Rubin, J. 1975. What the good language learner can teach us. *TESOL Quarterly* 9(1): 41–51.

Senior, R. 2006. *The Experience of Language Teaching*. Cambridge: Cambridge University Press.

Tsui, A. B. M. 2009. Teaching expertise: approaches, perspectives and characteristics. In A. Burns and J. Richards (eds.), *Cambridge Guide to Second Language Teacher Education*. Cambridge: Cambridge University Press. 190–7.

Tudor, I. 1996. *Learner-Centredness as Language Education*. Cambridge: Cambridge University Press.

Victori, M., and W. Lockhart. 1995. Enhancing metacognition in self-directed language learning. *System* 232: 223–34.

Waters, A. 2012. Trends and issues in ELT methods and methodology. *ELT Journal* 66(4): 440–9.

Wen, W. P., and R. Clement. 2003. A Chinese conceptualisation of willingness to communicate in ESL. *Language, Culture and Curriculum* 16(1): 18–38.

20 Teachers, approaches, and methods

Introduction

We have seen throughout this book that approaches and methods reflect particular assumptions and beliefs about how learners should learn – assumptions that may need to be reviewed based on the roles of autonomous learning, learning strategies, learning style preferences, and technology-mediated learning. Approaches and methods also prescribe how teachers should teach. They reflect assumptions about the nature of good teaching, the practices and techniques teachers should make use of, the teacher's role in the classroom, the kinds of language and resources they should use, and the kinds of grouping arrangements and interactions that should occur in their classrooms. When new approaches or methods are introduced, they are promoted as reflecting sound theory and principles and as being the best solution to the language teaching problem. They are often based on the assumption that the processes of second language learning are fully understood. Many of the books written by method gurus are full of claims and assertions about how people learn languages, few of which are based on second language acquisition research or have been empirically tested. Researchers who study language learning are themselves usually reluctant to dispense prescriptions for teaching based on the results of their research, because they know that current knowledge is tentative, partial, and changing. As Atkinson (2011: xi) comments: "It is increasingly apparent … that SLA is an extremely complex and multifaceted phenomenon. Exactly for this reason, it now appears that no single theoretical perspective will allow us to understand SLA adequately."

Much of SLA research does not support the often simplistic theories and prescriptions found in the literature supporting some approaches and methods. For example, in making their case for CLIL, Coyle, Hood, and Marsh (2010: 153–4) comment:

> CLIL has a significant contribution to make not only to providing learners of all ages with motivating experiences which are appropriate for knowledge creation and sharing, but also, fundamentally, to cultivating the "cosmopolitan identity" … where learning and using languages for different purposes generates tolerance, curiosity and responsibility as global citizens.

Commenting on this grandiose claim, Paran (2013: 140) observes: "Quite apart from the difficulty of any teaching programme to achieve this, it is not clear why CLIL can do this better than any other teaching, unless we accept that CLIL is 'better' than other language teaching, which is where the circularity of the argument comes in."

At any given time, some approaches and methods have become widely accepted and practiced, while others may have attracted much more limited interest. Some proposals are given wide support at local, national, and international levels when they are adopted as the framework for the national curriculum or supported by educational organizations, teacher-training institutions, academics, and decision-makers in ministries of education. Such was the case with Communicative Language Teaching (Chapter 5) and has also been true in some contexts for Task-Based Language Teaching (Chapter 9), Text-Based Instruction (Chapter 10), CLIL (Chapter 6), and the Common European Framework of Reference (Chapter 8). From the descriptions given in this book, it is also clear that some approaches and methods are unlikely to be widely adopted because they are difficult to understand and use, lack clear practical application, require special training, are not readily compatible with local traditions and practices, and necessitate major changes in teachers' practices and beliefs.

However, approaches and methods generally offer very *different* proposals for how to teach. This sometimes creates a dilemma for teacher educators, teachers, program coordinators, and decision-makers in ministries of education: on what basis should an approach or method be selected? And what are the alternatives? In this chapter we will consider three options that are available to teacher-educators, teachers, and other decision-makers and consider the assumptions and implications of each. These options are (a) to match teaching to the method; (b) to adapt the method to local needs; or (c) to develop a personal approach or method.

Match your teaching to the method

An assumption of all of the instructional designs discussed in this book is that the chosen approaches or methods work, that they are more effective than other approaches and methods, that they are applicable in many different situations, and that adopting them will produce successful learning outcomes in language programs. Hunter and Smith (2012) comment on the fact that historical accounts of methods and current debates about appropriate methodology tend to present new methods as evidence of progress – as one set of theories, ideas, and practices is replaced by another and presumably more appropriate and up-to-date set. Presented with a new approach or method such as Task-Based Language Teaching, CLIL, or Text-Based Instruction, the teachers' task is to study the method and its principles and then apply the procedures it recommends to their own teaching. To be able to do this, teachers need to acquire new beliefs and practices.

New beliefs

Before changing his or her practices, the teacher needs to acquire a new set of beliefs – some of which may run contrary to the teacher's own beliefs and understandings (Borg 2006). Based on the assumption that practices will not change unless the teacher's beliefs also change, those promoting the adoption of new approaches and methods face the task of bringing about changes in a teacher's beliefs. This is normally addressed in a number of ways:

- By persuasion: philosophical or ideological reasons may be used to support the new beliefs, such as arguments in favour of the value of learner autonomy or collaborative learning.
- By citing theory and research that supports the new method: this has characterized promotion of the Natural Approach and Task-Based Language Teaching as was also true of earlier methods such as Audiolingualism.
- By citing evidence of successful learning outcomes: this is often seen in discussions of CLIL and Content-Based Instruction.
- By appeals to authorities: support from credible experts and authorities can also be persuasive, such as recommendations from leading academics, "gurus," educational authorities and organizations, and so on. Support of this kind was crucial to the acceptance of Communicative Language Teaching in the 1970s (Richards 1984).

Much of the focus of graduate courses in language teaching is directed toward reshaping teachers' knowledge and beliefs through the study of some of the vast body of research and theorizing on second language learning and teaching. However, teachers' beliefs are often resistant to change. Clark and Peterson (1986) noted the following:

- The most resilient or "core" teachers' beliefs are formed on the basis of teachers' own schooling as young students while observing teachers who taught them. Subsequent teacher education appears not to disturb these early beliefs, not least, perhaps, because it rarely addresses them.
- If teachers actually try out a particular innovation that does not initially conform to their prior beliefs or principles and the innovation proves helpful or successful, then accommodation of an alternative belief or principle is more plausible than in any other circumstance.
- For the novice teacher, classroom experience and day-to-day interaction with colleagues has the potential to influence particular relationships among beliefs and principles and, over time, to consolidate the individual's permutation of them. Nevertheless, it seems that greater experience does not lead to greater adaptability in our beliefs and, thereby, the abandonment of strongly held pedagogical principles. Quite the contrary, in fact. The more experience we have, the more reliant on our "core" principles we become and the less conscious we are of being so.

New practices

In addition to acquiring a new set of beliefs and understandings, teachers adopting a new method also need to acquire a new set of practical skills. They may need to become familiar with a new set of procedures for teaching lessons, to learn to use different kinds of teaching materials and resources, or to change the kinds of interactions they have with learners. A shift from teacher-directed teaching to the use of group-based activities, for example, requires not only a change in the teacher's mind set but the learning of new routines for organizing a lesson. Practices of this kind are often the focus of training sessions, micro-teaching, workshops or demonstrations designed to show teachers how to teach a lesson based on the principles of approaches and methods such as Communicative Language Teaching, Cooperative Language Learning (Chapter 13), Total Physical Response (Chapter 15), Text-Based Instruction, or Task-Based Language Teaching. Videos are often available demonstrating how the method should be used. Teachers may later be assessed according to how closely their teaching reflects the model they are being trained to use (Barduhn and Johnson 2009). When teachers have difficulty in applying the method correctly, from a training perspective the issue is either to improve the system of transmission and delivery (how teachers are taught about the method), or to find out what went wrong at the receiving end. Did the teacher use the correct procedures? Did the teacher follow the correct sequence of stages recommended when using the method? Accounts by teachers using the new method can also be used to induct novice teachers into the method. For example, in Edwards and Willis (2005: 3) accounts are provided of how teachers implement TBLT. Donald Freeman, endorsing the book, cited in the book comments:

> In adopting task-based teaching ... the contributors to this collection write about their classroom practices from a common point of view, creating in a sense a shared "grammar" of the classroom. This approach then makes their accounts very readable, and I would think, very replicable by readers.

The metaphor of a "shared grammar" is interesting since it suggests how the method is conceived as a system of rules that teachers need to internalize and apply in their own practice.

Criticisms of matching teaching to the method

But a number of objections can be made to the practice of presenting teachers with the "pre-packaged expert-designed" teaching product that methods often seem to represent and inviting teachers to adopt it as the source of their classroom teaching. One criticism is that methods are suitable for only inexperienced teachers. Another is that they restrict the teacher's contribution to teaching.

Methods are only suitable for novices

It could be argued that presenting teachers with a pre-packaged method may be appropriate for novice teachers but not for more experienced teachers. Many experienced teachers typically began their professional training with a certificate-level training course in which they were taught to teach according to the methodology presented in their course – be it the PPP lesson model of the older RSA Certificate or an integrated-skills "communicative" lesson format found in more recent training programs (Richards, Ho, and Giblin 1996). As they gain experience, many teachers report that they no longer use the methods they were trained to use but adapt a much more flexible approach to methodology (Richards, Gallo, and Renandya 2001). For entry-level teachers with little professional or practical knowledge, the use of methods in programs like these is intended to provide trainees with a level of security. Methods, it could be argued, solve many of the problems beginning teachers have to struggle with because many of the basic decisions about what to teach and how to teach it have already been made for them. Therefore, for novice teachers, methods are probably necessary. Moreover, method enthusiasts create together a professional community with a common purpose, ideology, and vernacular. This provides adherents with a cohort group of like-minded teachers with whom they can share ideas and experiences. Like the "PPP" prescription of Presentation, Practice, and Production (Chapter 3), a method offers to the novice teacher the reassurance of a detailed set of sequential steps to follow in the classroom. Nevertheless, in recent years, even for novice teachers, schools are somewhat less rigid than they had been in the past in prescribing a method and teaching techniques.

In the case of experienced teachers, methods can restrict the teacher's options and choices and discourage the teacher from developing a personal teaching approach. They can limit creativity and encourage teachers to focus on the method rather than on the learners. Therefore, the practice of encouraging experienced teachers to match their teaching to a method has come under significant criticism.

Methods presents a deficit view of teaching

A "follow the method" strategy has also been described as reflecting a deficit view of teaching, one that suggests that teachers are generally deficient in their understanding of teaching and that this problem can be rectified through the use of a method that was designed by experts. Teachers have to accept on faith the claims or theory underlying the method and apply them to their own practice. They are therefore seen as involved in the application of other people's theories and principles, rather than engaged in developing theories and principles of their own. The roles of teachers and learners, as well as the type of activities and teaching techniques to be used in the classroom, are generally prescribed and not open to negotiation. Absent from the traditional view of methods, described above, is a concept of learner-centeredness and teacher creativity: an acknowledgment that learners bring different learning styles and preferences to the learning process, that they should be consulted in the process of developing a teaching program, and that teaching methods must be flexible and adaptive to learners' needs and interests and reflect the teacher's thinking.

Adapt the method to your teaching context

A more flexible way of considering approaches and methods is to see them as a resource that can be tailored to the teacher's needs. This view of the relationship between teachers and methods assigns a greater role to teacher creativity and individuality and positions a method in a supporting rather than a controlling role. The method is viewed as providing a core set of principles and procedures that can be adapted and modified according to the teacher's teaching context. Questions teachers might ask from this perspective, ones where the answers may require some creativity, would include:

> How can I use a communicative approach in a class of 70 students?
> How can I use Cooperative Language Learning in an exam-driven curriculum?
> What principles from the Silent Way can I use in teaching speaking?
> How can I adapt Total Physical Response to use in a business English course?
> How can Task-Based Language Teaching be used with young learners?

With this view of methods, the ways in which teachers individualize, localize, personalize, and adapt methods is valued. Although the use of a particular method or approach might be part of the overall teaching philosophy of a school, teachers are encouraged to develop their own personalized interpretations of it. Teacher development may focus on how teachers achieve their individual uses of a method. An example of how this can take place is with the *Lesson Study Approach* (Lewis and Tsuchida 1998; Tasker 2009). Teachers work together in a group and co-plan a lesson that focuses on a particular piece of content or unit of study and that reflects their shared philosophy of teaching and the method that they or their school has adopted. During this process they engage in extended conversations while focusing on student learning and the development of specific outcomes. Once the plan has been developed, one member of the team volunteers to teach it, while the others observe. (Sometimes outsiders are also invited to observe.) After the lesson, the group discuss their findings in a colloquium or panel discussion. Typically, the teachers who planned the lesson focus on their rationale for how they planned the lesson and their evaluation of how it went, particularly focusing on student learning. The planning group then re-convene to review the lesson and revise it, and then a different teacher teaches it to a different class. The cycle culminates in the team publishing a report that includes lesson plans, observed student behavior, teacher reflections, and a summary of the group discussions. These are then made available to others.

When teachers adapt methods to their local contexts of use, the adaptations they make will reflect both the teacher's personal understandings, beliefs, and teaching style but also adjustments due to local factors such as the class size, classroom resources, learners' proficiency level, age, backgrounds, needs, learning styles, goals, and so on. The teacher's role is to align the method to their classroom and school context. In this way there is a better fit between the method and the contexts of its use – the culture of learning in which a teachers works. Jin and Cortazzi (2011: 571) describe this in relation to the learning in Chinese classrooms:

> "Cultures of learning" describes taken-for-granted frameworks of expectations, attitudes, values and beliefs about successful learning and teaching, about learning and using different language skills in classrooms, and about how interaction should be accomplished. For students, this includes ways of preparing for English exams, self-study practice and classwork. It includes giving great importance to the teacher, to the book, to models and explanations, to mimicking and memorizing, to practising and performing ... It also includes deeper values of the importance of learning and study; their respect for teachers for their knowledge, cultivation of learning and morality; their awareness of teachers' guidance, care, concern, devotion and sacrifice (cognitive, social and affective dimensions). It includes a deep belief that making a continuous effort leads to success (not just having talent), that success is possible, and that difficulties and hardships can be endured and surmounted.

Thus, an important task for the teacher is to adjust the methods he or she has been trained to use to the culture of learning in which they are used.

Develop a personal approach or method

Another way of characterizing the relationship between teachers and methods is to shift the focus from methods to the teacher. This can be seen as a change in agency – from methods that change teachers, to teachers that are engaged in the process of developing their own teaching methods and approaches. This changed perspective on methods has been characterized as "post-method" (Kumaravadivelu 1994, 2003). The following are characteristics of a post-method philosophy.

Using principled eclecticism

In language teaching the blending of methods into the teacher's own method has long been a recommendation of methodologists. Jin and Cortazzi drawing on Brown, Larsen-Freeman, and others offer the following summary (2011: 561):

> This approach would be flexible, based on an analysis of local circumstances and needs, with a theoretical rationale and coherent principles and a philosophy of exploration and reflection. Interestingly, there is some tradition of being eclectic in this way among prestigious language teachers. It was advocated by Rivers, who cites Henry Sweet (1889): "A good method must, before all be comprehensive and eclectic. It must be based on a thorough knowledge of the science of language" and general principles rather than the "one absolutely invariable method" and Harold Palmer's "multiple line of approach", which "embodies the eclectic principle"; "we use each and every method, process, exercise, drill, or device … to select judiciously and without prejudice all that is likely to help us in our work. Conversely, inflexibility is likely to become dysfunctional" And "Any method ceases to be efficient when it is applied inflexibly, according to set procedures, in every situation" (Rivers, 1981, 27).

In a survey of teachers' view of methods in Turkey, Griffiths (2012: 473) reports:

> Although the need to be aware of a variety of methods was acknowledged, several respondents also stressed the need to be able to choose methods appropriate to the needs of their students. Overall, the preference of the teachers in this study seemed to be for an eclectic approach to methodology, which leaves the teacher free to choose from a variety of methods in order to help their students achieve success in language learning.

However, with an eclectic approach of the kind referred to here the principles the teacher draws on are derived from external sources – from the methods the teacher is familiar with. The teacher's task is to review, select, and blend different principles and practices. For example, a teacher might ask the following:

> Are there aspects of Audiolingualism that are compatible with Communicative Language Teaching?
> How can Grammar-Translation be used in a text-based approach?
> How can I combine a task-based and a text-based approach?
> Can cooperative learning and competency-based approaches be used together?

In comparing form-based and meaning-based methods, Lightbown and Spada (2006: 180) recommend eclecticism: "it is not necessary to choose between form-based and meaning-based instruction. Rather, the challenge is to find the best balance between these two orientations."

Using personal principles and practical knowledge

Another post-method approach to teaching is when teachers are encouraged to develop their own teaching philosophy, teaching style, and instructional strategies. This leads to a knowledge base that is sometimes referred to as "principles" or as "personal practical knowledge" (PPK) (Golombek 2009). PPK has been characterized as "a moral, affective, and aesthetic way of knowing life's educational situations" (Clandinin and Conelly 1987: 59). The concept of PPK describes how from their experience and understanding of teaching as well as from the methods they have experienced, teachers develop a set of personal values and beliefs that shape their approach to teaching. We see these in the following example of a teacher's account of how she approaches her teaching (author data):

> I think it's important to be positive, as a personality. I think the teacher has to be a positive person. I think you have to show a tremendous amount of patience. And I think if you have a good attitude, you can project this to the students and hopefully establish a relaxed atmosphere in your classroom, so that the students won't dread to come to class, but have a good class. I feel that it's important to have a lesson plan of some sort ... because you need to know what you want to teach, and how you are going to go from the beginning to the end. And also taking into consideration the students, what their ability is, what their background is and so on. I have been in situations where I did not understand what was being taught, or what was being said, and how frustrating it is, and so when I approach it, I say, "How can I make it the easiest way for them to understand what they need to learn?"

Teacher training, teaching experience, as well as the teacher's personal philosophy and understanding serve as a source of principles and practical knowledge that can be applied across different situations as well as in specific situations, such as when teaching large classes, teaching young learners or adults, teaching mixed-ability classes, or teaching specific content such as grammar or reading skills. The following are examples of principles that are part of teachers' PPK (Bailey 1996; Richards 1996):

- Engage all learners in the lesson.
- Make learners, and not the teacher, the focus of the lesson.
- Provide maximum opportunities for student participation.
- Develop learner responsibility.
- Be tolerant of learners' mistakes.
- Develop learners' confidence.
- Teach learning strategies.
- Respond to learners' difficulties and build on them.
- Use a maximum amount of student-to-student activities.

- Promote cooperation among learners.
- Practice both accuracy and fluency.
- Address learners' needs and interests.
- Make learning fun.

Teachers refer to these principles and core beliefs at different stages of teaching – prior to teaching, during the planning phase of a lesson, during the lesson itself (i.e., interactive or on-the-spot unplanned decisions), and after teaching a lesson when they reflect on what happened during the lesson. Golombek (2009: 157) cites research by Tsang on how teachers access PPK:

> Tsang (2004) investigated how the PPK of three pre-service "English as an additional language" teachers of ESL in Hong Kong affected their interactive decision making. The results showed that the teachers referred to their PPK in describing their interactive decision making in the classroom in approximately half of the instances. On the other hand, teachers more frequently called upon their PPK while describing their post-active decision making, enabling changes to be made in future lesson plans and future on-line teaching, and new understandings of their teaching philosophies.

It is perhaps due to the influence of teachers' core beliefs and PPK that teachers transform the methods they may have been trained to use. Research on teachers' use of methods has often found that at the level of classroom practices, methods are often more similar than different. Swaffar, Arens, and Morgan (1982: 25) commented: "One consistent problem is whether or not teachers involved in presenting materials created for a particular method are actually reflecting the underlying philosophies of these methods in their classroom practices." Swaffar and her colleagues studied how teachers using different methods implemented them in the classroom and found that many of the distinctions used to contrast methods, particularly those based on classroom activities, did not exist in actual practice:

> Methodological labels assigned to teaching activities are, in themselves, not informative, because they refer to a pool of classroom practices which are used uniformly. The differences among major methodologies are to be found in the ordered hierarchy, the priorities assigned to tasks.
>
> (Swaffar et al. 1982: 31)

Brown (1997: 3) makes a similar point:

> Generally, methods are quite distinctive at the early, beginning stages of a language course, and rather indistinguishable from each other at a later stage. In the first few days of a Community Language Learning class, for example, the students witness a unique set of experiences in their small circles of translated language whispered in their ears. But within a matter of weeks, such classrooms can look like any other learner-centered curriculum.

Thus, the ordered hierarchy that Swaffer refers to involves assigning greater or lesser priority to tasks, according to the approach chosen – a hierarchy that tends to disappear as the class gets underway or as the language level of the students increases. It is, perhaps, for this reason that video samples of different approaches and methods typically demonstrate the first lesson (or an early lesson) of a foreign language class. There are no convincing video "demonstrations" with intermediate or advanced learners, perhaps because, as Brown points out, at that level there is nothing distinctive to demonstrate.

Theorization of practice

A related dimension of teacher learning involves the theorization of practice. While method-based teaching can be seen as an application of theory to practice, a different way of conceptualizing teacher learning is to view it as involving the theorization of practice, that is, the development of a theoretical understanding of teaching from experiences of teaching.

> A theory of practice reflects a teacher's negotiation of multiple sources of knowledge including personal beliefs and values, pedagogical and content knowledge, knowledge of children, and the expectations of the school culture where he or she works when making instructional decisions. It is continually tests and modified as the teacher attempts to maintain coherence between what she or he thinks and what she or he practices.
>
> (Dubetz 2005: 235)

Teachers begin their experience of teaching with varying levels of theoretical as well as practical knowledge, and their familiarity with one or more approach or method is part of this knowledge base. Over time, however, the teacher's knowledge and beliefs change as a result of new understandings of themselves and their learners, their understanding of their classroom context and the curriculum, as well as their acquisition of new kinds of professional knowledge obtained from reading, from the Internet, from workshops, and from colleagues as well as other sources. The classroom thus becomes a site for learning and for the development of deeper and more extensive theoretical understandings of teaching. These may lead the teacher to develop new teaching strategies. As they try them out and review their impact on learning, they become part of the teacher's knowledge base. The teacher now has a more fully developed schemata to support his or her teaching through the theorization of practice in this way.

Options for teacher education

Teacher education courses reflect a variety of different positions concerning the role they attribute to the study of teaching approaches and methods. Some of these differences reflect whether the course has a "teacher-training" approach and is intended for pre-service teachers or a "teacher-development" perspective and is aimed at experienced teachers completing more advanced courses, perhaps at the MA level. The contexts where the trainees will work after completing a course also affect the status of method analysis in the curriculum.

Some courses contain international students who will work in very different teaching contexts from those courses after they complete their program, often in situations where a particular teaching approach is recommended by the ministry of education. Some courses may be targeted at teachers who will work within a particular institution (such as a private institute) or in a school system that has a mandated curriculum and an established approach or method in use. Other teacher education programs may be for experienced teachers who have well-developed understandings and practices and are interested in how these can be better understood or evaluated in the light of current theory and research. A number of options are available as outlined below.

Familiarity with one established method

One option for teacher education programs is immersing teachers in a particular approach or method (such as Communicative Language Teaching or Text-Based Instruction). This strategy is more typical with entry-level courses for new teachers, as mentioned earlier. Training is designed to develop teachers who are skilled users of a particular method. Assessment may be based on how well the teacher can use the principles and procedures of a method such as CLT. For example, Richards et al. (1996) describe a study of five trainee teachers completing what was then called the UCLES/RSA Certificate in TEFLA – a short introductory teacher-training program based on a blend of CLT and the use of a PPP lesson format. During the course the trainees study the required teaching principles and procedures, apply them in lessons during teaching practice, and receive feedback on their performance by the trainer and other trainees. This strategy is also common in contexts where a curriculum reform or change requires teachers to familiarize themselves with a new approach or method, such as when Singapore adopted TBI as the basis for a national English language curriculum. Courses and workshops are provided to familiarize teachers with the method.

However, teachers and teachers in training need to be able to use approaches and methods flexibly and creatively, based on their own judgment and experience. In the process, they should be encouraged to transform and adapt the methods they use to make them their own. Training in the techniques and procedures of a specific method is probably essential for novice teachers entering teaching, because it provides them with the confidence they will need to face learners and with techniques and strategies for presenting lessons. In the early stages, teaching is largely a matter of applying procedures and techniques developed by others. An approach or a predetermined method, with its associated activities, principles, and techniques, may be a useful starting point for an inexperienced teacher, but it should be seen only as that. As the teacher gains experience and knowledge, he or she will begin to develop an individual approach or personal method of teaching, one that draws on an established approach or method but that also uniquely reflects the teacher's individual beliefs, values, principles, and experiences. This may not lead to abandonment of the approach or method the teacher started out using but to a modification of it as the teacher adds to and adjusts the approach or method to the realities of the classroom.

Familiarity with a variety of different methods and a focus on eclecticism

This approach is seen in many graduate programs designed for teachers who may teach in many different locations after completing the course. The focus is typically on preparing teachers to teach flexibly and creatively, drawing on relevant methods and procedures according to the teaching contexts they find themselves in. The typical "methods" courses in such programs consist of a survey of current and past approaches and methods, observation of the methods in use (either through video or through the use of micro-teaching), practical experience in teaching lessons using the procedures of different methods, critical reflection on the method, and discussion of how to adapt them to different teaching contexts. (The present book is often used in this way to support the teaching of methods courses.) Since approaches and methods have played a central role in the development of our profession, we believe it will continue to be useful for teachers and student teachers to become familiar with the major teaching approaches and methods proposed for second and foreign language teaching. Mainstream approaches and methods draw on a large amount of collective experience and practice from which much can be learned. Approaches and methods can therefore be usefully studied and selectively mastered in order to:

- learn how to use different approaches and methods and understand when they might be useful;
- understand some of the issues and controversies that characterize the history of language teaching;
- participate in language learning experiences based on different approaches and methods as a basis for reflection and comparison;
- be aware of the rich set of activity resources available to the imaginative teacher;
- appreciate how theory and practice can be linked from a variety of different perspectives.

A post-methods approach

This strategy is also favored in some graduate programs or in courses for experienced teachers. The focus is on developing a framework of theory and principles that can be used to support an individual and personal teaching approach. Methods are looked at critically in order to detect the assumptions they are based on and the interests they are seen to represent. Alternatively, the study of methods may have no role in the program at all. Sometimes the stance of Critical Language Pedagogy (CLP), a philosophy that eschews reliance on methods, underlies this approach. As described by Allwright and Hanks (2009: 54):

> CLP questioned why the world of language teaching was so full of competing methods, and speculated about whose interests this served ... The conclusion was that the dominant interests were commercial and political (introducing the controversial notion of "linguistic imperialism") rather than educational.

This theme has been elaborated by Kumaravadivelu (2012: 18–19).

> These Center-based [or Western] methods [see Chapter 1] (such as audiolingual, communicative) have been aptly characterized as product of "interested knowledge" (Pennycook 1989) ... That is, these methods highlighted and promoted the native-speaker's language competence, learning styles, communication patterns, conversational maxims, cultural beliefs, and even accent as the norm ...These assumptions have since come under severe strain leading to calls for an alternative to the concept of method.

This alternative to the study of approaches and methods, in a CLP approach, involves having teachers engage in critical reflection, exploratory practice, classroom research, and related procedures. They are encouraged to develop a healthy skepticism concerning the claims of methods, and they take part in activities that help them identify and review the basis of their own knowledge, beliefs, and practice and to develop a personal methodological framework that is relevant to their own teaching context (Allwright and Hanks 2009).

Conclusion

In this chapter, we have considered three major ways in which teachers can approach the selection of an approach or method. They may consider matching their teaching to the method, adapting a method to their teaching context, or developing a personal approach or method. Each of these philosophies offers various options for teacher education programs. The relationship between approaches and methods and teachers is complex, simply because methods do not teach: teachers do. The extent to which the assumptions and principles underlying different method philosophies shape the thinking, decision-making, and practices teachers make use of in their teaching depends on a number of factors, including the teaching context, the teacher's theoretical and practical knowledge base, the teacher's experience, and his or her core principles and beliefs. Although within the language teaching profession the nature of approaches and methods has had a central place in accounting for trends and practices in language teaching, at the level of teachers' classroom practices teaching is a much more complex and dynamic process than methods often represent. Most teacher-training programs are designed on the assumption that knowledge of principles and practices of one or methods provides teachers with a useful set of techniques and strategies that they can use in their classrooms or adapt for their own needs. But there is sometimes the underlying assumption that good teaching cannot be achieved without the structure and guidance that methods are believed to provide. However, the adoption of new practices by teachers is problematic – on both practical and ideological grounds – since it undervalues the contributions teachers make to teaching. If the study of approaches and methods is included in a teacher education program, an appropriate focus for the inclusion of such study is needed, one in which these approaches and methods are presented not as prescriptions for best practice but rather as a source for reflective review of the teacher's own core principles, theoretical understanding, and personal practical knowledge.

Discussion questions

1. Does the country where you teach have a prescribed national curriculum? If so, does it favor or require the use of one particular teaching method or approach? On what basis was this selected?

2. If your country does have a national curriculum, which of the methods of changing teachers' beliefs on page 348 was used when the latest version of the national curriculum was implemented?

3. It is said (p. 348) that teachers' core beliefs are resistant to change. Consider your own development as a teacher.

   • How have your beliefs about learning changed over the years?
   • And your beliefs about *teaching*?
   • How are these different from the ways in which you were taught and learned when you were young?
   • If you have been teaching for a while, when was the last time in your career that you made a significant change in the ways you teach?

   Share your experiences with a colleague.

4. Read the experience of one teacher below (author data). If you are currently teaching, have you ever attempted to change a major aspect of your teaching? How did you experience this change?

   > I first became interested in learner autonomy a few years ago after attending a conference. I liked the idea of giving my learners more control over their learning, especially as many of my students go overseas and will need to continue to improve by themselves. After some time I realised that, despite my enthusiasm, in some ways my teaching hadn't really changed. I would, for instance, tell students they could choose what materials to work on, but in hindsight I only let them choose from materials that I provided. Assessments also didn't really change – it would still be marking students' work, not students assessing themselves or each other, for example. It took me a long time to really change my teaching practices, and in some ways I have learned that I am still not fully comfortable with giving up too much control of the classroom.

5. You have read arguments for and against the adoption by teachers of methods. What is your personal view? Is there room for methods? Do you agree that methods might be more suitable for novice teachers? In what other situations might you recommend use of methods?

6. What would you say to the teachers asking the questions below. Give reasons for and against using the approaches and methods mentioned in these situations.

   "How can I use a communicative approach in a class of 70 students?"
   "How can I use co-operative learning in an exam driven curriculum?"
   "What principles from the Silent Way can I use in teaching speaking?"

"How can I adapt TPR to use in a business English course?"
"How can Task-Based Language Teaching be used with young learners?"

7. Read the description of the Lesson Study Approach on page 351 of the chapter. Would this approach work in your context where you are teaching or studying a language? Why (not)?

8. "... an important task for the teacher is to adjust the methods he or she has been trained to use to the culture of learning in which they are used" (p. 352). Choose another country you are familiar with. Give an example of how you could adjust a particular method if you were to teach in that country?

9. On page 352, Rivers talks about a "philosophy of exploration and reflection." In what ways do you explore and reflect in your own teaching? What opportunities and encouragement are there in your place of work for this?

10. Post-method perspectives on teaching consider that teachers develop "personal practical knowledge" (PPK) or a set of principles that guides their teaching. Read the quote by a teacher on page 353. How would you summarize your PPK? Compare your answer with a colleague's.

11. Review below the list of teachers' principles that was presented in the chapter. For each of these, indicate how strongly you agree with them and believe you implement them in your teaching. Next, ask your learners to rate your teaching in terms of each of these. Are there any differences?

Principles	1 (I don't do this) 5 (I do this all the time)	1 (My teacher doesn't do this) 5 (My teacher does this all the time)
Engage all learners in the lesson.		
Make learners, and not the teacher, the focus of the lesson.		
Provide maximum opportunities for student participation.		
Develop learner responsibility.		
Be tolerant of learners' mistakes.		
Develop learners' confidence.		
Teach learning strategies.		
Respond to learners' difficulties and build on them.		

(Continued)

Use a maximum amount of student-to-student activities.		
Promote cooperation among learners.		
Practice both accuracy and fluency.		
Address learners' needs and interests.		
Make learning fun.		

12. "As they gain experience, many teachers report that they no longer use the methods they were trained to use but adapt a much more flexible approach to methodology" (p. 349). Using the comparison of approaches and methods in the Appendix at the end of the book, ask a colleague to observe one of your classes and identify which elements of each of these are used.

(Aspect of) approach or method	Classroom activity

References and further reading

Allwright, D. and J. Hanks. 2009. *The Developing Language Learner: An Introduction to Exploratory Practice*. New York: Palgrave Macmillan.

Atkinson, D. (ed.). 2011. *Alternative Approaches to Second Language Acquisition*. London: Routledge.

Bailey, K. M. 1996. The best laid plans: teachers' in-class decisions to depart from their lesson plans. In K. M. Bailey and D. Nunan (eds.), *Voices From the Language Classroom*. Cambridge: Cambridge University Press. 115–40.

Barduhn. S., and K. E. Johnson. 2009. Certification and professional qualifications. In A. Burns and J. C. Richards (eds.), *The Cambridge Guide to Second Language Teacher Education*. Cambridge: Cambridge University Press. 155–62.

Borg, S. 2006. *Teacher Cognition and Language Education*. London: Continuum.

Brown. H. D. 1997. *Teaching by Principles*. New York: Longman.

Clandlinin, D. J., and F. M. Connelly. 1987. Teachers' personal knowledge: what counts as "personal" in studies of the personal. *Journal of Curriculum Studies* 19: 487–500.

Clark, C. M., and P. Peterson. 1986. Teachers' thought processes. In N. M. Wittrock (ed.), *Handbook of Research on Teaching*. 3rd edn. New York: Macmillan. 255–96.

Coyle, D., P. Hood, and D. Marsh. 2010. *Content and Language Integrated Learning*. Cambridge: Cambridge University Press.

Dubetz, N. E. 2005. Improving ESL instruction in a bilingual program through collaborative, inquiry-base professional development. In Diane J. Tedick (ed.), *Second Language Teacher Education: International Perspectives*. Mahwah, NJ: Lawrence Erlbaum. 257–60.

Edwards, C., and J. Willis. 2005. *Teachers Exploring Tasks in English Language Teaching*. London: Palgrave Macmillan.

Golombek, P. 2009. Personal practical knowledge in L2 teacher education. In A. Burns and J. C. Richards (eds.), *The Cambridge Guide to Second Language Teacher Education*. Cambridge: Cambridge University Press. 91–101.

Griffiths, C. 2012. Focus on the teacher. *ELT Journal* 66(4): 468–76.

Hunter, D., and R. Smith 2012. Unpackaging the past: 'CLT' through ELTJ keywords. *ELT Journal* 66(4): 430–43.

Jin, L., and M. Cortazzi 2011. Re-evaluating traditional approaches to second language teaching and learning. In E. Hinkley (ed.), *Handbook of Research in Second Language Teaching and Learning*, Vol. II. New York: Routledge. 558–75.

Kumaravadivelu, B. 1994. The post-method condition: emerging strategies for second/foreign language teaching. *TESOL Quarterly* 29: 27–48.

Kumaravadivelu, B. 2003. A post-method perspective on English language teaching. *World Englishes* 22: 539–50.

Kumaravidivelu, B. 2012. Individual identity, cultural globalization, and teaching English as an international language: the case for an epistemic break. In L. Alsagoff, S. L. McKay, G. Hu, and W. A. Renandya (eds.), *Principles and Practices for Teaching English as an International Language*. New York: Routledge. 9–27.

Lewis, C., and I. Tsuchida. 1998. A lesson is like a swiftly flowing river: how research lessons improve Japanese education. *American Educator* (Winter): 12–17.

Lightbown, P., and N. Spada. 2006. *How Languages Are Learned*. 2nd edn. Oxford: Oxford University Press.

Paran, A. 2013. Review of *CLIL: Content and Language integrated Learning*, by D. Coyle, P. Hood and D. Marsh. *ELT Journal* 67(1): 137–41.

Richards, J. C. 1984. The secret life of methods. *TESOL Quarterly* 18(1): 7–23.

Richards, J. C. 1996. Teachers' maxims in language teaching. *TESOL Quarterly* 30: 281–96.

Richards, J. C., B. Ho, and K. Giblin. 1996. Learning to teach in the RSA Cert. In D. Freeman and J. C. Richards (eds.), *Teacher Learning in Language Teaching*. New York: Cambridge University Press. 242–59.

Richards, J. C., P. Gallo, and W. Renandya. 2001. Exploring teacher's beliefs and the processes of change. *PAVC Journal* 1(1): 85–92.

Swaffar, J., K. Arens, and M. Morgan. 1982. Teacher classroom practices: Redefining method as task hierarchy. *Modern Language Journal* 66(1): 24–33.

Tasker, T. 2009. Teacher learning through lesson study: an activity theoretical approach toward professional development in the Czech republic. In K. E. Johnson and P. R. Golombok (eds.), *Research on Second Language Teacher Education*. New York: Routledge. 204–22.

Tsang, W. K. 2004. Teachers' personal practical knowledge and interactive decisions. *Language Teaching Research* 8(2): 163–98.

Williams, M., and R. Burden. 1997. *Psychology for Language Teachers: A Social Constructivist Approach*. Cambridge: Cambridge University Press.

21 Approaches, methods, and the curriculum

Introduction

In describing language teaching approaches and methods in this book, we have focused on the classroom processes that constitute different instructional designs in language teaching and the theories and principles that they are based on.[1] We have seen that approaches and methods reflect different assumptions about *what* is learned, *how* it is learned, and what the *outcomes* of learning are. In educational planning, issues related to the inputs to teaching, to teaching processes, and to the learning outputs that result are elements of the process of curriculum development. The term *curriculum* refers to the overall plan or design for a course and how the content for a course is transformed into a blueprint for teaching and learning which enables the desired learning outcomes to be achieved.

> Curriculum takes content (from external standards and local goals) and shapes it into a plan for how to conduct effective teaching and learning. It is thus more than a list of topics and lists of key facts and skills (the "input"). It is a map of how to achieve the "outputs" of desired student performance, in which appropriate learning activities and assessments are suggested to make it more likely that students achieve the desired results.
>
> (Wiggins and McTighe 2006: 6)

In this chapter, we will examine how the approaches and methods we have examined reflect different understandings of how the elements of a curriculum are related and the processes by which they are arrived at. We will consider three alternative strategies that are reflected in the approaches and methods we have described in this book. As we noted in Chapter 8, one strategy is to first make decisions about *what* to teach (input), then to determine *how* to teach it (process), and finally to assess *what* was learned (output). We refer to this as *forward design*. Another strategy is to start with teaching processes or methodology and to let these determine input and output. We refer to this as *central design*. A third strategy is to start with learning outcomes or output and work backward to determine issues of process and content. This is known as *backward design* (Wiggins and McTighe 2006).

---

[1] This chapter reproduces material from Richards, J. C. (2013) "Curriculum approaches in language teaching: forward, central and backward design," *RELC Journal*, 44(1): 5–33.

Input, process, and output in a language curriculum

In language teaching, *input* refers to the linguistic content of a course. It seems logical to assume that before we can *teach* a language, we need to decide *what* linguistic content to teach. Once content has been selected, it then needs to be organized into teachable and learnable units as well as arranged in a rational sequence. The result is a syllabus. We have seen in this book that there are many different conceptions of a language syllabus. Different approaches and methods reflect different understandings of the nature of language and different views as to what the essential building blocks of language proficiency are, such as vocabulary, grammar, functions, or text-types (i.e., different syllabus types).

Once input has been determined, issues concerning teaching methods and the design of classroom activities and materials can be addressed. These belong to the domain of process. Process, or what is generally referred to in language teaching as methodology, encompasses the types of learning activities, procedures, and techniques that are employed by teachers when they teach. Once a set of teaching processes has been standardized and fixed in terms of principles and associated practices, it is generally referred to as a method, as in Audiolingualism or Total Physical Response. Therefore, it could be said that a method is the standardization of a methodology. In this book we have suggested how these procedures and principles relate to theories of the nature of language and of second language learning and the roles of teachers, learners, and instructional materials found in different approaches and methods. Output refers to learning outcomes, that is, what learners are able to do as the result of a period of instruction. This might be a targeted level of achievement on a proficiency scale (such as the ACTFL Proficiency Scale) or on a standardized test such as TOEFL. Today, desired learning outputs or outcomes are often described in terms of objectives or in terms of performance, competencies, or skills. In simple form the components of curriculum and their relationship can be represented as in Figure 21.1:

Input	Process	Output
Syllabus	Methodology	Learning outcomes

Figure 21.1 Dimensions of a curriculum

The relationship between approaches, methods, and the curriculum can be seen to reflect two important aspects of curriculum development:

- Curriculum development in language teaching can start from input, process, or output.
- Each starting point reflects different assumptions about both the means and the ends of teaching and learning.

Conventional wisdom and practice tend to assume that decisions relating to input, process, and output occur in sequence, each one dependent on what preceded it. Curriculum development from this perspective starts with a first-stage focus on input – when decisions about content and syllabus are made; moves on to a second-stage focus on methodology – when the syllabus is "enacted"; and then leads to a final stage of consideration of output – when means are used to measure how effectively what has been taught has been learned. However, this view of the curriculum does not, in fact, reflect how language teaching has always been understood, theorized, and practiced in recent times. Much debate and discussion about effective approaches to language teaching can be better understood by recognizing how differences in the starting points of curriculum development have different implications and applications in language teaching. This leads to the distinction between forward design, central design, and backward design referred to above. *Forward design* means developing a curriculum through moving from input, to process, and to output. *Central design* means starting with process and deriving input and output from classroom methodology. *Backward design*, as the name implies, starts from output and then deals with issues relating to process and input. The three different processes of curriculum development can thus be represented in simple form as in Figure 21.2.

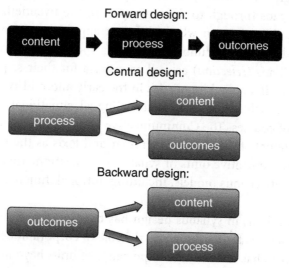

Figure 21.2 Curriculum design processes

Each of these curriculum development approaches will now be illustrated and examples given of how they relate to approaches and methods in language teaching.

Forward design

Forward design is based on the assumption that input, process, and output are related in a linear fashion. In other words, *before* decisions about methodology and output are determined, issues related to the content of instruction need to be resolved. Curriculum design is seen to constitute a sequence of stages that occur in a fixed order. Wiggins and McTighe (2006: 15) give an illustration of this process with an example of a typical forward design lesson plan:

- The teacher chooses a topic for a lesson (e.g., racial prejudice).
- The teacher selects a resource (e.g., *To Kill a Mockingbird*).
- The teacher chooses instructional methods based on the resource and the topic (e.g., a seminar to discuss the book and cooperative groups to analyze stereotypical images in films and on television).
- The teacher chooses essay questions to assess student understanding of the book.

A similar example would be a teacher planning a unit around "narratives" in a writing class. The starting point would be an understanding of the nature of narratives and their linguistic and discourse features. Models of different kinds of narratives would then be studied as preparation for students writing their own narrative texts. Assessment tasks might involve reviewing and correcting poorly written narratives or writing further texts based on the features that had been taught and practiced.

Forward design starts with syllabus design. Syllabus design was a growth industry from the mid-1920s through to the latter part of the twentieth century and led to a number of key publications in which different approaches to syllabus design were proposed (e.g., Wilkins 1976; Munby 1978; Willis 1996). Debate over criteria for the choice of syllabus items (*selection*) as well as criteria for their sequencing (*gradation*) was a dominant issue in applied linguistics in the early and mid-twentieth century, and carefully developed syllabuses are seen in audiolingual, situational, communicative, and many other kinds of courses. The Communicative Language Teaching movement in the 1980s prompted attempts to shift from grammar and lexis as the primary components of a syllabus to communicative units of syllabus organization. This led to proposals for a number of different syllabus models, including notional, functional, lexical, text- and task-based models.

A more recent focus in syllabus design has been on the authenticity of the input that is provided as a basis for teaching and the role of corpora in determining linguistic input. Corpus analysis has revealed the importance of units beyond the level of vocabulary (e.g., phrases, multi-word units, and collocations) and provides information that can be used to update or replace the earlier generations of lists that have been used in syllabus design. O'Keefe et al. (2007: 22) suggest that "course book dialogues, and even entire syllabi, can be informed by corpus data." Another approach that has been used to provide authentic input to teaching is through the use of discourse analysis – a procedure for studying the nature of different text-types, the ways they are used, and their lexical, grammatical, and textual features. This is particularly important in the design of courses in English for Special Purposes where the identification of the lexical, syntactic, and textual structures of different genres is a prerequisite to teaching specialized genres (see Chapter 10).

Syllabus and methodology

With a forward design approach, decisions about teaching processes or methodology *follow* from syllabus specification. Ideally, the planner starts with a theory of language and a syllabus derived from it and then looks for a learning theory that could be used as the basis for an appropriate pedagogy. In some cases there has been a natural link between input and process, between content and method, such as the natural link between structural linguistics and behaviorist learning theory that led to both the Audiolingual Method and Situational Language Teaching. However, in theory a syllabus does not necessarily imply a particular methodology. A structural syllabus can be embodied in an audiolingual as well as a task-based course, and there are many different ways in which a text-based or functional syllabus can be taught. The point here is simply that with forward design, decisions about how to teach follow from decisions about the content of a course, and decisions about output or learning outcomes follow from decisions about methodology.

Forward design in language teaching

Many of the approaches and methods in this book, such as Audiolingualism and Communicative Language Teaching, reflect the process of forward design. Clark suggests that the communicative approach still reflects the same assumptions as Audiolingualism since they both start with a model of language that is broken down into smaller units – elements of knowledge and part-skills. These are then sequenced from simple to more complex and build toward the desired learning outcomes. This approach

> has had a powerful influence in recent years on the design of foreign language curriculum. It has given rise to the audio-lingual, audio-visual/situational, topic-based, and functional-notional approach to foreign language learning ... All of these approaches have sought to bring about an effective communicative ability in learners as their ultimate goal, but have conceptualized this ability and the way to bring it about in different ways, adopting different organizing principles in the design of the foreign language curriculum. The audio-lingual approach conceptualized a communicative ability in terms of good grammatical habits. The audio/visual situational approach focused on the ability to understand and produce appropriate phrases related to particular situations. Topic-based approaches emphasized the ability to cope with certain topics. The functional-notional approach has focused on mastery of formal means to interpret and express certain predetermined meanings
>
> (Clark 1987: 23)

Content-Based Instruction and its more recent variant CLIL are also examples of forward design. They seek to develop language proficiency as well the mastery of subject matter, critical thinking, and other cognitive skills through the use of a syllabus that integrates both language and subject matter (e.g., science, geography, history, environmental studies). As with other forward design models, the process of developing a curriculum typically starts with the design of a syllabus that contains both content and language components. This then leads to the choice of suitable instructional materials as well as selection of activities for delivering, reviewing, and assessing instruction (Crandall 2012: 150). The following example (from Mehisto, Marsh, and Frigolos 2008: 50–69) illustrates in summary form the procedures used to develop a one-week science unit on volcanoes and is similar to the example from Wiggins and McTighe cited above.

1. Content and language needed for the topic of volcanoes is identified.
2. Aims in terms of content learning, language learning, and skills learning are identified.
3. Resources chosen to facilitate a variety of whole-class, group-based and individual activities focusing on different aspects of content and language.
4. Informal assessment procedures used to assess student learning.

Like other communicative approaches, the instructional processes used in CBI/CLIL are varied and no specific teaching methods are prescribed. A range of teaching activities are used, depending on the type of course and its context:

> In CoBI [CBI or content-based instruction], teachers can draw on a range of relevant, meaningful, and engaging activities that increase student motivation in a more natural manner, activities that involve co-operative, task-based, experiential, and project-based learning ...

> CoBI lessons include the use of both authentic and adapted oral and written subject matter materials (textbooks, audio and visual materials, and other learning materials) that are appropriate to the cognitive and language proficiency level of the learners or that can be made accessible through bridging activities.

> (Crandall 2012: 151–2)

Implementing a forward design curriculum

The curriculum design process associated with forward design can be represented as in Figure 21.3:

Forward design:

content   syllabus   methodology   outcomes   assessment

Figure 21.3 The forward design process

In some contexts the planning and development of each stage in the curriculum development process is carried out by different specialists who have expertise in each process, such as specialists in syllabus design, methodology, and assessment.

Central design

While a progression from input, to process, to output would seem to be a logical approach to the planning and delivery of instruction, there are other routes that can be taken. The second route can be called *central design*. With central design, curriculum development *starts* with the selection of teaching activities, techniques, and methods rather than with the elaboration of a detailed language syllabus or specification of learning outcomes. Issues related to input and output are dealt with *after* a methodology has been chosen or developed, or during the process of teaching itself.

Clark (1987) refers to this as "progressivism" and an example of a process approach to the curriculum.

> We communicate, and if it is found useful we can look at the product of our efforts and discuss what has occurred by examining the exponents and attempting to relate them to particular notions and functions, or to lexical and grammatical categories. But this is an after-the-event way of breaking up the flux and flow of a particular discourse, rather than the means of predetermining what one may wish to say. This does not deny that the teacher and pupil may need to focus on particular elements of rhetorical, semantic, and grammatical content that arise in the discourse. It seems important to insist, however, that such focuses should arise out of language in use, rather than precede them, so that learners are enabled to discover rules of use, form–meaning relationships, and formal rules and systems against the backcloth of real contextualized discourse.
>
> (Clark 1987: 40)

Research on teachers' practices reveals that teachers often follow a central design approach when they develop their lessons by first considering the activities and teaching procedures they will use. Rather than starting their planning processes by detailed considerations of input or output, they start by thinking about the activities they will use in the classroom. While they assume that the exercises and activities they make use of will contribute to successful learning outcomes, it is the classroom processes they seek to provide for their learners that are generally their initial focus.

In general education this approach was advocated by Bruner (1966) and Stenhouse (1975) who argued that curriculum development should start by identifying the processes of inquiry and deliberation that drive teaching and learning – processes such as investigation, decision-making, reflection, discussion, interpretation, critical thinking, making choices, cooperating with others, and so on. Content is chosen on the basis of how it promotes the use of these processes, and outcomes do not need to be specified in any degree of detail, if at all.

> [The curriculum] is not designed on a pre-specification of behavioural objectives. Of course there are changes in students as result of a course, but many of the most valued are not to be anticipated in detail. The power and the possibilities of the curriculum cannot be contained within objectives because it is founded on the idea that knowledge must be speculative and thus indeterminate as to student outcomes if it is to be worthwhile.
>
> (Stenhouse 1975, cited in Clark 1987: 35)

And again:

> Education as induction into knowledge is successful to the extent that it makes the behavioural outcomes of the students unpredictable.
>
> (Stenhouse 1970, cited in Clark 1987: 35)

Clark's description of the features of "progressivism" (1987: 49–90) captures the essence of central design:

- It places less emphasis on syllabus specification and more on methodological principles and procedures.
- It is more concerned with learning processes than predetermined objectives.
- It emphasizes methodology and the need for principles to guide the teaching learning process.
- It is learner-centered and seeks to provide learning experiences that enable learners to learn by their own efforts.
- It regards learners as active participants in shaping their own learning.
- It promotes the development of the learner as an individual.
- It views learning as a creative problem-solving activity.
- It acknowledges the uniqueness of each teaching-learning context.
- It emphasizes the role of the teacher in creating his or her own curriculum in the classroom.

Central design in language teaching

Although language teaching in the first part of the twentieth century was shaped by teaching methods which reflected a forward planning approach as we saw above, some of the alternative methods that emerged in the second half of the twentieth century, such as the Silent Way, Community Language Learning, and the Natural Approach, rejected the need for predetermined syllabuses or pre-planned learning outcomes and were built instead around specifications of classroom activities. These new teaching methods and approaches started with *process* rather than input or output and, as we have seen, were often recognized by the novel classroom practices they employed. They reflected central design approach – one in which methodology is the starting point in course planning, and content is chosen in accordance with the methodology rather than the other way round. For example, we saw in Chapter 14 that Krashen and Terrel's Natural Approach (1983) proposed that communicative classroom processes engaging the learners in meaningful interaction and communication at an appropriate level of difficulty were the key to a language course, rather than building teaching around a predetermined grammatical syllabus.

> In setting communicative goals, we do not expect the students at the end of a particular course to have acquired a certain group of structures or forms. Instead we expect them to deal with a particular set of topics in a given situation. We do not organize the activities of the class about a grammatical syllabus.
>
> (Krashen and Terrell 1983: 71)

Like other central design proposals, there is no need for clearly defined outcomes or objectives. The purpose and content of a course "will vary according to the needs of the students and their particular interests" (Krashen and Terrell 1983: 65). Goals are stated in very general terms such as "basic personal communication skills: oral" and "basic personal communication skills: written." The fact that the Natural Approach was not input- or output-driven (i.e., not built around a predetermined syllabus and set of learning outcomes) meant that it could not provide a framework for the design of instructional materials and textbooks. Hence, there are no syllabuses or published courses based on the Natural Approach.

Gategno's Silent Way (1972) can be understood as another example of central design in language teaching. Language input is not the starting point in the Silent Way. As we saw in Chapter 16, rather than beginning with the development of a linguistic syllabus, Gategno's starting point was a view of learning which saw it as a problem-solving and creative process of discovery. Curran's Community Language Learning (Chapter 17) is another central design method. Like other examples of central design approaches, there is no predetermined syllabus and no specific linguistic or communicative goals. These are specific to each class and an outcome of the social interaction that occurs during the lesson. Students typically sit in a circle and express what they want to say. Translation by the teacher is used to help express the learner's intended meaning. Later, interactions and messages are recorded and revisited as a source of reflection, analysis, and further practice.

Some early versions of Task-Based Language Teaching (e.g., Willis 1996) also reflect a central design approach (Chapter 9). Tasks drive the processes of second language learning, and linguistic and communicative competence are the outcomes of task work (Willis 1996). There is no predetermined grammatical syllabus and the goals are to develop general language ability rather than the ability to use language in specific contexts and for specific purposes. A more recent example of the use of central design in language teaching has been labeled "Dogme" (a term taken from the film industry that refers to filming without scripts or rehearsal) by Scott Thornbury – who introduced the approach to language teaching (Meddings and Thornbury 2009). It is based on the idea that instead of basing teaching on a pre-planned syllabus, a set of objectives and published materials, teaching is built around conversational interaction between teacher and students and among students themselves. As Meddings and Thornbury (2009) state: "Teaching should be done using only the resources that the teachers and students bring to the classroom – i.e. themselves and what happens to be in the classroom."

Thornbury's (2012) web posting on the topic clarifies the concept as follows: Thornbury explains that Dogme considers learning as "experiential and holistic" and that language learning is "an emergent jointly-constructed and socially-constituted process motivated both by communal and communicative imperatives." The syllabus or language focus is not pre-planned, and language and content emerge from the processes of interaction and negotiation that the teacher initiates.

The approach we referred to as post-method teaching in the previous chapter also illustrates central design. This refers to teaching which is not based on the prescriptions and procedures of a particular method but which draws on the teacher's individual conceptualizations of language, language learning and teaching, the practical knowledge and skills teachers develop from training and experience, the teacher's knowledge of the learners' needs, interests, and learning styles, as well as the teacher's understanding of the teaching context (Kumaravadivelu 1994). The teacher's "method" is constructed from these sources rather than being an application of an external set of principles and practices. The kinds of content and activities that the teacher employs in the classroom as well as the outcomes he or she seeks to achieve will depend upon the nature of the core principles that serve as the basis for the teacher's thinking and decision-making.

Tsui (2005, cited in Graves 2008: 168) contrasts approaches of this kind with traditional approaches by comparing the kinds of questions a teacher might ask working within what is described here as a forward design and central design approach.

- *Forward design issues:*
  What linguistic forms do we want to teach?
  How do we represent these items in the form of tasks or activities?
  How do we get learners to use the target items to complete the tasks or activities, either individually or in pairs/groups?
  Are there any gaps between the target-language structures/functions and those produced by the students?

- *Central design issues:*
  What opportunities are afforded for learners to participate in meaning making?
  What kind of shared understanding needs to be established among the learners?
  What kind of participation framework is being set up and what are the role configurations for the group and for the individual learner over time?
  What opportunities have been created by learners in the process of participation?

Interaction between the elements of central design

What central design approaches and methods have in common is the priority they attribute to learning processes, classroom participation, and the role of the teacher and the learners in creating opportunities for learning. The syllabus or learning input – rather than being something that is predetermined or prescribed and regarded as essential in initiating curriculum development – is rather an *outcome* of teaching and learning (Figure 21.4).

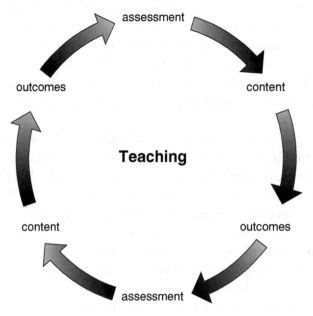

Figure 21.4 The central design process

Backward design

The third approach to curriculum design is to begin with a specification of learning outputs and to use these as the basis for developing instructional processes and input. Backward design starts with a careful statement of the desired results or outcomes: appropriate teaching activities and content are derived from the results of learning. This is a well-established tradition in curriculum design in general education, and in recent years it has reemerged as a prominent curriculum development approach in language teaching. It was sometimes described as an "ends–means" approach, as seen in the work of Tyler (1949) and Taba (1962), who viewed instruction as the specification of ends as a prerequisite to devising the means to reach them. The process consists of:

> Step 1: diagnosis of needs
> Step 2: formulation of objectives
> Step 3: selection of content
> Step 4: organization of content
> Step 5: selection of learning experiences
> Step 6: organization of learning experiences
> Step 7: determination of what to evaluate and of the ways of doing it

(Taba 1962: 12)

The role of methodology was to determine which teaching methods were most effective in attaining the objectives, and a criterion-referenced approach would be used for assessment (i.e., one linked to the attainment of specified levels of performance). There is no place for individually determined learning outcomes: the outcomes are determined by the curriculum designer.

Examples of the use of backward design in language teaching are detailed below.

Backward design through objectives

From the 1950s, educating teachers in how to describe learning outcomes in the form of objectives became a minor industry, and since then generations of teachers have been taught to begin lesson planning by first developing statements of objectives rather than from considerations of methodology. Wiggins and McTighe (2006), who argue for starting with a clear description of learning outcomes as the basis for curriculum planning, state that three steps are required with backward design:

1. Identify desired results.
2. Determine acceptable evidence of learning.
3. Plan learning experiences and instruction.

The planning process begins with a clear understanding of the ends in mind. For Wiggins and McTighe, it explicitly rejects as a starting point the process or activity-oriented curriculum in which participation in activities and processes is primary. A variety of teaching strategies can be employed to achieve the desired goals, but teaching methods cannot be chosen until the desired outcomes have been specified. From this perspective many of the central design methods or activity-oriented approaches discussed earlier fail to meet the criterion of good instructional design.

> The error of activity-oriented design might be called "hands-on without being minds-on" – engaging experiences that lead only accidentally, if at all, to insight or achievement ... activity-oriented curricula lack an explicit focus on important ideas and approach evidence of learning ... [learners] are led to think the learning *is* the activity instead of seeing that the learning comes from being asked to consider the *meaning* of the activity ... The shift, therefore, is away from starting with such questions as "What book will we read?" or "What activities will we do?" or "What will we discuss" to "What should [the learners] walk out the door able to understand [or do] regardless of what activities or tests we use? And "What is evidence of such ability?" and, therefore, "What texts, activities, and methods will best enable such a result?"
>
> (Wiggins and McTighe 2006: 16, 17)

In language teaching a number of curriculum approaches have been advocated that reflect the principles of backward design.

Needs analysis

Identifying learning outcomes or objectives is often seen to depend upon a systematic analysis of the learners' communicative needs, and this approach emerged in the 1960s as part of the systems approach to curriculum development – an aspect of the prevalent philosophy of educational accountability from which the use of objectives was also derived (Stufflebeam et al. 1985). Needs analysis is part of the process by which aims and objectives are determined: needs analysis is also the starting point for curriculum development in some versions of Task-Based Language Teaching and is used to determine an inventory of target-tasks learners need to be able to master in the target language.

> The design of a task-based syllabus preferably starts with an analysis of the students' needs. What do these students need to be able to do with the target language? What are the tasks they are supposed to perform outside of the classroom? Using different sources and different methods (such as interviews, observations, and surveys) a concrete description of the kinds of tasks students will face in the real word is drawn up. This description, then, serves as the basis for the design and sequencing of tasks in the syllabus.
>
> (Van den Branden 2012: 134)

Thus, if a task-based program begins with a cataloguing of outcomes, or tasks to be performed outside the classroom, it would be an example of backward design. The methodology of this approach to TBLT is then built around activities or tasks that require communicative language use, and it is from these that the learners' need for particular aspects of language are derived.

Competency-Based Language Teaching (see Chapter 8) is another widely used example of backward design and one in which the starting point of curriculum design is a specification of the learning outcomes in terms of "competencies" – the knowledge, skills, and behaviors that are involved in the performance of everyday tasks and activities and which learners should master by the end of a course of study. Like other backward design approaches, CBLT makes no assumptions about teaching methods, since any set of classroom activities can be used that enables students to master the desired competencies. However, since student learning is assessed on the basis of performance and the ability to demonstrate mastery of pre-specified skills and behaviors, teaching is generally based on helping learners acquire the communicative skills needed for specific situations, tasks, and activities. As with other backward design approaches, needs analysis is the starting point in curriculum development.

A related approach to backward design is through the use of standards (also known as benchmarks, core skills, performance profiles, and target competencies; see Chapter 8). Standards are descriptions of the outcomes or targets students should be able to reach in different domains of curriculum content, including language learning, and are generally specified in very general terms. The primary motivation for an increased emphasis on statements of learning outcomes in the design of language programs and particularly the use of "standards" as ways of identifying learning targets across a curriculum is described by Leung (2012: 162):

> the prominence of outcomes-based teaching in the past thirty years or so can be associated with the wider public policy environments in which the twin doctrines of corporatist management (whereby the activities in different segments of society are subordinated to the goals of the state) and public accountability (which requires professionals to justify their activities in relation to declared public policy goals) have predominated.

The use of standards in curriculum planning thus involves the following sequence of activities:

- Identifying the domains of language use the learners need to acquire (e.g., listening, speaking, reading, writing)
- Describing standards and performance indicators for each domain
- Identifying the language skills and knowledge needed to achieve the standard
- Selecting teaching activities and materials.

Perhaps the most widespread example of backward design using standards in current use is the Common European Framework for Reference for Languages (Council of Europe 2001), which is designed to provide a "common basis for explicit description of objectives, content and methods of the study of modern languages, within a wider purpose of elaboration of language syllabuses, curriculum guidelines, examinations, textbooks across Europe" (Council of Europe 2001: 1) – see Chapter 8. CEFR describes learning outcomes in terms of "can do" statements linked to six levels of achievement. No specifications are given for input or process. It is the teacher's or course designer's responsibility to work out how the outcomes can be achieved and to develop teaching strategies and materials and content relevant to the context in which they are teaching. The lack of a syllabus or specification of content that would enable the outcomes in CEFR to be achieved has been identified as problematic in using the framework and has led to the development of the English Profile project:

> The aim of the English Profile is to create a "profile" or set of Reference Level Descriptions of English linked to the CEF. These will provide detailed information about the language that learners can be expected to demonstrate at each level, offering a clear benchmark for progress that will inform curriculum development as well as the development of courses and test materials to support learners, teachers and other professional involved in the learning and teaching of English as a foreign language.
>
> (English Profile n.d.)

Figure 21.5 represents what backward design with CEFR involves.

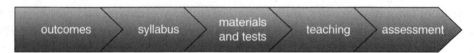

Figure 21.5 Backward design with CEFR

Conclusion

A question teachers and planners often ask when presented with alternative ways of addressing an issue is, "Which approach is best?" However, it is safer to assume that there is no best approach to curriculum design, and that forward design, central design, and backward design might each work well but in different circumstances. Each approach has advocates and practitioners who can cite examples of their successful implementation. They might also work concurrently in some circumstances.

Each approach, however, makes different assumptions about the context for the curriculum. These include, for example:

- whether intended for large-scale or small-scale implementation;
- the role of instructional materials and tests;
- the level of training of teachers;
- the roles of teachers and learners;
- teachers' proficiency in English;
- the demands made on teachers;
- the level of teacher autonomy assumed for teacher;
- the amount of support provided for teachers.

A forward design option may be preferred in circumstances where a mandated curriculum is in place, where teachers have little choice over what and how to teach, where teachers rely mainly on textbooks and commercial materials rather than teacher-designed resources, where class size is large, and where tests and assessments are designed centrally rather than by individual teachers. Since forward design can be used to develop published materials, there will generally be a wide range of teaching resources and materials to choose from. Forward design may also be a preferred option in situations where teachers may have limited English language proficiency and limited opportunities for professional development, since much of the planning and development involved can be accomplished by specialists rather than left to the individual teacher.

Central design approaches do not require teachers to plan detailed learning outcomes, to conduct needs analysis, or to follow a prescribed syllabus; hence, they often give teachers a considerable degree of autonomy and control over the teacher learning process. In the case of method-based approaches, however, teachers may be required to understand the sometimes obscure theory underlying the method as well as to master techniques and procedures that may initially prove difficult. Or they may simply adopt the practices without worrying about their claims and theoretical assumptions since they offer a supposedly "tried and tested or expert-designed" teaching solution. Adoption of a central design approach may also require a considerable investment in training, since teachers cannot generally rely on published coursebooks materials as the basis for teaching. With post-method and learner-community approaches, teaching strategies are developed according to the teacher's understanding of the context in which he or she is working as well as on his or her individual skill and expertise in managing the instructional process and in developing teaching materials and forms of assessment. High levels of professional knowledge as well as of language proficiency are probably a prerequisite.

A backward design option may be preferred in situations where a high degree of accountability needs to be built into the curriculum design and where resources can be committed to needs analysis, planning, and materials development. Well-developed procedures for implementing backward design procedures are widely available, making this approach an attractive option in some circumstances. In the case of large-scale curriculum development for a national education system, much of this development activity can be carried out by others, leaving teachers mainly with the responsibility of implementing the curriculum. In other circumstances such as a private institute developing company-specific courses, a more bottom-up approach may be adopted and the work required may be carried out by a well-trained and skillful individual teacher or group of teachers working together.

In conclusion, any language teaching curriculum contains the elements of content, process, and output. Historically, these have received a different emphasis at different times. Curriculum approaches differ in how they visualize the relationship between these elements, how they are prioritized and arrived at, and the role that syllabuses, approaches, methods, materials, teachers, and learners play in the process of curriculum development and enactment. The notion of forward, central, and backward design provides a useful metaphor for understanding the different assumptions underlying each approach to curriculum design as well as for recognizing the different practices that result from them.

Discussion questions

1. Which of the three approaches to curriculum development (forward, central, backward design) do each of these sequences of steps describe?

   - Outcomes > syllabus > materials and tests > teaching > assessment
   - Content > syllabus > methodology > outcomes > assessment
   - Teaching > selection and organization of content > selection and organisation of learning experiences > outcomes > assessment

2. If you are currently teaching, which of these three best describes how your curriculum was developed?

3. List two potential downsides and two advantages of forward, central, and backward design.

Forward design	
Downsides	Advantages
1	1
2	2
Central design	
Downsides	Advantages
1	1
2	2
Backward design	
Downsides	Advantages
1	1
2	2

4. Central design is sometimes said to provide a "learner-centered" approach to curriculum development. Explain why this claim is made, and why you agree/disagree with it.

5. A teacher has called in sick and the substitute is not available either. You have been asked to look after his or her students for the day. You know very little about them, except that they are 18- to 20-year-old students from overseas on a two-week intensive EFL programin your school, with a focus on communication skills. There is no time before the class starts to find out more. In terms of the approaches described in this chapter, which one would you choose, how would you prepare, and why would you use that approach?

6. Which of the three approaches is most common in commercially published materials? Why?

7. In which of the three approaches do teachers have the greatest degree of freedom? Why?

8. Input is often associated with syllabus, process with methodology, and output with learning outcomes. For which of the three aspects (input, process, output) of curriculum development will the following be most useful?

> The Academic Word List
> The Common European Framework of Reference for Languages
> Game-based learning theory
> The British National Corpus

9. For each of the main approaches and methods described in this book (you can use the table of contents page), choose whether they predominantly used a forward, central, or backward design.

10. For each of these groups, describe which curriculum development process you think would be best and give reasons:

- A group of engineers taking an intensive ESP course
- A group of primary school students of Spanish as a second language for whom this will be their first experience with the language
- A group of call center telephone support staff who will be working for a credit card company's helpline.

11. Work with a colleague. One of you reads the three statements below while the other responds with a counter-argument. Change roles until you have three counter-arguments.

> "It is impossible to decide what to teach unless you have decided what is worth learning."
> "It is impossible to know beforehand what learners will learn; learning is a creative, unpredictable process and the learners' needs come first."
> "It is impossible to be a successful teacher unless you know exactly what learning outcomes you are aiming for."

References and further reading

Basturkmen, H. 2010. *Designing Courses in English for Specific Purposes*. New York: Palgrave Macmillan.

Berwick. R. 1989. Needs assessment in language programming: from theory to practice. In R. K. Johnson (ed.), *The Second Language Curriculum*. New York: Cambridge University Press. 48–62.

Bruner, J. 1966. *The Process of Education*. Cambridge MA: Harvard Educational Press.

Burns, A., and J. C. Richards (eds.). 2009. *Cambridge Guide to Second Language Teacher Education*. Cambridge: Cambridge University Press.

Burns, A., and J. C. Richards (eds.). 2012. *The Cambridge Guide to Pedagogy and Practice in Language Teaching*. New York: Cambridge University Press.

Clark, J. L. 1987. *Curriculum Renewal in School Foreign Language Learning*. Oxford: Oxford University Press.

Council of Europe 2001. *Common European Framework of Reference for Languages: Learning, Teaching, Assessment*. Cambridge: Cambridge University Press.

Crandall, J. 2012. Content-based language teaching. In Burns and Richards (eds.), 149–60.

English Profile. n.d. http://www.englishprofile.org/; accessed August 31, 2012.

Gattegno, C. 1972. *Teaching Foreign Languages in Schools: The Silent Way*. 2nd edn. New York: Educational Solutions.

Graves, K. 2008 The language curriculum: a social contextual perspective. *Language Teaching* 41(2): 147–81.

Krashen, S., and T. Terrell. 1983. *The Natural Approach: Language Acquisition in the Classroom*. Oxford: Pergamon.

Kumaravadivelu, B. 1994. The postmethod condition: emerging strategies for second/foreign language teaching. *TESOL Quarterly* 28(1): 27–48.

Leung, C. 2012. Outcomes-based language teaching. In Burns and Richards (eds.), 161–79.

Mackey, W. F. 1965. *Language Teaching Analysis*. London: Longman.

McKay, P. 2000. On ESL standards for school-age learners. *Language Testing* 7(2): 185–214.

Meddings, L., and S. Thornbury. 2009. *Teaching Unplugged: Dogme in English Language Teaching*. Peaslake, UK: Delta Publishing.

Munby, J. 1978. *Communicative Syllabus Design*. Cambridge: Cambridge University Press.

Mehisto, P., D. Marsh, and M. Frigolos 2008. *Uncovering CLIL*. Oxford: Macmillan.

Reppen, R. 2010. *Using Corpora in the Language Classroom*. New York: Cambridge University Press.

Richards, J. C., and T. Rodgers. 2001. *Approaches and Methods in Language Teaching*. 2nd edn. New York: Cambridge University Press.

Stenhouse, L. 1975. *An Introduction to Curriculum Research and Development*. London: Heinemann.

Stufflebeam D., C. McCormick, R. Brinkeerhoff, and C. Nelson. 1985. *Conducting Educational Needs Assessment*. Hingham, MA: Kluwer-Nijhoff.

Taba, H. 1962. *Curriculum Development: Theory and Practice*. New York: Harcourt Brace and World.

Thornbury, S. 2012 (January 22). A is for approach. *An A–Z of ELT: Scott Thornbury's Blog*. http://scottthornbury.wordpress.com/2012/01/22/a-is-for-approach/; accessed October 8, 2012.

Trim, J. 2012. The Common European Framework of References for Languages and its background: a case study of cultural politics and educational influences. In M. Byram and L. Parmenter (eds.), *The Common European Framework of Reference: The Globalisation of Language Education Policy*. Bristol: Multilingual Matters. 14–34.

Tyler, R. 1949. *Basic Principles of Curriculum and Instruction*. Chicago: University of Chicago Press.

Tyler, R. 1950. *Basic Principles of Curriculum and Instruction*. Chicago: University of Chicago Press.

Van den Branden 2012. Task-based language education. In Burns and Richards (eds.), 140–8.

West, M. 1953. *A General Service List of English Words*. London: Longman.

Wier, C. J. 1990. *Communicative Language Testing*. New York: Prentice Hall.

Wiggins G., and J. McTighe. 2006. *Understanding by Design: A Framework for Effecting Curricular Development and Assessment.* Alexandria, VA: Association for Supervision and Curriculum Development.

Wilkins D. 1976. *Notional Syllabuses.* Oxford: Oxford University Press.

Willis, J. 1996. *A Framework for Task-Based Learning.* Harlow: Longman.

22 Postscript

From the survey of approaches and methods presented in this book, we have seen that the history of language teaching in the last one hundred years has been characterized by a search for more effective ways of teaching second or foreign languages. The most common solution to the "language teaching problem" was often seen to lie in the adoption of a new teaching approach or method. One result of this trend was the era of so-called designer or brand-name methods, that is, packaged solutions that can be described and marketed for use anywhere in the world. Thus, the Direct Method was enthusiastically embraced in the early part of the twentieth century as an improvement on Grammar Translation. In the 1950s the Audiolingual Method was thought to provide a way forward, incorporating the latest insights from the sciences of linguistics and psychology. As the Audiolingual Method began to fade in the 1970s, particularly in the United States, Communicative Language Teaching (CLT) as well as a variety of guru-led methods emerged to fill the vacuum created by the discrediting of Audiolingualism. While minor methods such as the Silent Way, Total Physical Response, and Suggestopedia had declined substantially by the turn of the century, new proposals for the organization of language teaching and learning have continued to influence language teaching policies and practices in different parts of the world. As noted in this text, these include Task-Based Language Teaching, Text-Based Instruction, CLIL, and the Common European Framework of Reference. And CLT continues to be considered the most plausible basis for language teaching in many contexts today, although, as we saw in Chapter 5, CLT can be applied and interpreted in a variety of ways. As Waters observes (2012), for some, CLT has taken the form of Task-Based Language Teaching (TBLT), for some, it is best reflected in a CLIL approach, while for others it is reflected in Dogme ELT, "a materials-light, conversation-driven philosophy of teaching that, above all, focuses on the learner and emergent language" (Meddings and Thornbury 2009: 103). Reviewing developments in approaches and methods since 1995, Waters (2012) concludes that at the level of classroom practice, since the 1990s methodology has been relatively stable.

This book describes approaches and methods in language teaching. We have described an approach as a set of beliefs and principles that can be used as the basis for teaching a language. An approach, however, does not lead to a specific set of prescriptions and techniques to be used in teaching a language. Approaches such as CLT, Content-Based Instruction (CBI) and CLIL are characterized by a variety of interpretations as to how the principles can be applied. Because of this level of flexibility and the possibility of varying interpretations and application, approaches tend to have a long shelf life. They allow for individual interpretation and application. They can be revised and updated over time as new practices emerge. On the other hand, a method such as Audiolingualism or Community Language Learning refers to a specific instructional design or system based on a particular theory of language and of language learning. It contains detailed specifications of content, roles of teachers and learners, and teaching procedures and techniques. It is relatively fixed in time and there is generally little scope for individual interpretation. As we discussed in Chapter 20, methods are learned through training. The teacher's role is to follow the method and apply it reasonably precisely according to the rules. Compared to approaches, methods tend to have a relatively short shelf life. They are often linked to very specific claims and to prescribed practices and tend to fall out of favor as these practices become unfashionable or discredited. The heyday of methods – particularly the "innovative" or "designer methods" – can be considered to have lasted up till the late 1980s.

However, methods offer some advantages over approaches, and this doubtless explains their appeal. Because of the general nature of approaches, there is often no clear application of their assumptions and principles in the classroom, as we have seen with a number of the approaches described in this book. Much is left to the individual teacher's interpretation, skill, and expertise. Consequently, there is often no clear right or wrong way of teaching according to an approach and no prescribed body of practice waiting to be implemented. This lack of detail can be a source of frustration and irritation for teachers, particularly those with little training or experience. Methods tend to be more prescriptive and less open to interpretation.

Yet the notion of approaches and methods has come under criticism since the 1990s promoted by ideological objections and by charges of oversimplification, as well as by greater recognition of the roles of learners and teachers in the learning process. Ideological objections often reflect a "critical theory" perspective, arguing that Western-based educational philosophies are liable to the charge of "native-speakerism" and "cultural imperialism," imposing assumptions about teachers and learning that may be incompatible with local cultures. For example, we saw in Chapter 5 that attempts to introduce CLT in countries with very different educational traditions from those in which CLT was developed (i.e., Britain and the United States and other English-speaking countries) have sometimes been unsuccessful. Some have referred to the import of Western teaching methods as an aspect of "cultural imperialism" because the assumptions and practices implicit in CLT are viewed as "correct," whereas those of the target culture are seen as in need of replacement. (See, e.g., Phillipson 1992; Kumaravidivelu 2012.) Similarly, approaches and methods such as Community Language Learning, Cooperative Language Learning, and TBLT all make assumptions about the roles of teachers and learners that are not necessarily culturally universal.

The charge of simplification has also been made by some observers who have suggested that describing teaching in terms of approaches and methods – and by labeling teaching proposals as such – presents methods "as fixed sets of procedures and principles, with little attention being paid to the contexts in which these developed, the way alternatives were debated at the time, or indeed the extent to which there was continuity with previous periods" (Hunter and Smith 2012: 430). The status of methods has also been reviewed in the light of a focus on both learner and teacher autonomy, as outlined in Chapters 19 and 20. Hence, the term "post-methods era" is sometimes used to describe a current perspective on teaching, the characteristics of which are reflected in Chapters 19 and 20. In Chapter 20 we also discuss different options for including a focus on approaches and methods in teacher education courses for language teachers.

Looking forward

How do we feel the language teaching profession will move ahead in the near, or even more distant, future? The approaches and methods surveyed in this book have identified a number of issues that we expect to continue to shape the future of language teaching in different ways. Some of the responses to these issues may take the form of new approaches and methods; others may lead to a refining or reshaping of existing approaches and methods as the teaching profession responds to the findings of new research and to developments in educational theory and practice. The initiatives for changing programs and pedagogy may come from within the profession – from teachers, administrators, theoreticians, and researchers. Incentives or demands of a political, social, or even fiscal nature may also drive change, as they have in the past. Particular personalities and leaders in the field may also shape the future of language teaching. Change may also be motivated by completely unexpected sources. We close, therefore, by identifying some of the factors that have influenced language teaching trends in the past and that can be expected to continue to do so in the future.

- *Government policy directives.* Increased demands for accountability on the part of funding agencies and governments have driven educational changes on a fairly regular basis for decades and are likely to continue to do so in the future. The standards movement, a focus on competencies in language programs, and the Common European Framework of Reference (CEFR) are examples of top-down influences on language teaching.
- *Trends in the profession.* The teaching profession is another source for change. Professional certification for teachers, as well as endorsement of particular trends or approaches by professional organizations and lobby groups promoting particular issues and causes, can have an important influence on teaching. CLIL and TBLT are benefiting from support of this kind in some parts of the world.
- *Guru-led innovations.* Teaching has sometimes been described as artistry rather than science and is often shaped by the influence of powerful individual practitioners with their own schools of thought and followers. Just as Gattegno, Lozanov, and Krashen inspired a number of teachers in the 1970s and 1980s, as did Gardner in the 1990s, so doubtless new gurus will attract disciples and shape teaching practices in the future.
- *Responses to technology.* The potential of the Internet, the World Wide Web, and other computer interfaces and technological innovations is likely to capture the imagination of the teaching profession in the future, as it has in the past, and will influence both the content and the form of instructional delivery in language teaching.

- *Influences from academic disciplines.* Disciplines such as linguistics, psycholinguistics, and psychology have shaped theories of language and language learning and support particular approaches to language teaching. As new theories emerge in disciplines such as these, they are likely to have an impact on future theories of teaching. Just as in the past Audiolingualism and cognitive-code learning reflected linguistic theories of their day, so new insights from functional linguistics, corpus linguistics, psycholinguistics, or sociolinguistics, or from sources now unknown, may play a dominant role in shaping language pedagogy.
- *Research influences.* Second language teaching and learning is increasingly a field for intensive research and theorizing. Second language acquisition research provided impetus for the development of the Natural Approach and TBLT, and it will doubtless continue to motivate new language teaching approaches.
- *Learner-based innovations.* Learner-based focuses recur in language teaching and other fields in approximately ten-year cycles, as we have seen with individualized instruction, the learner-centered curriculum, learner training, learner strategies, and Multiple Intelligences. We can anticipate a continuation of this trend.
- *Crossover educational trends.* Cooperative Language Learning, Whole Language, and Multiple Intelligences represent crossovers into second language teaching of movements from general education and elsewhere. Such crossovers will doubtless continue because the field of language teaching has no monopoly over theories of teaching and learning.
- *Crossovers from other disciplines.* Encounters with cognitive psychology, psychotherapy, communication science, ethnography, and human engineering have left their imprint on language pedagogy and exemplify the way that such diverse disciplines can influence a field that is always looking for inspiration.

Despite changes in the status of approaches and methods, we can therefore expect the field of second and foreign language teaching in the twenty-first century to be no less a ferment of theories, ideas, and practices than it has been in the past.

Discussion questions

1. Why do you think language teaching practices have often been described in terms of approaches and methods? What do you think are the advantages or limitations of this way of describing teaching?

2. Examine some recent commercial textbooks, either for the teaching of general English or a specific skill area. To what extent do the books claim to reflect the principles of a particular teaching approach or method? If so, how is this reflected in the design and contents of the book?

3. To what extent do coursebooks in use in your country (or in a context you are familiar with) reflect local cultural and educational traditions?

4. In what ways is technology influencing language teaching in your school or classroom? Do you see changes in the way an approach or method is implemented (consider areas such as roles of teachers and learners, and procedure) as a result of technology?

5. Take a look at one of the promotions for computer-based language learning systems such as Fluenz, the Pimsleur Method, TELL ME MORE, Rosetta Stone, Transparent Language® (http://www.transparent.com). In terms of descriptions in this text, how would you describe the approach or method underlying the product?

6. Review the above list of factors that have influenced approaches to language teaching. Can you give examples of some of these influences from your own experience? Which of the factors listed do you feel have been the most important?

References and further reading

Bailey, K. 1996. The best-laid plans: teachers' in-class decisions to depart from their lesson plans. In K. Bailey and D. Nunan (eds.), *Voices from the Language Classroom*. New York: Cambridge University Press. 15–40.

Brown, H. D. 1994. *Teaching by Principles*. Englewood Cliffs, NJ: Prentice Hall/Regents.

Brown, H. D. 1997. English language teaching in the "post-method" era: toward better diagnosis, treatment, and assessment. *PASAA* (Bangkok) 27: 1–10.

Clark, C. M., and P. Peterson. 1986. Teachers' thought processes. In M. Wittrock (ed.), *Handbook of Research on Teaching*. 3rd edn. New York: Macmillan. 255–96.

Holliday, A. 1994. *Appropriate Methodology*. Cambridge: Cambridge University Press.

Hunter, D., and R. Smith 2012. Unpackaging the past: 'CLT' through ELTJ keywords. *ELT Journal* 66(4): 430–9.

Kumaravadivelu, B. 1994. The post-method condition: emerging strategies for second/foreign language teaching. *TESOL Quarterly* 28: 27–48.

Kumaravadivelu. B. 2012. Individual identity, cultural globalization, and teaching English as an international language: the case for an epistemic break. In L. Alsagoff, S. L. McKay, G. Hu, and W. A. Renandya (eds.), *Principles and Practices for Teaching English as an International Language*. New York: Routledge. 104–22.

Meddings, L., and S. Thornbury. 2009. *Teaching Unplugged: Dogme in English Language Teaching*. Peaslake: Delta Publishing.

Nicholls, A. H., and H. Nicholls. 1972. *Developing Curriculum: A Practical Guide*. London: George Allen and Unwin.

Nunan, D. 1989. *Understanding Language Classrooms: A Guide for Teacher Initiated Action*. New York: Prentice Hall.

Pennycook, A. 1989. The concept of method, interested knowledge, and the politics of language teaching. *TESOL Quarterly* 23: 589–618.

Pennycook, A. 1994. *The Cultural Politics of English as an International Language*. London: Longman.

Phillipson, R. 1992. *Linguistic Imperialism*. Oxford: Oxford University Press.

Prabhu, N. S. 1990. There is no best method – why? *TESOL Quarterly* 24: 161–76.

Richards, J. C. 1998. Teachers' maxims. In J. C. Richards, *Beyond Training*. New York: Cambridge University Press. 45–62.

Richards, J. C. 2000. *Curriculum Development in Language Teaching*. New York: Cambridge University Press.

Skehan, P. 1996. Second language acquisition research and task-based instruction. In J. Willis and D. Willis (eds.), *Challenge and Change in Language Teaching*. Oxford: Heinemann. 17–30.

Swaffar, J., K. Arens, and M. Morgan. 1982. Teacher classroom practices: redefining method as task hierarchy. *Modern Language Journal* 66(1): 24 –33.

Waters, Alan 2012. Trends and issues in ELT methods and methodology. *ELT Journal* 664(4): 440–9.

Appendix: Comparison of approaches and methods

Chapter and method	Key characteristics	Influence on current language teaching	Teacher role	Learner role	Common classroom activities

3
The Oral Approach / Situational Language Teaching
	• More scientific approach to vocabulary selection
	• Grammar seen as "sentence patterns," systematically categorized to form the basis of teaching
	• Target language is the language of instruction
	• Emphasis on spoken language
	• Language is introduced through situations
	• Automatic use of sentence patterns
	• Teacher control
		• Emphasis on target language as the language of instruction
		• Use of PPP
			• Expert
			• Linguist
			• Guide
				• Recipient
				• Imitator
					• Guided repetition and substitution activities:
					  ○ choral repetition
					  ○ dictation
					  ○ drills
					  ○ controlled oral-based reading and writing tasks

Chapter and method	Key characteristics	Influence on current language teaching	Teacher role	Learner role	Common classroom activities
4 The Audiolingual Method	• Language taught through speaking • A focus on sentence patterns • Repetition and drills lead to habit formation • Linguistic analysis and contrastive analysis inform syllabus content and sequencing • Little focus on writing • Focus on avoidance of errors and an emphasis on grammatical accuracy • Teacher control	• Teach the language, not about the language • A language is what its native speakers say, not what they ought to say • Importance of practice • Use of the target language	• Expert • Provides error correction • Linguist	• Developing linguist • Imitator	• Pronunciation activities • Pattern drills • Mimicking native-speaker speech • Repetition-based tasks • Acting out dialogues

Chapter and method	Key characteristics	Influence on current language teaching	Teacher role	Learner role	Common classroom activities

5 Communicative Language Teaching	• Focus on meaning
	• Focus on *functional* aspects of language
	• Emphasis on interaction
	• Emphasis on authenticity of input
	• Learning by doing through direct practice
	• Learner-centered
		• Most characteristics (e.g., authentic communication, pair work, and group work) still influence current teaching practice
		• Changes since approach was introduced:
		  ○ Balance of fluency and accuracy has been refined
		  ○ Learner autonomy, diversity, and teachers as co-learners now play more important role
			• Communication facilitator
			• Encourages fluency
				• Active communicative participant
				• Collaborator
					• Collaborative learning through pair and group work; negotiation of meaning
					• Activities focusing on communication, e.g., jigsaw, task-completion, information-gathering, information-sharing
					• Activities focusing on fluency, with a high degree of tolerance for errors
					• Information gap, opinion, and reasoning activities
					• Role plays

Chapter and method	Key characteristics	Influence on current language teaching	Teacher role	Learner role	Common classroom activities
6 CBI and CLIL	• Language learning combined with subject learning • Focus on exchange of information through communication • Closely tied to learners' needs • Importance of comprehension • Development of intercultural awareness	• Strong awareness of subject matter • Awareness of students' real-life purpose for learning the language	• Subject and language knowledge; may be materials developer • Collaborator (with subject teachers) • Needs analyst • Learner-centered facilitator	• Active creator of knowledge and understanding • Autonomous learner • Collaborative learner	• Performance-oriented activities • Discussion activities • Collaborative work • (Critical) meaning-oriented activities

Chapter and method	Key characteristics	Influence on current language teaching	Teacher role	Learner role	Common classroom activities
7 Whole Language	• Language taught as a whole, not through discrete parts • Language learning is experiential learning; learner is at center and takes responsibility • Focus on meaning and authentic language • Integrated skills through collaborative learning • Use of literature	• Learning is experiential activity; needs to relate to learners • The emphasis on self-directed learning	• Facilitates learning process • Active participant • Facilitates negotiation with learners	• Collaborator • Evaluator • Self-directed learner • Selector of learning materials and activities	• Collaborative activities, e.g., small-group reading and writing • Reading and discussion of literature; use of parallel texts • Writing portfolios
8 CBLT and standards-based instruction	• Focus on explicit, measurable outcomes • Outcomes related to real-life needs; described as overt behaviors and "can do" statements • Instruction student-centered and individualized	• The attention to clear goals and objectives • Real-life objectives • The use of standards	• Needs analyst • Identifies and communicates learning objectives • Provides continuous feedback in relation to learning objectives	• Self-monitors learning against target competencies • Strategic communicator • Active participant in transferring knowledge to new situations	• No specific activities are suggested

Chapter and method	Key characteristics	Influence on current language teaching	Teacher role	Learner role	Common classroom activities
9 Task-Based Language Teaching	• Use of tasks as core units of planning and instruction • Use of real-world outcomes • Focus on lexis and speaking, and integration of skills	• The use of activities with real-world outcomes • A focus on authenticity • A focus on form combined with meaning-oriented activities	• Creates authentic, meaning-focused tasks • Provides interactional support • Encourages focus on form	• Collaborator • Risk-taker • Language user	• Information gap, jigsaw, problem-solving and other collaborative tasks • Communication activities
10 Text-Based Instruction	• Use of authentic spoken and written texts in their social and cultural context as the main source of input • Explicit teaching of structures and grammatical features	• The use of and explicit focus on different text-types, or genres	• Needs analyst and syllabus designer • Discourse and conversation analyst • Provides scaffolded guidance	• Discourse analyst • Self-monitor	• Analysis of different text-types • Text modeling • Text deconstruction and joint construction

Chapter and method	Key characteristics	Influence on current language teaching	Teacher role	Learner role	Common classroom activities
11 The Lexical Approach	• Centrality of lexis, particularly multi-word units or chunks • The importance of strategies for learners to deal with chunks	• Focus on multi-word chunks • The use of corpora	• Language analyst • Facilitates data-driven and discovery-based learning	• Data and discourse analyst • Discoverer • Strategic learner	• Awareness-raising activities • Corpora-based activities • Data-driven learning • Text chunking • Strategy instruction
12 Multiple Intelligences	• Learner differences impact learning and need to be taken into account in teaching • Learners have multiple intelligences • Learners are supported in becoming better designers of their own learning	• Awareness of learner differences • The use of a wide range of classroom learning activities	• Supports students' learning • Orchestrates multisensory learning experiences • Develops students' multiple intelligences	• Designer of his/her own learning • Works on self-improvement (not only in terms of language)	• Multisensory activities • The use of realia

Chapter and method	Key characteristics	Influence on current language teaching	Teacher role	Learner role	Common classroom activities
13 Cooperative Language Learning	• Focus on collaboration through pair and group work • Focus on establishing an inclusive classroom atmosphere • Focus not only on language but also on broader cognitive, social, and psychological development • Teaching of strategies and critical thinking skills • Frequent interaction in target language	• The importance of pair and group work • The importance of affective factors • The focus on critical thinking skills	• Facilitator • Groups learners • Organizes group work • Structures cooperative tasks • Encourages critical thinking	• Active participant • Facilitates an inclusive social environment • Interdependent participant with other learners for learning outcomes	• Cooperative projects and problem-solving • Jigsaw tasks • Peer assessment • Question Matrix – cooperative activities that encourage critical thinking

Chapter and method	Key characteristics	Influence on current language teaching	Teacher role	Learner role	Common classroom activities
14 The Natural Approach	• Strong focus on *meaning* • Lack of explicit instruction on *form* • Emphasis on input over practice • Attention to emotional preparedness for learning • Receptive before productive skills • View of second language learning as a naturalistic process similar to L1 acquisition • Prominence given to vocabulary	• The importance of affective factors	• Source of comprehensible input • Lowers students' affective filter • Selects rich base of activities and materials based on learners' needs	• Communicative participant	• Listening activities • Teacher questioning, progressing from nonverbal, to yes/no, to more complex responses • "Acquisition activities" focusing on exchange of meaningful information through role play, games, and problem-solving

Subject index